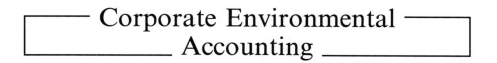

Corporate Environmental
Accounting

About the Authors

Dr. Stefan Schaltegger is currently Assistant Professor at the Center of Economics and Business Administration (WWZ), University of Basel, Switzerland. He is a member of the board of the environmental management program at Herning School of Business Administration and Technology, Denmark, and of the advisory board of the Sustainable Development Fund, Bank Sarasin and Cie. He has consulted and provided executive training courses at numerous companies and governmental agencies including Ciba-Geigy Ltd, the Swiss Environmental Protection Agency (BUWAL), and has given academic lectures and courses at various business schools and universities including Norwegian School of Management BI, Norway, and Insead, France.

Kaspar Müller is a founder and partner of Ellipson Ltd, management consultants. Prior to this, he was a financial analyst and Head of the corporate finance department at a Swiss private bank. He is Co-Chairman of the Commission on Accounting of EFFAS (European Federation of Financial Analysts' Societies), and is a member of the board of the Swiss Association of Financial Analysis and Investment Management, a member of the Accounting Standard Setting Committee of Switzerland (Swiss-GAAP/FER), and between 1987 and 1994 was Chairman of the Swiss Shareholder Information Committee.

Henriette Hindrischsen is a research assistant with Dr Schaltegger and a graduate student at the Norwegian School of Management BI, Oslo.

SPONSOR

As sponsor of this book on *Corporate Environmental Accounting*, the European Institute for Financial Analysis and Portfolio Management (EIAM) wishes to support important initiatives to introduce environmental questions into financial analysis. The EIAM was established in September 1993 by the European Federation of Financial Analysts' Societies (EFFAS) and the Fondation Genève Place Financière (FGPF). The European Institute supports the investment community throughout Europe, by participating in and co-ordinating the development and diffusion of techniques, norms and information.

Corporate Environmental Accounting

Stefan Schaltegger
University of Basel

with

Kaspar Müller
Henriette Hindrichsen

JOHN WILEY & SONS
Chichester · New York · Brisbane · Toronto · Singapore

Other Wiley Editorial Offices

John Wiley & Sons, Inc., 605 Third Avenue,
New York, NY 10158-0012, USA

Jacaranda Wiley Ltd, 33 Park Road, Milton,
Queensland 4064, Australia

John Wiley & Sons (Canada) Ltd, 22 Worcester Road,
Rexdale, Ontario M9W 1L1, Canada

John Wiley & Sons (Asia) Pte Ltd, 2 Clementi Loop #02-01,
Jin Xing Distripark, Singapore 129809

Library of Congress Cataloging-in-Publication Data

Schaltegger, S. (Stefan), 1964–
    Corporate environmental accounting / Stefan Schaltegger with
Kaspar Müller and Henriette Hindrichsen.
        p.   cm.
    Includes bibliographical references and index.
    ISBN 0-471-96784-X
    1. International business enterprises—Environmental aspects—
Accounting.   2. Industrial management—Environmental aspects—
Accounting.   3. Natural resources—Accounting.   I. Müller, Kaspar.
II. Title.
HF5686.I56S33   1996
658.4′08—dc20   96–22619
                                                          CIP

British Library Cataloguing in Publication Data

A catalogue record for this book is available from the British Library

ISBN 0-471-96784-X

Typeset in 10/12pt Times from the author's disks by Dobbie Typesetting Ltd, Tavistock, Devon
Printed and bound in Great Britain by Biddles Ltd, Guildford
This book is printed on acid-free paper responsibly manufactured from sustainable forestation, for which at least two trees are planted for each one used for paper production.

Contents

Preface

Accounting standards and standard setting have become essential to modern corporations worldwide. By providing the first comprehensive overview of the emerging field of environmental accounting this book sets a standard.

First, this book lays out the environmental issues and tools in managerial, financial and other accounting systems. Potentials for profits and cost savings by applying sound accounting practices are discussed very thoroughly. Furthermore, a comprehensive overview of existing standards and guidelines dealing with environmental accounting is given. From my viewpoint this variety of partly conflicting standards shows that the time has come for international standard setting to tackle environmental issues explicitly. Consistent standards embracing financial and ecological issues are required by business leaders. In the future listing requirements for stock exchanges might entail ecological data.

The second group of topics covered in this book raises issues that have never or hardly been discussed so far. It is shown excellently how accounting practices can be applied to tackle environmental impacts of firms. The so called "ecological accounting" has become part of daily business practice. The range of applied tools are discussed in a very innovative and professional way.

Thirdly, tools for the necessary integration of traditional financial and managerial accounting with ecological accounting are presented. The integration of financial figures with figures of environmental impacts make it possible to operationalize the eco-efficiency of firms.

As with financial accounting, external ecological accounting will benefit from making explicit the underlying assumptions and conventions, and by defining internationally applicable standards. By defining the necessary international standards of ecological accounting now the expensive experience made in setting the international financial standards may be avoided.

Prof. Dr. Eiichi Shiratori
Former Chairman of the International Accounting Standards
Committee (IASC) and retired Arthur Andersen Partner

Foreword

The relationship between corporations and their environment is of great and growing importance. Although this is already true as a result of its financial consequences, the effects of this interaction are not limited to this sphere and can embrace a much wider domain. Environmental accounting is therefore concerned with a very real set of problems that have a close bearing on actual practice.

Environmental accounting is the basis for taking environmentally relevant facts into consideration in corporate decision-making. It is a fundamental requirement for communication between the company and its stakeholder groups. Accounting necessarily presumes the existence of a set of figures without which outsiders cannot include this area in their decision-making process. Ultimately, environmental accounting is also the key to corporate environmental policy. Environmental problems can be discussed only on an objective, problem-oriented basis. A means of quantifying and describing them is therefore needed. This applies to the situation at a given moment and also to its development over a period of time.

A substantial number of publications already exist in this field, but tend to focus more upon environmental reporting than upon environmental accounting. In the existing literature different problems are examined from a number of angles, and individual approaches to their solution are proposed. But what is now needed is an approach that integrates the different instruments and establishes their position against a common notional and technical background. Only in a synthesis is it possible to understand and further develop the basic requirements, instruments, possibilities and limits of environmental accounting. The present book represents such an approach, and is therefore of special value from both the practical and the theoretical viewpoint. On the one hand it gives a useful overview of the spectrum of environmental accounting, thus effectively opening the door to this frequently somewhat inaccessible material. It should therefore become an indispensable working basis and reference book for students and academics. As a result of the operational applicability of the presented approaches, the same is true of companies and the professions which advise them. This book will also be of value to financial analysts and other groups who advise companies on investment decisions, as well as to interested members of the public.

On the other hand, however, the present work will be of interest to standard setters, namely to bodies governing national accounting standards and in particular to the International Accounting Standards Committee (IASC). Its special value as a conceptual starting point lies in its proposal of a broad overall approach which incorporates rather than isolates itself from traditional accounting. This integration permits a further discussion of fundamental conceptual aspects. With the need to reach agreement on the fundamental concepts that should be adopted against the background of individual proposals, environmental accounting is experiencing a similar development to that of accounting in general. From a certain point in time, standard setting requires a conceptual framework without which it is not possible to establish consistent, internationally valid and recognised standards.

Recognised standards can thus be arrived at only by way of a conceptual discussion. International standards, for their part, are a *sine qua non* for an international comparability at a level which transcends that of the individual company. As experience in international accounting has shown, it is comparability rather than individual good examples that will permit a wave of expansion to take place in the application of environmental accounting. Once this has been achieved, a breakthrough for environmental accounting and reporting will be only a short step away.

Prof. Dr. Ann-Kristin Achleitner
European Business School

Personal Acknowledgements

We are very grateful to the European Federation of Financial Analysts' Societies (EFFAS) and the Swiss National Science Foundation which have financially supported the project. Without the generous support of Prof. Dr. René L. Frey, chairman at the Center of Economics and Business Administration (WWE) of the University of Basel, it would not have been possible to finish this book.

Special thanks to Andreas Bürge, Matthias Blom, Thomas Braun, Eric Ohlund, Ruedi Kubat and two anonymous reviewers for their valuable comments which helped substantially to improve earlier drafts.

In addition, we are grateful to Frances Follin, James Griffin and Robert Williamson for their copy-editing. We would also like to thank Richard Baggaley, the publisher and his assistant Lynne Barc as well as Jenny Mackenzie who was the production editor. Many thanks also to Inge Hochreuthener who helped to establish the contact with Wiley.

This book is especially dedicated to Vivian, Oliver and Gregory Schaltegger who had to spend many evenings and weekends without their husband and father.

Abbreviations

AAA	American Accounting Association
AAF	Accounting Advisory Forum of the EU
ABC	Activity Based Cost Accounting
ACN	Association Canadienne de Normalisation
AICPA	American Institute of Certified Public Accountants
AIPP	American Institute of Pollution Prevention
BCG	Boston Consulting Group
BCSD	Business Council for Sustainable Development (now WBCSD)
BSI	British Standards Institute
BS 7750	British Standard 7750
BUWAL	Bundesamt für Umwelt, Wald und Landschaft (Swiss Environmental Protection Agency)
CEFIC	European Chemical Industry Council
CERES	Coalition for Environmentally Responsible Economies
CHF	Swiss Francs
CICA	Canadian Institute of Chartered Accountants
CM	Contribution Margin
COD	Chemical Oxygen Demand
COM	Commission of the European Communities
CRI	Chemical Release Inventory
DEM	Deutschmark
DOE	Department of Ecology, Washington, USA
EEC	European Economic Council
EFFAS	European Federation of Financial Analysts' Societies
EI	Emission Inventory
EIA	Environmental Impact Added
EITF	Emerging Issues Task Force of FASB
EIU	The Economist Intelligence Unit
EMAS	Environmental Management and Eco-Audit System
EPA	Environmental Protection Agency
EPM	Eco-Rational Path Method

EPP	Ecological Payback Period
ERR	Ecological Rate of Return
EU	European Union
FASB	Financial Accounting Standards Board
FEE	Fédération des Experts Comptables Européens
FER	Fachkommission für Empfehlungen zur Rechnungslegung (Swiss Commission for Accounting Standards)
GAAP	Generally Accepted Accounting Principles
GEMI	Global Environmental Management Initiative
HMIP	Her Majesty's Inspectorate of Pollution
IAS	International Accounting Standard(s)
IASC	International Accounting Standards Committee
ICC	International Chamber of Commerce
ICCR	Interfaith Center on Corporate Responsibility
IISA	International Institute for Sustainable Development
INSEE	Institut National de la Statistique et des Etudes Economiques
IRRC	Investors Responsibility Research Center
ISO	International Standards Organization
ISO 14000	International Standard 14000
LCA	Life Cycle Assessment
NPRI	Canadian National Pollutant Release Inventory
NPV	Net Present Value
OECD	Organisation for Economic Co-operation and Development
PER	Polluting Emissions Register
PERI	Public Environmental Reporting Initiative
PRTR	Pollution Release and Transfer Register
RONA	Return on Net Assets
SBU	Strategic Business Unit
SEC	Securities and Exchange Commission
SETAC	Society for Environmental Toxicology and Chemistry
TQEM	Total Quality Environmental Management
TQM	Total Quality Management
TRI	Toxic Release Inventory
$	Dollars
UBA	Umweltbundesamt (German Environmental Protection Agency)
UN	United Nations
UNEP	United Nations Environment Programme
US	United States (of America)
VOC	Volatile Organic Compounds
WBCSD	World Business Council for Sustainable Development
WCED	World Commission on Environment and Development
WICE	World Industry Council for the Environment
WWF	World Wide Fund for Nature
33/50	US 33/50 Program

PART A
Introduction and Framework

The main focus of this book is placed on accounting as it is or could be practiced within firms, choosing a micro-economic approach. It is not intended to discuss macro-economic (national) environmental accounting, although several references to such links are made.

At the conceptual level, the book presents an integrated framework, around which the discussion is centered. The book is organized in the following way.

Part A gives an introduction to the basic concept of this book, namely the stakeholder approach, and explains why different accounting systems emerge (Chapter 1). A review of important stakeholders trying to influence the agenda of environmental accounting is also given. The overall framework of the book is then presented (Chapter 2). This is the conceptual centerpiece of the book, and it is therefore referred to throughout the text.

Part B deals with the implications the incorporation of environmental issues has for traditional accounting systems (Chapter 3). Based on the introduction in Part A, a further examination is made of those stakeholders who attempt to influence financial accounting. The traditional accounting systems—managerial, financial and other accounting systems—treat information in terms of monetary units (Chapters 4, 5, and 6).

Part C deals with ecological accounting systems, where the environmental impacts of the company on the natural environment are sought for and measured, and where data are expressed in physical units (Chapter 7). The structure corresponds to that of traditional accounting and a distinction is made between internal, external and other accounting systems (Chapters 8, 9 and 10).

Part D shows how traditional and ecological accounting systems can be integrated and how the resulting figures can be used for strategic decision making (Chapter 11). Afterwards, the link between environmental accounting and environmental management systems is established (Chapter 12). Finally, the concept of eco-controlling is discussed in the context of environmental accounting. The book concludes with a discussion of the outlook (Chapter 13).

The structure of the text is shown below and is repeated several times throughout the book.

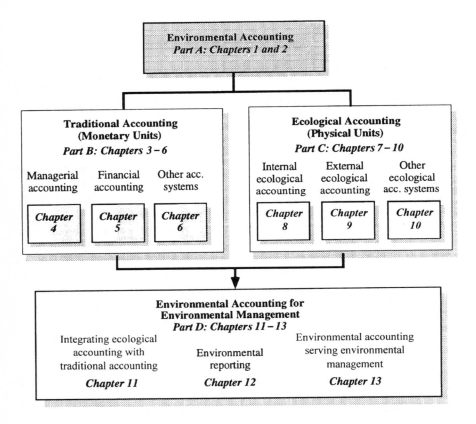

Figure 1   Structure of the book

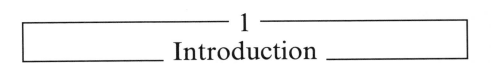

1
Introduction

Chapter 1 gives an introduction to the topic of environmental accounting. In developed countries, environmental accounting has become a major issue in corporate management. Sections 1.2 and 1.3 discuss the emergence of ecological accounting as a result of information demands of various stakeholders of the company.

Chapter 2 examines the framework of environmental accounting in the light of many different, sometimes conflicting goals of important stakeholders.

1.1 ENVIRONMENTAL ISSUES

Despite the progress made by some parts of the business community with regard to environmental performance since the rise of environmentalism in the late 1960s and early 1970s, environmental degradation is continuing at an alarming pace. As shown by scientific findings (e.g. about the ozone layer and also climatic change), the human impact on the natural environment now is not only local or regional but poses a threat to the global ecosphere (see for example Worldwatch Institute 1995).

Environmental protection agencies are creating more and more regulations, and market-based approaches working through the price mechanism are increasingly seen as a means of coping with the problems. In society, awareness of environmental issues has been rising dramatically during the last 20 years and environmental pressure group membership has been growing in most countries if seen over an extended period.[1] International and business organizations are increasingly dealing with environmental issues, as shown by the growing number of international agreements and public statements from business leaders (see for example Schmidheiny 1992).

All this has a major impact on business and has made a growing number of firms realize that it can very well pay to become "green", and that it can also hurt financially to be an environmental laggard. By increasing the environmental performance of a company, many benefits may be obtained. Some will have direct financial impacts such as decreasing liabilities and costs, while others will be of a more intangible nature such as better employee morale and an improved corporate image, the anticipation of future legislation and the development of future markets in the fields of environmentally more benign products.

There are many ways to give the outside world a greener image of a firm. However, these positive effects usually last for only a short time, if there is no action behind the words. Whereas most managers are concerned about the increasing level of environmentally induced financial costs, a growing part of the business community is also seriously engaged in finding and implementing more sustainable management practices. In this book it is shown that accounting is a necessary tool for learning more about the influence of environmental issues on companies' profits and about the effects of firms on the natural environment. (Throughout this book, company, firm, corporation and entity are used interchangeably.)

A strong tendency to internalize external costs and environmental impacts characterizes the political landscape of developed countries. However, this has so far not led to the total reflection of environmental impacts in accounting. Usually environmentally induced opportunities and threats, costs and revenues, assets and liabilities etc. are not explicitly reflected in companies' accounts. These influences nevertheless lead to a change in accounting figures, and because their monetary impact has been rising in many industries during the last decades they should be adequately and correctly reflected in accounting practices in order to improve management decisions. Today, rigorous cost management requires the thorough consideration of environmentally induced costs.

At the beginning of the century thick dark smoke and stinking water were regarded as a necessary evil of economic welfare. Today, society demands eco-efficiency and sustainable development (Section 1.2). In this connection, accurate recording and analysis of current and expected environmental impacts and of the use of resources are essential. They are a prerequisite not only for improving corporate environmental performance, but also for estimating possible future market opportunities (mountain bikes instead of motor bikes) and costs due to regulations (e.g. no CFCs), taxes (e.g. on CO_2), etc. Environmental impacts are perceived in different ways by various social groups, so recorded data should be interpreted using different assessment concepts. Also, not all groups demand the same things, so that adequately designed information, analysis and communication systems are needed.

In the past, costs induced by ecological issues were lower than the costs of collecting the respective information for the firm. This has changed as the costs of corporate impacts on the environment, and environmentally induced financial impacts on firms, are rising rapidly while the possibilities of data management have improved enormously. Such a change in the relative costs lays the ground for the emergence of environmental accounting (Section 1.3).

Environmental accounting embraces all of the above. In addition, its purpose has been changing for the last decade. Environmental accounting is no longer what it was in its earliest stages. Instead of being used to placate external activists, it is now an important source of information for company managers.

Environmental accounting can be defined as a sub-area of accounting that deals with activities, methods and systems for recording, analysing and reporting—used interchangeably with "disclosure" in this book—environmentally induced financial impacts and ecological impacts of a defined economic system (e.g. a firm, plant, region, nation, etc.). In this book, current issues and modern concepts of environmental accounting are discussed with a focus on firms and their environment.

1.2 STAKEHOLDERS INFLUENCING THE ACCOUNTING AGENDA

A stakeholder of a company is any individual or group who has an interest in the company because he can affect, or is affected by the company activities (Freeman 1984, p. 41). The term "stakeholder" indicates that these groups or individuals have a stake in the corporation. Stakeholders are, for example, management, employees, tax agencies, shareholders, environmental pressure groups, suppliers, customers or geographical neighbors (see Figure 1.1). Stakeholders can be divided into *internal* and *external* stakeholders, the two being separated by the boundaries of the firm. Management and employees are generally regarded as internal stakeholders having most of the influence on the firm. External stakeholders are, for example, shareholders, suppliers, customers or government agencies. The company's success depends on the stakeholders' cooperation, because they provide the resources needed to ensure the viability of any company (see for example Susskind and McKearnan 1995). Companies need both material and immaterial resources (e.g. information and services) in order to perform, and these will be supplied by individuals and groups as long as relations are perceived as favorable and fair. To verify if this

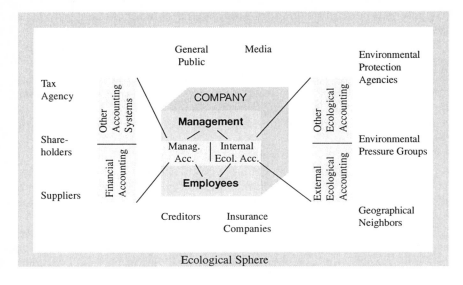

Figure 1.1 Accounting Systems and Stakeholders

is the case, stakeholders require information which must be continuously collected, organized and reported.

The stakeholder concept helps to explain

- why today's organizations have to consider a multitude of different interests to become economically successful, and
- how differing accounting systems have evolved and will evolve in the future.

For more than a hundred years, accounting has been the most important corporate system of information collection and analysis. This is also reflected in the notion "accountable", which means that someone has the duty to give an explanation. Precisely this duty, on the other hand, shows that someone has the right to receive the information collected. The process of "being held to account" determines, reflects, strengthens and solidifies the power relationship between the accountee and accountor (Maunders and Burritt, 1991). Accounting systems are designed in such a way as to make management and employees accountable for their activities, whereby the transparency of the organization is increased through the diffusion of information and in general leads to an expansion of the right of co-determination.

This ongoing process of "give and take" between management and its stakeholders leads to the development of different accounting systems, because different accounting information is required by different stakeholders. Not every stakeholder receives exactly the requested quality and quantity of information. The accounting systems and practices, and the information provided, are a result of the actual distribution of power between the relevant stakeholders and management. The relative power of a stakeholder group is reflected in the process of setting the accounting standard as well as in the accounting standards themselves. In turn, the question of who gets which information is also important considering the role accounting systems play in the political context of a firm as well as in society. A group with relatively better and more adequate information will always have an advantage in lobbying processes.

Because of the ongoing environmental degradation and the problems associated with it, growing importance is attached to environmentally related information for stakeholders. Accounting, as one of the most important information gathering systems, therefore has to be adapted to the new requirements. The creation of new accounting practices dealing specifically with environmental problems is one possible mode of responding. The *traditional accounting systems*, focusing on monetary aspects, can be supplemented by *ecological accounting systems* that collect information on the firm's impact on the natural environment. These supplementary systems can be used for communication with both internal (within the organization) and external stakeholders. Excellent companies do not just ask what information is required by stakeholders. Sometimes it is argued that, by increasing the transparency of firms' financial and ecological impacts, management will lose its power or will have to change its behavior to keep power. However, modern management argues that it increases its power because society is better informed about the firm. In this way, management conforms more to the demands of society, supports personal accountability and creates more positive feedback from the stakeholders. The most important stakeholder influencing environmental accounting will be mentioned throughout the book.

The internal stakeholders traditionally derive much of their corporate financial information from *managerial accounting*, which is shown within the boundaries of the firm in the box in the center of Figure 1.1. Usually, the information collected by this accounting system will be subjected to compromises for external accounting purposes. Though we acknowledge that this is not always the case, the internal collection of data should cover a much wider field than the requirements of external stakeholders alone. Managerial accounting is designed to facilitate internal decision making and therefore provides necessary data mainly to inform management.

The second internal accounting system shown in Figure 1.1 is *internal ecological accounting*. It is designed to fulfil the management's need to be informed about the environmental impacts of the firm.

Both internal accounting systems should be prerequisites for external accounting, regardless of whether they are of a financial or ecological nature. Internal and external stakeholders might demand the same kind of information, but the amount and the degree of detail of the required information may vary.

Among both internal and external stakeholders, some will primarily be interested in the financial impacts of environmental activities while others will demand information about the impact the firm has on the natural environment. The first view could be called an "outside-in" view: which aspects from the outside have an impact on the organization? The other is an "inside-out" view: (What impacts does the organization have on the natural environment?). Ideally, both kinds of impacts should be integrated in the same accounting approach. However, this would only be possible if all environmental impacts were internalized. In Figure 1.1 the external stakeholders are divided in two groups: the first being primarily interested in the environmentally induced financial impacts on the firm (to the left in Figure 1.1), the second in the ecological impacts of the firm on the natural environment (to the right in Figure 1.1). The external accounting systems are shown as interfaces for communicating and dealing with external stakeholders.

Traditional financial and other traditional accounting systems are shown on the left with the main addressees: shareholders, suppliers, tax agencies, etc. External ecological and other ecological accounting systems face to the right in Figure 1.1, towards their main addressees, namely environmental protection agencies, environmental pressure groups and geographical neighbors. It must be stressed, however, that this distinction between addressee groups is not necessarily very clear in reality. Shareholders, for example, sometimes are most certainly interested in the environmental impact of a firm.

Changed attitudes of stakeholders are a necessary but not a sufficient precondition for the emergence of environmental accounting. The next section shows how the relative costs and benefits of environmental accounting have changed over time.

1.3 THE EMERGENCE OF ENVIRONMENTAL ACCOUNTING

Most companies employ accounting systems that were designed before anyone could anticipate the present-day importance of environmentally induced costs and impacts. Before the 1980s, environmental compliance costs and

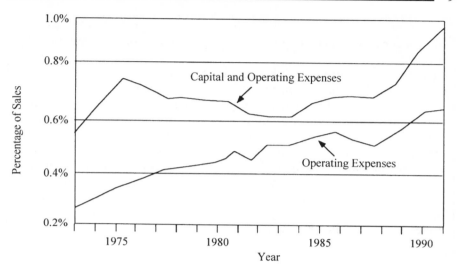

Figure 1.2 Development of Compliance and Pollution Control Costs in the US.
Source: Ditz *et al.* 1995

environmental impacts were marginal for most manufacturing firms. At the same time, the costs of measurement and recording were relatively high.[2]

In the past decade, this relationship has been reversed through a stricter enforcement of the widely accepted "polluter-pays" principle. Today environmental compliance costs are huge and still increasing for many firms, whilst information systems for tracking those costs have become relatively cheaper.

Figure 1.2 shows the development of the capital and operating expenses of US manufacturers for pollution abatement and control over the last twenty years (see Ditz *et al.* 1995, OTA 1994 and for a discussion of the expected future development, see Colby *et al.* 1995). The fines for environmental non-compliance are also much higher than they have ever been before.[3] In the USA, industry spends about 30% more than government for pollution abatement and control (*The Economist*, 1995, p. 62).

In other words, the opportunity costs of neglecting environmental issues have been rising substantially. (This change in importance of environmental costs can be compared to the rise in importance of workers' salaries. A hundred years ago these were not regarded as worth accounting for separately, because labor was cheap and they constituted no critical cost factor. Today this has changed.) The reason why firms now introduce environmental accounting is a logical consequence of changed relative costs rather than green idealism (Box 1.1).

Box 1.1
Economic Rationality of Introducing Environmental Accounting

Figure 1.3 summarizes why it has become economically rational, for the last decade, to introduce environmental accounting systems.

The marginal costs of collecting environmental data (MC_{EA} = marginal costs of environmental accounting) decrease with higher environmental impacts (from left to right). During the last decade, those costs have also decreased thanks to advanced accounting and information systems and skills (see arrow line MC_{EA}). The same has happened with the marginal costs of reducing environmental impacts (MC_{REI}), in this case thanks to advanced pollution prevention and abatement technologies (see arrow line MC_{REI}). Thus, the total marginal costs of pollution prevention have been decreasing (arrow line MC_{TREI}).

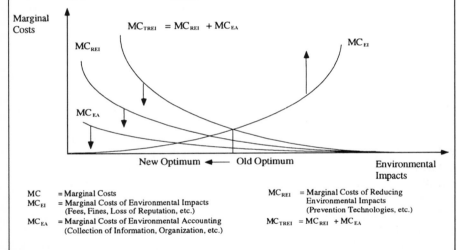

MC	= Marginal Costs	MC_{REI}	= Marginal Costs of Reducing
MC_{EI}	= Marginal Costs of Environmental Impacts		Environmental Impacts
	(Fees, Fines, Loss of Reputation, etc.)		(Prevention Technologies, etc.)
MC_{EA}	= Marginal Costs of Environmental Accounting	MC_{TREI}	= MC_{REI} + MC_{EA}
	(Collection of Information, Organization, etc.)		

Figure 1.3 Marginal Cost Curves for Environmental Accounting and Environmentally Induced Financial Impacts

The marginal costs of environmental damage, on the other hand, increase with growing environmental impacts (MC_{EI}). Due to stricter regulations (fines, fees, etc.), the marginal costs of environmental impacts have been increasing for the last decade (arrow line MC_{EI}).

Hence, the optimal point for the environmental policy of a company has been sliding to the left on the axis "environmental impacts". This means that from an economically rational perspective many more firms should introduce environmental accounting and eliminate more environmental impacts than a decade ago.

Chapter 2 discusses the framework of environmental accounting and the main issues of the different environmental accounting systems, which are later dealt with in depth in special chapters.

2

The Framework of
Environmental Accounting

2.1 THE FRAMEWORK

Stakeholders may be interested in two main groups of information with regard to environmental issues:

- environmentally induced financial impacts
- environmental impacts of the firm.

Not surprisingly then, many different perceptions and examples of "environmental accounting" exist (Schaltegger and Stinson 1994). According to the generally applicable "Tinbergen rule" in economics and public policy, a tool becomes inefficient and ineffective as soon as it is expected to pursue different goals which are not absolutely complementary (Tinbergen 1968). None of the goals would be achieved effectively and efficiently. Therefore, different tools should be applied to deal with non-complementary issues. With regard to accounting, this is why separate accounting systems should be used to deal with different sets of issues. Every accounting system provides specific information for different groups of stakeholders.

Figure 2.1 shows the most important stakeholders and different accounting *categories* and *systems*. While examples of various stakeholders are shown on the vertical axis, the horizontal axis is divided between *two different categories of accounting:*

- traditional accounting
- ecological accounting.

As shown with the areas shaded light and dark grey, both accounting categories deal with environmental issues and therefore are part of "environmental accounting". The fact that environmental accounting covers issues in traditional accounting (environmentally differentiated accounting), as

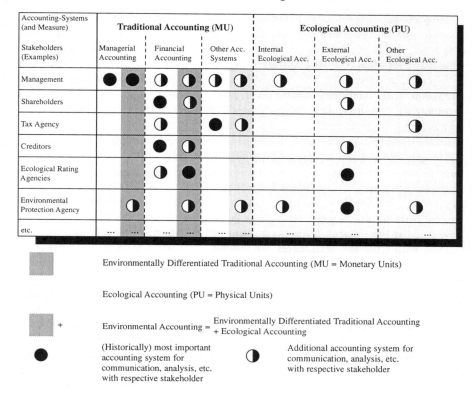

Accounting-Systems (and Measure)	Traditional Accounting (MU)			Ecological Accounting (PU)		
Stakeholders (Examples)	Managerial Accounting	Financial Accounting	Other Acc. Systems	Internal Ecological Acc.	External Ecological Acc.	Other Ecological Acc.
Management	● ●	◐ ◐	◐ ◐	◐	○	○
Shareholders		● ◐			◐	
Tax Agency		○	● ◐			○
Creditors		● ◐			○	
Ecological Rating Agencies		◐ ●			●	
Environmental Protection Agency	◐	◐	○	◐	●	○
etc.	... ...	... ...	... ...	...	...	...

Environmentally Differentiated Traditional Accounting (MU = Monetary Units)

Ecological Accounting (PU = Physical Units)

+   Environmental Accounting = Environmentally Differentiated Traditional Accounting + Ecological Accounting

● (Historically) most important accounting system for communication, analysis, etc. with respective stakeholder

◐ Additional accounting system for communication, analysis, etc. with respective stakeholder

Figure 2.1   The Framework of Environmental Accounting

well as the category of ecological accounting, is indicated by the areas shaded grey in Part B in the overview–figures introducing Parts B, C and D.

2.1.1   Environmentally Differentiated Accounting

The dark gray shaded areas in the traditional accounting category of Figure 2.1 are the *environmentally differentiated traditional accounting systems*. Being part of traditional accounting, they measure the environmentally induced financial impacts on the firm in monetary terms. The rest of the traditional accounting category which does not deal with environmental issues remains white. The category of traditional accounting is further divided into three accounting systems:

- traditional managerial accounting
- traditional financial accounting
- other traditional accounting.

Managerial accounting (also called management accounting or cost accounting) is the central tool and basis of most internal management decisions, and is not usually required by external stakeholders (see Figure 1.1). The managerial accounting system deals with questions such as: What are environmental costs and how should they be tracked and traced? How could environmentally induced costs be treated—should they be allocated to products or "counted as overhead costs"? What are the responsibilities of a management accountant?

In addition to this system, *financial accounting* is typically designed to satisfy the information requirements of external stakeholders of firms with respect to financial impacts. On the other hand, issues in financial accounting include, for example, whether environmentally induced outlays should be capitalized or expensed; or, what standards and guidelines regarding disclosure of (contingent) liabilities exist, and what recommendations do they provide on how to treat these liabilities in accounting. In addition, some possible ways of dealing with emission certificates are shown.

"Other traditional accounting systems" is a term used to cover several additional, mostly more specific, accounting systems such as tax accounting and bank regulatory accounting. Tax accounting is mandatory for all regular businesses, as the governmental tax agencies require tax "reports", whereas bank regulatory agencies, for example, have special accounting and reporting requirements only for banks. Each of these traditional accounting systems deals with different aspects of how environmental issues influence organizations (see also Schaltegger and Stinson 1994). The topics in other accounting systems vary. Tax accounting considers the effect of subsidies on pollution abatement devices, possibilities and impacts, examines how the costs for the remediation of landfills can be deducted from taxes, and looks at the effects of accelerated depreciation on clean production technologies and the consequences of various environmental taxes (e.g. a CO_2 tax, a VOC tax, etc.). Environmental issues in other traditional accounting systems include the insurance of product liabilities, mortgages, bank credits, etc.

2.1.2 Ecological Accounting

As pointed out above, many and often very different internal and external stakeholders are interested in environmental issues. Therefore, the traditional accounting category has not only to incorporate the financial impacts of environmental issues but should also be enlarged by a category of *ecological accounting systems* (shaded light grey in Figure 2.1). The distinction between the ecological accounting category and the traditional accounting category is necessary for several reasons.

- From a material point of view, the focus of ecological accounting is very different from that of traditional accounting. The focus of ecological accounting is on environmental interventions whereas that of traditional accounting is on financial impacts.

- Environmental information often stems from other sources than financial information.
- Environmental information is often required for different purposes and by different stakeholders compared with financial information.
- Environmental information has different measures of quality and quantity (e.g. kilograms) than economic information.

The category of ecological accounting, which is shaded dark gray in Figure 2.1, measures the ecological impact of a company on the environment. Its measurements (unlike those of environmentally differentiated traditional accounting) are in physical terms: the term "PU" stands for "Physical Units" (e.g. kilograms or joules). The category of ecological accounting can also be divided into three systems, corresponding to the structure in the traditional accounting systems:

- internal ecological accounting
- external ecological accounting
- other ecological accounting.

The *internal ecological accounting system* is designed to collect ecological information for internal managerial purposes in terms of physical units. It is complementary to traditional managerial accounting. Methods of measuring the impact of a company's products and processes on the natural environment are necessary to make possible good management decisions, and various ways of examining pollution discharges and damage to ecological capital have been developed over the last decade. More or less sophisticated internal ecological accounting is a necessary precondition for any environmental management system.

The counterpart of traditional financial accounting is *external ecological accounting*, where data for environmentally interested external stakeholders—namely the general public, the media, shareholders, environmental funds and pressure groups—are collected and presented. For the last ten years hundreds of firms have published external environmental reports thus giving a public stocktaking of their environmental impacts. Many of them are extensive annual reports with detailed data on discharges of pollutants.

Other ecological accounting systems, which measure data in physical units, are a means for regulators to control compliance. Also, those accounting systems are necessary for the correct assessment of environmental taxes such as a CO_2 tax or a tax on volatile organic compounds (VOC). For example, without information about discharges, environmental tax rates could not be multiplied by the respective releases of pollutants. Apart from the tax agency and the environmental protection agencies, which are primarily interested in

---

Box 2.1
Definition of Environmental Accounting

Environmental accounting is a sub-area of accounting that deals with

- Activities, methods and systems
- Recording, analysis and reporting
- Environmentally induced financial impacts and ecological impacts of a defined economic system (e.g. a firm, plant region, nation, etc.)

---

specific information on discharges of specific pollutants, an increasing number of stakeholders such as banks as lenders of money and insurance companies, etc. require reliable information on the environmental impacts of firms.

Figure 2.1 shows how the information collected by the various environmental accounting systems is of different value for various stakeholders. The historically most important accounting system for each stakeholder has been marked with a black filled circle, while additional systems designed for communication or analysis are indicated with a circle filled half white and black. Ecological accounting systems are relatively young and have only recently become important information tools for many stakeholders. An exception are government agencies in charge of environmental protection. The category of ecological accounting systems therefore contains relatively few completely filled circles.

As both the environmentally differentiated traditional accounting systems and the ecological accounting systems process environmentally induced information, they constitute—taken together—the *environmental accounting systems*. The definition of environmental accounting used throughout this book is shown in Box 2.1. (For other definitions or descriptions of environmental accounting, see Gray *et al.* 1993, p. 6).

The fact that with traditional and ecological accounting two different accounting categories have been established is not a problem. The results and information of both accounting categories can be integrated as a separate analysis, making them available for the decision making of management and external stakeholders (Part D). The integration of different accounting systems, as well as the integration of accounting information with environmental management concepts, is discussed in Chapter 12.

2.2 GOALS OF ENVIRONMENTAL ACCOUNTING

Because of the growing importance of environmental matters, issues of environmental accounting have attracted a lot of attention in recent years.

Table 2.1 Principal Stakeholder Groups Having Published Standards, Regulations, Guidelines or Recommendations Affecting Environmental Accounting

Stakeholder Group	Affected Accounting & Chapter	Specifications for Accounting	Characteristics
Regulatory Bodies			
SEC	Financial Acc. Part B, Chapter 5	Very specific	Legal, binding for firms listed on a US stock exchange
DOE Washington	Managerial Acc. Part B, Chapter 4	Very specific	Guideline accompanying a regulation
COM (EMAS/Eco-label)	Site-/ Prod.- or. Ecol. Acc. Part C, Part D	General	Voluntary
Professional Accounting and Financial Analysts' Associations			
EFFAS	Fin. Acc./Ext. Ecol. Acc. Part B, Part C	Specific	Statement and demand of financial analysts
CICA	Acc. Part B	Specific/general	Statement of professional accountants
Accounting Standardization Organizations			
IASC	Financial Acc. Part B, Chapter 5	Specific	Have not dealt with topic so far
FASB	Financial Acc. Part B, Chapter 5	Very specific	Strong influence of SEC
Other Standardization Organizations			
BSI	Man. Acc./Ecol. Acc. Part D, Part B/Part C	General	Focus on environmental management systems
ISO	Man. Acc./Ecol. Acc. Part D, Part B/Part C	General	Focus on environmental management systems
Industry			
ICC	Env. Acc. in general Part A	Very general	Starting point for environmental management
Chemical Industry (Responsible Care)	Ecol. Acc. in general Part C	Very general	Starting point for environmental management
"Green" Organizations			
CERES	Ext. Ecol. Acc. Part C, Chapter 9	Very general	Addresses environmental interests of potential investors

(*continued*)

Table 2.1 (*continued*)

WWF	Ext. Ecol. Acc. Part C, Chapter 9	Specific	Addresses "green" stakeholders
Scientific Certification Systems	Prod.-or. Ext. Ecol. Acc. Part C, Section 8.3, 9	Specific	Addresses "green" customers

Other International Organizations

UN	Env. Acc. Part A	Specific intentions	Addresses corporations in UN-countries
OECD	Ecol. Acc. Part C	Very general	Addresses multinationals in OECD-countries

Acc.	= Accounting
BSI	= British Standards Institute
CERES	= Coalition for Environmentally Responsible Economies
CICA	= Canadian Institute of Certified Accountants
COM	= Commission of the European Union
DOE	= Department of Ecology, Washington, USA
Ecol.	= Ecological
EFFAS	= European Federation of Financial Analysts' Societies
EMAS	= Environmental Management and Eco-Audit System
Env.	= Environmental
Ext.	= External
FASB	= Financial Accounting Standards Board
Fin.	= Financial
IASC	= International Accounting Standards Committee
ICC	= International Chamber of Commerce
ISO	= International Standards Organization
Man.	= Managerial
OECD	= Organization of Economic Cooperation and Development
Prod.-or.	= Product-oriented
SEC	= Securities and Exchange Commission (USA)
UN	= United Nations
US	= United States of America
WWF	= World Wide Fund for Nature

Many different interest groups are trying to influence the methods of environmental accounting as well as the respective reporting practices. Therefore, the emerging systems of environmental accounting are a result of different goals and perspectives as well as of the relative power of critical stakeholders.

Table 2.1 gives an overview of important stakeholder groups influencing different systems of environmental accounting. The specifications and characteristics of the published standards, regulations, guidelines and recommendations are discussed later in the respective chapters and sections.

All the different environmental accounting systems are developed to inform important stakeholders and to help firms to improve their environmental

Table 2.2 Examples Characterizing Environmental Accounting Systems

	Information Collection and Aggregation	Audit	Disclosure	Use of Information
Managerial Accounting	Many states require the collection of process costs	Regulators may be able to audit cost collection process	Cost information must be disclosed to regulator	Internal evaluation of profitability and communication
Financial Accounting	Company must estimate environmental liabilities	External auditor considers impact of environmental liabilities for client	Disclosure of certain environmental liabilities is required in some countries	Shareholder communication with financial reporting
Tax Accounting	Company must determine amount of environmental taxes	Tax authority can audit company to verify tax obligation	Various environmental tax obligations must be disclosed (paid)	Evaluation of tax burden and communication with tax authority
Internal Ecological Accounting	Emission/output monitoring	Usually no audit requirements because collection of information voluntary	Typically carried out for internal purposes	Evaluation communication
External Ecological Accounting	Environmental impacts are estimated	Regulator and verifiers can audit records and accuracy of monitoring	Records of monitoring must be disclosed to public and/or appropriate regulator	Public and shareholder communication with ecological reporting
Other Ecological Accounting	Basis for environmental taxes, emission allowances, etc. can be determined	Regulator can audit records and monitor accuracy	Records of monitoring must be disclosed to appropriate regulator	Communication with regulators' compliance audit

performance and thereby progress on the path of sustainable development (see Section 8.2).

The quantitative measurement of impacts and the calculation of comparable numbers is, in the opinion of many business leaders as well as of a large part of the scientific community, the only practical way to measure sustainable development and eco-efficiency (Part C). The comparison and aggregation of environmental impacts of various products, processes, firms, regions or nations is imperative, because it is the total amount of damage done which really matters for the environment. Nevertheless, the above quantitative accounting systems might well be supported by more qualitative assessments. As not all environmental impacts can (or should) be counted, supplementing quantitative environmental accounting with qualitative measures will become inevitable as business and the various stakeholders progress towards the state of a sustainable society. (For the concept of a sustainable society, see for example Karr (1993), and Section 7.2.)

Possible purposes of the development of environmental accounting are not only to measure environmentally induced financial impacts or the environmental damage done, but also to provide a means of developing closer relationships between organizations and society, transferring some power to society, and increasing the transparency of organizations (see Gray 1992, p. 415).

Today's companies have to consider different, sometimes conflicting interests of various stakeholders. In developed countries, ever more frequently, economically successful organizations have to adapt themselves to new needs and demands and new external as well as internal stakeholders.

Table 2.2 illustrates some goals and characteristics of environmental accounting systems with some examples of information collection and aggregation, audits, disclosure requirements and the use of the collected information.

The need for additional environmental information is changing the structure and behavior of organizations as they become more transparent. The requests for information of external stakeholders make internal organizational change necessary, as the required data have to be internally collected. However, it is important to note that environmental accounting by itself is not enough, but has to be embedded into the larger context of environmental management. Only this ensures that the information gathered by accounting is used efficiently, effectively and purposefully to improve the environmental performance of the company.

PART B
Traditional Accounting
and the Environment

Traditional accounting must consider environmental issues better because of their increasing influence on the economic success of a company. The notion of "environmentally differentiated accounting" describes the whole set of managerial, financial and other traditional accounting systems which are differentiated according to environmental criteria. Further specifications (managerial, financial, or other) are added if only a single specific accounting system is meant. (For example, "environmentally differentiated financial accounting" is used only when the environmental differentiation of financial accounting is meant.)

Chapter 3 prepares the discussion of environmentally differentiated accounting by outlining the nature and characteristics of environmental costs (Section 3.1). Section 3.2 reviews the customary and the current *environmentally oriented criticism* of traditional accounting. Despite some harsh criticism, traditional accounting has some uncontested advantages as a helpful management concept (3.3). In addition, traditional accounting can be differentiated so as also to consider environmental issues. This is why Section 3.4 provides an overview of systems of accounting environmentally induced financial impacts.

Chapter 4 treats the *environmental differentiation of managerial accounting*. The main issues are tracking and tracing (4.2) and allocation (4.3) of environmental costs as well as life-cycle costing (4.4), investment appraisal (4.5), and the influence of external stakeholders on managerial accounting (4.6).

Chapter 5 presents *environmental issues in traditional financial accounting*. Section 5.1 discusses the role of the main stakeholders who influence financial accounting. Standards are one of the main results of stakeholders' politics. A brief review is therefore given of the underlying assumptions and conventions of the international standards of financial accounting. On this basis, the following sections deal with the main environmental issues in financial accounting. An important question is whether environmentally induced outlays should be capitalized or expensed (5.2), and whether and how the respective costs (5.3) and financial impacts on company assets (5.4) should be treated and disclosed. In addition, the treatment of environmentally induced liabilities and contingent liabilities (5.5), as well as the special case of tradeable emission allowances (5.6) is discussed. Furthermore, the influence of environmental issues in the Management's Discussion and Analysis is treated (5.7). The chapter ends with conclusions (5.8).

After the main traditional accounting systems, namely managerial and financial accounting, Chapter 6 deals with environmental topics of *other traditional accounting systems*, such as tax accounting (6.2) and special regulatory accounting relationships (6.3).

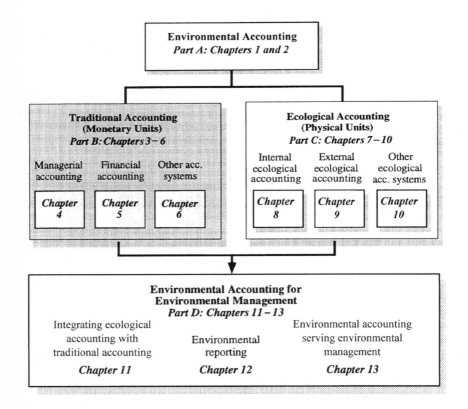

3

Introduction to Environmentally Differentiated Accounting

Issues of environmentally differentiated traditional accounting are examined following a discussion of environmental costs (3.1) and a review of the criticism of traditional accounting (3.2). Section 3.1 takes a macro viewpoint (in contrast to a corporate viewpoint) to show links between different kinds of environmental costs. The criticism and the discussion of the uncontested advantages of traditional accounting (sections 3.2 and 3.3) lead to the discussion of environmentally differentiated accounting. Readers in a hurry might prefer to skip Sections 3.2 and 3.3 and continue with Section 3.4 (accounting of environmentally induced financial impacts).

Today, every company faces environmentally induced financial impacts which are usually dealt with in traditional corporate accounting. However, to support economically rational decisions, these financial impacts should be explicitly reflected in traditional accounting and, therefore, differentiated from other financial impacts. For traditional accounting, environmentally induced costs are of main interest. For that reason, and to simplify this chapter, the focus is placed on "costs". However, expenses, assets, etc. will be discussed later where they become relevant for certain environmental issues.

3.1 THE NATURE OF ENVIRONMENTAL COSTS

When dealing with environmental issues of traditional accounting, a clear understanding of the nature of costs in general and environmental costs in particular is necessary. (Respective categories and definitions of revenue are not treated specifically.)

Costs are the valued use of goods and services. Every human presence and activity can cause costs for the economy, society and the natural environment (Figure 3.1).

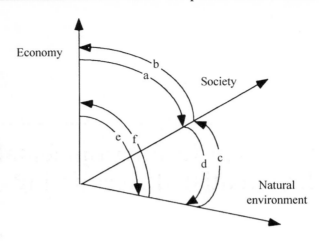

Figure 3.1   Costs for the Economy, Society and the Natural Environment

The three dimensions may interact:

−a→   Economic activities can cause social impacts (e.g. isolation of workers).
←b−   Social impacts can lead to economic costs (e.g. health costs, loss of jobs).
←c−   Social problems can accompany environmental impacts (e.g. deforestation due to poverty).
−d→   Environmental problems can induce social costs (e.g. deforestation can cause migration).
−e→   Economic activities can relate to environmental impacts (e.g. pollution).
←f−   Environmental impacts can result in economic costs (e.g. damage costs).

In reality many human activities affect all three dimensions. Sustainable development is characterized by an improvement in all three dimensions (see also Part C). However, this book focuses on environmental issues from a business perspective (arrows "−e→" and "←f−" in Figure 3.1).

In traditional corporate accounting, a distinction between *external* and *internal* environmental costs is crucial.

3.1.1   External Environmental Costs

For the last two decades, the concept of "external costs" has shaped the discussion of environmental costs. *External* costs (also called negative externalities) are costs borne by people other than those who cause the costs

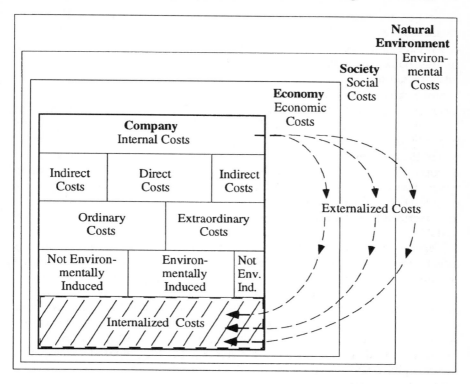

Figure 3.2 Environmental Costs

and receive the benefits.[1] Therefore, external costs, contrary to *internal* costs, are not reflected in the traditional accounting systems of the company (Figure 3.2). (For the distinction between pecuniary and technological externalities, see Baumol and Oates, 1988, p. 29ff.)

From a "deep green" (ecocentric) perspective, the natural environment has a value independent of mankind, and impacts on the environment must therefore be taken into account irrespective of whether human society is affected or not. Potential costs must be considered in decision taking but are not included in accounting. Ideally, accounting should therefore also consider indirect and potential effects on the natural environment.

Costs can be defined as the monetary value of the consumption of goods and services. From an all-embracing viewpoint, every use of the environment is a "consumption of goods and services" and can therefore be expressed as an *environmental cost* (Schreiner 1988, p. 199ff). As society is always part of the natural environment *all costs* are environmental costs (Figure 3.2). From this perspective, environmental accounting would have to capture completely all costs that can possibly exist. To attempt to do so would, of course, be utopian. In this book, the term "environmental costs" is therefore used in a more selective sense.

Some external costs affect society in a very direct way. This is the case, for instance, if the noise level near a road increases because of more traffic. The costs of reducing these adverse effects (e.g. by building a wall) are usually borne by the government, i.e. the taxpayers. If an anthropocentric approach is taken, the only important part of environmental costs is the part which results in costs for human society, now or in future. These are costs of degradation which have either a monetary or a non-monetary impact on the quality of life of at least one human being (Schreiner 1988, p. 199ff). In Figure 3.2 these costs are described by the term "*social costs*" (sometimes also described as "societal costs").

Negative external effects on the natural environment can also indirectly affect people. For example, future generations will have fewer opportunities (options) to observe wildlife. Lost opportunities to profit from nature induce *economic costs*, too. In Figure 3.2 these so-called "opportunity costs" are not shown directly as they are part of "economic costs". Furthermore, economic costs are part of social costs. For example, the extinction of species causes social and economic costs as the reduction of the pool of genes results in a loss of potential benefits from those genes (e.g. for the potential development of some pharmaceuticals)—even if nobody (or hardly anyone) ever saw these species (see Arber 1992). Biologists compare the loss of a gene with the burning down of a library before anyone could ever read the books (Arber, 1992).

The definition of environmental costs used here does not cover all costs for human beings. Society also faces costs which are not environmentally induced (e.g. due to social injustice). Environmental accounting in the sense defined in Part A does not capture the accounting of social development, injustice, etc. Hence, the focus of environmental accounting is rather on environmentally induced social (and economic) costs, or those monetary and non-monetary impacts on the natural environment that somehow affect society.

Externalities affecting the natural environment and society reduce the overall efficiency of an economy (Box 3.1). (Technological externalities are meant; for the distinction between technological and pecuniary externalities see, for example, Baumol and Oates, 1988). They are *not* considered in the traditional accounting system of the company which caused them. However, externalities may be "picked up" in the accounting systems of other, uninvolved companies if they alter their production costs (which is not necessarily the case).

Box 3.1
Externalities

CFCs contribute to the depletion of the ozone layer. Since stratospheric ozone shields the earth from ultraviolet radiation, the depletion of the ozone layer allows increased levels of radiation to reach the earth's surface. There is hard evidence that this results in increases in skin cancer rates and damage to crops and fisheries. Thus, using CFCs impacts the production function of farmers and fishers. Furthermore, with higher health costs and mortality substantial technological costs are borne by society.

These costs are not shown in the traditional accounting systems of the CFC users. However, they reduce the overall efficiency of the world economy. They are partially reflected in the accounting systems of farmers and fisheries (as decreased revenues), hospitals (as increased turn-over) and nations (as lower GDP).

Some environmental costs are internalized by governmental enforcement. Other external costs are "voluntarily" internalized, for example negotiating with important stakeholders who bear external costs. The difficulty of internalizing non-monetary externalities is that somehow they have to be assigned an artificial price (e.g. with an environmental tax) before they can be considered in traditional accounting. In spite of these difficulties, management should anticipate that more external costs will be internalized in the future. The pressure to internalize these costs increases with growing scientific evidence.

3.1.2 Internal Environmental Costs

Company-internal costs (also "private costs") can be divided into ordinary and extraordinary as well as into direct and indirect costs (Figure 3.2). Ordinary costs, in contrast to extraordinary ones, derive from the core business of the company.[2] Direct costs, unlike indirect costs, can be clearly identified with specific departments, products, or processes.

Both direct and indirect costs as well as ordinary and extraordinary costs can be environmentally induced or non-environmentally induced. For example, the costs associated with the production of cars are *ordinary* costs for a car manufacturer (e.g. fees for the waste water from production). An unexpected, exceptional accident, on the other hand, results in *extraordinary* costs (e.g. clean-up costs due to an unexpected explosion).

Direct environmentally induced costs could be, for example, costs of scrubbers directly linked to the production of a specific type of car. Costs of

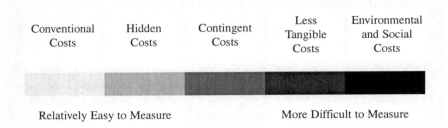

| Conventional Costs | Hidden Costs | Contingent Costs | Less Tangible Costs | Environmental and Social Costs |

Relatively Easy to Measure   More Difficult to Measure

Figure 3.3   The Spectrum of Environmental Costs. Source: Adapted from Spitzer and Elwood 1995, p. 14. Reproduced with permission

joint clean-up facilities, such as a waste water treatment plant, are *indirect* as they have to be specifically allocated to cost centers and cost carriers.

Among the most obvious environmental costs are conventional costs, such as capital and operating costs for clean-up facilities. There can also be hidden regulatory costs (e.g. reporting costs), contingent liabilities (e.g. expected clean-up costs), and less tangible costs such as damage to a company's image due to pollution. These are classified as environmentally induced internal costs. Figure 3.3 shows these costs on the spectrum between "easier to measure" and "more difficult to measure".

Conventional and hidden costs are mostly covered by traditional accounting. Contingent costs are sometimes included, whilst intangible costs usually are not directly reflected in accounting. Many social costs are not considered in traditional corporate accounting. (Examples of social costs considered in traditional accounting include: social security costs, costs of benefit plans, etc.) However, the last three categories of costs can easily have an indirect effect on the economic success of a company. Traditional accounting has been strongly criticized because it does not sufficiently reflect environmental costs (and social costs). The next sections deal with criticisms of traditional accounting.

3.2   CRITICISM OF TRADITIONAL ACCOUNTING

For the first time in accounting's sleepy history, there is a growing recognition among accountants and non-accountants alike that accounting, that value-free, balanced system of double entries, may be sending dangerously incomplete signals to business, to consumers, to regulators, and to bankers. (Rubenstein 1994)

Accounting systems are one of the most important management tools for every economy. The purpose of accounting is to reflect reality as accurately as possible. The information collected with an accounting system must provide a reliable basis for decisions of managers, investors and many other stakeholders. Yet, the reality is such a complex system that this objective cannot be achieved at reasonable cost. Hence, accounting systems represent *conventions* on how to reflect something.

Although absolutely necessary, these conventions have been sharply criticized. Some of the most extreme criticisms even go so far as to maintain that all the conventions, and the information collected with today's accounting systems, mirror just what economic leaders currently consider important for the economy and society.

Conventions reflect the distribution of power between different stakeholders such as shareholders, managers, future generations and others (see Section 1.1). Since the power-relations are constantly changing, accounting systems too are generally under constant pressure to change, expand or adapt. Moreover, accounting systems are not designed to provide information which is regarded as useless for the main (powerful) stakeholders. However, as a society moves ahead, new information and other stakeholders become important. This puts accounting systems under additional pressure to change (see Section 1.2). Consequently, the economic activities could also be reflected with other conventions. The main roots of the environmentally based criticisms of accounting systems are to be found here. Hence, the following sections point out not only the environmental criticisms, but also some other criticisms of traditional accounting.

The last section of this chapter finishes with the remark that, despite this criticism, traditional accounting has shown itself to provide uncontested advantages.

3.2.1 Environmentally Based Criticism

Historically, the first more or less complex accounting systems evolved in the Renaissance period in the sixteenth century. One of the most extreme criticisms directed at accounting points out an expected influence of this period of history. The belief that humans are external and superior to nature and that mankind is able to manage nature in a rational manner is seen to be still reflected in today's accounting. Although not immediately evident, this is considered to have led to some weaknesses of traditional accounting, in particular concerning the fundamental outlook of traditional accounting, its focus on the entity.

Also the *focus* of the traditional accounting *on entities* has been strongly criticized (see for example Maunders and Burritt 1991, p. 11 or Wainman 1991). The importance attached to the events happening within an entity and the ignorance of the events which take place outside lead to major problems for the accounting of environmental damage. From a legal point of view, the environment is outside the boundaries of a company, so that environmental impacts are often treated as "externalities" (Section 3.1). Therefore, they are dealt with in a company only in isolated instances.

Today accounting systems do not reflect environmental impacts caused directly or indirectly by a company. This will remain the same as long as organizations are treated as a "semi-closed system with hard (accounting) boundaries" (Maunders and Burritt, 1991). For example, if adverse health impacts occur because of the use of a product, this is not directly shown in the company's accounts. (Some may argue that it has shown excessively high revenues/profits in previous years). Nevertheless, in some cases, customers have the possibility of suing the company or of "punishing" it indirectly by not continuing to buy the company's products. In other cases product or other liabilities will lead to an *internalization* of the costs of environmental impacts. Society has other means of internalizing environmental costs such as through environmental taxes, the legal requirement for companies to have pollution control devices etc. Yet, it might take several years before some environmental impacts due, for instance, to products sold in the past, are recognized and the respective liabilities become material for a company, its suppliers or clients (see Box 3.2).

Box 3.2
Postponed Internalization of Environmental Externalities

- In the 1960s, the asbestos industry sold products that have been causing tremendous health damage in the 1980s and 1990s. Today, asbestos as a product is mostly phased out and the insurance companies (which have not caused the damage) are having to foot the financial bill. The financial liabilities for pollution, illnesses such as asbestosis, clean-up liabilities and related claims have to be borne by the insurance industry, i.e. today's premium payers. The claims are estimated to be $2 trillion alone in the USA, of which 11 billion is covered by reserves and provisions (Knight 1994, p. 48ff).

- The reinsurance industry faces a similar problem. They argue that they have huge cash outflows because of more frequent and severe storms which might be significantly correlated with the global warming effect. However, the insurance industry has never earned premiums to cover these costs (Knight 1994, p. 48ff).

Typical for both cases is that the costs have not been reflected in the accounting systems of those who caused them, although many years later, the negative financial consequences are internalized in the accounting systems of others (see also Section 3.1). The bulk of the consequences (financial and health effects) has not to be paid by the companies that caused the costs.

Traditional accounting systems do not provide information on how much the environment is harmed, no matter how high the social costs are, or whether the damage is irreversible or the carrying capacity exceeded. If the management relies only on traditional accounting information, it might very often not even recognize that the environment has been harmed. Therefore, it has been argued that adverse effects on the environment can be seen–to a certain extent–as a result of current accounting practices.[3] The impacts of current accounting practices can be divided (see Maunders and Burritt, 1991) into:

- *Direct* effects
- *Indirect* effects.

a) Direct Effects on the Environment

As accounting information is used for decision-making by both internal and external stakeholders, comprehensive information, as correct and as complete as possible becomes crucial. Decision-making and performance evaluation of activities with an environmental impact must rely on accounting information that often conforms to generally accepted accounting standards which can be regarded as conventions of financial reporting. The disregarding of externalities in these forms of accounting results in accounting information without external costs, which is used by financial and strategic management for decision-making. The internal costs are too low because the external costs are excluded so that the management favors the products and processes with the lowest internal costs–not the ones with the lowest total social costs.

b) Indirect Effects on the Environment

Indirect effects of traditional accounting on the environment are connected with the mental framework we unconsciously use when we view the world. Traditional accounting, for example, though it measures income does not question its distribution. Instead it accepts interpersonal, interregional and intergenerational distribution regardless of its moral or ethical flaws. For example, the traditional accounting system does not show who received the money spent by a company (interpersonal distribution), nor does it show where the supplier of the company is situated (interregional distribution) or if money is spent for the needs of future generations.

A further criticism points at the inherent discrepancy between the accounting system and the natural ecosystem. For accounting no upper limit exists—the word "enough" is never translated into numbers—whereas the natural environment has such a limit (carrying capacity). Compared to the macro-economic perspective this amounts to a criticism of the concept of the Gross National Product (GNP) as a measure of wealth and the related constant striving for higher GNP (see Gray 1992). Environmental damage is not considered in this quest for higher monetary income and wealth, as no value is put on most ("priceless") environmental goods. However, the same critics often see it as undesirable to give environmental goods an artificial price (Hines, 1991). Nature reacts according to completely different laws than accounting systems; it is based more on the interconnectedness and interaction of all substances and beings. Accounting systems, on the contrary, divide, separate and count everything independently. They use special accounts for every accounting item and finally put the many different items together again in a standardised format such as a balance sheet, a profit and loss account or a cash flow statement.

The interdependence of time is also ignored in traditional accounting systems. For example, outlays with future ecological benefits (e.g. pollution abatement expenditures) are often reflected negatively in current performance.

These procedures are not only seen to contribute to the above mentioned problems. They also cause problems for the financial analysis of companies, products, investments and production processes (see Chapter 4).

Maunders and Burritt (1991, p. 13) summarize their criticism of traditional accounting in the following way: "By providing the only quantified analysis available, it is not decision support which is provided [by traditional accounting], but rather conditioning."

3.2.2 Other Criticisms of Traditional Accounting

Criticism of traditional accounting is not limited to environmental argumentation. Its shortcomings are impressively underlined by long and never-ending discussions on "What is the relevant profit figure? How do profit figures have to be adjusted? What are the correct earnings per share?" and so on. There has been a passionate discussion about the shortcomings of traditional accounting. This discussion is dealt with extensively in the literature and is therefore not repeated here.

However, some aspects of the general criticism of traditional accounting are brought into context with environmental accounting. Accounting is criticized for encouraging us to live beyond our means and to control and suppress others.

Double-entry bookkeeping is seen to "recommend" that lending should be shown as a debt on the liabilities side of the balance sheet, and at the same time as cash on the assets side. This procedure enables companies and individuals to live beyond their means, or in other words at the expense of the natural environment and future generations. A company that wishes to expand despite having an insufficient operating cashflow can finance its debt as long as some debt ratios and rules are met. However, these additional financial resources lead to an incremental increase in sales, etc. and thus (in most cases) to an additional use of natural resources and to higher emissions. Consequently, less resources would have been used so far if debt financing were not allowed.

However, it is important to recognize that one of the main functions of debt-financing is to bridge time differences between savers and investors and thus to contribute materially to the wealth accumulated by many nations and individuals.

Feminist criticism takes a slightly different view (see Cooper 1992a,b or Gallhofer 1992). Accounting is seen to be a predominantly masculine (not necessarily male) discipline, used to control and suppress others. Traditional accounting lacks the strengths of the feminine way of dealing with life, such as non-competitiveness and giving (Cooper 1992a,b). The masculine way of thinking, which stresses the utility-maximizing goal of the unified, rational, and self-centered being, has been blamed for the environmental destruction we witness today (Cooper 1992a, p. 27). Therefore, the creation of a feminine libidinal economy is proposed, where feminine qualities, for example plurality and circularity, flourish. Cooper summarizes the feminist perspective the following way: ". . . we could perhaps imagine an accounting which is multiple, no debits or credits; which allows for many differences, these could not be added therefore there would be no totals; it would not be concerned with profits, and even less afraid of loss; it would be concerned with gifts, what was given; it would contain no phallocentric economic terms; and it would not be competitive." (Cooper, 1992a, p. 37).

Most critics miss the actual purpose and use of accounting by far. They could be taken as questioning anything society has created. This frustration about society in general is also reflected in the fact that none of the criticizing parties has been able to suggest a useful and superior information tool. However, to capture the environmental problems companies and society face today practical concepts for actual improvement are necessary. Thus, in contrast to the critique summarized, we will focus on concepts which are based on the strengths of accounting. The benefit of a pragmatic approach for the environment, society and economy is definitely greater than concentrating on idle talk.

Nevertheless, the discussed critique and shortcomings of traditional accounting systems and information can motivate stakeholders to a variety of reactions.

3.2.3 Stakeholder Reactions

In principle, three possible reactions exist whenever stakeholders do not agree with the present situation (Hirschman, 1970).

1 *Resignation and loyalty:* Stakeholders can accept (ignore) the deficiencies of traditional accounting and "indulge in the sweet side of life". With this reaction, no improvements are possible as no energy is expended to change the current situation.

2 *Voice:* As mentioned earlier, academics, professional accountants and managers have addressed weaknesses of accounting for many years. Even at the annual meetings shareholders have brought up environmental issues impacting on business. Many suggestions have changed the existing practices and systems and have contributed to improving accounting. "Voice" requires initiatives of important stakeholders, and the readiness of all involved parties to constructively contribute towards solving existing problems.

3 *Exit:* Investors and creditors can withdraw financial resources whenever they do not appreciate the accounting practices of a company. In addition, different models and groups exist that represent an escape to a separate social and/or economic system (colony model) with different rules of accounting. One way to exit the existing economic system is, for example, to live in a remote area. Another way is to establish "colony currency and accounting models". These models often work with negative interest rates to prevent people from striving for growth and to give incentives not to hoard money but to put it into circulation.[5]

Many environmental problems are too severe to be neglected (resignation) and too global in nature to allow a successful escape. Thus, following the second approach (voice) seems to be the only promising way to tackle them.

3.3 UNCONTESTED ADVANTAGES OF TRADITIONAL ACCOUNTING

We need dedicated, hardworking individuals, not armchair cynics. (Wainman 1991)

After having examined in detail the criticism of accounting, it must nevertheless be acknowledged that the existing accounting systems offer great and uncontested advantages.

Internal and external stakeholders need some kind of information system for decision making. In this connection, quantification can be seen as a widely accepted way to add precision to reasoning about the world. Of course, quantification cannot deal with issues of morality, beauty and love, but it is a powerful instrument when a society seeks to overcome poverty, fiscal deficits, or environmental degradation. The main principles of today's (quantitative) accounting systems have gained worldwide acceptance. Accounting can therefore be regarded as one of the most international "languages" spoken by many different stakeholders worldwide. This is also reflected in the growing economic importance of the accounting industry. This is reflected in its size. In 1994 the "big six" of the accounting industry employed more than 400,000 people worldwide and achieved a turnover of approximately $30 billion.

As accounting has shown itself to create many benefits, it should not be denied emotionally, but should be substantially improved. For accountants, much of the criticism seems rather exaggerated, for accounting does not really cause the problems mentioned. Accounting only reflects the human will to accumulate fortune, wealth and power measurable in monetary terms. However, every sensible accountant will also agree that traditional accounting systems are not sufficient to solve the enormous environmental problems of today and the future. Nonetheless, accounting is a necessary and important part of a pragmatic approach to the registration of environmental problems within the limits of possibility. In this connection it should be accepted that the suggested change in accounting practices will redefine and reinforce the relationships and power within an organization.

Among the main benefits of correctly considering environmental issues in traditional accounting are:

- to correctly consider the actual and potential economic consequences of environmental issues
- to adapt the economic effects of new environmental regulations (in advance)
- to take the economically superior measures of environmental protection
- to be able to respond to environmental issues raised by shareholders.

Considering the strengths, criticism and possibilities of accounting, the following questions remain.

- How can the traditional accounting framework be differentiated so as to effectively consider environmentally induced financial impacts (Part B)?
- How can the traditional accounting framework be enlarged so as to effectively and efficiently consider impacts on the natural environment (Part C)?

The first question is dealt with in the following chapters of Part B. First, an overview of the examined traditional accounting systems is given. Then it is shown how environmental issues influence traditional managerial, financial and other accounting systems.

3.4 ACCOUNTING OF ENVIRONMENTALLY INDUCED FINANCIAL IMPACTS

Traditional accounting should deal with environmental issues explicitly to provide correct information about the growing economic consequences of environmental issues and pollution prevention (see also Section 1.1 and 3.3).

Only with correct information management, can shareholders and creditors consider correctly the actual and potential economic consequences of

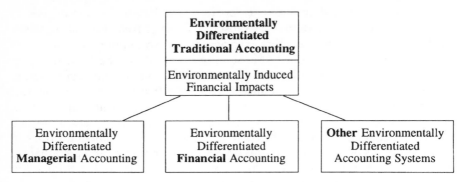

Figure 3.4 Environmentally Differentiated Traditional Accounting

environmental issues, adapt the economic effects of new environmental regulations and have a mutually fruitful discussion of how best to implement pollution prevention.

Traditional accounting that deals with environmentally induced financial information is called *environmentally differentiated traditional accounting* (see also Part A). It embraces environmentally differentiated *managerial* and environmentally differentiated *financial* accounting as well as other environmentally differentiated accounting systems (Figure 3.4).

Ideally, all impacts, including those borne by society and the natural environment, would be included in traditional accounting. As only a small part of the externalities are internalized, the strategic decisions of management may be based on incomplete information, which in some cases may even be economically misleading (e.g. when external costs are internalized after some time).

However, it would be even more misleading if the management internalized externalities in its traditional accounting as long as they are not part of the actual economic effects of business. Traditional accounting is a set of information systems for measuring the past economic performance (the economic profitability) of a company. A mixture of external and internal financial impacts (i.e. external and internal costs) would distort the actual figures so that they would no longer have the necessary informative value for making economic decisions.

Apart from its legal obligation to consider only actual internal financial impacts in financial accounting, the management must first of all be interested to know what environmentally induced (already internalized) financial impacts it faces. Hence, traditional corporate accounting should only consider internally relevant financial effects. To support economically rational decisions, these financial impacts should be explicitly reflected in traditional accounting (differentiated from other financial impacts).

In addition, as environmental issues often change and can quickly have substantial financial consequences, strategic management should use additional management tools for decision making and not rely only on accounting information.

Environmentally differentiated *managerial* accounting deals with environmentally induced costs and revenues.

Environmentally induced costs have been extensively dealt with (Section 3.1). They can be increased or reduced by taking steps to protect the environment. Additional costs include fines, fees, clean-up costs, the increased production of unwanted output, etc. On the other hand, savings might be achieved through the optimal use of resources, the decrease of unwanted output, fewer fines and fees, etc.

Environmentally induced revenues can be divided into direct and indirect revenues. Direct revenues, for example, include the gains from sales of recyclables, increased sales of products and higher prices of the products sold. Indirect effects are less tangible and can for example include an enhanced image, increased customer and employee satisfaction, the transfer of know-how and the development of new markets for environmentally benign products.

Environmentally differentiated *financial* accounting deals with revenues and expenses (shown in the income statement, also called profit and loss account), assets and liabilities (shown in the balance sheet).

Costs are classified as expenses if they have given a benefit that has now expired. Unexpired costs that can give future benefits are defined as assets, whereas property rights of creditors class as liabilities. Liabilities that can only be estimated are commonly called "provisions". If their occurrence is uncertain, liabilities are disclosed as "contingent liabilities" (also called "potential liabilities").

Environmentally induced expenses are, for instance, fines for illegal waste disposal or clean-up costs to restore land. (For example, a scrubber can be recognized as an *environmentally induced asset* if it secures future economic benefits (production can be continued) according to IASC 1995 [IAS 14, 16]). *Environmental liabilities* are future costs, such as for future remediation of landfills, legal cases, etc.

Other environmentally differentiated traditional accounting systems establish special, mostly regulatory, accounting relationships. Tax accounting, the most important example, deals with tax implications of environmentally induced expenses (including the topic of fiscal neutrality), assets and provisions and tax expenses (taxes) and tax subsidies of a company.

Environmentally induced taxes are, for example, expenses for a CO_2 tax, whereas subsidies for clean technologies are classified as *environmentally induced tax revenues*. Other issues include the accelerated depreciation of clean technologies, etc.

Information collected with environmentally differentiated managerial accounting is often used in financial accounting for communication with external stakeholders. Also, other environmentally differentiated accounting systems derive most information from managerial accounting.

The next chapter deals with environmentally differentiated managerial accounting.

4
Environmentally Differentiated Managerial Accounting

4.1 INTRODUCTION

This chapter is concerned with that part of traditional accounting which deals with environmentally induced financial impacts on the company's managerial accounting system, and which we call *environmentally differentiated managerial accounting* (see Figure 1.2). Managerial accounting " . . . is the identification, measurement, accumulation, analysis, preparation, interpretation, and communication of information that assists executives in fulfilling organizational objectives." (Horngren and Foster 1987, p. 2). Cost accounting can also be regarded as managerial accounting plus a small part of financial accounting. Here the term "cost accounting" is used as a synonym for managerial accounting. Other synonyms are internal accounting and cost accounting.

Managerial accounting is one of the most central tools for management. First, it supports planning, defined as the delineation of goals, predictions of potential results under various scenarios and ways of achieving goals. Second, it is a central basis for decisions on how to attain the desired results. Third, it allows control and feedback which is the action of accompanying the implemention of plans and the evaluation of performance (see also Horngren and Foster 1987, p. 3).

With this central function, managerial accounting must provide correct information to support the most economic way of managing the company. As environmental issues exercise increasing influence on the economic performance they must be considered most clearly in managerial accounting.

Ideally, managerial accounting lays the foundation for all other accounting systems and for communication with external stakeholders. For this reason managerial accounting is dealt with first and followed by traditional financial accounting and other, more specialised, accounting systems.

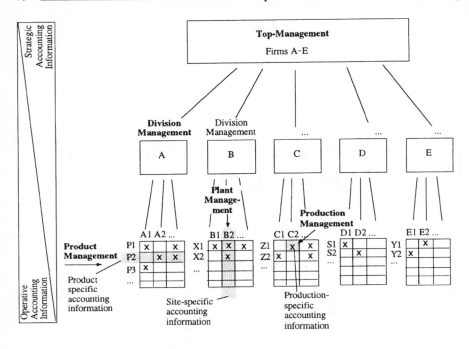

Figure 4.1   Each Management Level Focuses on Different Accounting Information

The basic purpose of environmentally differentiated managerial accounting is to account for the financial impacts of environmentally induced activities such as environmental protection activities and investments. The information is mainly used to facilitate decision-making by company-internal stakeholders, such as product, site and division managers and staff. In contrast to financial accounting (Chapter 5), managerial accounting is mostly voluntary and is not undertaken to satisfy requirements of external stakeholders. However, it is regarded as necessary for successful management.

Managerial accounting is not a uniform accounting system as it has to serve various management levels and functions which require different information. The information gathered in managerial accounting can be divided into accounting of products, of sites, of divisions and of the whole company. Product, site, division and top managers typically expect different information from accounting (Figure 4.1).

Product managers, for example, are interested in environmental product liabilities, site managers in issues such as site-specific clean-up costs, and division and top managers in the total of all environmentally induced financial impacts.

However, all levels of managerial accounting have the following issues in common:

- tracking and tracing of environmental costs (Section 4.2)
- allocation of costs to products and activities (Section 4.3)
- life-cycle costing (Section 4.4)
- investment appraisal (Section 4.5).

These issues are relevant for environmentally differentiated accounting as well as for ecological accounting (Part C). Their importance varies for both accounting categories at every level (product, site, whole company).

The following section deals with the identification, i.e. the tracking and tracing, of environmentally induced financial impacts. Tracking and tracing is a precondition for correct allocation to cost carriers (products) and cost centers (sites, production processes, etc.).

4.2 TRACKING AND TRACING OF ENVIRONMENTAL COSTS

As shown in Chapter 1, most companies employ accounting systems that were designed before anyone could anticipate the business costs of environmental compliance. Until recently, environmental compliance costs were marginal for many manufacturing companies. At the same time, the costs of tracking and tracing environmentally induced costs were very high. Therefore, many companies simply included all environmental protection costs in their general overhead costs, together with the president's salary, janitorial costs, and other expenses that were not traced back to individual manufacturing processes. A limited search on the Canadian Financial Database, which contained annual reports from 1983 to 1989 of more than 500 Canadian public companies, revealed that very few disclosed environmentally related costs separately (Hawkshaw, 1991, p. 24).

In the past decade, this practice has been reversed through new incentives, stricter environmental regulations and higher environmental awareness of important stakeholders.

In many countries, capital investments and expenditure for environmental protection enjoy subsidies, tax exemptions, or other advantages. On the other hand, today's environmental compliance costs are huge and still increasing for many companies, and the costs of the information systems to trace environmentally related costs are relatively small compared to those of not tracing (see Figure 1.3). Therefore, tracking and tracing of environmental costs have gained importance for the correct calculation of the profitability of products, production sites and companies.

Box 4.1
Environmentally Induced Costs Are Relevant

Kunert, a leading company in the textile industry, has traced its environmentally induced financial costs for its production site at Mindelheim (Germany). Kunert decreased pollution by 20% and production costs by one to two percent, which equals several million Deutschmarks.

(Source: Fritzler 1994, 20).

Others may argue that the position was not different in the past but rather unknown. Many companies did not (and some still do not) correctly calculate their environmentally induced costs. Thus, management simply could not know (and still cannot know) whether the marginal costs of collecting environmental information and reducing environmental impacts are smaller than the marginal costs of environmentally induced fees, fines, image problems, etc.

However, many examples have demonstrated that companies can benefit financially from correct tracing, tracking and allocation of environmentally induced costs (for an example see Box 4.1).

The most important task of tracking and tracing is to determine which costs should be classified as "environmental" in contrast to other costs. Generally, only those costs should be included which are specifically related to environmental issues and which are identifiable, and not those which relate to or are part of normal business activities. Box 4.2 shows a simple example where the costs of a waste incinerator are differentiated from other overhead costs.

The next question to be answered is, what (assets or expenses) internal costs should be recognized as environmental.

Among the most important problem areas in tracking and tracing of environmentally induced internal costs (and revenues) are:

- end-of-the-pipe technologies and integrated technologies
- research and development costs
- costs of past and future production
- environmentally induced assets and expenses.

Revenues are not treated here, because they can be considered in a similar way.

4.2.1 End-of-the-Pipe Versus Integrated Technologies

The identification of environmentally related internal costs is no problem, as long as they are incurred solely for the purposes of environmental protection.

Box 4.2
Tracing and Tracking of Environmentally Related Costs

The example in Figure 4.2 shows that costs of "joint environmental cost centers", such as incinerators, waste water treatment plants, etc., should be differentiated from other overhead costs.

A manufacturer has three production steps which all produce waste. The entire waste is treated in a jointly used incinerator on the production site. The costs of incinerating the waste from current production are $1600. The remaining share of overhead costs for general administration, salaries of top management, etc. are $9000.

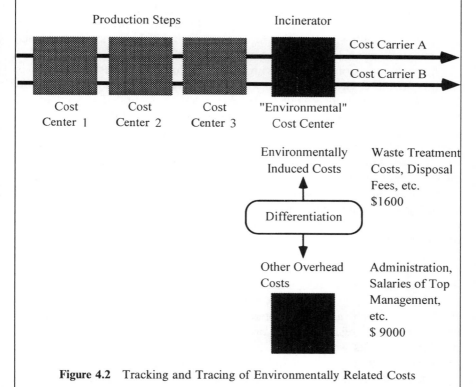

Figure 4.2 Tracking and Tracing of Environmentally Related Costs

This is the case with "end-of-the-pipe technologies", for example. End-of-the-pipe technologies are clean-up devices which have been installed mainly for cleaning purposes after the core production process. Scrubbers and waste water treatment plants are typical examples of end-of-pipe technologies. They can help to concentrate toxic substances and/or reduce toxic impacts. However, end-of-the-pipe technologies do not usually solve environmental problems at source, but they rather "catch" emissions before they are released uncontrolled into the natural environment. End-of-the-pipe technologies are nevertheless a way of internalizing externalities borne by human society or the environment. Another characteristic of technologies of this kind is that they shift emissions from one environmental medium to another (e.g. a scrubber shifts emissions from the air to the water and/or to the soil).

The identification and measurement of environmentally related costs is much more difficult with "integrated technologies" (also called "clean technologies"). Integrated technologies are more efficient production technologies which reduce pollution at source, or before it occurs (e.g. a new device uses 50% less energy and creates 20% less toxic effluent than the old one). Environmental issues were already integrated when the device was developed.

Because of this integration of environmental protection into the manufacturing device, the following question arises: What part of the device costs (assets) and maintainance expenditures are environmentally induced?

The main criterion for answering this question is the cost difference in relation to the environmentally next (less) favorable solution. For example, 20% of the capital costs may be traced as environmental if the integrated technology has caused 20% extra costs relative to a comparable device. Or the costs of depreciation of the old technology over two years may be considered as environmentally induced—if the integrated technology was installed two years earlier than would had been economically justified, simply to comply with environmental regulations.

However, the costs should not be considered as environmentally related if the integrated technology only represents present technological knowledge, and if it has been installed for no other reason than the regular replacement of an old device.

4.2.2 Research and Development Costs

As with research and development costs, the tracking and tracing of environmentally related costs presents difficulties. What research and development costs were incurred to improve the environmental performance of the company, its products and production processes?

In developed countries today, most research and development projects also consider environmental issues. However, environmental considerations are sometimes only minor ones in relation to others, and the actual benefit for the natural environment is often a "spin-off" of the main efforts to improve productivity and cost-effectiveness.

The problem of tracking and tracing research and development costs to specific cost categories is not new, nor is it specifically related to environmental questions. Nevertheless, the practices vary very much not only between industries but also among companies in the same industry. For example, some companies consider application costs as research and development costs while others do not.

Therefore, the general criterion needs to be interpreted case-by-case by management, so that only those costs are included which are specifically related to environmental issues and which are identifiable, and not those which relate to or are part of normal business activities.

4.2.3 Costs of Past and Future Production

Tracking and tracing environmentally related costs is further complicated by long term effects which are relatively more important for environmental issues than for many others.

Present costs can relate to past, current or future production activities. Examples of current costs of past production are today's clean-up costs, waste disposal and incineration costs, etc. Current costs of future production include present capital costs (e.g. interest payments for environmental protection investments).

Present production can relate to past, current and future costs. Past costs of present production are, for example, capital costs in past accounting periods. Future costs of present production are mainly liabilities and contingent liabilities.

Correct tracking, tracing and recognition of (environmentally induced) costs require that *all* (past, present and future) *costs are treated in the accounting period in which they accrue*, and not necessarily when they have to be paid (see Table 4.1). In other words, past, current and future costs of *present* production should be recognized in the *present* accounting period. As with the revaluation of assets, past costs of past production recognized in the present period should be counted as a loss in the present accounting period. On the accrual basis, the effects of transactions and other events are recognised when they occur, or when their potential occurrence arises, and not as cash or its equivalent is received or paid (IASC, 1995, 47 [IAS F22]). For the revaluation of assets due to unexpected technological or market developments see, e.g., Bührle (1993).

Table 4.1 All Costs Should be Recognized when they Accrue

| | | Recognition of costs | | |
		past	present	future
Production	past	X		
	present		X	
	future			X

Taking future costs into consideration is problematic since, especially with environmental issues, they are mostly unknown (e.g. contingent liabilities). One possibility is to insure environmental risks. Then the insurance premium allows for accurate recognition in the present. However, many environmental risks cannot be insured. Then, comparisons with similar cases in the past or similar cases in other companies can be made in order to estimate the probable liabilities. In the last decade, contingent environmental liabilities have become an important issue in financial accounting (see Chapter 5). The main problem is that the disclosure of contingent liabilities might attract the attention of certain stakeholders and thus have undesirable legal and economic consequences.

Unexpected current costs related to past and future production should be separately accounted for in the period when they occur (or when they are realized), so as not to distort the calculation of the profitability of present production.

Also, present costs of past production should be considered as losses (extraordinary costs) to prevent the distortion of the correct calculation of the operational profitability of present production.

4.2.4 Environmental Assets and Expenses

When tracking and tracing environmentally induced costs we are sooner or later faced with the question of whether they should be recognized as assets or expenses. The decision whether an environmentally induced cost item is identified as an asset or as an expense has a major impact on managerial decision making. The difference is crucial for environmentally differentiated accounting in general. As demonstrated in Box 4.3 the distinction between assets and expenses is often not clear in practice.

To answer this question, the following distinction of environmental costs may be useful:

- costs of improving the environmental record of a company (reduction, repair, prevention)
- costs of environmental impacts caused (fines, fees).

The first point covers costs incurred for the conservation of natural resources, or costs of steps taken to prevent, reduce or repair damage to the environment which result from a company's operating activities.

Expenditure for environmental impacts caused includes extraordinary costs of non-compliance, such as fines, costs of litigation, etc. as well as ordinary costs for omitted environmental protection, such as fees for waste disposal and environmental taxes.

As a general rule, costs for impacts caused are a result of omissions and therefore apt to be treated as expenses. On the other hand, costs to improve the environmental record of a company tend to be recognized more easily as assets.

Box 4.3
Asset or Expense?

A company has been legally dumping hazardous waste on a landfill for many years. Now the contaminated site has to be cleaned up because of new legal requirements. The management decides to use the property in future for other purposes. Are the incurred clean-up costs expenses or should they be considered as assets because they enhance the value of the property?

Standards, regulations and guidelines for financial accounting and reporting have a major impact on how this issue is treated in managerial accounting. If, for example, an outlay has to be counted as an asset in financial accounting, it will, for reasons of consistency, mostly be treated the same way in managerial accounting.

The question whether to expense or to capitalize an environmentally induced outlay is therefore dealt with in greater depth in Chapter 5 (financial accounting).

Nevertheless, the financial accounting guidelines leave management a certain discretionary latitude. It will account for environmental costs in a way most appropriate for economic decision making. Two contradictory effects are to be considered.

- Environmentally induced outlays which are recognized as assets increase the value of the company. The assets will be depreciated over several accounting periods. Thus, capitalization allows costs to be spread over a longer time period. In consequence, the earnings per share ratio will be affected over a long period.
- If the outlay is regarded as an expense the profits will be impacted only for a *short term* (the accounting period), although to a greater extent than if it had been regarded as an asset.

Once environmentally related financial impacts are tracked, traced and recognized, they have to be allocated to cost centers and cost carriers.

4.3 ALLOCATION OF ENVIRONMENTALLY INDUCED COSTS

It has been shown in Chapter 2 that financial impacts of environmental costs have been rising substantially. It therefore makes sense for any company to track and trace these costs to determine how much the company is affected by

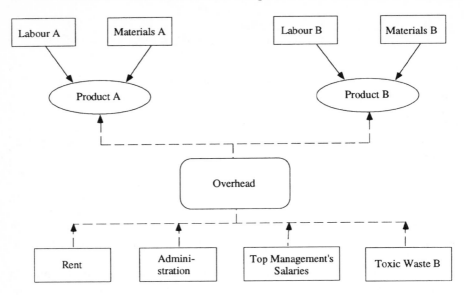

Figure 4.3   Traditional Cost Accounting. Similar to Todd (1993)

environmental issues. In addition, to calculate the actual contribution margins created, the environmentally related costs should be allocated correctly.

Traditionally, *full cost accounting* is the dominant approach of management accounting (see also Box 4.4). However, it has been discussed extensively that full cost accounting is too much oriented towards past instead of present and future activities (See, for example, Johnson and Kaplan 1987a, b). Another popular approach, direct costing, is less decision oriented than activity based accounting, which concentrates on calculating the costs of specific business activities. Hence, the focus of this chapter is on activity based accounting (also called "process costing" or "activity based costing: ABC").

4.3.1   Traditional Allocation of Environmentally Related Costs

Internal environmental costs are often treated as overhead costs and divided equally between all cost carriers. Figure 4.3 gives an example. The costs of treating the toxic waste of product B are included in the general overhead costs, and the overhead is allocated in equal parts to product A and B.

However, "dirty" products cause more emissions and require more clean-up facilities than "clean" products. Equal allocation of those costs therefore subsidizes environmentally more harmful products. The clean products, on the other hand, are "punished" by this allocation rule as they bear costs which they did not cause.

Table 4.2 Example of Correct and Wrong Cost Allocation. Source: Hamner 1993, 3

	"Clean" Process 1	"Dirty" Process 2
Revenues	$200	$200
Production Costs	$100	$100
Environmental Costs	$0	$50
True Profit	$100	$50
If environmental costs are overhead	$25	$25
Then the book profit is	$75	$75
Which is incorrect by	−25%	+33%

The simple example in Table 4.2 illustrates how equal allocation can lead to suboptimal management decisions. Two processes are compared: process 1 is "clean" and does not cause any environmentally induced costs for the company, while process 2 causes $50 of extra costs because it is environmentally harmful. If these costs are assigned to general overheads and allocated equally, both processes seem to create a profit of $75. (If $50 is allocated to overhead, $25 will implicitly be allotted to each process. This leads to a profit of $75 (= $200 − $100 − $25).) In reality, however, process 1 has created a profit of $100, while process 2 only has only contributed $50 to the company's profit.

4.3.2 Activity Based Accounting

Whenever possible, environmentally induced costs should be allocated directly to the respective cost centers and cost carriers. This means, for the example in Figure 4.4, that the costs of treating the toxic waste of product B should be allocated directly and exclusively to product B.

Many terms are used to describe this correct allocation procedure, such as "environmentally enlightened cost accounting", "full cost accounting" or "activity based costing (ABC)" (see Box 4.4).

In this book the term "activity based accounting" or "activity based costing" is adopted, although "full cost accounting" or "process costing" are often used in practice, Spitzer et al. (1993, p. 1) and the references there. However, the term "full cost accounting" can be misleading as it also describes methods which consider external environmental costs. Activity based accounting represents a method of managerial cost accounting that allocates all internal costs to cost centers and cost carriers on the basis of the activities which caused the costs. The activity based costs of each product are calculated by adding the joint fixed and the joint variable costs to the direct costs of production. The strength of ABC is that it enhances the understanding of the business processes

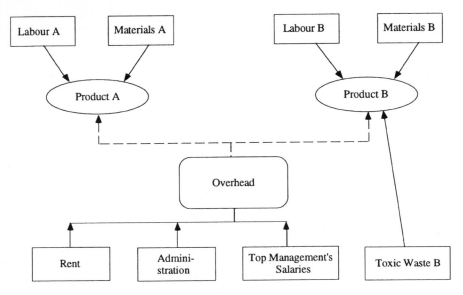

Figure 4.4 Activity Based Accounting. Similar to Todd (1993)

associated with each product, Spitzer *et al.* (1993, p. 6) and their reference to Gunn. It reveals where value is added and where value is destroyed.

The example in Box 4.5 illustrates the method of activity based accounting. It shows two steps of allocation, first, from joint environmental cost centers to the "responsible" cost centers (i.e. production processes), and second, from the production cost centers to the respective cost carriers (i.e. products A and B).

Today, it is definitely wrong to include all environmentally related costs in the general overhead costs. Nevertheless, some environmentally induced costs remain overhead costs. These are costs clearly related to general overhead activities, such as costs for a new insulation of the head-office building. Also costs of past production that are clearly related to strategic management decisions of the whole company might qualify as general overhead costs (e.g. liability costs of products that have been phased out).

At present, even in advanced managerial accounting systems, only the visible (direct) costs of environmental cost centers are directly allocated to production cost centers and cost carriers. However, additional costs are environmentally induced although they do not relate directly to a joint environmental cost center (e.g. an incinerator). Yet, some indirect costs could be saved if less waste was created. Waste occupies manufacturing capacities, requires labour, increases administration, etc. If no waste were produced, the machine would not have to be depreciated as quickly, and less would have to be paid in salaries.

Box 4.4
Environmentally Differentiated Managerial Accounting

Activity Based Costing (ABC), Activity Based Accounting (Process Costing)
Activity based accounting, also referred to as "enlightened cost accounting" (Todd 1992, p. 12ff), is a product costing system ". . . that allocates [costs typically allocated to] overhead in proportion to the activities associated with a product or product family" (Gunn 1992, p. 104ff; Spitzer *et al.* 1993, p. 6).

Full Cost Accounting
A method of managerial cost accounting that allocates environmental costs (direct and indirect) to a product, product line, process, service or activity. (White and Becker 1992).
"Not everyone uses the term 'full cost accounting' in the same way. Some include only a company's private costs (i.e. those costs that affect the company's bottom line) (White and Becker 1992) while others (MacLean 1989) include the full range of costs throughout the life cycle of the product, from raw material extraction to product disposal, some of which do not show up directly or even indirectly in the firm's 'bottom line'." (Spitzer *et al.* 1993, p. 5).

Full Cost Pricing
"A less-used term again used as a synonym for full cost accounting or life cycle costing." (Washington Post 1992, H1; Spitzer *et al.* 1993, p. 6).

Life Cycle Costing
A method in which all costs are identified with a product [process or activity] throughout its lifetime, from raw material acquisition to disposal (see also Spitzer *et al.* 1993, p. 6). Life Cycle Costing can focus on internal costs, or it may attempt to consider both internal and external costs.

Total Cost Accounting
"A hybrid term sometimes used as a synonym for either of the definitions given to 'full cost accounting', or as a synonym for 'total cost assessment'." (Spitzer *et al.* 1993, p. 6).

Total Cost Assessment
Long-term, comprehensive financial analysis of the full range of internal (i.e. private) costs and savings of an investment (White and Becker 1992; Spitzer *et al.* 1993, p. 7).

Box 4.5
Twofold Allocation of Environmentally Related Costs

After tracking and tracing (Box 4.2), the costs of joint environmental cost centers such as incinerators, sewage plants, etc. have to be allocated to the "responsible" cost centers and cost carriers.

Total input of production is 1000 kg, of which 200kg are treated as waste in the incinerator. Total costs of incineration are $1600. The cost key to determine the cost contribution of different kinds of waste should consider the costs of incineration which those kinds of waste cause. The treatment of one kilogram would cost $8 if every unit of waste caused the same costs.

In a first step, the costs of the incinerator have to be allocated to the three cost centers (allocation 1): $800 to cost center 1 ($8 × 100kg of waste) and $400 to cost centers 2 and 3, respectively ($8 × 50kg each).

In a second step (allocation 2), the costs have to be allocated to the cost carriers (e.g. products A and B). The cost key should reflect the costs of waste treatment which the respective product has caused at each production step.

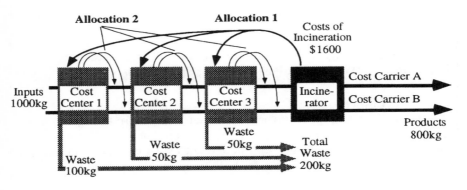

Figure 4.5 Allocation of Environmentally Related Costs

For instance, in the example in Box 4.5, 200 kg of the 1000 kg of inputs were purchased only to be emitted without creating any value. Thus, the respective waste has caused 20% more purchasing cost, higher costs of depreciation and administration, etc. Therefore, a third allocation step is necessary. As shown in the example in Box 4.6 this third allocation step can motivate management to realize huge efficiency gains by improving the environmental record at the same time!

Box 4.6
A Third Allocation Step

This example illustrates the third step of allocation on the basis of the example used in Box 4.2 and Box 4.5. 1000 kg of inputs have been purchased to create 800 kg of products. Of the 200 kg of waste, 100 are caused in step 1, and 50 each in steps 2 and 3. With the first and second allocation steps, the costs of the environmental cost center ($1600 for incineration) have been traced, tracked and allocated to the cost centers and carriers.

However, environmentally induced costs are much higher. Some inputs were purchased "just to be thrown away", without having created any value. Therefore, the management should also account for other environmentally induced costs, such as increased depreciation, higher costs for staff, etc. which are not directly related to joint environmental cost centers but which nevertheless vary with the amount of throughput. To take these environmentally induced costs into consideration, a third allocation step is necessary.

The environmentally induced indirect costs can be calculated as follows:

Cost center 1: Physically, 100 kg of waste show up in cost center 1. Economically, however, the waste which later shows up in cost centers 2 and 3 already causes costs in cost center 1. In all 200 kg (100kg + 50kg + 50kg) of the 1000 kg of inputs ($= 20\%$) purchased cause indirect costs (e.g. the production device is worn out faster) in cost center 1. The additional, environmentally induced indirect costs at cost center 1 are therefore:

$$20\% = (200\text{kg of }1000\text{kg}) \text{ of } \$9,000 = \$1800$$

Cost center 2: 900 kg of material enter cost center 2, but only 800 kg will finally leave the company as products. Thus, 100 kg of the 900 kg (11.1%) which enter cost center 2 only cause waste. The indirect waste costs are therefore:

$$11.1\% = (100\text{kg of }900\text{kg}) \text{ of } \$9,000 = \$999$$

The respective costs in *cost center 3* are:

$$5.9\% = (50\text{kg of }850\text{kg}) \text{ of } \$9,000 = \$531$$

In summary, calculated with activity based accounting, the total of all environmentally induced indirect costs is $3330 ($1800 + $999 + $531), whereas the total of all (direct and indirect) environmentally induced costs is $4930 ($1600 + $3330).

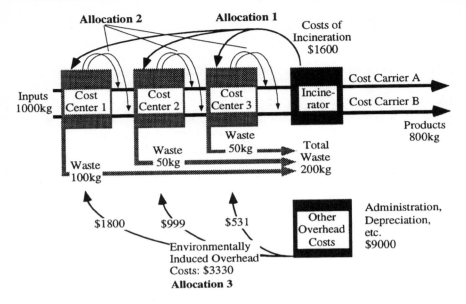

Figure 4.6 Allocation of Other Environmentally Induced Costs

The next section deals with allocation keys for environmentally related costs.

4.3.3 Allocation Keys

The choice of an adequate allocation key is crucial for obtaining correct information in cost accounting. The advantages and pitfalls of different allocation keys have been discussed extensively in the accounting literature (see for example Young 1985). This section is therefore kept short.

It is important that the chosen allocation key is closely linked with the actual, environmentally related costs. In practice mainly the following four groups of allocation keys are discussed for environmental issues.

- Volume of emissions, waste, etc. treated.
- Toxicity of emissions and waste treated.
- Environmental impact added (volume times impact per unit of volume) of the emissions treated.
- Induced relative costs of treating different kinds of emissions.

One possibility is to allocate the environmentally induced costs based on the volume of hazardous waste caused by each cost carrier (e.g. volume treated/ hour, waste/kg of output, and emissions/working hour of machine).

This is a rather arbitrary key in cases where the capital cost (interest and depreciation of construction costs) as well as the variable costs are not related to the total volume treated. Due to higher safety and technological requirements, the construction costs and the variable costs often increase substantially with a higher degree of toxicity of the waste treated. In many cases, these additional costs are due only to a small percentage of the waste. Thus, the costs of a treatment or prevention facility are often not clearly related to the overall volume treated, but rather to the relative cleaning performance required.

Another possibility is to allocate according to the potential environmental impact added of the treated emissions. The environmental impact added is calculated by multiplying the volume by the toxicity of the emissions.

However, this allocation key is often not appropriate as the costs of treatment do not always relate to the environmental impact added.

Hence, the choice of the allocation key must be adapted to the specific situation, and the costs caused by the different kinds of emission treated should be assessed directly. Sometimes a volume related formula best reflects the costs caused, while in other cases a key based on environmental impact is appropriate. The appropriate allocation key depends on the variety and the kind of emissions treated or prevented. Also the time of occurrence may be relevant (past, current or future costs).

4.3.4 Conclusion

For most businesses, economically rational management requires the direct allocation of environmentally induced costs to the "responsible" cost centers and cost carriers.

Management accountants have several responsibilities with respect to environmentally induced costs. First, the environmentally induced costs must be tracked and traced. Second, only those costs that relate to the same production period should be added together (i.e. all past, current and future costs which relate to current production should be considered together). Third, the environmentally induced costs should be allocated as directly as possible to the responsible cost centers and costs carriers. With activity based accounting this can be done according to the activities caused. Fourth, no general rule for the ideal allocation key exists. The suitability of an allocation key depends on the variety and kinds of emission prevented or treated. However, the allocation key should reflect the costs actually caused by an activity.

The implementation of these steps does not require a revolution in a company but is necessary more from a business perspective. Nevertheless, their implementation may meet with opposition although they make logical sense. The change of allocation rules leads to a redistribution of power in a company. Line managers with currently profitable products tend to refuse allocation rules whenever they expect losses, whereas the "company-internal lobby" for the clean products is often not established and still small.

The next section deals with life cycle costing, a costing approach which is often promoted by environmentalists.

4.4   LIFE CYCLE COSTING

The basic idea of life cycle costing is to consider the costs caused over the whole life cycle of a product. The approach has been developed by the Society of Logistics Engineers (SOLE) with the idea of taking all monetary internal and external costs into account.

All costs for the economic actors in a product life cycle are identified with the product throughout its whole lifetime. The costs should preferably be measured in quantified terms, but if this is not possible, qualitative judgments may be added (Spitzer *et al.* 1993, p. 6). With life cycle costing the accounting boundaries of the company as well as the time horizon of accounting are enlarged. Thus the focus on the entity is given up and broadened to the whole life cycle of a product.

The method of life cycle costing should not be confused with the much more popular concept of life cycle assessment (LCA), which focuses on the environmental impacts of a product life cycle (see Part C, Section 8.3).

Although extensively discussed in academic circles, life cycle costing has not gained much attention. First, the price mechanism in a competitive market should already include the internalized environmental costs of suppliers if the products are priced correctly (through correct identification and allocation). In addition, the external costs can only be estimated very roughly, so that the informative value may be very low.

Second, the concept of life cycle costing suffers from major problems in practice. The collection of necessary information from economic actors outside the company (suppliers and customers, disposal, etc.) usually results in:

- low quality of information
- inconsistent data quality
- high costs of data collection.

To initiate life cycle costing, management must define the boundaries of the life cycle system under consideration. Thereby, management has a large discretionary latitude in setting the boundaries of the investigated system. So far, no generally accepted criteria exist.

In most cases, the collection of company-external information results in poor data quality. Unless a very powerful company can require and verify the received information, the economic actors of other companies have little incentive to provide the information needed in a consistent quality. Some information might be of strategic importance or part of the business may be secret. In addition, most companies have established different information systems which provide various qualities of data. Life Cycle Assessment, in ecological accounting, faces similar problems (see Chapter 8.3).

Despite its substantial deficiencies, the basic idea of life cycle costing can be helpful as a way of thinking in strategic management, especially for early identification of contingent liabilities or of ecological weaknesses and strengths in the "value chain" of an industry.

External as well as long term effects of managerial decisions result mainly from investment decisions. Therefore, the next section deals with investment appraisal as a tool for managerial decision support.

4.5 INVESTMENT APPRAISAL

Investment appraisal (capital budgeting) is one of the most important managerial activities. (Other terms used in this context are "Economic Feasibiliy Analysis", "Total Cost Assessment", "Benefit Assessment", "Investment Appraisal" and "Financial Analysis of Waste Management Alternatives", Spitzer *et al.* 1993, p. 7.) The basic idea is to compare different investment alternatives.

"Just as there is no single method of evaluating investment opportunities, there can be no single way of incorporating environmental considerations into investment decisions." (Gray 1993, p. 153). The shortcomings of methods such as the payback period, annuity method, or the internal interest rate (IRR) are discussed in any textbook on corporate finance. However, the task of investment appraisal has been complicated with the increasing importance and uncertainty of environmentally induced future costs (see Box 4.7). Although not discussed here, the same holds true for financial investments.

Possible steps to include environmental consideration into investment appraisal are:

- expansion of cost inventory
- correct allocation of costs
- extension of time horizon and use of long-term financial indicators (net present value and option value).

For similar suggestions, see Spitzer (1992).

An *expanded cost inventory* considers four categories of costs; see also Section 3.1.

- Direct costs (capital expenditures, operation, maintenance, expenses, revenues, waste disposal, energy, etc.).

- Indirect costs (administrative costs, regulatory compliance costs, training, monitoring, insurance, deterioration, depreciation, etc.).
- Potential liabilities (contingent liabilities, potential fees, fines, taxes, etc.).
- Less tangible costs (image, absent workers, morale, etc.).

Box 4.7
Future Consequences of Investment Decisions

Estimates of future costs are uncertain because nobody can be fully informed about the future. Because of substantial uncertainties of future costs, management is inclined to underestimate potential future costs which are not proven.

Lack of adequate information about the future has forced many companies to phase out products which were warmly welcomed at the time of their introduction (i.e CFCs).

However, the investment decisions which took place under uncertainty strongly influence future activities. Once investments are made, a big financial incentive exists to delay phasing out as much as possible.

Chlorofluorocarbon (CFC) production of DuPont*

1986	1987	1988	1989	1990	1991	1992	Goal 1995
100%	117%	119%	112%	66%	51%	45%	0%

*"Based on a request from the US government, DuPont could produce in 1995 in the USA as much as 25% of its 1986 CFC production levels. DuPont will base production on customer commitments." (DuPont 1993, p. 5)

First, delayed phasing out extends the depreciation period, which increases the short term profit potential. Second, the last companies in the business have no other competitors and will benefit from exceptionally high profit margins (e.g. DuPont with CFCs, see DuPont 1993). These advantages have to be weighed against a potential bad image, legal requirements and pressure from stakeholders.

The calculation of direct costs is part of any method of investment appraisal. However, environmentally related costs are sometimes hidden in general overhead costs and therefore not considered (see Section 4.3). Indirect costs, potential liabilities and less tangible costs especially are often difficult or impossible to identify, measure and allocate. Nevertheless, these costs can very much influence the profitability of an investment.

The rules of allocation applied for environmentally related costs can substantially influence investment decisions. As discussed in Section 4.3, three steps of *correct allocation* can be distinguished in the allocation of:

- costs of joint environmental cost centers (e.g. incinerators) to production cost centers
- costs of production cost centers to cost carriers
- other environmentally induced costs to production cost centers and cost carriers.

Box 4.8
Correct Allocation in Investment Appraisal

This example shows how correct allocation, compared with the mode of allocation often employed, can substantially influence the result of an investment appraisal. The calculations are based on the example which has already been used in Boxes 4.2, 4.5 and 4.6.

The total costs of the environmental costs center (e.g. the incinerator) are $1600 whereas the total of all indirectly caused costs is $3330. The total of all environmentally induced costs are shown in Figure 4.7 for each cost center as well as for the whole company.

Pollution prevention activities do not create the same economic benefit in every cost center, even if they achieve the same reduction of emissions. Pollution prevention investments in cost center 1 are most attractive as they impede waste related costs at subsequent cost centers. The management should therefore emphasize pollution prevention activities for the first manufacturing steps.

Many economically profitable investments, especially for pollution prevention, would not be implemented if management relied on traditional allocation rules which only consider the direct costs of environmental centers. For example an investment with annual costs of $1000 would not be introduced in cost center 1, even it would reduce (in all other cost centers) environmentally induced costs by $1600 per year.

The application of this three-step allocation procedure in investment appraisal has a large influence on what investments, including pollution prevention investments, are economically favorable (see Box 4.8).

First empirical studies have demonstrated that between 6 to 10 times higher savings could be realized if investment decisions for pollution prevention were based on correct allocation rules. For an economy, total economic loss of retained environmental investments can easily run up to billions of dollars. An example from the German metal industry is given in Table 4.3.

It may seem surprising that cost savings due to more pollution prevention have not been realized. However, the collection and analysis of the respective (accounting) information also causes costs. In the past, the costs of environmental accounting were expected to be larger than the benefits from being better informed (see Chapter 1, Box 1.1).

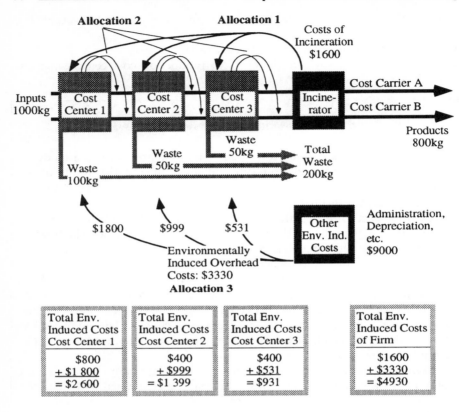

Figure 4.7 The Correct Calculation of All Environmentally Induced Costs

With the growing knowledge about these saving potentials those companies that fail to realize them will face competitive disadvantages. A third step for the inclusion of environmental considerations in investment appraisal is to extend the time horizon and to use long-term financial indicators.

Environmental investments often have longer payback periods than other investments, because the relevant benefits and losses often lie many years in the future. However, this is not always true, as the example in Box 4.9 shows.

Nevertheless, the application of long-term financial indicators is useful, especially with high contingent liabilities and high potential future benefits.

New regulations which require the internalization of former external costs can suddenly evolve. The US Superfund legislation under CERCLA (Comprehensive Environmental Response, Compensation and Liability Act of 1980) is an excellent, well-known example, as it shows the enormous and unexpected financial impacts environmental issues might cause (see Section 5.5).

Table 4.3 Example of the Significance of Correct Calculation of Environmentally Induced Costs. Source: Wagner 1995

Usual Way of Calculating Environmentally Induced Costs		Correct Way of Calculating Environmentally Induced Costs	
Costs of Waste Disposal		*Costs of Waste Disposal*	
Fees	500,000	Fees	500,000
Disposal Costs	300,000	Disposal Costs	300,000
		First Total	800,000
		Environmentally Induced Costs in Production	
		Logistics and Transportation	150,000
		Additional Personnel	250,000
		Additional Depreciation	200,000
		Storage	100,000
		Second Total	1,500,000
		Excess Material Input	
		Purchase	4,500,000
Total	800,000	*Correct Total*	6,500,000

The application of long term financial indicators might help future financial impacts to be considered in advance. In particular, two long term financial indicators are discussed in the context of environmental accounting:

- net present value
- option value.

The *net present value* (NPV) is calculated by the following formula:

$$NPV = \Delta F / (1 + r)^n$$

whereas F = Future value (revenues − costs)
   r = Discount rate
   n = Number of periods

Box 4.9
Short Payback of Environmental Investment at Ciba

The Swiss multinational company Ciba-Geigy Ltd. installed a computerised environmental monitoring and internal billing system within its plant in Huningue in France. The costs were approximately CHF 2.4 million. The system saved energy costing more than CHF 0.8 million per year. Therefore, from a static perspective, the payback period was three years.

Box 4.10
Option Value Versus NPV

Pollution prevention equipment adds an extra $4 million to capital spending on a new factory costing $20 million. New equipment could prevent soil pollution that would have to be cleaned up in ten years at estimated costs of $10 million.

The pollution prevention investment is not economical if the method of NPV is strictly applied. The discounted value of the clean-up costs is $3.9 million (discount rate of 10%), which is lower than the prevention costs of $4 million. Therefore, the value of the company is $0.1 million higher without the new equipment. However, in ten years, soil contamination might completely prevent further operations. Thus, the NPV method might lead to wrong decisions in strategic management, if the option value is not considered as well.

(Source: Koechlin and Müller 1992)

The opportunity costs of capital (the lower value of future cash flows or the loss of value over time) are considered by the application of the discount rate of financial markets. The sum of all discounted future cash flows determines the value of a project. Projects with a positive NPV should be executed. Projects with negative NPV should be cancelled.

Some may argue that the concept of discounting is fundamentally unethical as a lower value is assigned to the needs of future generations. This is in sharp contradiction to the conservation of assets for future generations and to sustainable development in general (see also Box 4.11). Others may argue that discounting is a necessity for economics to function but, acknowledging its flaws, propose a social discount rate for environmentally related investments which is lower than the market based interest rate. Thus, investments are given a longer time horizon to pay off, and the time horizon of the company is extended.

The omission of discounting and the manipulation of the discount rate are problematic as the calculated results do not reflect the actual economic situation. Furthermore, investment appraisal should indicate the economic value of alternative investment opportunities. Other, non-economic aspects might be considered separately but should not distort the economic analysis.

However, the NPV method also has flaws, as the discussion in Box 4.10 shows.

The *option value* takes the net present value as well as the strategic value of investments into account (see for example Brealey and Myers 1991, Dixit and Pindyck 1993 or 1995). An option entails the right but not the obligation to do something. It can also be defined as the right *not* to undertake a follow-on investment. The price of the option is determined by the price of the underlying stock (free cash flows of the project), the exercise price (the follow-on investment), the time to maturity (the date when the decision has to be made) and also by the risk of the stock and the risk-free interest rate. "Opportunities are options—rights but not obligations to take some action in the future." (Dixit and Pindyck 1995).

The strict application of the net present value method very often ignores the value of creating or exercising options or the costs of impeding future options. The NPV method was conceived for the valuation of bonds with constant cash streams over a determined period. Not undertaking a project with a negative NPV today might result in a follow-on project becoming too expensive or completely impossible (see Box 4.11).

Some investments create a special value in the context of other investments of the company. Sometimes an investment that appears uneconomic might be crucial if, in fact, it can create an option that enables the company to undertake other investments in the future (see for example Brealey and Myers 1991 or Dixit and Pindyck 1993). A negative NPV only shows that the project as such (in isolation) does not pay off. However, the project could be very important in the context of other projects a company envisages. This effect is called the "strategic value" of a project and can be expressed as a call option.

Because of new scientific evidence about environmental problems, new issues with huge effects on an industry can emerge very quickly. Many environmentally crucial projects (e.g. the launch of a green product line or the introduction of an integrated environmental management programme in the company) are of a strategic nature because of their long time horizon as well as their effect on

---

Box 4.11
High Clean-Up Costs in the Far Future

The management of a company has to decide between paying clean-up costs of $100 million in 50 years caused by an activity which increases its cash inflow today by $1 million.

According to the concept of NPV this management must be advised to choose the option that creates the cash inflow today, because the discounted value of the costs in 50 years (discount rate 10%) is lower than the cash inflow of $1 million today.

This means that the company should use resources now, cash in today and postpone disposal. However, the damage of $100 million can be disastrous for future generations as well as for the company. The damage caused may reduce options and prevent the company from making future investments. The effects on future business options should therefore be carefully considered too.

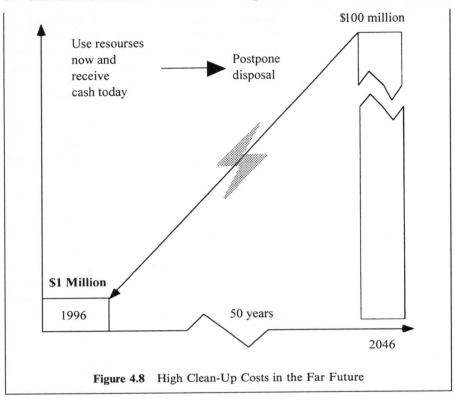

Figure 4.8   High Clean-Up Costs in the Far Future

public perception (signals for the general public and for customers). The capacity to adapt quickly to new circumstances also clearly represents an option value.

Just as in financial markets, the value of the strategic option increases with the variability of the project's cash flows and the risk of the project, respectively. With stricter legislation and increasing risk investments to prevent environmental liabilities, or to start green product lines to create new markets, have an option value. They entail the option to stay in the market.

The strategic value of going further than mere compliance with regulations increases with the probability of future environmental laws. The option value can therefore exceed the NPV of pollution prevention equipment (Koechlin and Müller, 1992).

Future free cash flows of environmental management activities are often worth less than the present actual costs. If a company receives free cash flows of $100 million in 50 years but has to invest $1 million today, it will have a negative NPV. However, the respective investments might create options for future economic activities which are not taken into consideration in the calculation of the NPV.

Box 4.12
Free Cash Flows in the Far Future (Precious Woods)

Precious Woods is an example of a company with an environmental strategy which will create free cash flows in the far future. Sustainable forestry in Costa Rica and Brazil is expected to create free cash flows in 20 to 25 years whereas considerable costs for reforestation have to be borne today.

This project is possible because the shareholders consider the option value and because they are especially long-sighted. However, the shares of Precious Woods will soon be quoted on the stock exchange. Therefore, it is crucial that the management can communicate its long-term strategy to make sure that the valuation on the stock exchange is as high as possible. In the case of a low valuation of the shares, the company could be taken over and the forests cut down after ten years. The profit at the date of the take-over could be higher than the price for the shares although even higher profits could be realized a decade later.

To protect the company from a possible unfriendly take-over, Precious Woods has placed restrictions on the transfer of its shares.

Not only foregone options due to high future costs can be ignored. Also free cash flows in the far future tend to be underestimated if the option value is not taken into consideration (see Box 4.12). Short-term profits are possible, for example, if the value of the shares of a green company is less than the present value of the current assets. Thus, the management of green companies going public must inform the investors about the expected future cash flows.

It has been shown that environmental issues involve special problems in investment appraisal. These environmentally induced issues are often not known to management. Some external stakeholders have therefore started to influence management to consider environmental aspects more carefully in investment appraisal and in managerial accounting in general.

4.6 EXTERNAL STAKEHOLDERS INFLUENCE MANAGERIAL ACCOUNTING

Managerial accounting is designed for internal decision-making, which means that management cannot be forced to account for environmental impacts in a specific way.

Financial accounting standards naturally exert a strong influence on managerial accounting. Investors should be interested in a change of accounting practices to enhance their future financial return. Standards of financial accounting are therefore changing (see Chapter 5). Nevertheless, some additional stakeholders, while having no effective power to tell management how to account internally, have substantially influenced managerial accounting practices so as to consider environmental issues better. Two of the most active stakeholders are the State of Washington (USA) Department of Ecology (DOE), and the United States Environmental Protection Agency (EPA), (DOE 1992a, 1993a or Spitzer 1992).

DOE has established a regulation which requires companies to carry out investment appraisals for pollution prevention plans. Even a guideline for investment appraisal for pollution prevention has been published.

The results of this regulation and the guideline are impressive (DOE 1992a or 1993a). Many economically favorable pollution prevention plans have been developed and implemented on the basis of the enforced investment appraisals, although no additional pollution prevention activities were required. The regulation forced the management to be better informed about the economic consequences of pollution prevention plans. Obviously, information costs as well as some prejudices had prevented management from informing itself earlier. Hence, more pollution prevention activities were implemented as soon as the financial information was available, and after the costs of information were spent.

The US environmental protection agency (EPA) has issued guidelines on activity based costing and capital budgeting to educate managers on how to carry out investment appraisals of alternative pollution prevention plans. Furthermore, the EPA provides information on probable contingent liabilities as well as on new approaches to environmental accounting (Spitzer 1992 or Spitzer and Elwood 1995a).

Furthermore, by making future and external environmental costs of a firm explicit and by assigning a monetary value, the introduction of environmental taxes and tradeable emissions allowances simplifies managerial accounting (see also Sections 5.6, 6.1, 6.2 and 10.2). External costs are known, internalized and considered better in decision-making. First, because uncertainties in the quantification of these costs are substantially reduced with "official" or "market-based" valuation, and second, because allocation is simplified.

Thus, advanced companies, as well as banks and insurance companies, can reduce their information costs when these policy tools are established. In consequence, advanced companies should support the introduction of market-based environmental policies.

4.7 SUMMARY

The rapid emergence of environmental issues has prevented many managers from being adequately informed about potential and actual environmentally induced costs and benefits. Furthermore, most management incentive systems are not adapted to the new situation.

In any case, economically rational management in developed countries requires early consideration of the actual and potential financial consequences of environmental issues. It has been shown that many economically favorable investments are neglected if traditional rules of allocation and traditional methods of investment appraisal are applied without taking environmental issues into account.

The adaptation and environmental differentiation of managerial accounting is crucial, for it is necessary to provide correct incentives for management to be most profitable. Accounting practices are extremely important because they strongly influence management activities. Correct accounting for environmentally induced costs and revenues enhances future profits. First, because the costs and revenues are correctly reflected in the accounting system. Second, because only correct information allows the most profitable management decisions to be taken.

Every management level is interested in different information. Product managers require other information than site, division or top managers. Managerial accounting should provide information for all levels of management. Nevertheless, it is up to the respective managers to decide which information to collect and to use for analysis.

5
Environmentally Differentiated Financial Accounting

This chapter deals with environmental issues in financial accounting (see Figure 1.2). Financial accounting and reporting are used by the management to communicate the company's economic situation to external stakeholders, i.e. to shareholders and creditors.

Environmentally differentiated financial accounting deals with the recognition, measurement and disclosure of environmentally related economic impacts in financial accounting. The series on environmental accounting published by Price Waterhouse gives an insight into the current issues and practices in the USA (Price Waterhouse 1991, 1992a, 1993, 1994).

Section 5.1 discusses the role and influence of standard setters and regulators for financial accounting practices. The question of whether and in which cases environmentally induced outlays should be classified as assets or as expenses is dealt with in Section 5.2. The next sections of Chapter 5 deal with the recognition, measurement and disclosure of:

- environmentally induced expenses (5.3)
- environmentally induced financial impacts on assets (5.4)
- environmental liabilities, contingent liabilities as well as environmentally related reserves, provisions and charges to income (5.5)
- tradeable emissions allowances (5.6).

Section 5.7 addresses environmental issues in management's discussion and analysis. However, environmental reporting covers more than the mere communication of the environmental performance of a company, and also addresses issues such as environmental policies and targets, stakeholder relations, comments regarding public policy, etc. Environmental reporting is treated explicitly in Part D to emphasize its importance as part of a comprehensive environmental management system.

5.1 STAKEHOLDERS INFLUENCE FINANCIAL ACCOUNTING

The main stakeholders in managerial accounting are members of different management positions (e.g. top, product, and site managers). Being an internal information system, managerial accounting faces almost no external regulations.

Financial accounting, on the contrary, is strongly standardized and regulated. Investors (shareholders) and many other external stakeholders have a strong economic interest in receiving true and fair information about the actual economic performance of a company. Hence, standard-setting bodies and regulatory agencies have been established to make sure that the requested information is supplied with the desired quality. Accounting systems are standardised conventions on how one should treat (recognize, measure and disclose) specific items. The result of the information collected is that the stakeholders are supported in their decision-making process.

Figure 5.1 contrasts providers ("suppliers") of accounting frameworks and users ("customers") of corporate financial accounting information. On the left side, examples of prominent providers of regulations, standards, guidelines and recommendations for financial accounting are shown. Some of the main customer groups of financial accounting information are depicted on the right side. These include shareholders, potential investors, financial analysts, rating agencies, banks, regulators, suppliers, the media, pressure groups, etc.

Financial reporting should provide useful information to external stakeholders, i.e. investors and creditors. "The objective of financial statements is to provide information about the financial position, performance and changes in financial position of an enterprise, that is useful to a wide range of users in making economic decisions." (IASC [1994, IAS 12]). These objectives change with the economic, legal, political and social environment. Furthermore, the content and quality of useful information depends on the specific context of the company (e.g. on the industry).

The standards and regulations supplied to companies should serve as tools for solving problems and for serving the public interest in providing even-handed information that facilitates efficient functioning of capital and other markets.

Until recently, environmentally induced financial impacts have been considered to be adequately covered by the existing accounting and reporting standards and regulations. However, the increasing number of environmental issues has resulted in substantial financial consequences for companies. Therefore, various customers of financial accounting information have started to influence standard-setting bodies and regulators to alter existing and create new accounting standards, regulations and guidelines.

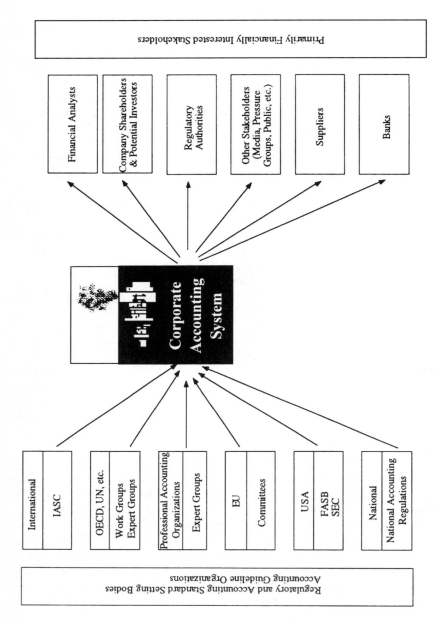

Figure 5.1 Different Standard Setting Bodies and Financially Interested Stakeholders

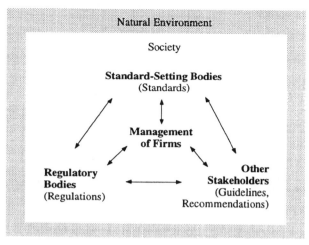

Figure 5.2 Stakeholders Defining Guidelines, Standards and Regulations for Financial Accounting

Also, the most important regulators, standard setters, professional organizations and other key stakeholders of financial accounting have started to acknowledge that existing standards may have to be amplified, and that new guidelines should offer explanations.

Figure 5.2 shows the three main groups ("providers") which directly influence how the management of companies considers environmental issues in financial accounting.

- Regulatory bodies (e.g. the US Securities and Exchange Commission: SEC; founded in 1929 in response to the Wall Street crash, the SEC supervises the US bourses (Arthur Andersen *et al.* 1994, p. 39)).
- Standard setting bodies (e.g. the International Accounting Standards Committee: IASC, or the Financial Accounting Standards Board: FASB[6])
- Other stakeholders (e.g. professional accounting organizations, international organizations)

Regulators have the strongest direct influence on the management of companies as they create legally enforceable regulations. Nonetheless, regulators and jurisdictions are strongly influenced by organizations which create standards for financial accounting (standard setting bodies). In addition, other stakeholders, such as organizations of professional accountants and financial analysts, or expert groups of international organizations (e.g. UN, OECD), publish guidelines and recommendations which are used by standard setters and management. Furthermore, environmental protection agencies

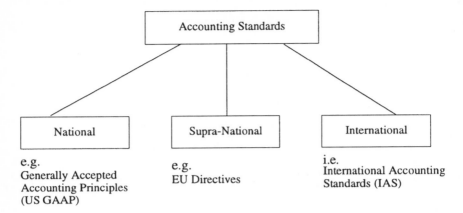

Figure 5.3 National, Supra-national, and International Accounting Standards and Regulations

exercise influence on standard setters. For the last couple of years, some of these organizations have started to deal with the recognition, measurement and disclosure of environmentally related financial impacts on companies. Most comprehensive and important for companies are the national, supra-national and international sets of accounting standards (Figure 5.3).

National accounting standards differ between countries. Hence, an increasing number of multinational companies apply international accounting standards. However, the US standards exercise a strong influence on other national as well as on supra-national and international standards. This is especially the case with international standards, which are mostly formulated when several national (i.e. US) standards are already in place. US regulations and standards are also more advanced with regard to environmental issues than the international accounting standards (IAS). They might thus provide valuable hints on the direction in which the international standards will have to go.

It can be expected that new standards will be issued which deal specifically with environmental issues. However, given the problem that too many standards increase the costs of reporting, new standards should only be issued if they are clearly advantageous to the present situation. Much of the externally available information could already be improved if the existing standards were adapted and if the existing accounting principles were enforced more consistently by regulators.

The International Accounting Standards Committee (IASC) is the only global standard setting body. It is therefore useful to take a look at the assumptions and conventions of the international accounting standards (IAS) (Figure 5.4).

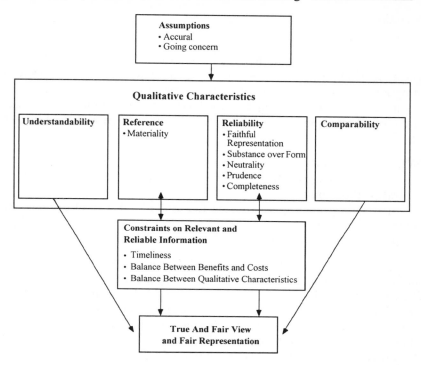

Figure 5.4 Assumptions and Qualitative Characteristics of Accounting Information Characteristics According to IASC 1995, pp. 47ff.

In order to meet the objectives of financial statements, they are assumed to be prepared on the basis of two assumptions (IASC [1995 IAS 21ff]):

- accrual
- going concern.

On the accrual basis, effects of transactions are recognized when they occur or when a potential future occurrence becomes likely (and not when cash or its equivalent is received or paid), and they are recorded and reported in the financial statements to which they relate. The assumption of a going concern implies that the company will continue in operation for the foreseeable future.

Furthermore, the information provided in financial reports should meet some qualitative characteristics (IASC [1995 IAS 25ff]):

- understandability
- relevance

- reliability
- comparability.

The disclosed information must be understandable if studied with due diligence, and relevant to the users of financial statements. The relevance of information is strongly determined by its materiality (prospective impact) for the financial position of a company. Furthermore, the usefulness of financial information depends on its reliability. Reliable information is characterized by being:

- faithfully represented
- substantially in contrast to just formally correct
- neutral (without bias)
- prepared with prudence, i.e. with the adoption of a degree of caution when making judgements
- complete (without omissions).

To support investment decisions, the information provided should be comparable with financial statements of other companies.

These qualitative characteristics are the main attributes that are thought to make information useful to readers of financial statements. However, the relevance and reliability of financial reporting information is influenced by its timeliness, the costs of collection and some trade-offs which often have to be made between of different qualitative characteristics.

Financial reports should give a true and fair view of the financial position of a company. The information provided as well as the fair representation of financial statements should be externally verifiable to be useful for the recipients.

However, the usefulness of given information varies with changes in the economic, legal, political and social environment. Thus, accounting standards have to be regularly updated to ensure that the information provided is still useful and that it reflects the changed requests and priorities of investors.

Today, environmental issues must be considered in financial accounting and reporting as well as in modern financial analysis—because they substantially influence risks and opportunities of companies. Examples of environmentally induced financial impacts on companies are environmental charges, fees, fines, site abandonment costs, lower value of polluting production devices, environmental liabilities, etc.

Companies operating in environmentally sensitive businesses should therefore recognize, measure and disclose environmentally related financial impacts separately from all other items.

Recognition is the formal recording of past or of probable future items (environmentally induced outlays) in the main body of the financial statements (Johnson 1993 p. 118), whereas measurement deals with the determination of the monetary amount of recognized outlays. Items which are relevant to the

---

Box 5.1
Definition of Recognition, Measurement, Disclosure and Elements

Recognition ". . . involves the depiction of the item in words and by a monetary amount and the inclusion of that amount in the balance sheet or income statement totals. Items that satisfy the recognition criteria should be recognized in the balance sheet or income statement. The failure to recognize such items is not rectified by disclosure of the accounting policies used nor by notes or explanatory material." (IASC 1995, p. 63 [IAS F82]).

"*Measurement* is the process of determining the monetary amounts at which the elements of the financial statements are to be recognized and carried in the balance sheet and income statement. This involves the selection of the particular basis of measurement." (IASC 1995, p. 63 [IAS F99] Emphasis is added here and in later boxes).

Disclosure ". . . is appropriate when knowledge of the item is considered to be relevant to the evaluation of the financial position, performance and changes in financial positions of an enterprise by the users of financial statements." (IASC 1995, p. 64 [IAS F88])

Elements: "Financial statements portray the financial effects of transactions and other events by grouping them into broad classes according to their economic characteristics. These broad classes are termed 'elements' of financial statements." (IASC 1995, p. 54 [IAS F47])

---

evaluation of the economic performance of a company are to be disclosed (see Box 5.1), or incorporated into the balance sheet or the income statement.

The US Securities and Exchange Commission (SEC) is the first and so far the only regulator that requires disclosure of all material effects of compliance with environmental regulations on required capital, expenditures, earnings and the competitive position of the company. The disclosure is required in the financial statement in the "Description of the Business" as well as in the material "Legal Proceedings" (SEC 101 and SEC S-K 103).

The topics dealt with in financial statements are grouped into "elements" in order to enhance understandability and comparability (Box 5.1). The elements related to the measurement of the

- financial position in the balance sheet are assets, liabilities and equity
- economic performance in the income statement are income and expenses.

Environmental issues do not influence all elements and procedures (recognition, measurement, disclosure) of financial accounting to the same extent. Thus the remaining sections of this chapter focus on some of the most important and most discussed issues and procedures (Table 5.1). The crosses in Table 5.1 indicate the emphasis given in the environmental context.

- Classification of environmentally induced outlays as assets or as expenses (Section 5.2).
- Environmentally induced expenses (e.g. costs of remediation and pollution prevention, fees, fines, etc.) (Section 5.3).
- Environmentally related financial impacts on assets (e.g. impaired inventory and production devices) (5.4).
- Environmental liabilities, contingent liabilities as well as reserves and provisions (5.5).
- Tradeable pollution permits (5.6).
- The management's discussion and analysis in financial reporting (5.7).

One of the main areas of concern is the adequate classification of environmentally induced outlays as assets or as expenses. The distinction is crucial in accounting, and financial accounting standards deal thoroughly with this topic. The next section deals with this topic with regard to environmentally induced costs.

Table 5.1 Issues and Topics of Environmentally Differentiated Financial Accounting

Procedures / Issues	Tracking, Tracing and Recognition (Differentiation)	Measurement and Estimation	Disclosure and Reporting
Capitalize or Expense?	XX		
Environmentally Related Expenses	XX	X	X
Environmentally Induced Depreciation and Devaluation of Assets	X	X	XX
Liabilities and Contingent Liabilities	X	XX	XX
Tradeable Pollution Permits	XX	X	X
Management's Discussion and Analysis			XX

X = Important, XX = Very Important

Box 5.2
Assets and Expenses

"An *asset* is a resource controlled by the enterprise as a result of past events and from which future economic benefits are expected to flow to the enterprise." (IASC 1995, p. 54 [IAS F49])

"*Expenses* are decreases in economic benefits during the accounting period in the form of outflows or depletion of assets or occurrences of liabilities that result in decreases in equity, other than those relating to distributions to equity participants." (IASC 1995, p. 60 [IAS F70])

5.2 ENVIRONMENTALLY INDUCED COSTS: ASSETS OR EXPENSES?

The issue of whether environmental costs should be capitalized or expensed is one of the most controversial subjects for accountants as well as for financial analysts, EFFAS (1994, p. 17).

The difference between an expense and an asset is clear in principle (see Box 5.2). An *expense* is a cost that has given a benefit and now has expired, while unexpired costs which can give future benefits, are classified as *assets* (Polimeni *et al.*, 1986 p. 10). However, what are the increased or decreased (economic) benefits of pollution prevention and emission reduction measures?

Environmental investments have been defined by the Canadian Institute of Chartered Accountants (CICA 1993) as those undertaken to:

- prevent or mitigate environmental damage or conserve resources
- clean up past environmental damage.

CICA identifies two approaches to the question of when to capitalize environmental costs (CICA 1993; see also Holmark *et al.* 1995).

- *Increased future benefits approach (IFB):* the disbursement must result in an increase in expected future economic benefits from the asset.
- *Additional cost-of-future-benefits approach (ACOFB):* environmental costs can be capitalised if they are considered to be a cost of the expected future benefits from the asset, regardless of whether there is any increase in economic benefits.

Financial statements are prepared to report the economic performance of a company and should not be distorted with issues which are not economically material. From a strict *economic perspective*, capitalization should only be allowed if the costs contribute to additional future economic benefits beyond the originally assessed standard of performance (IFB approach).

However, in special cases, costs for clean-up or pollution prevention may qualify as assets if they are absolutely necessary for the company to stay in business, even though they do not create additional economic benefits. (At least some of the costs should create assets in the future.) Less clear is the treatment of other costs which may enhance reputation but are not directly attributable to a specific economic benefit or investment.

From an *environmental point of view*, capitalization (and therefore the ACOFB approach) should be favored if pollution prevention creates future environmental benefits. Furthermore, capitalization allows amortization over a number of years, and therefore, enhances long-term thinking (Williams and Phillips 1994).

Nevertheless, it could also be argued that most environmental protection activities are expenses because they reflect a repayment of debt to society and nature. In this case, pollution is seen as an increase of the liabilities of a company (liabilities to nature). The costs of reducing liabilities should be expensed and not recognized as investments. Also the payment of liabilities that were not recognized when they occurred should not be regarded as investments.

The ACOFB approach may be favored if the rapid emergence of new environmental issues is considered to be unforseeable and likely to cause unexpected future liabilities. In this case, prudent economic management would require those costs of environmental protection which impede possible future economic problems to be considered as assets.

IASC has chosen the IFB approach (IAS 16, see Box 5.3) whereas the Fédération des Expertes Comptables Européens (FEE) and the Emerging Issues Task Force (EITF) of FASB have adopted the ACOFB approach.[7]

IAS 16, 14 allows the capitalization of environmentally related costs for property, plant and equipment if an increase of future economic benefits from other assets is expected and if the costs are recoverable. Capitalization is possible if the costs are necessary to *comply with environmental requirements* (see Box 5.3). However, it is not entirely clear if to "comply with environmental requirements" is limited to legal requirements, or if voluntary activities to comply with social requirements might also qualify for capitalization (the term "legal obligation" might be better).

IASC has much changed the perspective it expressed in earlier proposed standards. The term "expenditure" (in the proposed statement E43, 14 of May 1992) has been replaced with "property, plant and equipment" in IAS 16. The attribute "an improvement in the safety or environmental efficiency of an asset" in E43, 23 has been omitted completely from IAS 16. The most important change is the omission of paragraph 24 of the proposed standard E43 (see Box 5.3), which would have made explicitly clear that environmental clean-up costs and fines should be expensed if they do not result in an improvement of the originally assessed standard of safety or environmental efficiency of the asset.

FEE recommends that costs incurred to prevent future environmental impacts should be capitalized while clean-up costs for past environmental damage should be expensed.

Also, the Emerging Issues Task Force (EITF) of FASB has a consensus that treatment costs of environmental contamination should generally be expensed. (For the discussion of the treatment of costs of asbestos removal, see EITF Abstract Issue No. 89–13). Nevertheless, capitalization is possible if one of the following three criteria is met. (FASB EITF 1990, Issue No 90–8. For a discussion, see Williams and Phillips 1994, p. 329.)

- "The costs extend the life, increase the capacity, or improve the safety or efficiency of property owned by the company.
- The costs mitigate or prevent environmental contamination that has yet to occur and that otherwise may result from future operations of activities. In addition, the costs improve the property compared with its condition when constructed or acquired, if later.
- The costs are incurred in preparing for a sale of property that is currently held for sale."

Box 5.3
Capitalize or Expense?

"*Property, plant and equipment* may be acquired for safety or environmental reasons. The acquisition of such property, plant and equipment, while not directly increasing the future economic benefits of any particular existing item of property, plant and equipment, may be necessary in order for the enterprise to obtain the future economic benefit from its other assets. When this is the case, such acquisitions of property, plant and equipment qualify for recognition as assets, in that they enable future economic benefits from the related assets to be derived by the enterprise in excess of what it could derive if they had not been acquired. However, such assets are only recognized to the extent that the resulting carrying amount of such an asset and related assets does not exceed the total recoverable amount of that asset and its related assets. For example, a chemical manufacturer may have to install certain new chemical handling processes in order to comply with environmental requirements on the production and storage of dangerous chemicals; related plant enhancements are recognized as an asset to the extent they are recoverable because, without them, the enterprise is unable to manufacture and sell chemicals." (IASC 1995, p. 261 [IAS 16, 14]).

". . . [In] general, environmental contamination treatment costs should be charged to expense. Those costs may be capitalized if recoverable but only if any one of the following criteria are met.

1. The costs extend the life, increase the capacity, or improve the safety or efficiency of property owned by the company. For purposes of this criterion, the condition of that property after the costs are incurred must be improved as compared with the condition of that property when originally constructed or acquired, if later.

2. The costs mitigate or prevent environmental contamination that has yet to occur and that otherwise may result from future operations or activities. In addition, the costs improve the property compared with its condition when constructed or acquired, if later.

3. The costs are incurred in preparing for sale that property currently held for sale." (FASB EITF 1990, Issue 90–8)

"*Expenditure on repair or maintenance* of property, plant and equipment is made to restore or maintain the future economic benefits that an enterprise can expect from the originally assessed standard of performance of the asset. As such, it is usually recognized as an expense when incurred. For instance, the cost of servicing or overhauling plant and equipment is usually an expense since it restores, rather than increases, the originally assessed standard of performance. Similarly, the costs of cleaning the environment and the payment of fines for breaches of environmental regulations resulting from the operation are deferred as an item of property, plant and equipment. This is because they do not increase the future economic benefits arising from the related assets. The removal of contamination is also an expense except to the extent that the removal process results in an improvement in the originally assessed standard of safety or environmental efficiency of the asset." (IASC 1992a, p. 11 [IAS E43, 24] *omitted* in IAS 16).

In summary, IASC, FASB EITF and FEE recommend expensing fines, fees and costs of past environmental impacts. In any case, capitalization is allowed if a future economic benefit is expected to result from present costs. Costs of voluntary activities to comply with the requests of critical stakeholders of the company may not qualify for capitalization under IAS 16. EITF and FEE allow capitalization of costs which result in the improvement of the safety or efficiency of the company's property, even if no future economic benefits are expected and no legal requirements exist. However, EITF and FEE do not require capitalization of those costs so that the decision whether to capitalize or to expense is left to the management. (Arthur Andersen and Company has criticised this EITF FASB statement because it allows free choice on whether to capitalize or expense—FASB EITF 1990, 21 [Discussion Issue 90–8]. This results in lack of consistency in financial reporting.)

Depending on industry or the financial position, some companies may decide to expense while others would tend to capitalize environmental costs for voluntary pollution prevention. The management of other companies might want to change the treatment at their own discretion.

Although the method of treatment chosen has substantial implications, *consistency* in the treatment of environmental outlays is even more important for external stakeholders. Consistency reduces uncertainties about the contents of financial statements and adds quality to the disclosed information. Such consistency is provided by the international accounting standard.

Box 5.4 shows a case for the classification of "voluntary" clean-up costs.

Box 5.4
Case: Capitalize or Expense?

The management of company "Goodfellow" decides to respond to requirements of various local stakeholders (neighbours, employees, etc.) and customers and to clean up an old waste site. The company has no legal requirement to do so, nor does it intend to sell the site or to use it for other purposes.

First, the remediation of the contaminated soil is necessary. Thereafter a liner will be installed to prevent future contamination.

Should these outlays be classified as assets or as expenses in the financial statement of company "Goodfellow"?

Clean-up: IAS 16, 14 allows for capitalization if the environmental outlay is recoverable and if it increases the future economic benefit of the landfill. This would be possible, for example, if the company can use the site for building purposes after the clean-up.

The recommendation of EITF, on the contrary, clearly supports expensing of the refinement costs, because the life of the waste site is not extended by refining its soil. The condition of the soil after refining will not be improved compared to when the site was constructed or acquired. The refinement will also not mitigate or prevent future operations from creating toxic waste (FASB EITF 1990, Issue 90–8).

Installation of the liner: IAS 16, 14 allows capitalization (subject to recoverability) if the liner helps to create future economic benefits from the property. This is the case if the liner is installed because of environmental regulations. Voluntary installation, as here, does not necessarily allow capitalization, unless the site is intended to be sold or used for building purposes.

FASB EITF recommendation 90–8 allows capitalization because the liner improves the safety of the site (FASB EITF 1990, Issue 90–8).

The next section deals with the treatment of environmentally related expenditures which have been recognized as expenses. Section 5.4 discusses environmentally induced financial impacts on assets.

5.3 TREATMENT OF ENVIRONMENTALLY INDUCED EXPENSES

Environmental *expenses* are environmentally related costs that have given a *benefit* and have *now expired*. Expenses are set against revenues in the profit-and-loss account (income statement). (Environmentally induced revenues are not treated separately in this book.) Despite the magnitude of environmental expenses, no standard requires their separate recognition. For a definition of environmental costs, see Section 4.1.

Environmental issues are clearly part of the risk structure of a company, and thus should be disclosed separately. Otherwise, investors are not able to assess the company's risk accurately. The differentiation of environmentally induced expenditures from others would allow investors and other financially interested stakeholders to assess the economic performance better as well as the future opportunities and problems of a company.

Large fines and fees are a signal that a company is among the laggards. High insurance premiums paid might indicate that management has realized potential problems, but that it is not yet ready to tackle the problems at their source. Or they might also mean that measures for risk reduction are less economical than insurance. High environmentally induced operational costs might indicate that the economic costs of corporate environmental protection could be reduced by investments in more efficient pollution-prevention technologies.

However, some first moves towards requiring separate disclosure are in sight. (See also EFFAS 1994, p. 17).

The US Securities and Exchange Commission (SEC) has dealt with the increasing financial impacts of environmental issues for companies. The SEC asks for disclosure of environmental information that is economically material to the issuer. This includes financial effects that compliance with federal, state and local environmental laws may have upon capital expenditures and earnings.

The securities commissions of Ontario and Quebec (Canada) require disclosure in the annual report of ". . . the financial or operational effect of environmental protection requirements on the capital expenditures, earnings and competitive position [. . .] for the current fiscal year and any expected impact on future years" (Moore 1991, p. 55 and CICA 1993; see also Holmark *et al.* 1995, p. 75). This provides investors with information about the future strategy of a company (CICA 1993).

The accounting advisory forum of the EU recommends the disclosure of the amount of environmental expenditures charged to the profit and loss account. Expenditures should be analyzed in a manner appropriate to the nature and size of business and/or the types of environmental issues relevant to the enterprise (AAF EU 1994).

Nonetheless, the mere differentiation of environmental expenditures from other expenditures is not sufficient to inform investors adequately. Further distinction is necessary, at least between expenditures incurred to improve the environmental record of a company and expenditures for breaches of environmental law (fines).

Expenditures to improve the environmental record should be subdivided into outlays incurred for repair, reduction and prevention of environmental damage. For investors, there is a substantial difference if, for example, one company spends $1 billion on clean-up work while another spends $1 billion on pollution prevention (see also Section 4.2.1).

Environmental expenses are often recognized for the first time when they result in a cash outflow and not when the expenses occur. For the last decade, this practice has changed in some companies which have started to recognize contingent liabilities for potential fines and remediation costs for landfills. However, early recognition of such (potential) expenses requires the collaboration of the environmental protection agency. Recognition and disclosure of potential expenses are not encouraged as long as some agencies take disclosures of potential expenses as evidence of omitted prevention activities.

Standards of financial accounting also influence managerial accounting (see also Section 4.6). A further differentiation of environmental expenditures in financial accounting would therefore provide incentives to separate and to correctly allocate these costs. However, most important for investors is the consistent treatment of environmental expenditures.

5.4 TREATMENT OF ENVIRONMENTALLY INDUCED FINANCIAL IMPACTS ON ASSETS

Environmental issues can also have major financial impacts on the balance sheet, i.e. on assets and liabilities. However, it is not a simple matter to identify the "correct" amount of environmental impacts on assets and liabilities (see Section 4.2; environmental liabilities are discussed in Section 5.5).

So far, as with expenditures, no specific standards of financial accounting exist to clarify when environmentally induced assets must be recognized, measured and disclosed. Nonetheless, there are more general accounting standards which discuss if and when an asset should be recognized (see Box 5.5).

> **Box 5.5**
> **Recognition of Assets**
>
> "An asset is *recognized* in the balance sheet when it is probable that the future economic benefits will flow to the enterprise and the asset has a cost or value that can be measured reliably." (IASC 1995, p. 64 [IAS F89])

Unexpired costs which are expected to give future benefits are classified as *assets*. Ideally, it should be possible to measure the benefits reliably. When the benefits cannot be reliably measured, assets should be disclosed in the notes, explanatory material or supplementary schedules (IASC 1995, p. 64 [IAS 90–81]).

The influence of environmental issues on assets is most evident with:

- end-of-the-pipe and integrated technologies
- obsolete inventories.

End-of-the-pipe technologies to treat environmental impacts can easily be recognized as environmental assets. This is more difficult with pollution prevention which is integrated into the production technologies (5.4.1). Environmental issues and regulations can substantially influence consumer tastes and market conditions. This can result in impaired or even obsolete inventories (5.4.2).

5.4.1 End-of-the-Pipe and Integrated Technologies

As a rule, according to IASC (1995, p. 261), costs which do not lead to future economic benefits should be expensed. FASB EITF, however, allows capitalization if the costs mitigate or prevent contamination that is yet to occur and that otherwise may result from future operations or activities. In addition, the costs must improve the property, compared with its condition when constructed or acquired. Nonetheless, no additional future economic benefit has to be expected (FASB EITF 1990 p. 2 [Issue 90–8]).

End-of-the-pipe technologies (for a definition, see Section 4.2.2) definitely qualify as assets if they are necessary investments to obtain future economic benefits from other assets of the company. This is the case whenever the technologies are required for legal compliance (see Section 5.2). Differentiation and also measurement is usually no problem with end-of-the-pipe technologies as they can easily be identified.

So far, however, no standard exists that would require separate recognition, measurement or disclosure of end-of-the-pipe technologies. In addition to providing useful information to shareholders about the costs incurred for environmental protection, such a standard would create incentives for management to track, trace and correctly allocate the outlays for end-of-the-pipe technologies (see Section 4.2).

Integrated pollution prevention technologies are part of ordinary production assets. They are bought mainly for economic reasons. Therefore, these environmentally related assets are not considered as overhead costs even in companies lagging behind with their accounting practices. Correct allocation and classification as assets is likely.

The environmentally related part of integrated technologies often cannot be determined exactly. This leaves the management a discretionary latitude for recognition.

In the past, some companies felt pressed for image reasons to overstate the environmentally related part of their assets. Nevertheless, with increasing environmentally induced costs, firms are ever more confronted with demands from shareholders to improve the economic efficiency of the firm's environmental protection. In those circumstances, environmentally related assets tend to be underestimated.

Integrated technologies should be treated as normal capital investments (assets) because

- the investments have been made mainly for economic reasons
- it is difficult to determine exactly the environmentally induced part of the integrated technology.

Such recognition implicitly allows for capitalization of the environmental part of the investment. This provides an incentive to favor integrated pollution prevention technologies instead of end-of-the-pipe technologies as the latter often have to be expensed.

Investments in integrated technologies should be mentioned in the management's discussion and analysis of the financial statement. This allows the management to specifically report changes in environmental assets. The environmental improvements due to environmental assets are reported in external ecological accounting (see Part C).

5.4.2 Impaired and Obsolete Inventories

New, tightened environmental regulations, or a change of consumer tastes, can devalue inventories of products. In rare cases inventories of semi-manufactured or final products can also increase in value or become obsolete. Therefore, the exercise of prudence requires cautious valuations of assets such as inventories.

A decrease of the value of an inventory should be measured at the net realizable value if it cannot be sold at cost or higher.[8] The loss of value should be recognized as an environmentally related loss. This allows (potential) investors to judge the economic consequences of omitted environmental strategies.

Also, inventories of products which do not comply with new, tightened regulations, can decrease in value. Such inventories should be recognized as a loss, or be amortized faster than originally planned to reflect the real value of the assets to shareholders.

In extreme cases, inventories or other assets (e.g. land) can change into liabilities. For example, in the US, some creditors (banks) which held land as security for loans have become liable for clean-up costs which exceed the value of the land (see Section 5.5). In consequence, in countries like the US, a firm should depreciate property (i.e. land) which is being continuously contaminated. If the contamination happens through a single accident, the land should be revalued. In contrast, IASC (1992a, p. 629) has defined that "land normally has an unlimited life and is therefore not depreciated". IASC, in other words, assumes implicitly that "land" is equal to "space". Thus this standard only considers the economic life of the space and disregards the "ecological life" of the land. However, as the very high remediation costs in the US show, land is much more than space. The contamination of land can substantially impair the economic life of a property. These (internal) costs should be reflected in the financial statement either as an environmental impairment of assets or as an environmental liability.

There is already an exception which allows depreciation of land from which natural resources are being extracted. "When natural resources are involved, the land is amortized by means of a depletion expense. Depletion for GAAP is usually calculated using a units-of-production method, i.e., a certain rate per ton, barrel, cubic foot, or whatever". "For tax purposes, depletion is calculated quite differently, normally as some percentage of revenue rather than cost" (Young 1985, p. 183).

The next section treats environmental liabilities, which may be the main issue for many companies in dealing with environmental accounting.

5.5 TREATMENT OF ENVIRONMENTALLY INDUCED (CONTINGENT) LIABILITIES, RESERVES AND PROVISIONS

In the past, environmental issues often did not enter the priority list of management before they showed up as liabilities in the account books. Some environmental liabilities have exceeded the worst dreams of management. Among the major disasters in the 1980s were Bhopal (Union Carbide), Schweizerhalle (Sandoz), and Prince William Sound (Exxon), all of which had substantial financial consequences for the companies involved (see Box 5.6).

Box 5.6
Exxon's Environmental Liabilities—$16.5 Billion?

On March 24, 1989 the giant oil tanker Exxon Valdez ran aground in Prince William Sound on Alaska's west coast. Forty million liters of crude oil spilled into the sea, causing enormous damage to the marine flora and fauna.

On July 13, 1994 the jury of an Alaskan court ruled that the captain had been a reckless master, having a history of drinking, and that Exxon, which owned the tanker and the oil, had been equally reckless in allowing him to command the Exxon Valdez.

The announcement of the court's decision in the first of four stages of the proceedings led to a 4% fall in Exxon's share price, wiping out roughly US$3.1 billion of the firm's market capitalization (in the short term).

By then the company had already spent $2.5 billion on cleaning much of the 2,400 km of beaches soiled by the spill, and another $1.1 billion to settle several claims under criminal law.

In the second phase of the proceedings the compensation payments for the damages to the environment, fisheries and other impacted industries will be determined. Exxon has for example been sued for the losses suffered by fishermen. The court decided that Exxon will have to pay altogether only $268.8 million of the $895 million which were demanded by the fishermen. However, this is still two and a half times more than Exxon estimated the damage to be.

Third, the court will decide about the fine. The 10,000 fishermen and other people living at Prince William Sound (including a large group of indigenous people) demand a fine of $15 billion. So far, Exxon is confronted with a bill totalling $16.5 billion: $3.5 for clean-up, $1.5 billion in compensation and the rest as punishment.

In the fourth stage, the court will deal with the claims of thousands of individuals and groups that do not belong to those of stage three of the court case.

- How can the court account for the environmental damage of the Exxon Valdez spill when it has to determine compensation payments?
- What possibilities has Exxon to account for its contingent liabilities ($16.5 billion plus the yet unknown claims of stage four of the proceedings)?
- How should Exxon account for its compensation ($1.5 billion) and settlement payments ($1.1 billion)?

As mentioned above, financial markets react to environmental impacts of a company as soon as the impacts are monetarized and made material for the company. How can financial analysts assess and consider environmentally induced financial risks and opportunities?

(Sources: Aeschlimann 1994, 3; NZZ 1994a, 19; The Economist 1994a, 62; ibid 1994b, 20; Vaughan 1994, 175).

Furthermore, thousands of other companies have also been hit by major liabilities incurred through less spectacular spills, accidents, etc.

However, in the US, legislation has had more influence on environmental liabilities than some well-known accidents (Brüggemann 1994, p. 71ff). Notably the Resource Conservation and Recovery Act of 1976 (RCRA) and the Comprehensive Environmental Response, Compensation, and Liability Act of 1980 (CERCLA, often referred to as the "Superfund law"), which enable the US Environmental Protection Agency to enforce landfill remediation by companies, resulted in a major increase of environmental liabilities. Thus, environmental liabilities have become not only much more common but also much larger than ten years ago. A well known example is Monsanto which, in 1992, made a provision for liabilities to clean up waste sites which was almost 83% of its 1991 net income (McMurray 1992). CERCLA aims at cleaning up abandoned waste sites (Superfund sites). The liability is regarded as joint and retrospective for all costs incurred in the clean-up. All involved parties can be held liable for the total costs of remediating the landfill. The liability exists even if the activity which caused the environmental problem was legal and the Superfund legislation did not exist at that time. The EPA can require any person or company involved to carry the total of all remediation costs, no matter how much of them the respective party has actually caused. This shows that environmental liabilities are one way of internalizing external costs.

Even banks which have given mortgages or which manage closed properties can be held liable. The costs of cleaning up Superfund sites are expected to exceed $500 billion in the next 40 to 50 years, EIU (1993).

Less well known is that the Superfund amendments also require disclosure of environmental risks arising from the company's activities (see Newell *et al.* 1990, Dirks 1991 and Rabinowitz and Murphy 1992).

The main questions regarding the treatment of a company's environmental liabilities are as follows.

- What are (contingent) environmental liabilities?
- Should they be recognized? If yes, when?
- How can they be measured?
- If and when should they be disclosed?

5.5.1 What Are (Contingent) Liabilities?

An *environmental liability* is an obligation to pay future expenditures to remedy environmental damage that has occurred because of past events or transactions, or to compensate a third party which has suffered from the damage. Liabilities (see also Box 5.7) have three essential characteristics (CICA, 1993).

Box 5.7
Liabilities

"A *liability* is a present obligation of the enterprise arising from past events, the settlement of which is expected to result in an outflow from the enterprise of resources embodying economic benefits." (IASC 1995, p. 54 [IAS F49 b]).

- Liabilities ". . . embody a duty or responsibility to others that entails settlement by future transfer or use of assets, provision of services or other yielding of economic benefits, on a specified or determinable date, on occurrence of a specified event, or on demand.
- The duty or responsibility obligates the entity leaving it or [. . . avoiding] it.
- The transaction or event obligating the entity has already occurred."

The essential characteristic of a liability is that the enterprise has a *present* obligation. "An *obligation* is a duty or responsibility to act or perform in a certain way. Obligations may be legally enforceable as a consequence of a binding contract or statutory requirement. [. . .] Obligations also arise, however, from normal business practice, custom and a desire to maintain good business relations or act in an equitable manner" (IASC 1995, p. 57 [IAS F60]). Therefore, under some circumstances, voluntary pollution prevention and clean-up activities can also qualify as liabilities.

Future financial consequences of environmental issues are often not certain because of the strong influence of frequently changing regulations and political decisions. The first uncertainty is related to the occurrence of liabilities, whereas the second uncertainty concerns their amount.

- Will a liability become material or not? (Contingent liabilities.)
- How large will the liability be? (Measurement.)

Contingent liabilities (contingencies) are a common way of recognizing uncertain outcomes (see Box 5.8). A *contingent environmental liability* is an obligation to remedy environmental damage dependent on the occurrence or

---

Box 5.8
Contingent Liabilities

"A *contingency* is a condition or situation, the ultimate outcome of which, gain or loss, will be confirmed only on the occurrence, or non-occurrence, of one or more uncertain future events" (IASC 1995, p. 181 [IAS 10, 3]).

---

non-occurrence of one or more uncertain future events, or to compensate a third party which would suffer from such a damage.

Examples of (contingent) environmental liabilities which can emerge from corporate activities include the following.

- Soil contamination (e.g. from underground storage or spills).
- Groundwater contamination (e.g. from contaminated surface water or soil contamination).
- Surface water contamination (e.g. from point sources like industrial processes).
- Air emissions (e.g. from fugitive emissions and transportation activities, as well as from sound, noise, light, etc.).
- Energy emissions (e.g. heat, radioactive or electromagnetic emissions, noise).
- Visual impact (e.g. because of buildings).

Liabilities and especially contingent liabilities often contain large uncertainties. To secure consistency and reliability, liabilities must therefore possess certain characteristics in order to be recognized in the main body of a financial statement.

5.5.2 Recognition of Environmental Liabilities

So far, no specific standard has been issued purely for the recognition of environmental liabilities. Some may argue that the general accounting standards would be sufficient to cope with environmental liabilities, if they only were applied correctly (Hawkshaw 1991, p. 22ff).

The most important accounting standards specifying if and when to recognize (all) liabilities are presented in Box 5.9.

As a rule, environmental liabilities should be recognized in financial statements if they are material and if the liabilities

- or the events leading to the liabilities are probable
- can be reliably measured (or reasonably estimated).

However, liabilities must not be specially recognised if they are part of normal business risk. The US SEC also states that management may not delay recognition of an environmental liability until only a single amount can be reasonably estimated (Holmark *et al.* 1995; Price Waterhouse 1992a, p. 6). The words "probable" and "reliably measured" (or "reasonably estimated") are important for the interpretation of the main accounting standards.

"The word probable is used with its general meaning rather than in a specific accounting or technical sense, and refers to that which can reasonably be expected or believed on the basis of available evidence or logic but is neither certain nor proved." (Adams 1992, p. 16). Therefore, an environmental liability is probable if, for example:

> **Box 5.9**
> **Recognition of Liabilities**
>
> "A *liability is recognized* in the balance sheet when it is probable that an outflow of resources embodying economic benefits will result from the settlement of a present obligation and the amount at which the settlement will take place can be measured reliably" (IASC 1995, p. 65 [IAS F91]).
>
> "An estimated loss from a *loss contingency* [. . .] shall be accrued by a charge to income if both of the following conditions are met: (a) Information available prior to assurance of the financial statements indicates that it is probable that an asset had been impaired or a liability incurred at the date of the financial statements. It is implicit in this condition that it must be probable that one or more future events will occur confirming the fact of the loss. (b) The amount of loss can be reasonably estimated." (FASB 1995 Current Texts [FAS 5, 8]) For pre-acquisition contingencies of purchased businesses, see FASB 1995 Statement 38.

- a legal obligation exists
- the management wants to prevent, reduce or repair substantial environmental impacts (FEE 1993)
- a company in the US has been named by the US EPA as a Potentially Responsible Party (PRP) to clean up a US Superfund site (Price Waterhouse 1992a).

However, management has a large discretionary latitude in deciding when to recognize a liability even if it is likely to occur. Legal obligations can take years to finally emerge and become material for a company.

Even more difficult than the definition of "probability" is the formulation of criteria when an environmental liability or contingent liability is "reasonably estimable". Thus, the main problem with environmental liabilities is the measurement, or estimation, of their amount.

5.5.3 Measurement of (Contingent) Environmental Liabilities

A liability must be measured or reliably estimated in order to qualify for recognition in the main body of a financial statement. Key factors that can be considered when estimating environmental liabilities are (SEC 1993; Surma and Vondra 1992; Holmark *et al.* 1995; or Roberts 1994b):

- current laws and regulations
- the extent of regulatory involvement
- the number and viability of the parties involved

- prior legal, economic, political and scientific experience
- the complexity of the problem, existing technologies and technological experience.

Experience in estimating environmental liabilities has been gained especially in the US with the "Superfund Act". The most important questions to be answered in the estimation process for clean-up costs are as follows (Holmark *et al.* 1995, p. 73; Price Waterhouse 1992a, p. 15).

- What remedial action will be taken?
- What is the company's share of responsibility?
- What significant costs can be recovered from others?
- When will the remediation commence and how long will it take?
- If the planned remediation does not work, what further actions are necessary?

If a company has a probable and reasonably estimable contingent environmental liability, the *best estimate* should be recognized (see Box 5.10). If there is no best estimate within the range of loss which could occur because of the contingency, at least the minimum amount should be recognized (IASC 1995, p. 183 [IAS 10, 8]). The minimum amount is likely to be zero. For example, a company which has been informed by the environmental protection

---

Box 5.10
Measurement of Contingent Liabilities

"*The estimation of the amount of a contingent loss* to be recognized in the financial statements may be based on information that provides a range of amounts of loss which could result from the contingency. The best estimate of the loss within such a range is recognized. When no amount within the range is indicated as a better estimate than any other amount, at least the minimum amount in the range is recognized. Disclosure of any additional exposure to loss is made if there is a possibility of loss in excess of the amount recognized" (IASC 1995, p. 183 [IAS 10, 11]).

Among the factors taken into account by management in *evaluating the contingency* are the progress of the claim at the date on which the financial statements are authorized for issue, the opinions of legal experts or other advisers, the experience of the enterprise in similar cases and the experience of other enterprises in similar situations (IASC 1995, p. 185 [IAS 10, 20]).

"An *estimated loss from a loss contingency* shall be accrued by a charge to income if it is probable that a liability has been incurred and the amount of the loss can be reasonably estimated." (FASB 1993, FAS 5)

agency that its disposal site does not comply with legal regulations might still not know which technique of remediation will be necessary, and thus what costs the company will face. Then, at least the costs of the cheapest remediation should be recognized. An additional exposure to loss should be disclosed in a footnote and the management should mention that the amount cannot be estimated (Roberts 1994a, p. 4).

A special issue is whether *counterclaims* or claims against a third party should be *offset against a liability*. According to IASC an offset is allowed but not required (IAS 10, 13). Contrary to this, the US SEC has decided that companies must not record or offset potential insurance reimbursements against the liabilities until received (SEC interpretation SAB No. 92), SEC (1993, [SEC interpretation SAB No. 92]). The US Securities and Exchange Commission recommends that the amount of the liability and the anticipated claim for insurance recovery be separately displayed, as this most fairly presents the potential consequences of the contingent claim on the company's resources. The risks and uncertainties associated with the contingent liability are separate and distinct from those associated with the recovery claim (Napolitano 1995, p. 10 or SEC 1993 [SEC interpretation SAB No. 92]).

Furthermore, companies should *refrain from discounting accrued liabilities* to reflect the time value of money, unless the aggregate amount of the obligation and the amount and timing of cash payments are fixed or reliably determined. The SEC stipulates that the discount rate used should not exceed the interest rate on risk-free monetary assets and have maturities comparable with that of the environmental liablity (Napolitano 1995, p. 10; SAB 1993 [SEC interpretation SAB No. 92]).

Also, companies should *not anticipate technological developments*, but base their estimates of future expenditures on existing technology (Napolitano 1995, p. 10; SAB 1993 [SEC interpretation SAB No. 92]). The same is also true for the development of *exchange rates,* which should not be anticipated by management.

Liabilities may be recognized even if they cannot be reliably measured. This is usually done by making reserves, provisions or charges to income.

5.5.4 Environmental Reserves, Provisions and Charges to Income

Liabilities which can only be broadly estimated are often recognized as provisions (see Box 5.11). In principle, reserves for environmentally induced liabilities and contingent liabilities may be made according to the same rules as reserves for other liabilities. *Reserves, charges to income or provisions for liabilities* are intended to cover losses or debts which are clearly defined and which on the date of the balance sheet are either likely to be incurred or certain to be incurred but uncertain as to the amount or as to the date on which they will arise (IASC 1992a).

Box 5.11
Provisions and Liabilities

"Some liabilities can be measured only by using a substantial degree of estimation. Some enterprises describe these liabilities as provisions. In some countries, such provisions are not regarded as liabilities because the concept of a liability is defined narrowly so as to include only amounts that can be established without the need to make estimates." (IASC 1995, p. 51 [F64])

Today, the IASC has defined liabilities in a broader sense (see Box 5.7; IASC 1995, p. 54 [F49]).

The Canadian Association for Accounting Standards (Association Canadienne de Normalisation) has issued a special guideline for provisions for environmental liabilities in its *Canadian Handbook*, ACN (1993). "When reasonably determinable, provisions should be made for future removal and site restoration costs, net of expected recoveries, in a rational and systematic manner by charges to income", and "the accumulated provisions [should] be recorded as a liability" (ACN 1993, 3060.39).

The initial reaction to the issue of a "Handbook" recommendation on site restoration was mixed. Critics argued that more time should be taken to develop a proper understanding of the problem, and wondered whether it was practical to require entities to make provisions for environmental liabilities. However, the standard has been justified by the potential magnitude of the costs incurred with environmental liabilities, and with the need to achieve some consistency in practice (Hawkshaw 1991, p. 25, Moore 1991, p. 54). The Canadian standard has served as a guide for other national and international standards, as the examples of the newly issued regulations of SEC and FASB show. FASB has also started to deal with site restoration or exit costs of the nuclear and other industry groups (FASB 1994, p. 6). These new standards require companies to set up reserves to pay for future costs of environmental liabilities (Fenn 1995, p. 62ff).

The oil, gas and coal industry as well as some public utilities often view site restoration costs as part of operation costs. However, some argue that the oil and gas business is fundamentally different from a manufacturing facility because the latter does not have a similarly finite production life (Adams 1992, p. 18). Nonetheless, if site restoration costs are material and probable they should be recognized and provided for by reserves or charges to income.

If liabilities do not have the characteristics required for recognition (e.g. if they cannot be reliably measured), and if they are not apt to be considered as reserves, charges to income or provisions, they might nevertheless have to be disclosed (Section 5.5.5).

5.5.5 Disclosure of (Contingent) Environmental Liabilities

Disclosure is the process of incorporating elements of financial accounting (assets, liabilities, equity, expenses and income) into the balance sheet, the income statement or separate sections and papers of disclosure. All recognized items must be disclosed in the balance sheet.

Nevertheless, many environmental liabilities are difficult to estimate with any degree of certainty when they are associated with accidents or with the remediation of "Superfund sites". Such items often possess the essential characteristics of an element (e.g. an expense), but fail to meet the criteria for recognition, because, for example, their monetary amount cannot be determined (see Box 5.1). Thus, the environmental liabilities disclosed in the balance sheet tend to be incomplete. To correct this shortcoming, the respective information can be added in an off-balance-sheet statement.

As with recognition, no standards have been developed solely to specify when to disclose environmental liabilities. However, it can be argued that general standards are able to deal with environmental liabilities, as long as they are applied correctly or enforced by regulatory authorities.

IASC, for example, requires a *disclosure* of contingent losses even if they are not recognized *unless the probability of a loss is remote* (IASC 1995, IAS 10, 9). Hence, also non-recognized environmental liabilities which are relevant to the evaluation of the financial position should be disclosed in the notes, explanatory material or supplementary schedules of the financial statement.

In the USA, liabilities (including environmental liabilities) have to be accrued for if they are *material, probable, and reasonably estimable* (SFAS 5, see Box 5.9). However, the occurrences of environmental liabilities associated with accidents or eventual remediation of landfills are often difficult to estimate with any degree of certainty. Thus, they do not necessarily have to be recognized under the US GAAP (Abelson 1991, Roussey 1991). However, in some cases the SEC has determined that disclosures of environmental liabilities were not made when they should have been made (Zyber and Berry 1992; Williams and Phillips 1994, p. 31).

The SEC has therefore described four possibilities for disclosing environmental liability information in the financial statements (Holmark *et al.* 1995, p. 73ff):

- the Management's Discussion and Analysis
- notes to the financial statements
- the Description of Business
- in the context of legal proceedings.

The SEC requires disclosure in the *Management's Discussion and Analysis* (SEC 1989, 22428), even if disclosures are made in other sections of the annual report (e.g. in the notes to the financial statement). The Management's

---

Box 5.12
Disclosure of (Contingent) Liabilities

The IASC ". . . requires the disclosure of contingent losses that are not recognized unless the probability of loss is remote" (IASC 1995, p. 183 [IAS 10, 9]).

The US SEC requires disclosure in the Management's Discussion and Analysis of any "trend, commitment, event or uncertainty" that (SEC 1989, 22430):

(i) is "known"
(ii) cannot be determined to be "not reasonably likely to occur"—this double negative is in the regulations—and
(iii) is reasonably likely to have "a material effect on the [firm's] financial condition".

Discussion and Analysis must include any known trends or any known demands, commitments, events, or uncertainties that are reasonably likely to have material impact on earnings and liquidity (SEC S-K 303). Disclosure is required whenever management is unable to determine if material effects on future results of operations or the financial condition are "not reasonably likely" to occur (SEC 1989, Interpretative Release FRR 36).

A liability must be disclosed in the *notes of the financial statement* if it is probable that it has occurred, although no reasonable estimate can be made of the amount. Footnote disclosure of the contingent loss is appropriate if the likelihood of a loss is at least "reasonably possible". Only if the likelihood of loss is "remote" is no disclosure necessary (see Box 5.12)

Material effects on the required capital, expenditures, effects on earnings and competitive position of the registered company related to compliance with environmental regulations are required to be disclosed in the *Description of Business* (SEC 101).

Legal proceedings which might have material effects on the company must be briefly described (SEC S-K 103). The US Environmental Protection Agency (EPA) has agreed to supply corporate environmental information to the SEC. This particularly aims at companies which have been designated as Potential Responsible Parties (PRP) for the clean-up of Superfund sites, but which have not recognized or disclosed any information about environmental liabilities in the annual report.

So far, no regulations for the disclosure of environmental liabilities have been published outside the USA. However, some initiatives may be mentioned.

In the *European Union*, the Directive on Civil Liability for Damage caused by waste was introduced in 1993. This directive is similar to the Superfund law apart from not being retrospective. The financial implications for companies are therefore expected to be considerable.

The Intergovernmental Working Group of Experts on International Standards of Accounting and Reporting (ISAR) of the *United Nations* has issued the recommendation to include environmentally induced liabilities, provisions and reserves as well as contingent liabilities with an estimate of the amount involved in the notes to financial statements, unless the event is not likely to occur (ISAR 1991, p. 98).

Furthermore, the Canadian Institute of Chartered Accountants recommends the following (CICA 1993).

- Environmental liabilities should be disclosed separately in the financial statements.
- Environmental liabilities of individual materiality should be disclosed separately.
- A deferred charge should be disclosed in connection with the liability it relates to.
- The nature of any uncertainties of measurement should be explained.

Holmark *et al.* (1995, p. 75) propose a general form for disclosing liabilities in a structured manner (see Table 5.2).

In conclusion, the formulation of new accounting standards defining the disclosure of environmental liabilities might not be necessary. However, true and fair reporting to external stakeholders requires the rigorous enforcement of existing standards as well as consistent reporting practices based on clear, generally accepted and established guidelines. To ensure consistency in practice, management will often have to take precedent cases for guidance on whether and when to disclose environmental liabilities.

While the discussion about environmentally induced liabilities has attracted much attention, new topics have recently been emerging. One of the most

Table 5.2 Liability Disclosure Form. Source: Holmark *et al.* 1995, p. 75

Description	Amount of liability	Prior provisions	Counter-claims	Notes
Liability 1				
Liability 2				
. . .				
Liability n				
Total				

remarkable market-based regulations is emission trading. For many fields of application (i.e. stationary industrial emissions), emission trading is regarded as the most efficient way to regulate pollution, Frey *et al.* (1993), Hahn (1984), Pekelney (1993), Stavins (1992), or Tietenberg (1989). Tradeable emission allowances are established in the USA and have been introduced on a smaller scale in some European countries (Switzerland, Germany, the Netherlands). With this new regulatory instrument some tricky accounting issues have also emerged.

5.6 TREATMENT OF TRADEABLE EMISSION ALLOWANCES

In all countries, companies are allowed to pollute as long as they do not exceed legal emission standards. This right is usually implicit. However, the position is different if a system of emission trading is introduced where the right to pollute is specifically certified with emission allowances (pollution permits). The total amount of pollution is strictly limited by the total number of pollution permits and their respective amounts.

An emission allowance is a certified right that allows a company to discharge a certain amount of pollution into the natural environment within a specified time limit (see also Section 11.2). Thus, an emission allowance can be seen (a) as a (general) licence to pollute, and in addition (b) as a right to pollute by a specific amount in a limited period of time (e.g. a year). The right to a specified amount of pollution starts again every year (e.g. 100 t of SO_2 every year).

The idea of emission trading is not that the individual source of emissions is relevant for the environment but rather the acceptance of an absolute amount of emissions in a given region over a given period.

Pollution rights are mostly "grandfathered" by the government or the environmental protection agency. Thus, the allowances are given to companies on the basis of past emissions.

The companies can sell their allowances or buy additional permits, depending on whether their marginal costs of pollution prevention are lower or higher than the market price for the emission allowances. Companies facing high costs of pollution prevention are willing to pay a high price for emission allowances. On the other hand, companies with low marginal costs of pollution prevention will improve their environmental record to below legal standards and then sell their obsolete rights. In this way, a market for the right to pollute is created. With emission trading the marginal cost of pollution abatement of all involved firms will equalise after some time. For every firm as well as for the total economy, emission trading results in the lowest possible costs of pollution prevention.

With the introduction of emission allowances some questions have emerged as to how emission allowances should be recognized, measured and disclosed in financial accounting.

- Are emission allowances assets or expenses?
- How should emission allowances be recognized?
- How should the value of pollution permits be determined or measured, and how should they be disclosed in financial statements?

Emission allowances fit the definitions of an *asset* as formulated by IASC and FASB (see Box 5.2). Pollution permits are necessary for a company to receive future economic benefits as companies are not allowed to produce without such permits. Pollution permits have a capital value as they can be sold.

Some confusion might arise with the US Clean Air Act, which regards emissions allowances as "limited authorizations" and not as "property rights". However, these authorizations are owned by the company and holders are provided with substantial protection against expropriation. Emission allowances should therefore be recognized as assets.

Nonetheless, the question remains of how emission allowances should be *recognized* in the financial statement. Three main options have been discussed in this context (Ewer *et al.* 1992). Pollution permits can be classified in several ways.

- *Inventory*. Inventory comprises assets: (a) held for sale in the ordinary course of business, (b) in the process of production for sale, or (c) in the form of materials or supplies to be consumed in the production process or in the rendering of services (IASC 1995, p. 84 [IAS 2, 4]).
- *Securities*. Marketable securities are held with the intention of selling them in the short term, whereas investment securities are acquired and held for yield or capital growth purposes and are usually held to maturity (IASC 1995, p. 425 [IAS 30, 19]).
- *Intangible operating assets*. An asset is a resource controlled by the enterprise as a result of past events and from which future economic benefits are expected (IASC 1995, p. 47 [IAS 49]).

Tradeable emission permits possess some of the characteristics of all three classifications, but do not exactly match any of the definitions.

Pollution permits are *held for sale or consumption* and could therefore be classified as inventory. However, they lack other characteristics: they are *neither tangible nor necessarily held for current consumption*.

If classified as marketable securities, tradeable permits would have to be carried in two distinct portfolios. First, emission allowances are *non-current* securities (a general licence for pollution). Second, the pollution permits are also *current* securities as they are rights to pollute by a specified amount in the current accounting period.

Tradeable pollution permits possibly could eventually also be treated as options (*a right, but not an obligation* to do something: i.e. to pollute) for they can be sold in the same way (Ewer *et al.* 1992, p. 71). The certificates for future allowance rights will have to be treated as futures as an efficient futures market emerges (Adams 1992, p. 3 or Sandor and Walsh 1993). However, emission allowances also have a stronger *tangible* character. They are assets because they provide a right to actually produce.

Pollution permits possess some of the characteristics of intangible operating assets. For example, the rights are unrelated to the physical form and could be compared to licences. Thus, if pollution permits are recognized as *intangible* they should be carried as *non-current operating assets* in the same way as licences (Ewer *et al.* 1992, p. 71).

Another issue is the *measurement* of the value of emission allowances.

The main question is whether valuation based on historical cost or on current cost is most appropriate. Valuation according to the realizable (settlement) value should provide a similar result to the current cost method, because emission allowances have a market price.

The historical cost method values allowances according to the amount paid for them at the time of their acquisition. The current cost method assigns the amount of cash or cash equivalents that would have to be paid if the same or an equivalent asset was acquired in the current accounting period (IASC 1995, p. 67 [F100]).

The *historical cost method* does not give a proper indication of the actual value. In the beginning, most permits are grandfathered at no cost, and thus would not be recognized with this treatment (Adams 1992, p. 3). Historical costs do not reflect the market value and the contribution to the shareholder value of the company. Furthermore, no incentives are given to management to realize pollution prevention at low costs and to make a profit from selling unused permits.

From an economic and an environmental perspective the *current cost approach* must be clearly favored. The current costs equal the market value of the allowances. Furthermore, the market value reflects the opportunity costs which are relevant for managerial decisions. Only this treatment allows the marginal costs of pollution prevention to be contrasted with the present marginal (opportunity) costs of keeping the permits. If bought in the market, the cost of purchase should be expensed as the permits are sold or used.

The argument that a market price is not given when the allowances are grandfathered is not valid. Experience in the USA showed that pollution permits were already traded before they had been granted. Thus a market price existed before the allowances had to be accounted for (Feder 1993, NZZ 1994c).

Another reason to apply the current cost approach is the fact that pollution permits are usually devalued over time by the environmental protection agency (the certified amount of pollutants which may be emitted decreases over time). This devaluation could not be considered with the historical cost approach. From the viewpoint of prudence, it could also be argued that the lower of the two values (historic costs or current costs) should be considered.

Emission allowances should not only be reported with their monetary value but also the *number of permits* should be stated. The monetary value alone does not tell readers of financial statements whether, for example, the market price of the permits has changed, or whether more emission rights have been bought.

Obviously, many arguments can be found for dealing with emission allowances in various ways. Hence, a specific accounting standard is necessary to recognize and disclose them in a consistent manner separately from other items. This would also simplify treatment in managerial accounting (see Section 4.6).

As shown in the last two sections, not all economically important environmental topics can be recognized in the financial statement in monetary terms. The Management's Discussion and Analysis is therefore an important communications tool to disclose environmental issues in the financial report.

5.7 THE MANAGEMENT'S DISCUSSION AND ANALYSIS

Every financial report provides a discussion and analysis of the management's view of the company's position. The Management's Discussion and Analysis (MD & A) treats information which is not, or not clearly, recognized as a monetary value in the financial statement.

The formulations of the *MD & A requirements* are ". . . intentionally general, reflecting the [Securities and Exchange] Commission's view that a flexible approach elicits more meaningful disclosure and avoids boilerplate discussions, which a more specific approach could foster." (SEC 1989, p. 1577). This perspective is also reflected in the explanation of what information is required and what is *"optional forward-looking"* (Box 5.13).

In the MD & A, some companies give an outline of their environmental policy.[9] In the past it was usual to just state that the environment was considered to be a very important issue. Today, many companies specify how they endeavor to cope with environmental problems. Investors are interested in relevant and maybe quantifiable information on how efficiently a company spends its resources for environmental purposes. The lack of focus in the environmental protection activities of a company impedes rational decision making, and therefore lowers the value of the company. Financial analysts, for example, are less interested in the company's past achievements than in the potential problems and opportunities as well as in the programs to meet the requirements of the future.

Box 5.13
The Management's Discussion and Analysis (MD & A)

"*MD & A* requires a discussion of liquidity, capital resources, results of operations, and other information necessary to an understanding of a [firm's] financial condition, changes in financial condition and results of operations." (SEC 1989, p. 1577)

"*Required disclosure* is based on currently known trends, events, and uncertainties that are reasonably expected to have material effects" (SEC 1989, p. 1579).

"*Optional forward-looking disclosure* involves anticipating a future trend or event or anticipating a less predictable impact of a known event, trend or uncertainty." (SEC 1989, p. 1579)

"Where a trend, demand, commitment, event or uncertainty is known, management must make two *assessments*

(1) Is the known trend, demand, commitment, event or uncertainty likely to come to fruition? If management determines that it is not reasonably likely to occur, no disclosure is required.

(2) If management cannot make that determination, it must evaluate objectively the consequences of the known trend, demand, commitment, event or uncertainty, on the assumption that it will come to fruition. Disclosure is then required unless management determines that a material effect on the [firm's] financial condition or results of operations is not reasonably likely to occur." (SEC 1989, p. 1580)

Environmental issues, i.e. environmental liabilities (Section 5.5), are among the most important factors which can substantially influence the future economic performance of a company. Hence, the US SEC has emphasized the importance of the disclosure of environmental issues that might affect the company's financial conditions (i.e. environmental liabilities) in the Management's Discussion and Analysis (see also Section 5.5.5). For potentially responsible parties (PRP) the disclosure of the expected material effects of the clean-up of their sites is required (SEC 1989, p. 1580).

However, disclosure of most other environmentally induced issues is voluntary and subject to the discretion of the management. Issues which might be considered in the MD & A include the following. (For companies operating in environmentally sensitive areas, several of these points should be treated in more depth in an environmental report, see Part D.)

- The financial or operational effect of environmental protection measures on the organization's capital expenditures, earnings and competitive position for the current period and any expected impact on future periods (Moore 1991, p. 55, SEC 101 and SEC S-K 103).

- Treatment of different environmentally induced financial impacts (e.g. if environmental costs are expensed or capitalized) (EFFAS 1994, p. 19).
- Aggregate payments to be made in the longer term (e.g. in the next five years for future environmental expenditures) (CICA 1993).
- Environmental liabilities of individual materiality (CICA 1993).
- Contingent environmental liabilities which are either not probable (though the probability is not remote) or not reasonably estimable.
- The scope and methods of consolidation.
- The nature of any uncertainties of measurement.

A list of further recommendations on environmentally related issues which could be addressed in the Management's Discussion and Analysis has been made by the Intergovernmental Working Group of Experts on International Standards of Accounting and Reporting of the United Nations (ISAR UN 1991a, pp. 97ff). Apart from actual, expected and potential future financial consequences, ISAR also mentions ecological information which may not involve financial consequences directly. Among such environmental topics may be information on the following.

- The environmental issues that are relevant to the organization and the industry in which it operates.
- The environmental impact of the company's operations.
- The formal policy and programs the company has adopted with regard to environmental protection.
- Improvements made since the policy was introduced.
- Future targets and quantification of the targets.

5.8 CONCLUSIONS

Financial accounting is the tool for collecting the information requested by external stakeholders, i.e. investors, whereas the financial report is the "platform" for sharing the information. In the past, it was economically rational for management to ignore many environmentally related issues in financial reporting.

However, this has changed with the increasing magnitude of environmental costs, i.e. environmental liabilities. Environmentally related issues are of increasing importance for the financial position of a company. Thus, to support economically rational decisions, companies with sensitive businesses should explicitly disclose environmentally induced financial impacts in their traditional accounting. So far, worldwide, only a few companies have disclosed the respective financial impacts in a consistent manner. Recently, however, this has started to change. Correct consideration and environmental differentiation of financial accounting allows for better informed decisions.

Today, management still has a large discretionary latitude in deciding what environmental issues to recognize, how to measure and what to disclose. Environmental management has just started to become an issue in financial markets. The communication of the respective accounting issues between the preparers of financial statements and powerful external stakeholders is in an early phase. As with other issues, the requirements of those stakeholders will urge companies to provide clear and understandable reports to help investors to make informed decisions. The substantial environmentally related financial consequences for companies require a change in several of the current financial accounting practices. For some specific environmental questions, new standards and guidelines must be developed, primarily in order to ensure consistency of reporting (e.g. for the treatment of emission allowances).

Experience with advanced accounting practices in the USA suggests that more environmentally induced costs (i.e. liabilities) would be disclosed if clear international standards dealing with the main environmental topics were issued. Clear environmental accounting standards reduce costs for management. Furthermore, investors and other critical stakeholders would be better informed. Only internationally accepted standards for financial accounting allow investors and other stakeholders to compare companies reliably. As will be shown later, the same is the case with external ecological accounting. However, given the problem that too many standards increase the costs of reporting, new standards should only be issued if they bring a clear improvement on the present situation. Much of the externally available information could already be improved if the existing accounting principles were enforced more consistently by regulators.

Regulators are among the most powerful stakeholders. Some agencies, such as tax agencies and the environmental protection agencies, have established their own accounting relationships with companies. This allows for special treatment of those issues which are of most importance for the respective stakeholder. As discussed in the next chapter, these other accounting systems are also influenced by environmental issues.

6

Other Environmentally Differentiated Accounting Systems

Although managerial and financial accounting are generally regarded as important sources of information, some stakeholders have gained so much power that they obtain more financial information than others. These stakeholders commonly exert a major influence on the financial positions of companies.

This chapter deals with special environmentally differentiated accounting systems which have been established or are expected to be introduced by the tax agency, commercial banks, other creditors and by insurance companies.

Commonly, most companies must obey the conditions of these stakeholders once a relationship is established. Having little discretionary latitude, management must observe closely the environmental issues which influence these stakeholders. The focus of this chapter is therefore on developments which should be anticipated by companies as they might alter the accounting relationships with regulators, banks and insurance companies.

First the influence of the tax agency on corporate accounting is discussed (Section 6.1). Section 6.2 addresses environmental issues which influence the accounting relationships with creditors and insurance companies.

6.1 ENVIRONMENTAL ISSUES IN TAX ACCOUNTING

Environmental issues affect tax accounting in two ways. First, tax accounting is involved in *taxes*, *charges* and *fees* on environmental impacts and consumption of natural resources. Second, tax accounting is affected by regulations allowing companies to reduce their tax burden by such means as *tax credits*, *tax deductions*, *tax exemptions*, *faster depreciation* and *subsidies* for pollution prevention technologies.

The formulation of tax laws has a strong influence on how outlays are classified, recognized, measured and disclosed in companies. Although the information for both financial and tax accounting are collected in managerial accounting, an item can be treated in a completely different way in financial accounting than in tax accounting. This is legal and even purposeful, because the tax agency has different incentives and information interests than, for instance, investors.

Tax agencies, in their role of defining information requirements for taxing purposes, are to a certain extent standard setters, though legislators exhibit some power over the taxing agency. The incentives provided (or not provided) with tax regulations also substantially influence the ecological behavior of companies.

6.1.1 Environmental Charges, Fees and Taxes

Environmental taxes, charges and fees became a part of the business agenda in the last decade. Although there are distinct differences between taxes, fees and charges (see Box 6.1), the expression "tax" is also used as a general term for all three concepts. The purpose of *charges* is to change the behavior of economic subjects, whereas *fees* are used to cover expenses for specific projects such as for pollution prevention. The taxes treated here cover the area of "pollution" not "resource use". One example of the latter would be taxes used as policy instruments in fishery management (OECD 1994b, p. 56). Charges are often levied on emissions. Normally, these charges are subdivided according to the impacted environmental compartment: air, noise, soil, waste and water, or they are levied directly on products. (Deposit refunds are sometimes also viewed as charges, but they will not be dealt with here). *Taxes*, in contrast, are levied for financial reasons and flow into the general public budget. In practice it is often difficult to distinguish taxes, fees and charges, as in the political process many reasons for their introduction are usually set forth simultaneously. In most countries, the environmental protection agency is involved in controlling the correct payment of environmental taxes, charges and fees. Traditionally a supervisor of standards, the environmental protection agency has often taken on a new role as a collector of charges.

The main stakeholder in tax accounting is the tax agency. It has enforcement power if companies do not provide the required information.

The tax agency collects taxes from companies to serve the financial needs of the government. (Taxes collected from private persons—e.g. income taxes—are not discussed here.) Although most people agree that taxes are necessary, they are also regarded as an evil, creating incentives to find loopholes in the tax system. The formulation of tax laws is therefore a never-ending job as everybody tries to report biased information to evade taxes. Thus, tax accounting is changing continuously because the regulators are constantly trying to close the loopholes in regulations. A further reason for frequent changes of the tax system is that taxes represent a signal strongly characterizing the policy of every government. In addition, tax accounting varies widely between countries and even local districts. Tax accounting is therefore treated more generally in this chapter.

An important issue related to environmental taxes is the *tax base*: What should be taxed? Desired "goods" are hardly ever a good tax base as they create value for customers. Larger amounts of goods are preferred to a smaller amount. "Bads", by contrast, are undesirable. A smaller amount is better than a larger amount.

Therefore, it could be argued that preferably bads should be taxed and goods should be exempted from taxes. This is in contrast to present-day practice where most governments rely heavily on income taxes for fiscal purposes, while pollution taxes are still relatively seldom imposed. In consequence, it would seem much better to tax pollution than income. However, when analyzing in more depth, it becomes obvious that taxing bads can lead to substantial problems since, as the government relies on fiscal resources, it has no interest in reducing bads.

Taxes which are labelled as "environmental" are often taxes levied mainly for fiscal purposes. They hardly tend to be beneficial and may even be harmful for the environment. The government has no interest at all in curbing the environmental impacts as long as their main goal is to raise money.

"Real" environmental taxes are often referred to as "guidance taxes" because they actually influence behavior and therefore often have small financial effects. Four kinds of "real" environmental taxes can be distinguished:

- input based taxes
- output based taxes
- activity based taxes
- tariffs and import taxes.

Examples of *input based taxes* are taxes levied on the amount of energy, gasoline, electric power, or solvents used. *Output based taxes* are often related to the quantity of emissions discharged (e.g. a CO_2 tax). *Activity based taxes* are levied on certain activites undertaken such as using a motorway.

Von Weizsäcker has proposed a mixture of a guidance tax and an income tax with an increase in the tax rate over time (Mauch *et al.* 1992, von Weizsäcker 1992). As the environmental impacts declined over time, the tax rate would be increased accordingly to maintain government income. Ideally, this would result in a reduction of environmental impacts caused while maintaining fiscal income in the longer term.

Problems with this proposal are, first, that zero environmental impacts are impossible to achieve and are also economically inappropriate. (From an economic perspective, the marginal costs of pollution prevention should not exceed the marginal damage of environmental impacts—see also Section 11.2.) Second, in practice the political process in democracies is an obstacle to frequent changes in tax rates.

In summary, any change of prices should be fiscally neutral, to prevent the government from further increasing its budget. The temptation, in the absence of fiscal neutrality, is for the government to start relying on the income so that it has no incentive to encourage companies and households to decrease environmental impacts. The logical consequence is to request the introduction of *environmental charges* (and no fiscal taxes).[10]

Some suggest using the revenues of environmental taxes only for environmental purposes, such as the remediation of waste sites. However,

---

Box 6.1
Environmental Charges, Fees and Taxes

An example of a *charge* on air pollution is the Swedish NO_x-charge. It is levied on actual emissions (which are metered) of heat and power producers with a capacity of over 10 megawatts (MW) and production exceeding 50 gigawatt hours (GWh). Only final energy producers are charged, and the installations subject to the charge emit around 6.5% of total Swedish NO_x emissions. If the emissions are not metered, standard emission rates apply which exceed average actual emissions in order to encourage installation of measurement equipment. The charge revenues are redistributed to installations subject to the charge, on the basis of their final energy production. The redistribution between high emitting and low emitting plants ensures that continuous improvement is sought after. The incentive effect in Sweden is very positive, having surpassed expected emission reduction. The actual emission reduction is between 30%–40%, compared with an expected reduction of 20–25%.

Many European countries have established waste *fees* to finance waste collection and disposal (OECD 1994b, p. 60ff). For municipal waste, in most cases simply a flat rate, or a volume based rate (e.g. per waste bag), is employed for households. Some municipalities are experimenting with actually measuring the weight of household waste delivered. Firms, however, are more often charged according to the mass of waste actually caused.

Practically all countries levy *taxes* on petrol. Usually, no data are available and the actual incentive effects of these taxes have not been calculated (OECD 1994b, p. 58ff). Therefore, it can be expected that these taxes are levied mainly for fiscal purposes.

Table 6.1 Eco-Bonus Method Used for Redistribution of Environmental Tax Revenues

	Company A	Company B	Company C
Released Tonnes of CO_2	100t	50t	50t
Value Added	$500	$300	$400
CO_2-Eco-Efficiency = $ Value Added per Tonne of CO_2 Released)	$5/t CO_2 = 5	$6/t$CO_2$ = 6	$8/t CO_2 = 8
	Tax Rate = $1/t$CO_2$		
	Total Tax Revenue = $200		
	Total Value Added = $1200		
	Redistribution (According to Value Added)		
	$200/$1200 = **$0.16 per $ Value Added**		
Paid Tax Amount	$1/t CO_2*100t = $100	$1/t CO_2*50t = $50	$1/t CO_2*50t = $30
Received Tax Amount	500* − $0.16 = $ − 83.3	300*$ − 0.16 = $ − 50	400* − $0.16 = $ − 66.7
Net Tax Amount (− = net receipt)	**$16.7**	**$0**	**$ − 36.7**

this reduces flexibility in the use of government budgets, and also restricts more efficient allocation of resources. Furthermore, industries which benefit from government spending (e.g. the clean-up industry for hazardous waste) will lobby to impede any change of environmental policy even if the need for cleaning-up waste sites no longer exists.

Fiscal neutrality can be achieved by redistributing the revenues to the firms and households. Nevertheless, to maintain the desired incentive, the redistribution must be designed as an *"eco-bonus"* system in which the same average sum is redistributed to all taxpayers. ("Eco-bonus" is a translation from the German *Oekobonus*, describing this method of redistribution). Cleaner industries and households are rewarded by receiving back more than the tax they have paid. The relatively higher-polluting industries and households, on the other hand, pay more than they receive back.

The choice of the redistribution formula is very important in order to reward eco-efficiency. Redistribution according to the number of employees or working hours supports labor-intensive businesses, whereas redistribution according to the created value added favors economically successful companies. The latter may be the preferable re-allocation formula as it supports companies which are environmentally and also economically successful.

An example demonstrating the eco-bonus tax system is given in Table 6.1.

The taxed pollutant is CO_2, blamed for contributing to the greenhouse effect. Three companies A, B, and C release 100t, 50t and 50t annually, and create a value added of $500, $300, and $400 respectively. The CO_2 efficiencies of the companies ($ value added per tonne of CO_2 released) are $5/t, $6/t, and $8/t. With a total discharge of 200t of CO_2 and a tax rate of $1 per ton of CO_2, the total tax revenue is $200.

The tax revenue is redistributed according to the eco-bonus system. The chosen redistribution formula is based on the value added of each company (A = $500, B = $300, C = $400). Company A is least eco-efficient. It pays $100 and receives $ 83.3, thus making a net payment of $16.7. Company C is most CO_2 eco-efficient and is rewarded with a net revenue of $36.7. Company B receives as much as it paid, for its CO_2 eco-efficiency is the same as the average for the industry.

The introduction of an eco-bonus tax system (like any environmental tax system) requires an ecological accounting system reporting the taxed emissions of every firm. Furthermore, the respective information is necessary in managerial accounting to calculate the cost-benefit ratio of pollution prevention devices.

6.1.2 Environmental Costs and Tax Accounting

Tax rules may influence the treatment of environmental expenditures. In order to enhance "green behavior" some environmentally induced costs are subject to tax credits, tax deductions or tax exemptions. A *tax credit* reduces the company's tax liability dollar-for-dollar. *Tax deductions* reduce the company's tax liability by screening income from taxation (Polimeni *et al.* 1986, p. 674). *Tax exemptions* exclude assets or income from being taxed. A tax credit for a certain amount is therefore more valuable for the firm than a tax deduction or exemption for the same amount.

Tax credits, deductions and exemptions are effective in most cases. However, they may provide adverse incentives. For example, the tax agency might allow certain environmentally induced expenditures to be deducted or regarded as tax credits. If these costs relate to increased assets they could be classified as expenses in tax accounting and as assets in financial accounting.

Or, as another example, firms will increase their voluntary pollution prevention activities if the respective costs are tax deductible. However, tax deductions and tax credits equal an externalization of the respective costs because in the end it is society which pays by receiving smaller tax revenues.

Other costs, such as clean-up costs, are mostly treated as ordinary expenses, and therefore subtracted from income when calculating the taxable profit.

Certain expenditures are almost never tax deductible. These include, for instance, legally imposed costs such as *fines* for breaching environmental laws and some clean-up costs (see for example Young 1985, p. 202).

From an economic as well as from an environmental perspective, subsidies, tax deductions, tax credits, etc. are not recommendable. They increase government spending and lower the general price level, which results in a growth of consumption (assuming that personal income taxes do not increase). Taxes, on the other hand, are a better means of internalizing environmental impacts as they reduce the consumption of environmentally harmful goods. Redistribution ensures fiscal neutrality (see Section 6.1.1).

However, for politicians, subsidies provide more possibilities of increasing popularity. For management they may be welcome in that they enhance the profit margin in the short term. Nevertheless, subsidies of any kind involve the risk of becoming less competitive in the world market in the long run. Advanced firms should therefore support the establishment of environmental taxes and oppose the introduction of tax credits, deductions, exemptions and subsidies.

Environmental issues in tax accounting also have impacts on financial and *managerial* accounting. For example, customers may require a detailed calculation of product prices after they have been increased because of new environmental taxes or charges. However, neither financial nor managerial accounting is usually prepared for the respective information disclosure. Managerial accounting systems are often not designed to separate manufacturing costs from manufacturers' taxes. The management might also be reluctant to disclose the contribution margins of important products.

Furthermore, managerial accounting is influenced by taxes as they have to be considered as part of product costs. Environmental taxes often negatively influence the evaluation of product managers. Because the product margins rarely rise in the same proportion as the imposed taxes, it appears as if the performance of managers has fallen (see Stinson 1993).

The inclusion of environmental taxes in the overhead costs is not an acceptable solution to this problem. The true costs of the products would no longer be reflected in the accounting figures, leading to suboptimal management decisions (see Chapter 4).

One of the main obstacles discouraging management from adequately accounting for environmental measures is related to tax accounting. In many countries expenses are only tax deductible when paid, because tax accounting is very much focused on cash flows. Consequently, as *provisions* cannot be deducted from taxes, there is little incentive for enterprises to record their (contingent) liabilities by charging them to income (Moore 1991, p. 55).

Very polluting production plants or other environmentally harmful *assets* are rarely confronted with special taxes. More often, clean technologies are supported with subsidies. A separation of assets into environmental and other assets may be useful to detect better technologies which classify for tax credits or tax deductions.

6.2 SPECIAL ENVIRONMENTAL "ACCOUNTING" RELATIONSHIPS

Other stakeholders than the tax agency can also exert enough power to enforce the disclosure of especially desired information. Information in the financial statements is not sufficiently detailed for their needs. Creditors (especially banks) and insurance companies are two stakeholders exerting a strong influence on corporations (Hawkshaw 1991, p. 24).

With the growing costs associated with non-compliance, environmental taxes, changing consumer preferences and environmental liabilities, *banks* and other *creditors* are interested in the impacts on the financial position of customers borrowing money.

To lose money lent is part of the normal business risk of banks, but they have not in the past been exposed to the impact of environmentally induced risks. However, in the USA, in the context of the "Superfund law" (Section 5.5), some banks have been made liable even for the remediation costs created by customers who have become insolvent (*"lender liability"*). The financial consequences for lenders can be substantially bigger than the amount of the credit given (see Box 6.2).

For the first six years after the enactment of the Superfund law, lenders were specifically exempted from bearing any clean-up costs. However, in 1986 a Maryland district court ruled that if a company closes because of a contaminated site, the lender should be treated like an owner (Hector 1992, p. 107ff).

The amounts required for clean-ups can be many times greater than the credit, eventually forcing the bank itself into bankruptcy. Banks are therefore increasingly cautious about lending money to possible polluters (see Box 6.3).

Box 6.2
The Case of Montana-Butte

"In 1980 the Bank of Montana-Butte lent $275,000 to a local company that coated telephone poles with PCP and other chemicals to protect them against rot and insects. The company collapsed in 1984, leaving behind a heavily contaminated site. Regulators and courts prosecuted previous owners of the land, including Atlantic Richfield. However, they also pursued 'The Bank of Montana-Butte'. The projected cost of the cleanup, $10 million to $15 million, was several times larger than the bank's total capital of $2.4 million. So far, the bank has spent more than the amount of the loan defending itself against state and federal regulators" (Hector 1992, p. 107).

Box 6.3
Changed Lending Practices of American Banks

- 88.1% of the US banks had changed lending procedures to avoid environmental liability
- 62.5% had rejected loan applications because of the possibility of environmental liability
- 45.8% had discontinued loans to certain businesses because of fear of environmental liability
- 16.7% had abandoned property rather than taking title because of environmental concerns
- 13.5% had incurred clean-up costs on property held as collateral.

(Source: Simon 1991, p. 16.)

Especially smaller and medium-sized companies without the necessary resources to cover potentially large liabilities face difficulties in obtaining loans.

In 1990, a panel of federal judges ruled that if a bank, or any other secured lender, could influence management, it ought also be treated like an owner (Gray *et al.* 1993, p. 185). In consequence, some banks have increasingly started to deal with the management practices of their clients. To protect themselves from huge liabilities, banks have started to routinely run eco-audits before judging the risk of a site. A poor environmental record can create large difficulties in obtaining a loan (Hector 1992, p. 109). In any case, such audits as well as the legal costs involved significantly increase the price of financing.

Banks often rely on environmental consultants to assess the risk of environmental liabilities. The question of whether the consultants involved could be made liable as well has not yet been fully answered.

In April 1991 the US Environmental Protection Agency issued new regulations. These clarify a bank's right to conduct environmental audits and the circumstances under which it can foreclose on contaminated property or lend money to finance a clean-up without running the risk of being treated like an owner of the land. Nonetheless, most bankers doubt if the new regulation will help to end the loan freeze (Hector 1992, pp. 107ff).

While the above examples apply to US sites, the issue of lender liability has now started to attract attention in Europe, too. The effects of lender liability regulation as well as possible consequences of an introduction in Europe are being discussed in the financial sector (Advisory Committee on Business and the Environment 1993). The EU legislation on contaminated land, on civil liability caused by waste and the polluter-pays principle might change banks' lending practices considerably. So far, environmentally induced risks of credits are practically always connected with toxic waste and the remediation of disposal sites, production sites, etc. At present, the potential environmentally induced risk of credits due to other environmental impacts, such as emissions of greenhouse gases, are expected to be low even in the future (Mansley 1995).

Viewed in isolation, the Superfund law has not resulted in a major clean-up of disposal sites or in a major improvement in the environmental situation, but if anything has engendered substantial economic costs. However, when analyzed more in depth, the lender liability regulation and the respective reactions of the banking industry have provided the most powerful incentives to prevent future environmental liabilities (and environmental impacts).

Insurance companies are also taking environmental aspects into account more often when considering insuring risks. They want to be informed about the environmental performance of their customers, and the possible financial consequences of spills, accidents and remediation costs. The Superfund law has also influenced the insurance industry substantially. "The situation in the United States is so serious that it threatens the solvency of the whole insurance industry . . ." (Wheatley quoted in Gray *et al.* 1993, p. 218).

The main concern of insurance companies (as of banks) is of course to estimate risks and opportunities correctly. Environmental risks have started to become a substantial component of insurance premiums. Companies involved in the production and transport of chemicals, waste disposal sites, etc. are especially likely to face higher insurance premiums.

A main problem for (re-)insurance companies is that the risk of natural disasters has increased since the premiums were calculated. For example, insurance premiums to cover damages due to storms, floods and other natural disasters which are thought to be a consequence of the greenhouse effect, have never been calculated with today's risk rate (Schweizer Rück 1995).

As insurance companies will at some time have to cover these previously unexpected losses, today's clients will have to pay higher premiums than necessary to cover the costs incurred today. In consequence, external costs of past generations will have to be internalized and borne by today's generation. This effect is likely to continue. Management should therefore try to insure environmental risks early with long-term contracts and fixed conditions.

Many new insurance instruments to deal with environmental risks have evolved in recent years, because of the increasing environmental costs and liabilities as well as the inherent uncertainty associated with environmental issues.

An environmental insurance is a financial mechanism that reduces a company's exposure to environmental risk in exchange for the payment of a premium. Environmental cover falls into two categories:

- pure risk transfer
- a program combining risk management and risk transfer.

The first represents a physical transfer of risk from the company to the insurance company. Typically, third party physical injuries, property damage and losses emanating from the insured site are covered.

Environmental insurance can be part of the business strategy of a company. However, it will never entirely replace prevention activities as the insurance company is interested in reducing uncertainties and its own risk. Thorough environmental audits are conducted before an insurance contract is signed. Yearly monitoring before renewing the policy is the norm (EIU 1993, p. 86).

Second, risk-management risk transfer coverage is a company funded risk management program designed to cover clean-up and third party liabilities. Such programs are mostly used by large corporations with heavy environmental exposures. Any valid claims up to the annual insured limit are paid in full by the insurance company and recovered from the fund. If the losses are higher than the accumulated capital the insurance company will cover the additional costs over a defined period (EIU 1993, p 86). Such insurance tools help companies to hedge risks such as those emerging from the Superfund regulation. However, these tools are not widely known, so that several Member States of the EU have passed legislation forcing companies to take out a liability insurance or obtain financial guarantees for environmentally dangerous activities (EIU 1993).

Nevertheless, the reinsurance industry expects that major environmental risks might not be insurable in the future (Münchner Rückversicherung 1995). Hence, these risks will have to be borne by the companies themselves.

In consequence environmental issues will also increase uncertainties and risks for investors, creditors and other stakeholders. Management is therefore ever more challenged to prove the financial viability of the company. The best way to do so is by covering insurable risks and informing the stakeholders in an open and consistent way, as well as by establishing a convincing financial accounting system based on recognized international standards.

6.3 CONCLUSIONS AND OUTLOOK

Today, environmental issues are among the major topics influencing traditional accounting. In managerial accounting, correct tracing, measurement and allocation can uncover hidden sources of loss. Correct allocation improves information, often results in an improved environmental record, and allows the profitability of a company to be increased.

Environmental issues have also started to shape financial accounting. The main purpose of environmental accounting standards must be to improve the usefulness of the information supplied to investors.

Some powerful stakeholders, namely regulators such as tax agencies, have established special accounting relationships to enforce their interests. With liability issues, banks and insurance companies have also become increasingly involved in environmental issues.

In consequence, environmentally differentiated accounting is becoming ever more important for economic success as environmental issues have become a major source of financial impacts. This trend is expected to continue.

However, as long as external effects are not internalized, environmentally differentiated accounting is not sufficient for those stakeholders who require direct, unadulterated information about effects of corporate activities on the natural environment.

PART C
Ecological Accounting

"Responsible environmental management recognizes that 'what you don't know will hurt you'." (Friedman 1992, 63)

Although accounting has been criticized as creating environmental problems (see, e.g., Maunders and Burritt, 1991), it is also seen as a means of measuring corporate environmental impacts and as an opportunity to reduce and prevent them (see, e.g., Gray *et al.* 1993, Müller-Wenk 1978, Schaltegger 1993, Schaltegger and Sturm 1992a or Ullmann 1976).

Part C describes the main current developments in the emerging field of ecological accounting as the category of accounting which attempts to measure corporate environmental impacts and ecological efficiency. Ecological accounting deals with physical units and not with financial information. The presented non-financial accounting approaches are currently applied in a wide range of companies, including several international corporations (see, for example, Flierl 1993 or Schaltegger and Sturm 1995).

The introductory chapter (Chapter 7) addresses the emergence of this relatively new way of accounting, sustainable development and the measurement of ecological efficiency, as well as the nature of environmental impacts. Chapter 8 deals with internal ecological accounting, the corresponding tool of traditional managerial accounting. In Chapter 9, an overview of external ecological accounting is given. Here also, the applicability of the conventions of financial accounting to ecological accounting is investigated. Chapter 10 examines other (regulatory) ecological accounting systems which are established to supply information to special stakeholder groups, such as tax or regulatory agencies.

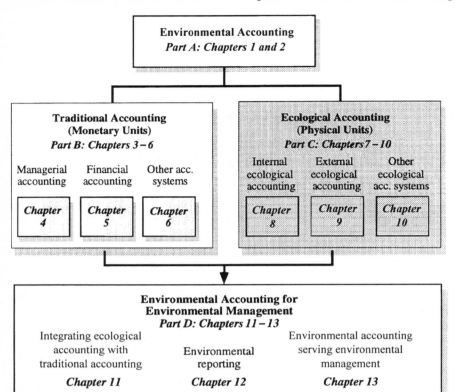

7

Introduction to Ecological Accounting

This chapter prepares the discussion of different ecological accounting systems, namely internal, external and other ecological accounting systems.

7.1 THE EMERGENCE OF ECOLOGICAL ACCOUNTING

Since the mid 1980s the business community has started to deal with the accounting of corporate environmental impacts, because an increasing number of stakeholders have urged firms to improve their environmental performance. Referring back to Figure 1.1, where it has been shown that some stakeholders primarily request information about the financial performance of the company, we recall that other stakeholders are mainly interested in the impact of firms on the environment.

The latter is what the category of ecological accounting attempts to ascertain. This distinguishes it from environmentally differentiated traditional accounting, which accounts for the environmentally induced financial impacts on the firm. Ecological accounting takes an "inside-out" view, its purpose being to determine what impacts the firm has on the natural environment. Today, ecological accounting demands (or allows) the measurement of environmental interventions in physical terms. Despite the fact that some environmental assets and impacts can been given a monetary value, it is not yet possible to measure all environmental impacts of a firm in monetary units.

Some stakeholders want to use the information derived from ecological accounting for further financial investigations. As has been shown in Part B, corporate environmental impacts very often have substantial financial impacts on the company. Examples are when toxic releases or hazardous waste sites lead to actual or potential liabilities, or when CO_2 releases are taxed, as is the case in some Scandinavian countries. Therefore, ecological accounting systems also provide valuable information for financially interested stakeholders. With the growing probability of a governmentally initiated internalization of external effects, financial investors are also becoming more interested in ecological accounting figures.

However, many other stakeholders care little about the financial position of the company, and tend to be interested only in the ecological impacts of the firm. Environmental pressure groups, geographical neighborhoods or environmental protection agencies are typical examples. No matter what attitude management has towards environmental protection, requests of these groups must always be taken seriously since they may have a substantial positive or negative influence on the operation and success of companies. A major demand of ecologically interested stakeholders is the disclosure of environmental impacts.

There are other reasons for the emergence of ecological accounting. Figure 7.1 shows, for a firm as well as for a nation, that the *marginal* internal costs of environmental impacts (additional costs due to additional impacts) increase with a growing number of impacts (due to fines, fees, taxes, employee leave, loss of consumer acceptance, etc.). In contrast, the marginal costs of accounting for environmental emissions, as well as the marginal costs of

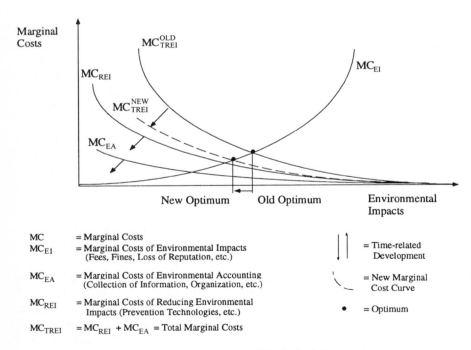

Figure 7.1 The Emergence of Ecological Accounting

reduction, are smaller with high impacts. This is because little environmental protection has taken place at a high pollution level. Therefore, the marginal costs of reducing (e.g. additional emissions) increase with every abatement activity. Historically, with few environmental impacts and high marginal costs of accounting for them, it used not to make sense to deal with environmental issues from an accounting perspective. However, the value of information on environmental impacts has increased (partly due to potential cost savings), while technological development has led to a decrease in the costs of preventing environmental impacts (the MC_{REI} curve in Figure 7.1). But also improved information technologies have reduced the marginal costs of information collection and ecological accounting. These changes are shown by the arrows in Figure 7.1. Ecological accounting also delivers fairly good information for product- and production-technology innovations. Therefore, today ecological accounting is recognized as important even if it is not explicitly requested by stakeholders.

Subsequently, the optimal point where the marginal costs of environmental impacts (MC_{EI}) are equal to the marginal costs of reducing these impacts (MC_{TREI}) has been moving to the left. This means that it has become economically advisable to further reduce environmental impacts.

Despite these developments, it is sometimes asked whether ecological accounting really is necessary. Is traditional financial accounting not much more accurate and does it not also recognize environmental impacts? The practical development towards more environmental reporting in companies gives a clear answer: measuring and reporting of corporate impacts on the environment is becoming a factor for success (Naimon 1995). But management theory and education have also realized the need for ecological accounting. Financial accounting is far from able to recognize all environmental costs, even if the boundaries and the time frame of financial measures are extended. It is true that ecological accounting (still) lacks a consistent set of international standards and widespread experience. Nevertheless, to some extent this also applies to financial accounting, as shown by the many discussions about the "correct" mode of financial reports (see Part B).

Some argue that if environmental impacts of firms require a separate accounting system, then so do other issues such as the social impact of firms. This is theoretically correct. However, ecological accounting, broadly defined, has already been established in a great many firms and by far exceeds social accounting in practical importance. In addition, several signs—such as the growing interest of regulators and financial markets—strongly indicate that it is becoming more attractive and necessary for companies to consider their impact on the natural environment.

However, what is the main indicator of a company's environmental performance? What does ecological accounting actually set out to measure? At first sight these are fairly easy questions to answer: the environmental impacts of a firm. Nevertheless, environmental impacts are only accounted for in order to achieve sustainable development. Perhaps the most important indicator of sustainable development is eco-efficiency. But, what is sustainable development (Section 7.2) and what is eco-efficiency (Section 7.3)?

7.2 THE AIM: SUSTAINABLE DEVELOPMENT FOR A SUSTAINABLE SOCIETY

The measurement of the environmental performance of a firm requires an overarching environmental goal as a target. The following concepts can be distinguished.

- *Sustainability*. The concept of sustainability stems from forest engineering and requires that the harvest of trees must not exceed the growth of new trees. The general interpretation of sustainability is that society must use no more natural resources than the natural environment can regenerate. (For other definitions of sustainability, see, for example, Gray *et al.* 1993, p. 290 footnote 20).
- *Qualitative (sustainable) growth*. Qualitative growth is considered to mean every sustainable increase of welfare per capita, and of society as a whole, which is achieved with a decreasing or constant use of natural resources as well as with a decreasing or constant amount of pollution (BfK 1985, p. 15; similar is the Brundtland Report 1987, p. 212).
- *Sustainable development*. Sustainable development (Brundtland Report 1987, p. 43; SustainAbility 1993; WWF 1993) is defined as the development that meets the needs of the present generation without compromising the ability of future generations to meet their own needs. It contains two key concepts:

  — the concept of "needs", in particular the essential needs of the world's poor and future generations, to which overriding priority should be given (see, e.g., Welford 1994)
  — the idea of limitations, imposed by the state of technology and by social organization, on the environment's ability to meet present and future needs.

- *Sustainable society*. A society is sustainable when it is structured and when it behaves in such a way that it can exist for an indefinite number of generations (Meadows *et al.* 1992, p. 250). "A sustainable society depends upon a life-support system with integrity. Such a system is characterized by stability, realization of inherent potential, capacity for self-repair, and minimal need for external support." (Karr 1993, p. 299). Production as well as consumption is sustainable.

The definitions of sustainable growth and sustainable development do not entirely match the biological approach based upon the carrying capacity of the earth or specific ecosystems, see for example Daly (1992), Daily and Ehrlich (1992). However, if a company is seen as a social system, its survival is a result of its economic performance. Sustainable growth and sustainable development describe processes towards the desirable situation of sustainability and a sustainable society. Nevertheless, "development" leaves more possibilities for interpretation than "growth" as it specifically recognizes social factors and does not exclude a "sustainable decrease" of economic productivity. The concepts of sustainable development and sustainable society include socio-political aspects, whereas sustainability is a concept of natural science. In conclusion, the overarching goal of ecological accounting is one step in measuring the progress of sustainable development towards a sustainable society.

This general goal has to be specified in order to operationalize the concept of sustainable development. More concise and measurable objectives and benchmarks are needed.

7.3 THE MEASURES: ENVIRONMENTAL IMPACT ADDED AND ECO-EFFICIENCY

The concept of eco-efficiency was first introduced and discussed in the academic press (Schaltegger and Sturm 1990). Eco-efficiency also covers the concepts of ecological efficiency and economic-ecological efficiency, as discussed later in this chapter. To measure ecological efficiency, tools for ecological accounting are needed. However, the term eco-efficiency did not become widely used until the Business Council for Sustainable Development (BCSD)—since 1995 The World Business Council for Sustainable Development (WBCSD)—and Schmidheiny published *Changing Course* at the UNCED conference in Rio in 1992 (see Schmidheiny 1992 or BCSD 1993). In practice, the terms are used with different meanings and with little precision. Therefore, it is very important to clarify the dimensions of eco-efficiency.

In general, *efficiency measures the relation between output and input*. The higher the output for a given input, or the lower the input for a given output, the more efficient is an activity, product, firm etc. Economically rational management is characterized by being efficient, as the purpose of economic behaviour is to manage scarcity in the best possible manner.

Efficiency is a multi-dimensional concept, because the units in which input and output are measured can vary. If input and output are measured in financial terms it is commonly referred to as *profitability* or *financial efficiency*. Some measures of financial efficiency are: contribution margin, return on sales, return on assets etc. Economic efficiency indicates whether, and for how long, social activities can be economically sustained. If efficiency is measured in technological terms the focus is usually placed more on physical units like kilograms. Technological efficiency is also called *productivity*. The difference between the best possible and the actually achieved efficiency ratio is described as *X-efficiency* (Leibenstein 1966). Efficiency is not bound to a financial or technological dimension: different dimensions can be combined by calculating *cross-efficiency* figures, such as the shareholder value created per employee.

As efficiency is the ratio between output and input, *ecological efficiency* can generally be defined as the desired output per caused total environmental impact added[1] (Schaltegger and Sturm 1990, 1992a).

$$\text{Ecological Efficiency} = \frac{\text{Desired Output}}{\text{Environmental Impact Added}}$$

Environmental impact added is the measure of all environmental interventions which are assessed according to their relative environmental impact. Environmental impact added is correlated with value added, as no economic activity is without environmental impacts.

Ecologically efficient management of a company is characterized by a favourable (high) ratio between products sold or functions accomplished and the resultant environmental impact added. Two kinds of ecological efficiency measures can be distinguished:

- ecological product efficiency
- ecological function efficiency.

Ecological product efficiency is a measure of the ratio between a product unit and the created environmental impact added over the whole or over a part of the product life cycle (Schaltegger and Sturm 1990, 1992a):

$$\text{Ecological Product Efficiency} = \frac{\text{Product Unit}}{\text{Environmental Impact Added}}$$

Managements of companies tend to show their environmental improvements by communicating their total product efficiency or a part thereof (e.g. number of cars produced per unit of energy consumption). Product efficiency can be improved with many pollution prevention techniques but also with end-of-the-pipe devices, reduced input or substitution of resources etc. Although the improvement of product efficiency is desirable in principle, some products will never be as ecologically efficient as others in fulfilling a certain demand. For example, a car will always be less ecologically efficient than a bicycle.

The second formula for ecological efficiency takes a broader view, measuring how much environmental impact has been caused in serving a specific function per unit time. A function could, for instance, be defined as the painting of one square meter of sheet metal or the transport of a person over a certain distance. The alternative that causes least environmental impact in serving the specific function has the best *ecological function efficiency* (Schaltegger and Sturm 1990, 1992a).

$$\text{Ecological Function Efficiency} = \frac{\text{Served Function}}{\text{Environmental Impact Added}}$$

Ecological function efficiency can be improved by substituting products with low product efficiency by highly efficient products (e.g. a bicycle instead of a car), by reducing the amount used to serve the function (e.g. car pools lead to decreased demand for cars), by prolonging the life span of products (e.g. longer corrosion guarantee of cars) and by improving product efficiency.

Environmental interest groups often prefer to measure the environmental record of a product according to its overall function efficiency (e.g. the ecological function efficiency of a car in transporting a person over the distance compared to the efficiency of a bicycle, public transport, etc.).

Both measures of ecological efficiency are useful and their adequacy depends on the purpose of the investigation. The two ecological efficiency ratios can be applied to different levels of aggregation, such as one product unit, a strategic business unit, total sales of a firm, etc. In this connection, it is important to consider total sales and the absolute environmental impact: a large number of ecologically efficient products can be more harmful than a small amount of ecologically inefficient items.

Ecological efficiency allows the relationship between environmentally sustainable activities, products, etc. to be measured.

The cross-efficiency between the economic and the ecological dimension—economic-ecological efficiency—is the ratio between the created value added and the caused environmental impact added (Schaltegger and Sturm 1990, 1992a).

$$\text{Economic-Ecological Efficiency (Eco-Efficiency)} = \frac{\text{Value Added}}{\text{Environmental Impact Added}}$$

Economic-ecological efficiency is often referred to as eco-efficiency.[2] In this connection, the measurement neither of the economic nor of the ecological dimension is fixed. The relation should be calculated by using the kind of measures that provide the best information in view of the aim of the analysis. (This might be the shareholder value, free cash flow, the contribution margin, the net profit etc. for the economic dimension. Possible measures for the ecological dimension are discussed in Section 8.2.3.) Economic-ecological efficiency provides a means of measuring the economic and ecological sustainability of the way in which the management of an organization acts. If, as shown above, both the numerator and the denominator of this ratio, are equally weighted, then economic and ecological concerns are considered to have the same importance. Depending on their values the stakeholder groups assign different weightings to economic and ecological performance.

The main relations between sustainable development and eco-efficiency are shown in Figure 7.2. The development of firms, products, nations, etc. can be demonstrated with the "eco-efficiency portfolio". (For a discussion of the eco-efficiency portfolio, see Ilinitch and Schaltegger 1995, Schaltegger and Sturm 1992a, 1995.)

The economic efficiency is shown on the vertical axis whereas ecological efficiency is measured on the horizontal axis. To include all dimensions of sustainable development a third measure for "social impacts" would be necessary. The current situation is defined as the point in the middle of Figure 7.2. Movements to the right of the diagonal *"eco-efficiency line"* indicate an improvement of economic-ecological efficiency. The ratio between economic and environmental performance has improved.

However, *economic and ecologically sustainable development* is characterized by movements towards the upper right *quadrant*. Environmentally sustainable

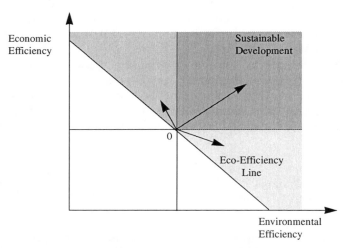

Figure 7.2   Eco-Efficiency and Sustainable Development

development does not allow an increase of environmental impacts, i.e. movements to the left of the vertical line through point 0. The same applies to economically sustainable development, which must be above the horizontal line through point 0.

Eco-efficiency is the measure used when economic and environmental efficiency are given the same weighting.

The definitions of ecological efficiency and eco-efficiency naturally present a major difficulty: how can environmental impact added be accurately measured (Sections 8.2.1)? And how can releases into the natural environment be adequately assessed (Section 8.2.3)?

The next section deals with information about environmental impacts in order to prepare us for the discussion of the perspectives, methods and tools of ecological accounting.

7.4 INFORMATION ON ENVIRONMENTAL IMPACTS

All environmental impacts originate from activities that are deemed to create value or utility (Figure 7.3). These economic activities cause *environmental interventions*, such as emissions, use of resources, etc. Environmental interventions represent the exchange between the anthroposphere (the economy) and the environment including resource extraction, emissions into the air, water or soil, and aspects of land use (Udo de Haes and Hofstetter 1994). The environmental interventions can be recorded in an inventory table (e.g. an emissions inventory). The emissions function describes the link between economic activities (i.e. value added) and environmental interventions. Because almost every activity has some influence on nature, it will never be possible to record all environmental interventions.

Due to transformation (dilution, dispersion, synergies, chain reactions, etc.) not every *environmental impact* causes the same change in *ambient environmental quality*. Today more impact chains (transformation functions) can be described and explained than ever before. (An impact chain is the conceptual, qualitative linking of an inventory to potential direct and indirect impacts (Research Triangle Institute 1993a, C-2).) Some of the impacts which have just become apparent were caused a long time ago (e.g. erosion in the Mediterranean area as a result of logging in ancient times). Others have been recognized because of new scientific evidence (e.g. the depletion of the stratospheric ozone layer).

Environmental impacts can be distinguished as follows (see Udo de Haes and Hofstetter 1994, Guinée 1994, p. 3, RTI 1993a, C-2, Schaltegger and Kubat 1994, pp. 88ff).

- Direct impacts are potential impacts that are directly attributable to an inventory item (e.g. photo-chemical smog as a direct impact of ozone emissions).
- Indirect impacts are potential impacts that are not directly attributable to an inventory item, but rather stem from another impact (e.g. human lung damage is an indirect impact of photo-chemical smog).
- Parallel impacts are impacts that potentially contribute to several problems.
- Direct impacts in series are impacts that potentially contribute to several successive impacts.
- Indirect impacts in series occur when an emission contributes to another impact through a metabolite of its degradation, or through the impact which it primarily causes.
- Impacts can also be divided into local, regional, continental or global impacts according to their spatial impact radius.

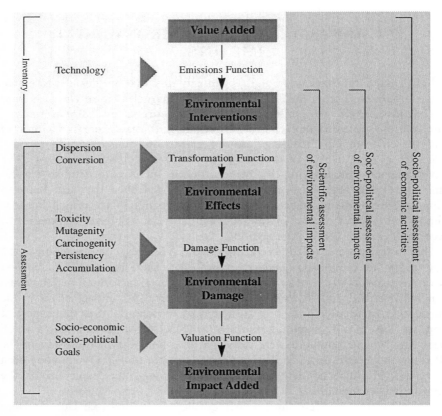

Figure 7.3 The Link Between Value Added and Environmental Impact Added. Source: According to Schaltegger & Sturm 1992a

Every environmental intervention causes an environmental impact (e.g. photochemical smog), but not every release or activity necessarily leads to an *environmental effect* (e.g. human lung diseases) and environmental *damage*. Environmental effects are the consequences of an environmental intervention in the environmental system. An environmental damage is a deterioration in the quality of the environment not directly attributable to depletion or pollution (Heijungs *et al.* 1992, p. 92.) Nature has the ability to adapt, but only so far as threshold levels, or the carrying capacity, are not exceeded. The damage function is influenced by factors such as persistency, mutagenic, carcinogenic, accumulation potential, etc. (For an introduction to eco-toxicity see, for example, Ottoboni 1991).

Some inherent characteristics of nature and environmental impacts such as large uncertainties due to changing conditions, or qualitative, fuzzy information, further complicate the analysis of impact chains.

Because of the sheer complexity of nature, in many cases, even among natural scientists, no agreement exists about what constitutes a specific case of environmental damage. In spite of the fact that science is making great strides this probably will never change.

The causal chain described so far is what some natural scientists attempt to assess. However, not all societies and people attach the same importance to environmental effects and environmental damage. Therefore, *environmental impact added must consider socio-political and economic preferences*. The *socio-political and economic valuation* functions attempt to consider these preferences.

In view of this very complex causal chain, we must ask ourselves to what extent ecological accounting can help to clarify the link between the value added created by a firm and the environmental impact added caused by its economic activity. In order not to reinvent the wheel, it is desirable to consider which concepts of traditional accounting can be taken over by ecological accounting.

First, the applicability of the basic structure of accounting systems is discussed. Thereafter, Chapters 8 to 10 examine different ecological accounting systems.

7.5 STRUCTURE OF ECOLOGICAL ACCOUNTING

Ecological accounting is an enlargement of traditional accounting as it has been visualized in Figure 1.1. It represents a set of *satellite accounting systems* to compute impacts of businesses on the environment. The notion "satellite accounting system" was first used in macro-economic accounting and originates from Hamer 1993 (see also Vaterlaus 1993). As a result of the matter recorded, its measurements are stated in physical terms (unlike in environmentally differentiated traditional accounting). The physical units can be of a quantitative or qualitative nature, but an endeavour to measure in quantitative terms is usually made.

Ecological accounting is that sub-area of environmental accounting that deals with activities, methods and systems for recording, analyzing and reporting impacts of a defined economic system on the natural environment (Schaltegger and Stinson 1994).

The basic structure of the traditional accounting category can also be applied to the category of ecological accounting, Schaltegger and Sturm (1992a). As shown in Figure 7.4 the ecological accounting category can be divided into:

- an internal ecological accounting system
- an external ecological accounting system
- other ecological accounting systems.

The *internal ecological accounting system* seeks to provide ecological information for internal managerial purposes. It is the enlargement of traditional managerial accounting, and is designed to satisfy the management's need to be informed about the environmental impacts of the firm. First, the use of natural resources as input factors for production is examined. Second, environmental interventions are recorded, such as pollution from emissions which are outputs of the production processes. The use of natural resources both as an input factor and as a dump for unwanted outputs can be increased or reduced. Firms that possess large environmental assets, such as land, forests etc. can also account for the growth and reduction of their ecological capital in a so-called "eco-asset sheet". Internal ecological accounting is a necessary precondition of any environmental management system (EMS) and, in principle, a prerequisite for external ecological accounting. Internal and external stakeholders may demand the same kind of information, but the amount and degree of detail of the required information will usually vary.

In addition, ecological accounting serves as a valuable input for environmentally differentiated managerial accounting. For instance, managers

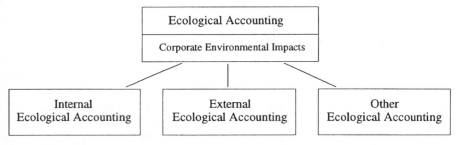

Figure 7.4 Ecological Accounting Systems Treat Environmental Impacts

cannot predict environmentally induced contingent liabilities if they have no idea about their actual environmental impacts today and in future. Furthermore, internal ecological accounting enables management to calculate the most cost-effective environmental protection measures.

External ecological accounting considers—like financial accounting—the information requirements of external stakeholders. For different reasons, many external stakeholders: customers, the general public, the media, shareholders, environmental funds, geographical neighbors as well as pressure groups and others, are interested in the environmental performance of firms. In principle, external accounting and reporting provides information of a more general and consolidated character than other accounting systems.

In the recent past, over 300 extensive annual environmental reports with detailed data on discharges of pollutants have been published (Naimon 1995). Effects on owned or otherwise influenced ecological assets are rarely reported. The main focus is on information on the increase and reduction as well as the total level of emissions.

Other ecological accounting systems are, for example, designed for the correct assessment of environmental taxes, such as a CO_2 or VOC tax. Without information about discharged effluents or used resources, environmental tax rates could not be multiplied by respective quantities. Apart from the tax agency and the environmental protection agencies—which are primarily interested in specific, regulated information on discharges of specific pollutants—an increasing number of stakeholders also require this information. These include banks (e.g. when lending money) and insurance companies (e.g. when underwriting contracts). Environmental laws and regulations already in force in the USA, in Europe and in some other countries have created a new area of substance "accounting" in the effluent monitoring reports that many firms must submit to regulators. Although these laws and regulations can impose substantial costs on individual businesses (and, indirectly, on society), several studies (summarised in Cairncross 1991) find that the benefits of these regulations to society, and indirectly to its businesses, are often even greater (see also Stinson 1993).

At the moment, ecological accounting is sometimes seen as a gadget for relatively proactive companies which are able to overcome institutional barriers and possess the resources to experiment. However, this situation is changing faster than is widely realised. In future, ecological accounting might even become highly regulated and mandatory. In Denmark, for example, Chapter 5 of the Danish Environmental Protection Act which requires firms to publicly disclose environmental impacts in green accounts has been established in 1995 (see for example Reuters 1995a). Ecological accounting systems have evolved because "green" thinking is increasing in almost every stakeholder group. There is no sign that this will change fundamentally as long as environmental degradation continues at the same pace as today. Regulatory bodies will continue to push for an internalization of external environmental costs, environmental pressure groups and media will not stop informing the general public, insurance companies will ask for relevant information from firms and consider environmentally induced costs when calculating their premiums, banks will further investigate potential costs and liabilities when lending money, and so forth.

7.6 PERSPECTIVES, SUBJECT MATTER AND FURTHER STRUCTURE OF ECOLOGICAL ACCOUNTING

Various *perspectives* can be taken into account with regard to environmental interventions. The main perspectives are (Figure 7.5) the:

- product perspective
- spatial perspective
- corporate perspective (business unit, respectively industry).

None of these perspectives is obsolete or wrong, but their appropriateness depends on the purpose and task of the analysis. Every perspective can be taken with a broader or more narrow focus. The smallest common denominator of all perspectives of ecological accounting—product, spatial

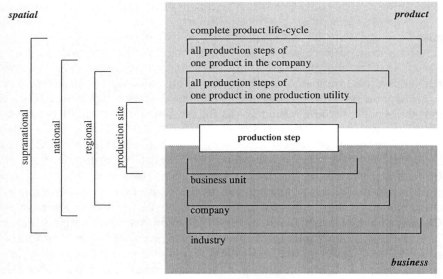

Figure 7.5 Different Perspectives and Foci of Ecological Accounting. Source: Schaltegger and Sturm 1994

(site) and industry (business)—is a single production step (Figure 7.5). Therefore, ecological accounting activities will usually start with the investigation of single production steps.

The *focus*, i.e. the *boundaries of the system considered*, can be widened in every perspective.

- From a product perspective, it is possible to consider one production step, all production steps in a specific plant, all production steps of that product in a firm or a complete product life-cycle, also incorporating transformation steps outside the boundaries of the firm.
- A spatial (geographical) perspective may cover one production step, a production site, a local region, a nation, or a supranational area.
- From an industry perspective one production step, a business (e.g. a strategic business unit), a firm, or an industry can be looked at.

In the theoretical extreme, all three dimensions would merge: the environmental interventions of all geographical regions (the world) would equal those of all corporations, businesses and industries (the world economy) and of all product life-cycles (the world output of products).

The *subject matter* of ecological accounting is independent of what perspective, focus or system boundaries are chosen. Ecological accounting collects, analyses and communicates information on ecological assets and interventions. As environmental interventions and assets are manifold, different aspects are considered.

- Resource use

    —Non-renewable material resources and energy carriers (e.g. ores, oil).
    —Renewable material resources and energy carriers (e.g. wood, water).

- Environmental interventions

    —Material emissions and pollution respectively (substances and substance combinations, e.g., CO_2, NO_x, VOC).
    —Energy emissions (energy informs such as heat, radiation, noise).

- Ecological assets (ecological capital goods).

    —Land, forests, biodiversity, etc.

According to the nature of the topics, the subject matter of ecological accounting can be broadly divided into:

- *assets* (stock) at a specific point of time
- *flows* per period.

This distinction defines the *main accounts* of ecological accounting systems (Figure 7.6). They should, in principle, include an:

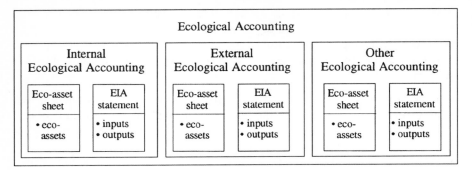

Figure 7.6 The Main Accounts of Ecological Accounting Systems

- *eco-asset sheet* listing all ecological assets at a specific point of time
- *enviromental impact added statement* (EIA statement) listing all flows (inputs and outputs) during a specific period of time.

Neither internal or external nor other ecological accounting systems are bound to a specifically different set of discussed perspectives, foci and subject matter.

Concerning an adaptation of the concept of a *balance sheet* to ecological accounting, various vague ideas and metaphors have been put forward. One such metaphor is the view that the "...environmental quality [is] a stock, a kind of capital that is 'depreciated' by the addition of pollutants and 'invested' by abatement activities" (Solow 1992, p. 13). In a figurative sense, this comparison is convincing. However, it raises the question of what the environmental liability is that corresponds to the environmental capital or the eco-assets. It is also not clear when environmental assets become environmental liabilities and vice versa. (For example, when is a stream so polluted that it is no longer an environmental asset, but an environmental liablility?)

A first attempt to consider the environment as a capital stock from an accounting perspective has been made by subdividing the total "capital" available to mankind into three categories (Gray *et al.* 1993, pp. 290ff.).

- Critical natural capital: demands of the biosphere which are essential for life.
- Other natural capital (sustainable, substitutable or renewable): elements of the biosphere which are renewable or for which reasonable substitutes can be found.
- Artificial capital: elements created from the biosphere which are made by humans (e.g. machines, buildings, roads, etc.).

Artificial capital has been expanded at the expense of the first two categories of (natural) capital. To achieve sustainable development the critical natural capital must not be diminished.

This approach has not gained any acceptance in the business community, perhaps because the distinction between the three categories of capital is difficult and arbitrary.

It does not seem possible or sensible to apply the concept of a balance sheet in a consistent manner to ecological accounting. The comparison of ecological assets and liabilities (land, forests etc.) does not provide any helpful information as all natural assets are "borrowed" from nature. Nevertheless, depending on the industry, firms own or influence considerable natural assets (e.g. mining firms, forest management, government agencies etc.). Therefore, ecological assets should be considered in ecological accounting when they are more or less directly affected. For this purpose an eco-asset sheet listing all ecological assets can be created. The respective assets at a certain point of time—the end of an accounting period—can be shown in this sheet.

There are distinctive differences between an eco-asset sheet and a balance sheet.

- The eco-asset sheet allows for comparisons between accounting periods (longitudinal comparisons), but does not counterbalance assets with liabilities and equity.
- An eco-asset sheet does not reflect a balance between items.
- All eco-assets come from only one "lender", namely nature.
- No concepts exist to aggregate eco-assets in one unit of measurement.

Several eco-asset sheets, although tagged with various names, have been drawn up for nations on the macro-economic level. Several OECD countries have tried to account for their physical resource endowments (OECD 1994a). Norway has classified its resources into material and environmental resources. Accounts have been developed for fish and forest reserves as well as for various minerals and energy resources (Alfsen *et al.* 1993, OECD 1994a, p. 13). Recent reviews of the accounts indicate, however, that the success of adjusted accounts has been uneven. France is the country with the most comprehensive system of accounting for resource endowments so far, and its objective is no less than to account for all interactions between the economy and the environment (INSEE 1986a, b). So far, it has only been implemented on a very partial basis. The Netherlands have adopted a system aimed at determining where a loss of function takes place in the environmental resources of water, air and land. Until now, environmental assessment has focused on problems related to natural resource destruction or depletion, and increasingly complex scientific methods and technologies are used for monitoring and assessment (UNEP 1991, p. 35).

The eco-asset sheet will only be discussed briefly in the section on internal ecological accounting because it is mainly the management and measurement of pollution which is of practical relevance for most industries.

The basic idea of the *environmental impact added statement* corresponds to the income statement in traditional accounting. Flows of material and energy inputs as well as the respective outputs into the natural environment are recorded and assessed for an accounting period. As shown in the next sections, ecological accounting deals mainly with flows of environmental interventions.

As in traditional accounting, the main work of ecological accounting also consists of the collection, recording, allocation, analysis and communication of data. The environmental interventions have to be assessed in physical terms as they usually have no market price. This procedure of ecological accounting is discussed in the section on internal ecological accounting, but also applies to external and other ecological accounting systems.

As has been shown in Section 7.5, the different ecological accounting systems serve as information tools to communicate with different groups of stakeholders. In the next chapter internal ecological accounting is discussed. Chapter 9 deals with external ecological accounting, whereas Chapter 10 looks at other regulatory ecological accounting systems.

8
Internal Ecological Accounting

8.1 INTRODUCTION

Chapter 8 deals with internal ecological accounting. This accounting system is designed to provide information for the decision-making of internal stakeholders, primarily management. After an introductory overview, the following aspects of internal ecological accounting are examined.

- Site-oriented accounting (Section 8.2) with the main activities of ecological accounting:

  — recording of environmental interventions (Section 8.2.1)
  — tracing and allocation of environmental interventions and environmental impact added (Section 8.2.2)
  — assessment of environmental interventions (impact assessment) (Section 8.2.3).

- Product-oriented accounting: LCA (Section 8.3).
- Environmental investment appraisal (Section 8.4).

The chapter ends with a discussion of links between internal and external ecological accounting and with some notes on the influences of external stakeholders on internal ecological accounting.

The approach of internal ecological accounting corresponds in principle to the concept of traditional managerial accounting. Therefore, internal ecological accounting serves as:

- an analytical tool to detect ecological weaknesses and strengths
- a decision support method concerning relative environmental quality and a basis for environmental measures such as eco-efficiency
- a tool to control directly and indirectly caused environmental effects
- a neutral and transparent base for internal (and therefore also indirectly external) communication.

In most cases, internal ecological accounting is voluntary, and is not undertaken specifically to satisfy demands of external stakeholders. Ideally, the internal ecological accounting system should—like the traditional managerial accounting system—lay the foundation for the external and all other ecological accounting systems. It is therefore the starting point for the discussion of ecological accounting systems including those designed for external purposes. This is why the first academic approaches to ecological accounting focused on internal measures. Seen from a historical and empirical angle, however, corporate internal ecological accounting started to develop and to be applied after powerful external stakeholders (i.e. environmental protection agencies) were able to force firms to inform about emissions. With growing environmental costs, as well as new regulations and more stakeholders requiring different information on an increasing number of environmental interventions, the need for an efficient internal environmental information system emerged. In the last couple of years, many companies have recognized that the structure of accounting systems might be useful to organize environmental information systems efficiently. However, because of a wide range of information needs, many different approaches to internal ecological accounting have been developed. Therefore, the focus of this chapter is on the most important perspectives and on the approaches adopted in contemporary internal ecological accounting practice.

Comprehensive internal ecological accounting provides useful information for all managers, regardless of their responsibilities and hierarchical level (Figure 8.1). Typically, different managers will have different perspectives and therefore place the emphasis on other aspects of information (see also Section 4.1). Also, the degree of specification and detail will have to be altered to satisfy different needs. A product manager has other information needs than, for example, a site or a division manager. This is why an internal ecological accounting system should be able to distinguish between site- or spatially-oriented accounting; product-oriented accounting; business-, company- or industry-oriented accounting.

- A *production manager* considers the contribution of his production activities (e.g. B2X2 in Figure 8.1). He wants to know, for instance, his share of the environmental interventions released by jointly used clean-up facilities. Sewage plants, incinerators, etc. usually treat the waste of several production processes and products. Therefore, the emissions released by these cleaning facilities have to be allocated to the production processes and products. The production manager has to ask the manager of the sewage plant to provide information on how much his product has contributed to the emissions of the sewage plant. He also has to speak with the managers of jointly used incinerators, etc.

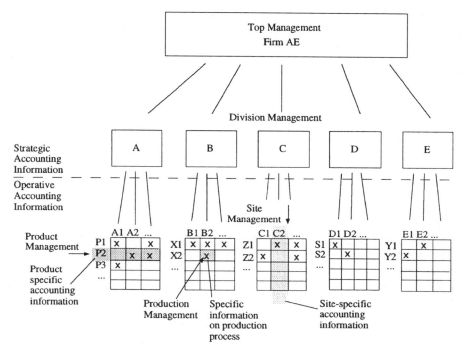

Figure 8.1 Perspectives of Internal Ecological Accounting

- A *site manager* wants to be informed about the impacts of his plant (e.g. site C2 in Figure 8.1), whereas a division manager needs is to know about the environmental interventions of all sites and products of his division (e.g. division C in Figure 8.1). Historically, ecological accounting started at the level of a plant and a firm.[3] Today, in English speaking countries "environmental impact assessment" (EIA) is the most common, though confusing, term used to describe generally regulated procedures for computing environmental impacts of sites.[4] Site-specific ecological accounting often also considers how the natural surroundings of a plant are impacted (Section 8.2).

- A *product manager* is interested in product-specific information. Therefore, he is bound to ask at every production step for the share of environmental interventions that are caused by his product (see, e.g., Product P2 in Figure 8.1). Extended further, this perspective is usually described with the term "life-cycle assessment" (formerly life-cycle analysis) or "LCA".[5]

- The *division management* requests information at the level of strategic business units (SBU). The respective environmental information has an aggregated strategic character and is, depending on the focus of analysis, site- or product-oriented.

- The *top management* (and the division management) is not particularly interested in details but primarily wants an overall picture and consolidated information on the whole firm (the whole division), including all sites and all products. Whereas most management levels are interested in information for operative management, the top and division management require accounting information for strategic management (Figure 8.1). However, in some cases (e.g. for media statements, meetings with pressure groups, etc.) top and division management require specific information from lower management levels.

Managers adjust the scope (focus) of their accounting to the goal and importance of their analysis. The process of specifying the boundaries of the accounting system is strongly influenced by the demands of important internal and external stakeholders, as well as the expected cost-benefit ratio of collecting and analyzing further information. For project-evaluation from an environmental perspective, all management levels are apt to use methods of ecological investment appraisal (Section 8.4).

No matter what perspective and focus (boundary of the accounting system) is chosen, internal ecological accounting always must deal with the following topics.

- *Recording, tracking and tracing* of environmental interventions. The purpose of recording is to have an inventory where all environmental interventions are registered in physical terms (kilograms, joules, etc. or more generally: physical units, see PU in Figure 2.1, Part A).
- *Allocation* of environmental impacts to products, processes and activities. In ecological accounting, allocation is a procedure for assigning environmental impacts to the production steps, sites and products that caused them.
- *Assessment* of the relative severity of environmental interventions and calculation of environmental impact added. Impact assessment is a technical, quantitative, and/or qualitative process of classifying, characterizing and assessing the effects of the resource requirements and the recorded releases of pollutants.

The following section deals with these joint topics of internal ecological accounting in the site-specific context.

8.2 SITE-ORIENTED ECOLOGICAL ACCOUNTING

The first approaches to "ecological bookkeeping" (Müller-Wenk 1978, Ullmann 1976) and "corporate ecological accounting" (Schaltegger and Sturm 1991, 1992a) describe information tools that deal with environmental externalities of production sites and firms from an engineering, or an accounting angle respectively. The main objective of these concepts, as well as of the modern management tool of eco-controlling, is to support site managers in the continuous, systematic registration, allocation and assessment of non-financially measured ecological impacts of production sites, plants and firms.

Today, several important environmental regulations encourage site-specific ecological accounting, above all the US Toxic Release Inventory (TRI) and the European Environmental Management and Eco-Audit Scheme (EMAS). The influence of both regulations on accounting is discussed in Chapter 10 (other ecological accounting systems) as these regulations establish ecological accounting relations with special stakeholders.

Historically, ecological accounting started at a plant and company level. In the Anglo-Saxon world site-specific ecological accounting of new projects is often referred to as "environmental impact assessment". (For a short introduction to environmental impact assessment as a preventive management tool, see for example Welford and Gouldson 1993.) This is a confusing term because, in Life Cycle Assessment, for example, it denotes the general procedure of assessment of environmental interventions. Interpreted in the regulatory sense, it usually describes a set of regulated procedures to compute environmental impacts of sites. Site-specific ecological accounting considers how the natural surroundings of a plant are impacted. Then, environmental impact assessment "... is essentially a process that seeks to identify and predict the impacts of a new development [e.g. a new production site] on the environment, to mitigate them where possible and to monitor the actual impacts"; (cited more fully in Gray *et al.* 1993, p. 80). The framework of environmental impact assessment "... is specifically developed to minimise the potential environmental impact of new developments at the earliest stage possible—the design and development stage" (Welford and Gouldson 1993, p. 31). In this traditional application, environmental impact assessment can be defined as the formal and systematic collection and analysis of information relating to the possible environmental effect of a new or significantly altered project. However, even where it is not required by law it is good business practice to undertake such an assessment anyway.

Site-specific ecological accounting has received increasing attention in Europe because of the EU Directive on Environmental Assessment (85/337). As will be shown in Section 8.2.3, the term "impact assessment" is also used for the weighting of environmental interventions.

The basic accounting activities are shown in Table 8.1. First, the role of environmental accounting has to be formulated in the environmental policy of the firm. Second, the accounting framework has to be defined and the data have to be collected (Section 8.2.1).

In a next step, environmental interventions have to be allocated to determine which production steps and products are "responsible" for the environmental impact caused (Section 8.2.2). To obtain an environmental impact added

Table 8.1 Basic Steps and Results of Ecological Accounting

Stage	Step	Result
Definition of goal	1. Goal definition	Defined goals
Accounting framework	2. Definition of accounts	Defined accounts
Inventory	3. Recording	Data sheets
	4. Allocation	Detailed inventories
	5. Aggregation	Aggregated inventory
Impact assessment	6. Classification	Impact categories
	7. Characterization	Indicators, eco-profile
	8. Valuation	Index, eco-balance
Improvement	9. Integration	Environmental management system
	10. Interpretation	Ecological weaknesses and potential of reduction
	11. Implementation and controlling	Improved situation

statement, the environmental interventions have to be aggregated and assessed according to their relative impacts. The procedure of impact assessment distinguishes three steps: classification, characterization and valuation (Section 8.2.3). For actual improvement, ecological accounting must be integrated with traditional accounting and into an environmental management system (Part D). Then the derived economic-ecological information can be interpreted to determine ecological weaknesses of the firm. The environmental management system must also support implementation and controlling to actually achieve an improved situation.

8.2.1 Recording

The purpose of recording is to arrive at an inventory where all environmental interventions are registered in physical terms.

Ecological accounting favors quantified data to measure the extent of environmental interventions (use of resources, material and energy emissions, or environmental impact added) and ecological assets (e.g. land, forests, water reserves, etc.). In addition, qualitative information can also be considered. First, the physical quantities of environmental interventions as well as of natural assets can be assessed according to their relative potential impact on nature (Section 8.2.3). Second, all internal and external accounting reports should be completed with qualitative information, as well as being explained to facilitate correct interpretation by the reader.

Ecological assets (e.g. forests, land) can be registered and described in an eco-asset sheet. Natural assets are rarely accounted for on the level of a firm as few industries own substantial amounts of unsealed land or other natural resources. However, some firms have recorded the fauna and flora of their sites and have actively started to create and manage habitats on roofs, open places, etc. (For examples of firms, see Buser and Schaltegger 1995.)

The *eco-asset sheet* is not a correct analogue to the financial balance sheet. Quite simply, the eco-asset sheet represents a "photograph" of a company's natural assets at a certain moment: all ecological assets that a company owns or occupies on a given date are listed. The eco-asset sheet contains all ecological assets and also includes an inventory of various species inhabiting land, forests, etc. Overharvesting reduces the values, while good maintenance and sustainable harvesting keep or even improve the eco-assets. Extinction of species, clear-cutting, soil erosion etc. represent devaluations of ecological assets (number of species, size of forests, etc.). Table 8.2 gives an example of an eco-asset sheet for a company. The list shows ecological values which are measured in a variety of physical units (kg, m^2, pieces, etc.). No one-dimensional method of comparing and aggregating ecological assets exists so far. The eco-asset sheet is an inventory list, nonetheless, it is often an eye-opener for management to recognize actual and potential ecological assets. The financial importance of the eco-asset sheet increases with the probability, amount and up-to-dateness of corresponding financial contingencies and liabilities as well as with the increasing scarcity of natural resources (see also, e.g., Bailey 1991; Haasis 1992; Hamner and Stinson 1992; McMurray 1992,

Table 8.2 Possible Contents of an Eco-Asset Sheet

Eco-Asset Sheet of a Firm	
Soil, Ground	*Surface Water*
• m^2 sealed	• m^3 of water flow
• Quantity of soil	• m of drainage
• Quality of soil (pH-value, concentration of heavy metals, etc.)	• Water quality (oxygen, pH-value, etc.)
• Resources (e.g. ores)	• Speed of water flow
• Wetness/dryness	• Height of water level
• ...	• ...
Air Quality	*Underground Water*
• Ambient air quality	• Height of water level
• ...	• Quality (oxygen, toxics, etc.)
Fauna, Flora, Habitats	• ...
• Number of species	*Landscape*
• Kind of species	• Kind of vegetation
• Kind of habitats	• Kind and size of constructions (e.g. chimney, electric power lines)
• Separation of habitats by roads, etc.	• ...
• ...	

p. 17; Ross 1985; Surma and Vondra 1992.) Recently, some companies (e.g. Dow Chemicals) started to explicitly create and express a financial value of ecological assets by, for example, establishing harvesting rights for rain-forests.

An eco-asset sheet can be related to the land *owned* by a company. This is a useful tool for mining and waste management companies or forest product industries. Nevertheless, for most companies, a broader perspective, looking at *influenced* ecological assets, might be of additional interest. In some cases, ratios between the currently known, economically accessible assets and the resources supplied to and used annually by the firm can be calculated. Observation over time shows the change in the relative scarcity of the resource. Also, the use of natural resources represents a flow of materials and energy and is therefore recorded in the environmental impact added statement. On a global scale, the accumulated use of natural resources represents a decrease of ecological assets. For many companies, this kind of information may not be of high priority, because plenty of the resources needed are available today. However, this might change in future.

After all, the eco-asset sheet is a very valuable tool, enabling management to obtain an overview and to communicate its "stock of environmental values" to interested stakeholders. Furthermore, it helps management to recognize actual and potential financial assets and liabilities that are related to the ecological assets. The importance of financial liabilities due to ecological assets has often been underestimated in the past (McMurray 1992, p. 17).

To account for *environmental interventions* requires them to be recorded, tracked and traced. The use of accounts to record and present financial flows is widely accepted. In view of the need for practical ways of handling data, and because efficient procedures of recording material and energy flows have been established with traditional accounting, it is sensible to use a similar procedure for ecological accounting. The main difference is that data on environmental interventions are recorded not in monetary but in physical terms (e.g. kg, m^3, l). However, an *input-output account* only considers direct environmental interventions, which have to be assessed before their relative environmental impact can be realized. Parallel, serial and indirect impacts can only be partially recognized in the assessment and are not considered in an input-output account (see Section 7.4).

In the USA, the main driving force for compiling corporate input-output accounts of environmental interventions is the "Toxic Release Inventory (TRI)". The TRI is further discussed in Chapter 10 for it establishes a specific accounting relationship between the environmental protection agency and firms. Similar regulations (though mostly less systematic and comprehensive) exist in other countries, too (e.g. in Germany and the Netherlands).

First of all, detailed material and energy flow diagrams must be prepared for the manufacturing processes. These can only be obtained in a comprehensive manner by detailed observation of actual production and by recording all material and energy flows. Table 8.3 shows an example of an input-output account.

On the left all material and energy inputs into production (natural resources, semi-manufactured goods, raw materials, etc.) are listed with an identification number. On the right all desirable and undesirable material and energy outputs of production (desired output, emissions, waste, etc.) are presented with an identification number. The material inputs are divided into mineral resources, biomass, water, energy carriers and other materials. Energy carriers (e.g. oil) are registered as material resources. That is why electric power, electromagnetic (light, heat, UV-rays, etc.) and ionizing rays, as well as mechanical energy and noise, belong to the category of energy inputs and outputs, which must be accounted for separately.

The recording of energies should be separated from the registration of material flows to avoid double-counting and confusion. According to the law of conservation of mass and energy, the total mass and energy on the input and output side of the account has to be the same. The left and the right side of the ecological account must be balanced as mass and energy cannot be destroyed. When many activities have to be computed, special accounts can be opened for all items listed in this "aggregate" account (e.g. an account for oil use, an account for CO_2 emissions, etc.). Depending on the purpose of the analysis, management will differentiate its ecological accounts according to single production steps, buildings, etc.

The transfer of effluents and energies from one account to a subsequent one or to the aggregate account can be done as in basic bookkeeping except that

Table 8.3 Example of an Input-Output Account. Source: Schaltegger and Sturm 1994

Group 10 Material Inputs	Group 20 Material Outputs
100 Mineral Resources	200 Products
101 Biomass	(Environmental Impact Added Carrier)
102 Water	201 Recyclates & Downcyclates
103 ...	203 Emissions
104 Fossil Energy Carriers	2050 Landfill
1040 Crude Oil	2051 Water Emissions
1041 Coal	20510 TOC
1042 Gas	20511 Sulfur
105 Regenerative Energy Carriers	20512 Water
106 Materials	20513 ...
1060 ...	2052 Air Emissions
1061 ...	20520 CO_2
107 Recyclates & Downcyclates	20521 NO_x
1070 ...	20522 VOC
1071 ...	20523 ...

the transactions are entered in their physical units of measurement (i.e. kilograms, joules). By this procedure the incoming and outgoing mass and energy flows can be aggregated and defined according to their origin. This is analogous to an income statement in traditional accounting. The registration of material and energy flows can be done at the end of an accounting period. In the case of many activities a journal can be used for continuous registration.

Table 8.4 shows an example of a journal for registering resource and energy use (as inputs into production processes) as well as environmental interventions (outputs). At least the following information should be recorded.

- The date.
- A short text describing the transaction.
- A note stating where the flow came from and where it went to.
- The input or output (ideally with its identification number).
- The quantity.
- The quality of the data used.
- The place.

Information on data quality is extremely important for the interpretation of the results as well as for the search for better alternatives. Possible categories of data quality are:

- measured data
- calculated data
- estimated data
- secondary data from literature (e.g. an industry average) or from suppliers.

Measured data usually reflect the specific situation in the best way. Nevertheless, it is helpful to note the analysis techniques to get an idea how reliable the data are, and how well they can be compared with other data. Even measured data are not always the same, even if the same analysis technique is used. Differences of measured data can occur, for example when a different time of measurement is chosen, or when an annual average instead of a monthly average of measurement results is presented, etc.

Economically, it makes no sense to aim for a full inventory of all mass and energy flows; in any case this goal can rarely be achieved. Usually, data collection protocols (journals) will be developed over several years, digging deeper each year until the marginal benefit of more detailed information matches the marginal costs of its collection.

In order to simplify the procedure of recording, a priority list of considered effluents can be set up. Such a list can also help to economize ecological accounting, as even in a medium or small manufacturing firm at least a few hundred substances and energy flows could be examined. The data collection definitely requires a computerized management information system, but even with computerization it is helpful to set priorities with regard to waste streams.

Table 8.4 Journal for Registration of Resource Use and Environmental Interventions

Date	Text	Prestep	Poststep	Input	Output	Quantity (kg)	Quality of Data	Place (EIA-Center)
1. Jan. 96	storage	supplier X		oil		100	measured	storehouse A
3. Jan. 96	burning	natural env.		O_2		200	measured	process B
3. Jan. 96	burning		natural env.		CO_2	200	calculated	process B
3. Jan. 96	burning		natural env.		SO_2	95	calculated	process B
3. Jan. 96	burning		natural env.		CO	5	calculated	process B
3. Jan. 96	discharge		natural env.		CO_2	200	calculated	scrubber
3. Jan. 96	discharge		natural env.		CO	5	calculated	scrubber
3. Jan. 96	discharge		natural env.		SO_2	95	calculated	scrubber

To obtain the necessary data in sufficient quality and full detail is a burdensome job that has to be done very carefully.

A special case of the described accounting of material and energy flows is the so called approach of "loss track accounting" (Pojasek and Cali 1991a, b). Manufacturing losses are considered to cause pollution and to lower the economic efficiency of production processes and products. The method of loss-tracking computes the losses of material or energy which are not part of the desired output. The loss-tracking system is a computer based tool that enables management to identify the location and circumstances of each process loss. In a subsequent step it allows the loss reduction performance to be monitored by detailed observation of the actual manufacturing process. Typically all units of measurement (volume, container units, weight, etc.) are converted to pounds of dry weight (Pojasek and Cali 1991a, b, pp. 119ff).

8.2.2 Allocation

In traditional accounting, the purpose of activity based cost accounting (ABC) is to calculate the total induced costs of a cost carrier (product, product group, etc.). ABC is pursued in order to find out where exactly the firm earns and where it loses money. The same task is also an issue in internal ecological accounting.

"Ecological activity based cost accounting" aims to show where environmental interventions are caused and which products, product groups, etc. contribute most to overall environmental impact added.

There is a major difference between managerial cost-accounting and internal ecological accounting. In ecological accounting environmental interventions are allocated before they are assessed. Only in a second step are the environmental interventions assessed according to their relative environmental impact, in order to calculate environmental impact added (EIA, see Section 8.2.3). In traditional cost accounting no assessment is necessary as the monetary values (prices and costs) already represent an assessment. In analogy to managerial cost accounting, internal ecological accounting distinguishes between the following.

- *EIA centers*
  Environmental impact added centers describe "places" where material and energy are processed or where the respective flows enter the natural environment. Examples of EIA centers are production steps, sites, incinerators, sewage plants, etc.
- *EIA carriers*
  Environmental impact added carriers are the analogue to cost carriers in traditional cost accounting. They describe a product, product group, division etc. that is seen to be responsible for the creation of value added as well as environmental impact added. EIA carriers should ideally correspond to the cost carriers, because only then can eco-efficiency be calculated (see Section 7.3).
- *EIA drivers*
  Environmental impact added drivers initiate environmental impacts. Examples of EIA drivers are CO_2 emissions which cause the greenhouse effect, or VOC emissions that cause photochemical smog.
- *EIA allocation rules and EIA allocation keys*
  EIA allocation rules formulate general procedures allocating environmental interventions in order to allow a correct allocation. EIA allocation keys describe the relation between an EIA carrier and environmental interventions caused.

Allocation is not usually an issue when the boundaries of the accounting system are defined according to spatial (geographical) criteria or if the focus is on the whole firm. Obviously, allocation of environmental interventions is more an issue for middle and lower management levels (product and production managers) than for higher management levels (top and division management). Furthermore, allocation is not an issue when putting together an eco-asset sheet. Spatial accounting then considers the environmental interventions only as a whole, or assets in their respective regions.

However, this changes with narrower system boundaries (e.g. a production step) as well as with product-oriented accounting. In developed countries, clean-up facilities, such as sewage plants and incinerators, are the EIA centers where most emissions are released into the natural environment (e.g. EIA center 3 in Figure 8.2). But these facilities are not the cause of the environmental interventions. Ecological EIA carrier accounting attempts to answer questions such as: which carriers actually cause the major environmental interventions and impacts?

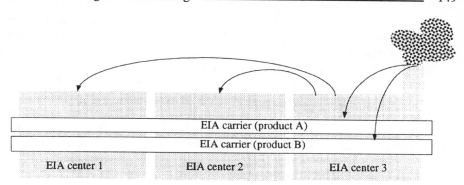

Figure 8.2 EIA Centers, EIA Carriers and Allocation

EIA center accounting helps to answer the question of where (in EIA center 1 or 2 in Figure 8.2) "overhead environmental interventions" of jointly used clean-up facilties (EIA center 3) actually are created, or where they actually occur. In a further step, *EIA carrier accounting* answers the question of which products, processes or activities cause the environmental interventions that have been allocated to EIA centers (EIA carrier A or B in Figure 8.2). The same questions are answered in managerial accounting when costs are allocated to cost centers and to cost carriers.

EIA carrier accounting is primarily a tool for the management's internal use. It focuses on the products and product groups that correspond to specific environmental interventions. This accounting sets out to determine, for example, how much pollution each product or product group causes by estimating the environmental impact added of each carrier. To estimate the environmental interventions caused by a carrier—for example, the "jointly" caused environmental interventions from multi-purpose clean-up facilities such as scrubbers, sewage plants, etc.—these have to be traced and allocated to the carriers "responsible". To do so as accurately as possible, representative EIA drivers and allocation rules have to be defined. Correctly assigning the environmental interventions makes it possible to determine how much different EIA carriers have contributed to the environmental impact added of these clean-up facilities. This calls for basically the same allocation procedure as in cost-accounting. The utmost care must be taken not to double-count waste flows when they are processed through on-site treatment, storage and disposal units (Pojasek and Cali 1991a, b, p. 123).

In traditional cost accounting calculating the contribution margin of a product unit requires the allocation of all related costs. Correspondingly, in EIA carrier accounting to calculate the EIA caused by a specific product, it is necessary to calculate all environmental interventions associated with the responsible EIA carrier.

The importance of the chosen allocation rule is particularly evident when considering its influence on the contribution margins of products as well as on directing capital investments.

The example in Figure 8.3 illustrates a typical allocation problem in ecological accounting. The term "environmental impact added units (EIA units)" is used in order to generalize and to simplify the example.

Production waste of product A is burnt in a large incinerator. The total environmental impact added of the incinerator is 66 EIA units (40 air emissions plus 26 sewage emissions). 26 EIA units in the form of hot waste water leave the incinerator. The installation of a new heating system for production plant P would result in emissions of 30 EIA units. Plant P discharges 20 EIA units after using the waste water for heating. Emissions of 6 EIA units result from the leaking pipe.

Much waste is treated in incinerator A. When focusing on the incinerated waste of one specific product, the question arises of how much and what emissions this product generates. This allocation problem regularly arises when dealing with product oriented ecological accounting and life cycle assessment. In our example, the burning of a product results in air emissions of 40 EIA units.

A variety of *allocation rules for environmental interventions* have been formulated (Schaltegger and Sturm 1992a, p. 180). For the example in Figure 8.3, several rules for tracing and allocating discharged pollutants are possible and have been proposed.

- *Full charge:* all environmental interventions are charged to the product. The EIA of product A would be $40 + 6 + 20 = 66$.
- *Passing on:* as the incinerator "produces" heating water for plant P, the end-user is responsible for all emissions. The environmental impact added of our product is calculated as 0, while plant P is charged 66 EIA units.
- *Partition allocation:* as all parties of our example are involved, the pollution added has to be allocated proportionately to all steps. The pollution added of the incinerator in this case is 50% of $66 = 33$. The 33 EIA units of the incinerator are charged to the product. The environmental impact added of production plant P is also 33. If another party were involved the total EIA would be divided by three.
- *Substitution bonus:* the environmental impact added of the incinerator is reduced by the EIA which would be caused if plant P had its own water heating (30 EIA units) but the leakage is a result of the transport to plant P which would be unnecessary if it had its own heating system. The pollution added of the incinerator is therefore calculated as $66 - 30 + 6 = 42$, and only the actually released pollution (20) is actually charged to plant P.
- *Difference bonus:* because the decision not to install a heating system for plant P only reduced pollutants that would arise from that heating

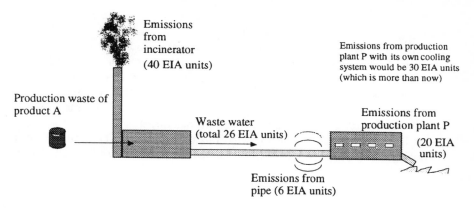

Figure 8.3 Allocation of Environmental Interventions

installation (e.g. SO_2), the incinerator may not be relieved of all of its emissions but only by the difference of actually saved pollutants (e.g. SO_2 but not NO_x). The environmental impact added of the incinerator would thus be smaller than 60 ($< 60 = 40 +$ the pollution that is untypical for the heating system [< 20]). The EIA of plant P would be smaller than 26, that is 6 from the pipe plus less than 20 from the heating system's typical pollution. ($< 26 = 6 + < 20$).

- *Cascade-use bonus:* the waste water of the incinerator which is forwarded to plant P is treated as a raw material. No waste water emissions of the incinerator are charged to the product. The incinerator, and therefore the product, is assigned responsibility for all air emissions from the incinerator (40). Production plant P is charged its own waste water emissions plus the emissions of the waste water pipeline ($26 = 6 + 20$).

While all allocation rules address important aspects, it is essential to be aware of the incentives created for all parties affected. The management of the incinerator should have an incentive to further use or recycle the waste water, while the management of production plant P should be encouraged to find and implement ways to use the waste water. To establish a trade, suppliers and "buyers" are needed. "Full charge" and "Passing on" create incentives for one party only. "Partition allocation" creates somewhat perverse incentives. For example, someone using or recycling 10% of the incinerator's waste water is "punished" with 50% of the total pollution, which therefore diminishes his options. With the "Substitution" and the "Difference" rules, the calculated incremental EIA may exceed the actual releases. *Considering the incentives created for all parties involved, the cascade-use bonus allocation rule seems to be the most useful allocation rule* (Schaltegger and Sturm 1992a, p. 180).

Allocation rules provide a general procedure and some criteria for allocation. For example, the cascade bonus allocation rule states that the pollution of the incinerator should be allocated to all products which are burnt in the incinerator. However, usually several products are burnt in an incinerator at the same time. The question then arises of how much of the respective environmental interventions should be allocated to product A, or to product B, C, etc. which are also treated in the incinerator. To actually carry this allocation process through, concrete *allocation keys* are needed. Allocation formulae have to be specifically defined for every case. Possible allocation keys for product A in the example of Figure 8.3 are as follows.

- *Used capacity* of the incinerator such as burning time, etc.
  Product A burns for ten minutes in the incinerator and uses the full burning capacity during this time. Therefore, the pollution which the incinerator releases in ten minutes should be allocated to product A.
- *Total weight or volume* of product A.
  Product A weighs 100 kg which is 1% of the total freight that is burnt in the incinerator. Therefore, 1% of the pollution of the incinerator should be allocated to product A.
- *Weight or volume of key pollutants* such as heavy metals, etc. which are caused by product A when burnt.
  The main driver of the total EIA of the incinerator is the discharge of heavy metals. Burning product A in this incinerator causes 0.5% of the total release of heavy metals of the incinerator. Therefore, product A is allocated 0.5% of *all* emissions of the incinerator.
- The *activity* that causes environmental interventions.
  Traditional full-cost accounting has been criticized for not giving an accurate picture of reality as the allocation of costs are not necessarily related to activities which can be influenced by management and employees. Therefore, activity based accounting (ABC) has been proposed. ABC "... allocates overhead costs in proportion to the activities associated with a product or product familiy" (Gunn 1992, pp. 104ff.). Accordingly, activity based ecological accounting allocates overhead environmental interventions in proportion to the activities associated with a product or a product family (also see Part B).

As discussed in Section 4.3, environmentally induced costs of joint clean-up facilities (e.g. costs of a sewage plant) can also be allocated to EIA centers (e.g. different production facilities) according to the environmental impact added of the waste water released by different production processes. However, as has been shown in Section 4.3, the EIA is not necessarily the best indicator for the induced clean-up cost, because the costs do not necessarily relate to the severity of the environmental impacts. Thus, the approach of ecological activity based accounting seems to be most promising.

After all the environmental interventions have been allocated to their respective EIA centers and EIA carriers, *aggregation* can be carried out. The same kind of environmental interventions are aggregated in their physical units.

Table 8.5 shows a typical example of a *departmental EIA account* with the aggregated environmental interventions of an EIA center (production site). The production site, the time period and the place are identified in the heading of the table. The data from the journal (Table 8.4) are aggregated in the respective categories of inputs and outputs. In order to avoid confusion, every input and every output is marked with an identification number. In the second and third column the quality of data and the EIA center before (prestep for inputs) or after the site "river" (poststep for outputs) are indicated. In the column to the right the used quantities (inputs) and the quantities that have been released or passed on to another EIA center (outputs) are filled in. This accounting system has proved to be useful in practice as all relevant information is summarized.

A special use of EIA carrier accounting is the comparison of the results with an *EIA standard calculation*. An increasing number of institutions have published basic inventory data (industry average environmental interventions) for the manufacturing of basic materials and products, such as steel, aluminum, glass, paper, packaging materials, energy systems, etc. (see for example BUWAL 1991, ESU 1994, Fritsche *et al.* 1989). These data can be used to establish *environmental impact added benchmarks* for the manufactured goods (Schaltegger 1994a). The computed environmental interventions, for example for the production of a specific product of the firm, can then be compared with such a benchmark, i.e. the best or an "average" equivalent production process for this product. As comparative data become increasingly available, comparisons with the cleanest comparable production processes will become more common.

As in traditional accounting, the choice of allocation rules also substantially influences the result in ecological accounting. The possibility of distortions of the end results is higher with an increasing number of allocation activities. The tasks of analysis and the system boundaries should be defined in such a way, therefore, as to ensure that internal ecological accounting provides information of the highest accuracy. As shown in Section 8.3, this means that site- and company-oriented accounting tend to provide more accurate information than product oriented accounting.

Sometimes a complete inventory provides enough information to see what the main environmental problems are and where they are created. In such a

Table 8.5   Example of a Departmental EIA Account for a Production Site

Production site		"River"		
Time period		One month, from May 1 to June 1, 1995		
Production quantity of period:		869.09 t		
N.B.: Air pollution is cleaned in a multi-purpose scrubber, measured twice per day.				

ident. no.	inputs/ outputs	quality of data	step before/ step after	tons per period
1	**Inputs**			
101	propylene	measured	production site A	3,111.04
102	sulfur	calculated	production site A	960.00
103	copper	calculated	production site A	69.60
104	sodium bicarbonate	measured	supplier Bart	2,000.00
105	compressed CO_2	measured	supplier Neal	5.60
106	ethane	measured	supplier Sela	20.00
107	cooling water	estimated	pumping station	2,000,000.00
108	water	measured	pumping station	96,000.00
10	***Total Input***			*2,102,166.24*
2	**Outputs**			
201	product A	measured	drying	*869.09*
210	***By-Products***			
211	waste water consisting of:			
212	water	estimated	waste water plant	89,760.00
213	TOC	calculated	waste water plant	3,014.40
214	AOX	calculated	waste water plant	0.56
215	Cu	calculated	waste water plant	0.08
				92,775.04
220	***Recycled and Downcycled By-Products***			
221	cooling water	measured	recycling	*2,000,000.00*
230	***Emissions***			
231	*air pollution* from scrubber:			
2311	CO_2	measured	environment	2,002.40
2312	N_2O	measured	environment	101.60
2313	SO_2	measured	environment	78.40
2314	particulates	measured	environment	7.20
2315	Cu	measured	environment	0.08
				2,189.68
232	*disposal*			*0.00*
20	***Total Output***			*2,095,833.81*
30	*Difference between In- and Output (10–20)*			6,332.43

case priorities for environmental protection, pollution prevention etc. can be defined on the basis of the inventory. However, in most cases the inventory provides an enormous amount of unassessed detailed information that cannot be accurately interpreted by management. An impact assessment of the inventory data is then necessary.

8.2.3 Impact Assessment

If, as often happens, the inventory table is overloaded with detailed information and if the comparison of the environmental interventions is ambiguous, then the decision makers need a concrete approach to assess the relative harmfulness, i.e. impact, of different environmental interventions.

Impact assessment is a technical, quantitative, and/or qualitative process of classifying, characterizing and assessing the effects of the resource requirements and the environmental loading recorded.

Ideally, assessment should address ecological impacts, human health impacts and resource depletion, as well as other effects such as habitat modification and noise pollution. The ecological assessment of environmental interventions, and therefore the reduction of many physical measures to a few units or one unit of measurement, should only follow after aggregation on an EIA center or an EIA carrier account has been carried out. The advantage of this approach is that different assessment methods can be based upon the same inventory data and can be compared with each other. For this reason, ecological accounting is not restricted to today's level of knowledge about the environmental harm of environmental interventions, but allows an approach adopting a new weighting to be applied at any time.

It would be desirable if impact assessment considered direct, indirect, parallel and serial impacts as well as spatial, time and social, political and economic aspects. So far, however, the complexity of the material allows only some of the criteria to be considered.

Today, many scientific disciplines (i.e. natural sciences, engineering, economics), universities, research institutes, environmental consultants, environmental protection agencies, and working groups with an international scope, deal with measures and criteria for environmental impact assessment and try to promote their concepts. The American, Canadian, Danish, Dutch, German, Norwegian and Swiss environmental protection agencies are among the most active in the area of ecological accounting. The Society for Environmental Toxicology and Chemistry (SETAC) is the most influential working group in setting standards of impact assessment for product-oriented accounting, though it has no enforcement power. Over the last decade impact assessment has proved to be a highly *interdisciplinary* research field. In the recent past, new interest groups, especially professional accounting associations, standardization organizations, and regulatory bodies,[6] have begun to indirectly influence this arena in various ways. The most important approaches of these newcomers—who are mainly trying to shape the procedure and practical methods of Life Cycle Assessment (LCA)—are discussed in more detail in Section 8.3.

So far, no consensus exists among researchers or users, although much work has been done. Moreover, the proponents of different assessment approaches

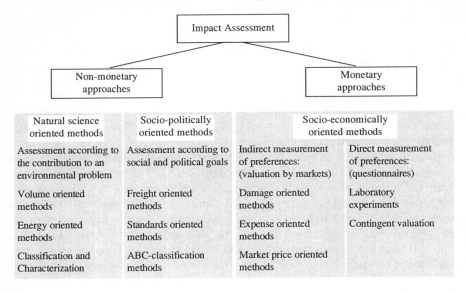

Figure 8.4 Categories of Impact Assessment Approaches. Source: Schaltegger *et al.* 1996

are competing vigorously. The competition is not merely scientific, because several groups are strongly lobbying regulators, environmental protection agencies as well as national and international organizations and opinion leaders. This is particularly obvious, for example, in a brochure from the Swiss Environmental Protection Agency where the concept of eco-scarcity has been published (BUWAL 1992); or in publications of SETAC Europe, where the CML method, see below, is supported. As a result of the lack of an acknowleged ecological accounting standard setting committee, no standards exist today only recommendations and guidelines.

Figure 8.4 surveys the main *categories of impact assessment approaches*. Many different published approaches deal with impact assessment and numerous variations are used in practice (for an overview see Schaltegger and Sturm 1994). The differences between the concepts are mainly because different scientists (sciences) ask different questions. When comparing various impact assessment methods it is therefore important to realize that they *provide answers to different questions*. In corporate ecological accounting and LCA non-monetary methods are usually applied, whereas socio-economic studies (e.g. on the external costs of traffic) commonly use monetary approaches.

A first *group* of assessment approaches covers the *non-monetary impact assessment* concepts. These methods can be distinguished in natural science oriented and socio-politically oriented methods. The former can be subdivided into energy and volume oriented as well as into classification/characterization approaches.

With the slogan "megatons instead of nanograms", scientists of the renowned Wuppertal Institute in Germany have recently proposed concentrating on the measurement of *volumes of material* and natural resources which are shifted for the production of one unit of good. The focus should not be on the measurement of smaller and smaller quantities of toxics but more on large material flows. They reason that every transport of material needs energy and has a negative influence on the environment and that therefore, above all, the volume should be reduced.

A majority of environmental impact studies shows that energy use is the main cause of most environmental interventions. Therefore, some scientists propose focusing on the measurement and reduction of energy use and energy losses (see, e.g. Frank and Ruppel 1976, Grittner 1978). *Energy oriented* methods do not focus on the measurement of energy carriers (oil, gas, electric power, etc.) but on the energy contents of material flows (Grittner 1978). The basis for this is the physical law of thermodynamics which has been applied to economic activities by Georgescu-Roegen (1971). The valence of energy is measured by energetic entropy. High energetic entropy means that the availability of energy is low. The law of thermodynamics says that entropy can only be increased, and never decreased. The target should therefore be to minimize the creation of entropy due to economic activities (Georgescu-Roegen 1971, Daly 1968, Rifkin 1985). Energy and volume oriented assessment concepts have not been applied widely, perhaps because they do not recognize toxicity or parallel, indirect, serial, social, political and economic aspects. In addition, energy oriented methods in particular require a great deal of scientific skill.

Classification and characterization methods attempt to answer the question of what has been contributed to a specific environmental problem (e.g. the greenhouse effect, depletion of the ozone layer, acidification, etc.) by an activity, product, site, etc. Classification and characterization methods consider indirect impacts concerning the respective environmental problem, but cannot take into account parallel or direct and indirect impacts in series. In particular, the classification and characterization concept of the Center for Milieukunde (CML) in Leiden, Netherlands, has attracted much attention. The following definition of impact assessment with three main steps has been proposed (see for example Udo de Haes and Hofstetter 1994, Schaltegger and Kubat 1994).

- *Impact assessment* is a quantitative and/or qualitative process to characterise and assess the effects of the environmental interventions identified in the inventory table. The impact assessment component consists in principle of the following three steps: classification, characterisation and valuation.

- *Classification* is the first step, within impact assessment, which identifies the impacts and, as far as possible, attributes the environmental interventions to a number of predefined *impact categories* (e.g. greenhouse effect). Environmental interventions contributing to more than one impact category are listed more than once.
- *Characterization* is the second step in which quantification (and eventually analysis and aggregation) of the impacts within the given impact categories takes place. This step results in effect scores (environmental indicators or environmental impact added indicators) of the *environmental impact added profile*.
- An *environmental indicator* (also environmental impact added indicator or effect score) is the aggregated contribution of environmental interventions to one impact category. The figure with the environmental indicators for all impact categories is called the environmenal profile.
- *Valuation* is the third step which weighs the effect scores of the environmental profile against one another in a quantitative and/or qualitative way as a basis for drawing conclusions. The valuation step can result in an *environmental impact added index*.

This structure of a general procedure for impact assessment is shown in Figure 8.5.

The result of classifying inventory data is *impact categories* (e.g. the category "greenhouse effect", or the category "depletion of the ozone layer").

The *characterization* of the grouped data leads to *environmental impact added indicators* (also effect scores) with one number for each environmental problem considered (e.g. the contribution to the greenhouse effect and the depletion of the ozone layer are measured with the indicators "greenhouse warmth contribution" and the "ozone depletion contribution" respectively). The 16 impact categories defined by CML (e.g. greenhouse effect, photochemical smog, etc.) and the respective characterization factors are listed in Heijungs *et al.* (1992). Mathematically, these indicators are calculated by multiplying the physical quantity of released environmental interventions (e.g. CO_2, CH_4, etc.) that have been classified in the same impact category (e.g. greenhouse effect) with weighting factors (e.g. 1 for CO_2, 11 for CH_4, factors taken from Heijungs *et al.* (1992) for a time frame of 100 years) that assess the relative contribution to the respective environmental problem (e.g. the contribution to the greenhouse effect measured in CO_2 equivalents).

The figure that integrates several environmental indicators is called an *environmental profile*.

So far, no approach for the (socio-political and economic) valuation of environmental profiles to calculate one single *environmental impact added index* has prevailed. The valuation methods that have been developed in the past do not rely on classification and characterization but only refer to an inventory of

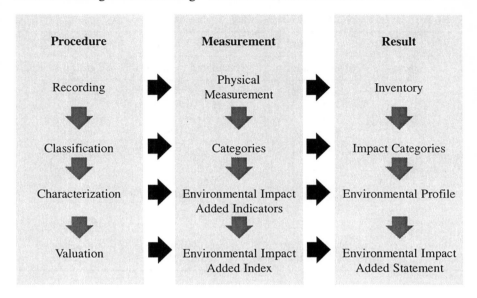

Figure 8.5 Impact Assessment Procedure

environmental interventions. Recently, however, many discussion papers have taken this as a topic and have proposed different approaches.[7]

Socio-politically oriented impact assessment concepts are another *group* of assessment approaches. These valuation methods attempt to weight environmental interventions according to politically determined targets (no classification or characterization takes place). General environmental goals (such as maintaining atmospheric balance) are broken down into specific objectives (such as reducing gases that contribute to the greenhouse effect by x%). These targets can, for example, be defined by regulators and governments as environmental standards (e.g. ambient concentration values) or as loads of interventions (e.g. loads of emitted pollutants). Mainly for company-internal reasons, goals can also be determined by management to carry out an ABC analysis.

Standards-oriented and loads-oriented approaches are among the first impact assessment concepts to have been developed (see, e.g., BUS 1984). The logic behind these methods is that managements of firms orientate themselves according to the priorities set by regulators or the government. The basic idea is to make explicit the relations between socio-political targets for various environmental interventions (e.g. ambient standards, or targets concerning

Table 8.6 Example of a Standards-Oriented Assessment Approach

	Standard Based Weighting Factors		
	Ambient Standard	Calculated in mg/mol	Weighting Factor
Air			
CO_2	579 mg/m^3	13.701272	1
CO	8 mg/m^3	0.189152	72
NO_x	0.03 mg/m^3	0.000709	19,316
Water			
Aluminum	0.1 mg/l	0.001803	7,599
Iron	1 mg/l	0.018031	760
Mercury	0.001 mg/l	0.000018	759,852
Landfill			
Aluminum	1 mg/l	0.018031	760
Cadmium	0.01 mg/l	0.000180	75,985
Tin	0.2 mg/l	0.003606	3,799

total loads). These targets represent the relative importance that is assigned to the respective interventions.

Table 8.6 gives an example of the methodical approach to the concept of quality standard relations (Schaltegger and Sturm 1992a).

The ambient standards of different pollutants are listed in milligrams per cubic meter in the second column. The standards presented here serve only for illustration. They are taken from regulations of the Swiss Environmental Protection Agency (for more details see Schaltegger and Sturm 1992a). In the third column milligrams of pollutant per mol—one mol of a substance is 6×10^{23} particles (molecules or atoms)—environmental media are used as a common unit of measurement (e.g. mg SO_2/mol air or mg mercury/mol water). Bringing the different units of measurement to a common denominator of one mol environmental media facilitates a comparison between the relations of standards in all environmental media. After converting the standards of each pollutant into the relation mg/mol, the second step is to make the ambient standard of one pollutant (e.g. CO_2 as leading substance) equal to one. The relations of all the other standards measured in mg/mol are then normed according to their relation to the leading pollutant CO_2. The result is a scale representing the relations between the ambient standards of all pollutants which permits a fairly comprehensive weighting method based on emissions primarily.

Socio-politically oriented approaches have attracted much attention in the past. To look at the prevailing legal obligations, and to follow the ongoing environmental debate in the public and legislative bodies closely, is one way to anticipate coming regulations. In this way possible liabilities can be anticipated. Though this might be a suboptimal environmental decision, it takes financial aspects into account. The company thereby moves on a socially accepted path.

However, socio-political assessment approaches are also very much questioned because they accept the political (non-scientific) nature of concentration-based or load-based standards. In addition, they carry the odium of political expediency (and not up-to-date regulations). They also reflect the weight given by regulators to different environmental media. The weighting scheme therefore varies between countries (Grimsted *et al.* 1994). Furthermore, standards-oriented assessment methods do not explicitly consider indirect, parallel or serial environmental impacts.

The approach of an *ABC analysis* (not to be confused with activity based accounting, ABC accounting) has been implemented in some very advanced firms, notably in Germany (see for example Hallay 1989, Lehmann 1990, Lehmann and Clausen 1991). The underlying assumption of an ABC analysis is that few (A-) interventions cause most of the impact (e.g. 20% of all activities or interventions cause 80% af all impacts) and that many (B-) and (C-) aspects or interventions contribute only little to the impacts. Figure 8.6 illustrates this approach.

The ABC analysis has only a limited operational area because management has a large discretionary latitude in the assessment procedure and there is no proof of having applied a high or "objective" standard. Furthermore, ABC methods do not explicitly consider indirect, parallel or serial environmental impacts. Nevertheless, this approach can be very valuable for internal purposes.

The *group* of *monetary impact assessment* concepts has evolved from socio-economic research and can be broadly split into direct and indirect methods of measuring people's preferences for environmental quality (for an overview see, for example, Botkin 1990, Hautau *et al.* 1987, Himelstein and Regan 1993, Staehelin-Witt 1993). The first group of concepts is based on market valuations of environmental damage, or on expenses and market prices of goods and services for protection against environmental interventions. The latter approaches attempt to measure the people's preferences directly by using laboratory experiments or contingent valuation methods. With two exceptions (Tellus, 1992 and Steen and Ryding, 1992) monetary approaches have not so far been applied for impact assessment and ecological accounting at the corporate level.

Damage oriented impact assessment methods measure the monetary loss due to environmental damage (e.g. loss of species) or the replacement value of environmental goods (e.g. a forest). They are economic ex-post measures which are mostly used to prove the severity of environmental interventions to politicians.

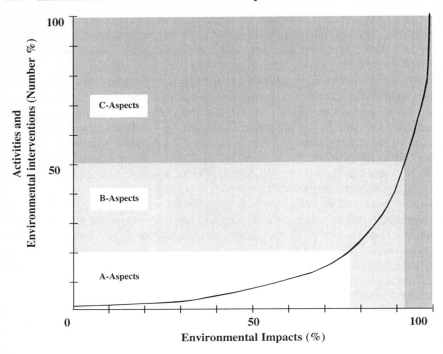

Figure 8.6 Underlying Assumption of the ABC Analysis

The *expense oriented* assessment method provides an answer to the question of what direct costs and opportunity costs people actually accept, or use to protect specific environmental assets (e.g. a lake).

The *market price method* asks what costs people will accept to repair (repair costs) or prevent environmental damage (prevention costs), or to protect themselves against environmental interventions (e.g. by buying noise protection devices, etc.).

People can also be asked about their preference for environmental quality. This can be done directly in an artificial *laboratory* situation or with *contingent valuation* approaches by asking in concrete situations when and where the activities or problems occur (for example see Hautau *et al.* 1987 and Schulz 1985).

The main underlying questions of socio-economic assessment methods are summarized in Box 8.1.

Monetary assessment methods (Box 8.1) do not explicitly take indirect, parallel or serial environmental impacts into account although they might

Box 8.1
Monetary Assessment Approaches

Expense	What costs do people accept to use or protect a specific environmental asset?
Willingness to pay	How much are people ready to pay for the reduction of a specific environmental problem?
Willingness to accept	How much has to be paid for people to be willing to accept a deterioration of environmental quality?
Prevention costs	How much money do people spend to protect themselves against environmental problems? How much are they ready to spend for prevention measures?
Damage costs	What are the (monetary) costs of environmental impacts for the society?

theoretically be considered in the "willingness-to-pay" or the "willingness-to-accept" of citizens.

Nonetheless, it can be assumed that time and spatial differences of environmental impacts are included in the valuation. All monetary assessment methods have to contend with the problem that the derived monetary values can hardly be linked to single environmental interventions. In comparison to non-monetary concepts the results are not disaggregated enough. However, it is possible to link them with non-monetary assessment approaches to derive monetary values for environmental interventions. This can be done by determining monetary values for specific environmental impact classes (e.g. the greenhouse effect). Then, the classification and characterization approach allows the relative contribution of different interventions (e.g. CO_2, methane, etc.) to be traced back to that environmental problem. In this way a monetarization of the impact of environmental interventions concerning specific environmental problems is possible (see Schaltegger *et al.* 1996). However, this scientific discussion has not so far manifested itself in corporate practice.

The distinction between the scientific, socio-political and socio-economic assessment concepts is based on the differences between the question pursued by the respective scientific disciplines. In this connection it is important to state that no assessment concept is generally superior to another weighting method, but that the various assessment concepts provide answers to different questions. This is why the choice of an assessment method should depend on the aim of analysis. Various methods should be employed if several questions are of interest.

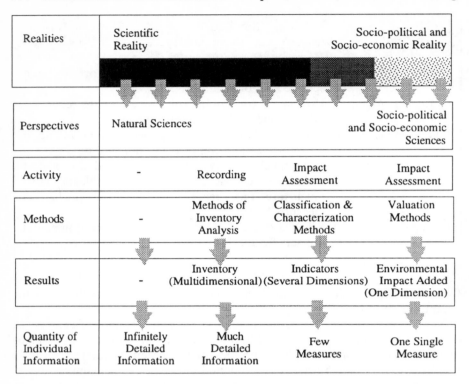

Realities	Scientific Reality			Socio-political and Socio-economic Reality
Perspectives	Natural Sciences			Socio-political and Socio-economic Sciences
Activity	-	Recording	Impact Assessment	Impact Assessment
Methods	-	Methods of Inventory Analysis	Classification & Characterization Methods	Valuation Methods
Results	-	Inventory (Multidimensional)	Indicators (Several Dimensions)	Environmental Impact Added (One Dimension)
Quantity of Individual Information	Infinitely Detailed Information	Much Detailed Information	Few Measures	One Single Measure

Figure 8.7 Environmental Impact Added Between Scientific Reality and Socio-Political or Socio-Economic Reality

Figure 8.7 shows the continuum from absolutely objective, experimentally provable scientific knowledge to the socio-political and socio-economic judgement of the environmental harmfulness of environmental impacts. The different steps of ecological accounting as well as the groups of assessment methods are plotted in the figure. At the right end of the spectrum is subjective information with high disagreement among individuals.

On the other hand, no assessment method can give an absolutely objective reflection of reality. As has been discussed in Section 8.2.1, subjective judgements have to be made even for the *recording* of environmental impacts (e.g. What environmental interventions are considered? All emissions of more than one gram, one milligram, one nanogram? What techniques of analysis are employed? Are the data measured, estimated, calculated, taken from literature? Are the measurements of average data, specific data, annual or monthly data? etc.).

The influence of social, political and economic aspects increases with every step towards the calculation of environmental impact added and with a further reduction of the number of measures.

The classification and characterization methods result in multi-dimensional environmental profiles (e.g. one value for the contribution to the greenhouse effect, one value for the contribution to photochemical smog, etc.), which are oriented towards scientific reality. On the other hand, the socio-political and socio-economic assessment methods better reflect the social, political and economic judgement of environmental problems.

The state of the art in impact assessment can be summarized as follows.

- No overall accepted standard for impact assessment exists. Many different concepts and research institutions compete with each other and new developments are continuously taking place. However, agreement may be reached that classification, characterization and valuation are the steps of the procedure of impact assessment. (This is a consensus of researchers at SETAC (Society of Environmental Toxicology and Chemistry); see, e.g., Udo de Haes and Hofstetter 1994.)
- It has to be stressed that today's weighting models are designed mostly for emissions. It must also be pointed out that the number of EIA units only represents one part of the environmental impacts, namely those resulting from pollution. Extinction of species, clearing virgin forests, soil erosion, etc. affect ecological integrity (Karr 1993), and represent a "devaluation" of ecological assets (number of species, size of forests, etc.). These ecological impacts are not included in the number of EIA units but may be represented in the eco-asset sheet. However, no weighting scheme for ecological assets exists so far.
- Regulators, and to a certain extent also traditional standardization organizations, have partially entered the arena of impact assessment.

The following conclusions can be drawn for firms.

- Of course, no impact assessment concept is perfect. Nevertheless, the fact that some approaches have a socio-political or socio-economic perspective must not be rejected as being non-scientific. Moreover, the user of an assessment concept must ensure that the method employed has been designed to answer the relevant question.
- The choice of an impact assessment method should be guided by the following questions.

  — What information is of interest for the firm (e.g. the contribution to specific environmental problems, or the socio-political preferences)?
  — Which approaches attempt to answer these questions best?
  — Which impact assessment approach is preferred by the communication partners (stakeholders)?

- Management ought to carry out a sensitivity analysis of the result to see how robust the derived information is and to make sure that the information is useful for decision taking.

8.2.4 Conclusions

This section discusses the main activitites of ecological accounting in a site-specific context. Internal ecological accounting allows environmental weaknesses to be detected. The entity-focused EIA carrier accounting and EIA center accounting discussed above create a necessary foundation for continuous ecological accounting. Site-specific accounting is also a basis for external ecological accounting. External accounting can also be enlarged by product-oriented accounting. With regard to longitudinal comparisons (over time) and for comparisons between sites as well as for external purposes, it is important that the same range of environmental interventions are taken. Also the data quality, the allocation rules and the assessment methods employed should not vary between the EIA statements.

No method of impact assessment matches the ideal of experimentally testable scientific information. Some concepts focus on natural scientific information whereas others stress socio-political or socio-economic information. However, no method considers differences in when and where environmental interventions occur. The development of assessment approaches is an ongoing process. Therefore, management ought to make a sensitivity analysis and consider several assessment approaches to provide answers to the relevant questions.

The next section deals with product-oriented ecological accounting which relates to EIA carrier accounting.

8.3 PRODUCT LIFE CYCLE ASSESSMENT (LCA)

We have seen in the last section that EIA carrier accounting is a helpful tool to ascertain what products have created most environmental impact added in a site or a firm. In addition, EIA carrier accounting is a good analytical tool for product management, management of technological innovations and for better allocation of environmentally induced costs to the cost carriers.

However, accounting has been heavily criticized as causing adverse environmental effects, due to accounting conventions which do not consider the principles of ecology (see also Section 3.2). One main critique addresses the "entity concept". Often, major environmental impacts (externalities) occur outside the boundaries of the company. However, the recognition of these "external effects" in the firm's accounting systems is in contrast to the current accounting philosophy and conventions. Therefore, several authors have called for a survey of all discharges over the whole life cycle of products (see for example Fava *et al.* 1991, Nordic Council of Ministers 1995). The Life Cycle Assessment (LCA) approach takes a broad view of the product life cycle and therefore largely corresponds with the philosophy of "deep greens" (see Maunders and Burritt 1991 or Gray 1992).

Despite having several issues in common, the concept of Life Cycle Assessment usually does not refer to accounting. A broad range of objects, such as infrastructure, processes or activities can be examined by using an LCA, but the most common application still focuses on products.

LCA corresponds to life cycle costing in traditional managerial accounting (Section 4.4), but the difference is that LCA calculates environmental impacts in physical terms, while life cycle costing attempts to measure the (financial) costs of a product during its whole life-time in monetary terms.

Today, the main motivation for firms to implement LCA are eco-labelling norms and regulations (see, e.g., EEC 1992) as well as the market success of some eco-labels (see for example Scientific Certification Systems 1992). The first eco-labelling schemes were devised in Germany (1978), Canada, Japan, Norway and Austria. In 1992 an eco-labelling regulation was passed in the EU (EEC 1992). LCA is mainly an issue for middle management, i.e. product and marketing managers. Nevertheless, division management—and in very rare cases also top management—may be involved in the assessment of the life cycle of important products which are of high public interest.

8.3.1 Evolution and Approach of LCA

Holistic thinking is often regarded as a must for assessing all environmental interventions of the whole life cycle of all products of a firm (Gray 1992, Gray *et al.* 1993). Therefore, the accounting boundaries need to be expanded. LCA tries to capture all environmental interventions, or the environmental impact added, caused by a product, process, service, etc. during its total life cycle, from "cradle to grave". Henn and Fava (1984, p. 548) use the term "cradle to cradle" to describe the ". . . rebirth, or reincarnation, of the resources being used for a subsequent product's life-time". Thus, LCA is a special case of ecological accounting. In addition to the environmental interventions ascertained by site-oriented internal ecological accounting, it is also necessary to consider data from suppliers, the suppliers of those suppliers, etc. as well as from customers, disposal firms, and so on.

Consequently, EIA carrier accounting would have to be enlarged by supplementing and connecting the site-specific data with data on the environmental impacts of the respective pre-life and post-life cycle steps outside the entity. Figure 8.8 illustrates the *environmental impact added life cycle chain* for a product during its life-time.

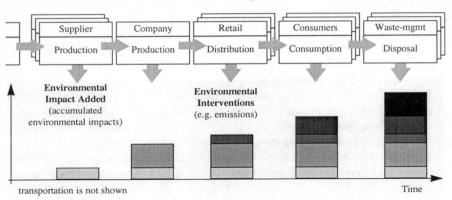

Figure 8.8 Environmental Impact Added Life Cycle. Source: Schaltegger and Sturm 1992a

The goal of LCA has been defined the following way: "The life-cycle assessment is an objective process to evaluate the environmental burdens associated with a product, process, or activity by identifying and quantifying energy and materials used and wastes released to the environment, to assess the impact of the energy and materials uses as well as the releases to the environment, and to evaluate and implement opportunities to affect environmental improvements. The assessment includes the entire life-cycle of the product, process, or activity, encompassing extraction and processing of raw material, manufacturing, transportation and distribution, use/re-use/ maintenance, recycling, and final disposal."; (SETAC 1991, p. 1).

The first attempts at developing Life Cycle Assessment (LCA) were in the 1960s and 1970s when studies calculated energy requirements or chemical inputs and outputs associated with various production processes, energy systems or packages (see for example Basler and Hoffmann 1974, EPA 1978 or Henn and Fava 1984). In the beginning, LCA stood for product life cycle *analysis*. Many other terms describing the idea of LCA have also been used: life cycle systems analysis, eco-balancing, eco-profiles, resource and environmental profile analysis (REPA), product life cycle assessment, etc. Today the expression "life cycle assessment (LCA)" is used for those approaches of product-oriented ecological accounting that attempt to consider all environmental interventions during the whole life cycle of products, services or infrastructure. By contrast, the term "life cycle analysis" covers a broad range of methods with economic, social, political and ecological tasks (see for example Henn and Fava 1984).

LCA has been a research topic for more than three decades. Many regulators (e.g. US EPA, the German UBA, the EU), national and international

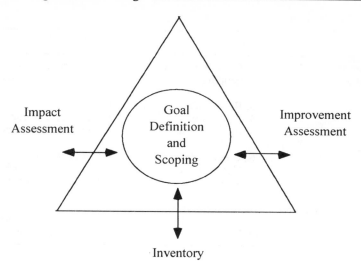

Figure 8.9 SETAC Framework of Life Cycle Assessment (LCA)

organizations (e.g. SETAC; the Nordic Council of Ministers) deal with LCA in one way or another. Even national and international standardization organizations have started to deal with LCA (e.g. ISO which has published a draft standard for the process of making an LCA, but not concerning the contents, assessment approaches, etc.; e.g. the standards ISO 14040ff, see ISO 1994b). The most active international research organization is the Society of Environmental Toxicology and Chemistry (SETAC), which has published a wide range of papers and guidelines concerning LCA.[8] The concepts which are published under the aegis of SETAC (traditionally, SETAC has dealt with questions of environmental chemistry and toxicology, but one section specifically covers LCA) are widely accepted as they often reflect a consensus of many LCA experts. Nevertheless, SETAC is strongly influenced by some scientists of the Center for Environmental Sciences of the University of Leiden, Netherlands (see, e.g., Heijungs *et al.* 1992).

Commonly the structure of LCA is shown in a triangle (see Figure 8.9) with inventory, impact assessment and improvement assessment at the sides and goal definition and scoping in the middle (SETAC 1991). The terms are explained in Table 8.7.

Discussions on impact assessment long dominated LCA research. In contrast, improvement analysis has not been thoroughly discussed in the context of LCA. This is unfortunate, for improvement assessment is a core activity in actually managing and reducing environmental impacts. (However, research in business administration has resulted in the development of various

Table 8.7 The Process of LCA

Stage	Step	Result
Goal Definition and Scoping	1. Goal definition 2. Scoping	Defined goals of analysis Defined system boundaries
Inventory	3. Recording 4. Allocation 5. Aggregation	Data sheets Detailed inventories Aggregated inventory
Impact Assessment	6. Classification 7. Characterization 8. Valuation	Impact categories Effect scores, eco-profile Effect score, eco-balance
Improvement Assessment	9. Interpretation 10. Prevention activities	Ecological weaknesses and potential for reduction Improved situation

helpful environmental management tools to assist managers to increase the eco-efficiency of their companies, see Part D). Currently, the focus has switched more to inventory analysis and the recording of data.

The triangle is a very popular way to summarize LCA as it symbolizes several aspects of the methods. For example, the bottom and the wide part of the triangle represent the inventory with highly detailed information. With the narrowing of the triangle the improvement assessment is based on less detailed information. However, in some cases, an improvement assessment can also be employed directly on the basis of the inventory without assessing impacts. This is why the side "improvement assessment" is not only shown as a subsequent phase of impact assessment but is also connected with the side "inventory". Goal definition and scoping are in the middle of the triangle as all stages of LCA must continuously be seen in the light of the goals and boundaries defined in the beginning.

The four main stages of LCA (see Box 8.2) can be further subdivided into steps and (intermediate) results as shown in Table 8.7.

In the way it is carried out today, LCA is a special case of ecological accounting. The general stages and steps of LCA are analogous to these of ecological accounting in general, with the differences that (a) the scope is over product life cycles and (b) that no explicit integration with traditional accounting and no integration into an environmental management system is yet planned.

Hence, the main accounting activities (definition of EIA centers, carriers and drivers, recording, allocation, aggregation and assessment) are the same as described for site-specific ecological accounting (Section 8.2). Nevertheless, some characteristic aspects of LCA, namely those concerning goal definition,

---

Box 8.2
Steps of LCA

Goal Definition and Scoping are activities that initiate an ". . . LCA, defining its purpose, boundaries and procedures. The scoping process links the goal of the LCA with the extent or scope of the study, i.e. the definition of what will or will not be included." (Udo de Haes and Hofstetter 1994)

The Life Cycle *Inventory* (LCI) is a technical, data-based process of quantifying energy and raw material requirements, air emissions, water-borne effluents, solid waste and other environmental releases throughout the life of a product, process, or activity.

Life Cycle *Impact Assessment* is a technical, quantitative and/or qualitative process of characterizing and assessing the effects of the resource requirements and the environmental loading identified in the inventory component. Ideally, the assessment should address ecological impacts, human health impacts and resource depletion, as well as other effects such as habitat modification and noise pollution.

Life Cycle *Improvement Analysis* is a systematic evaluation of the needs and opportunities to reduce the environmental burden associated with energy, use of raw materials and waste emissions throughout the whole life cycle of a product, process, or activity. This analysis may include both quantitative and qualitative measures of improvement, such as changes in product design, raw material use, industrial processing, etc.

(Sources: Battelle 1993; Udo de Haes and Hofstetter 1994; Schaltegger and Kubat 1994; SETAC 1991).

---

inventory data and consolidation of data, still remain to be examined. The integration of ecological accounting into environmental management is discussed in Part D.

8.3.2 Special Characteristics and Present Approach of LCA

In contrast to the ecological accounting concepts discussed so far, the LCA approach is not designed for continuous accounting but rather to carry out a single ecological investigation of a product. Today's LCA practice can be regarded as making *ecological one-time single case calculations* of the environmental impacts of a product. Special characteristics of the present approach of LCA are goal definition and scoping as well as the collection and use of background inventory data. These characteristics distinguish LCA from other approaches of ecological accounting. Issues in common with site-specific ecological accounting, such as impact assessment, are discussed in Section 8.2.

a)   Goal Definition and Scoping

The first step in every LCA is goal definition and scoping. These are extremely important, but are often neglected when carrying out an LCA. Goal definition includes the clarification of the object (e.g. product or process) to be examined and which time period it should cover. The *definition of the object of investigation* includes first of all the description of the object (e.g. coloring pigment Y). Here it is also important to describe why this object, and not another one, has been selected for examination. By choosing one item for examination and leaving others out, a qualitative judgement has already been made. Priority objects should include those that provide the greatest opportunity for reducing waste, and that are considered to have very adverse effects on the environment.

An *analysis of the time dimension* then has to be made because products have varying life times with different effects on the environment.

In order to define the functional efficiency (see Section 7.3) it must be established which function is to be fulfilled and what is to be understood by a *functional unit* (e.g. red dyeing of one m^2 of textile.)

The fourth step contains the definition of the *system boundaries* of the object investigated. For an LCA all the pre-steps and post-steps are to be listed. Boundary problems especially arise when ecological product investigations are made in an attempt to record the environmental impact added of many, and ideally "all", steps of a product life cycle. When setting the boundaries by excluding important pre-steps or post-steps in a product LCA, considerable distortion of the results may have to be taken into account. This especially applies when pre-steps dealing with the generation of electric power are excluded. On the other hand, the inclusion of several connected but actually independent environmental impacts forms a never ending "environmental impact added conglomeration" and should be avoided. In this context it may be asked whether the environmental impacts of the production of plant and manufacturing buildings should be assigned to a product. In the extreme case the whole world could be included. (For example, the extraction of raw material requires a certain machine whose parts have to be produced, as well as the building in which it was manufactured, etc.) Additionally, the problem can arise that a defined product (e.g. paint) has been used for its own production (e.g. the paint on the machine which extracts raw materials for the production of that paint). A further boundary placing problem arises for products which are jointly produced or combined (e.g. chlorine is a by-product of the production of sodium hydroxide and used for products of the chlorine industry such as PVC or CFCs). The question of how many pre-steps should ideally be included has not yet been definitely answered.

Apart from a few proposals—see for example Büchel (1996), Schaltegger and Sturm (1992a, 1994), SETAC (1991)—no standards exist to determine where the examination boundaries of the product life cycle assessment should be drawn. Also, LCA practices vary substantially. Therefore, the comparability of different analyses is rarely given. The following list shows *possible criteria* defining the system boundaries of an LCA (Schaltegger and Sturm 1992a, 1994).

- The consideration of further preliminary steps is not necessary when a raw material is extracted from the natural environment.
- When several products are manufactured in the same process (e.g. sodium hydroxide and chlorine) then only those products manufactured with the intention of creating an input of the product investigated (e.g. CFCs, PVC for sodium hydroxide) should be taken into account. The distinction between a product and a by-product is that a product has an unsubsidized market price.
- When continually including preliminary steps, the boundaries of a system can be defined as where the direction and control of effluents by human beings cease. This is the case when an output is discharged into the natural environment.
- When a connected product or remaining material finds a buyer, it represents a valuable material for other economic players and therefore achieves a market price.
- If, for the production of a specific product, additional environmental impact added is created through the production, operation or disposal of installations, machines and buildings, this does not have to be taken into consideration if the difference of environmental impact added for production and disposal between two installations is minimal. This means that the use of different installations has no great influence on the total environmental impact added of a product.
- A specific production step may only be excluded if the step is negligible, or if the effects of the step on a comparable object not considered are the same.

In practice, the following procedures depend on management's possibilities of influence.

- First: boundary placement in the in-house calculations.
- Second: inclusion of post-steps.
- Third: inclusion of the preliminary steps to extend an LCA over the environmental impact added chain.

It has commonly been stated that relying on the first two steps may lead to suboptimization (see e.g. Gray *et al.* 1993, p. 167). Some even argue that truly valid statements can only be made if an ecological account contains all product life cycle steps (for example Fava *et al.* 1991). In this connection, process calculations form the starting point of every ecological account (see also Figure 7.4, Section 7.6).

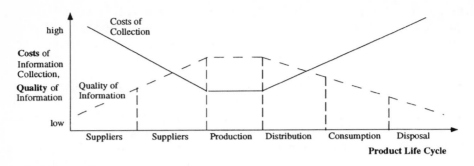

Figure 8.10 Costs of Collection and Quality of Information in LCA

It must be carefully borne in mind that only sufficiently defined objects (same boundaries and life cycle steps) permit valid comparisons.

Finally, the value of a completed LCA can be seen in the transparent presentation of the boundary criteria as well as in all considered, and especially non-considered, pre-steps and post steps.

b) Collection and Use of Background Inventory Data

For a comprehensive LCA all data concerning the environmental interventions induced by a specific product in an environmental impact added chain must be collected. However, with the increasing "distance" to the firm the collection of data becomes more difficult and costly (Figure 8.10). Thus, a comprehensive LCA is extremely time consuming and expensive to conduct. An extensive product life cycle analysis for the whole life of the product components can be undertaken only in isolated cases, for example when products attract society-wide notoriety as did styrofoam cups or milk-packaging.

In addition, compared with internal surveys, the quality of the computed data decreases dramatically with the declining influence of the firm on distant life cycle steps. In practice, it is not rewarding enough and far too inefficient for one firm to collect all the product-specific data of its suppliers, customers, etc. The fact that the benefits of "remote" data are small (low quality and low representativeness), and that the costs of collection are exorbitantly high, were reasons enough for various companies to refrain from conducting LCAs after their first experiences. It was mostly small and medium sized firms that discontinued LCA. Among the companies still experimenting with LCA is Procter and Gamble. This firm was among the first to carry out an LCA, comparing disposable nappies with traditional towelling diapers (for more examples see Gray *et al.* 1993, p. 171ff., Schaltegger *et al.* 1996).

To overcome the problem of the high costs of collecting information on distant life cycle steps, several institutions have started to publish data with average environmental interventions for the manufacturing and disposal of basic materials and products. The collected, so-called *background inventory data* (also called basic inventory data or service data) mostly represent the average environmental interventions which are related to the respective material (e.g. kg of CO_2 to supply 1 kg of PVC). Their public availability allows small and medium sized businesses to carry out LCAs, and ensures that most LCA applications are based on the same or similar data for inputs and waste of pre-steps (e.g. resources, materials, semi-manufactured goods) and post-steps (e.g. waste water in publicly owned treatment plants). In fact the costs of carrying out an LCA have declined with the improved availability of background inventory data. The use of background inventory data is therefore enjoying increasing popularity.

The best known examples of such "background inventory data bases" are for packaging materials (see, e.g., BUS 1984, BUWAL 1991), plastics (PWMI 1992), and energy systems (e.g. generation of electric power, extraction and precombustion of coal, etc., see, for example, ESU 1994, Fritsche *et al.* 1989).

At first sight the demand for an assessment of all environmental impacts of the whole life cycle of all products of a firm seems to make very good sense. But when the practicability of this demand is considered, LCA in its present state of practice and development proves to be an inefficient approach to curbing environmental impacts. This is so even if the process of conducting an LCA is seen to be more important than the arithmetic result of the LCA.

8.3.3 Inefficiency of the Present Approach of LCA

LCA can be useful if used as a general tool for strategic management. However, when used *as an accounting tool*, the present method of LCA of products, and especially the use of background inventory data, are confronted with major flaws which drastically impair the ecological efficacy and the economic efficiency of the approach.

- *Ecologically,* the information provided with LCA may result in wrong decisions, first because inventory data lack representativity, relevance and precision, and second because consolidation (aggregation) of environmental intervention data usually ignores spatial and time differences.
- *Economically,* the present approach of LCA causes perverse incentives for the stakeholders involved, as well as high costs for the firm to potentially create a small hypothetical benefit.

A *first* major drawback of LCA is the *lack of representativeness, relevance and precision of data collected* which are often connected with the use of background inventory data. As shown in Figure 8.10, many errors, uncertainties and lack of precision of inventory data increase with the distance from the information collector (the firm). With the collection and use of background inventory data this gets even worse. As the epoch-making work of Johnson and Kaplan (1987a, b) has shown for management accounting, the relevance of information is no longer assured when data is *outdated*, widely aggregated and distorted (average data instead of specific data).

The industry average represented in background inventory data hides the highs and lows of especially good and bad manufacturers. One reason why practitioners and scientists are increasingly apt to forget about the constant small differences and changes which make up most of the environmental degradation, is probably their growing preoccupation with statistical aggregates. These show a much greater stability than the movements in different places and periods. The statistics with background inventory data which are centrally collected are (and have to be) arrived at precisely by abstracting from minor (but crucial) differences. Environmental interventions, which, for example, differ in place or time of occurrence, are lumped together as figures of one kind, although their local and time-specific environmental impact may be very significant for many decisions.

It has even been acknowledged in the LCA community that the calculated data are of disputable quality (Fava *et al.* 1992). The consequence is that the "... total error of an LCA can easily become larger than the calculated differences of ecological impacts of products and services." (Pohl *et al.* in Schaltegger (Ed.) 1996, p. 13).

LCA is of value for decision makers only if the information has been externally audited in accordance with generally accepted, standardized procedures. So far, such procedures have only been standardized for the environmental management of sites and firms.

Second, today's LCA practices suggest the *consolidation (aggregation) of environmental interventions at various points of time and with different spatial impacts.* However, aggregated figures of local emissions do not provide valuable information as they tell nothing about potential or even actual environmental impacts. One kilogram of mercury emitted in one hour at one place may kill many people, but the same amount emitted over a year at a hundred places may be without any appreciable impact. The LCA inventory shows aggregated data of interventions with local impacts at very different places. "What environmental significance can be attributed to an LCA inventory total of 30 tonnes of COD, made up of 10 tonnes discharged in Australia, 15 tonnes discharged in Holland and 5 tonnes discharged in Mexico?" (Perriman 1995, p. 4). Hence, the sum of these local interventions has little meaning. Only global interventions can meaningfully be aggregated on a global level (Müller *et al.* 1994).

The same is true with the current methods of *impact assessment*. The various product-related production, consumption and disposal activities in an environmental impact added chain occur at different times and are spread over different places. Therefore, the respective environmental interventions impact different habitats which are characterized by distinct ecological absorption capacities, etc.

Most concepts for impact assessment completely fail to consider local circumstances and habitats although they have a spatial dimension. The assessment approaches either rely on national environmental targets (socio-political methods) or economically and culturally inclined budgets (socio-economic approaches), or they relate to the spatial dimension of specific environmental problems (classification and characterization).

In conclusion, from an ecological perspective LCA is of little use as it does not provide information on actual (or potential) but rather on hypothetical environmental impacts.

Third, the data collector depends on the information provided by different firms of the respective industry. From an economic perspective, background inventory data suppress initiatives to be an industry leader. Likewise, advanced manufacturers are punished for being members of a "dirty industry" whereas the laggards benefit as freeriders of the advanced firms in the same industry.

Moreover, the only inherent incentive given by background inventory data is for the industry to hand out biased or at least favorable (and at all events unchecked) inventory data. The suppliers of data have—without cheating—a large discretionary latitude as to what data they specifically want to pass on. Possibilities include annual, monthly or hourly average data; calculated or measured data; average data of several production processes or of the best production process; data under ideal production conditions, etc. The quality of the estimated and calculated data, as well as the quality of the data received from different firms, naturally varies substantially. Thus, the derived industry average is an artificial figure without any meaning.

Furthermore, the published data represent an industry average. Hence, the users of background inventory data and the purchasers of raw materials cannot distinguish suppliers by their environmental performance. However, "dirty" suppliers of a "clean" material often pollute more than "clean" suppliers of a "dirty" substitute material. Thus, the choice of a supplier is sometimes environmentally more relevant than the choice of an input such as a raw material or a semi-manufactured product (Pohl *et al.* 1995, p. 11).

Fourth, even if the quality of the information provided by industry were standardized and regulated, building-up and maintaining such inventory databases would still cause high *costs.* The basic concept underlying the current LCA-development *must fail because the organizational approach is too centralistic.* The attempt to collect background inventory information through one central authority on various steps of a life cycle and on different firms of the same industry (and therefore from many different economic actors with conflicting goals) causes extremely high collection costs. This is also reflected in the need for ever larger computer systems to handle inventory data. Due to technological development and continuous changes of production equipment, background inventory data must be regularly updated. Today, the respective costs are mostly borne by public institutions, i.e. the taxpayers, which is contrary to the "polluter pays" principle.

Several other problems—without completing the list—show that today's LCA practices and developments prove to be immature as they cannot help to effectively curb environmental impacts in practice.

- LCA is regarded as a typical interdisciplinary field of research. This has led to an increasing specialization of the researchers involved and of the topics dealt with in LCA. Increased specialization has also resulted in a methodological procedure which is packed with many additional conceptual steps (characterization, classification, normalization, etc.). For practitioners this development has not only improved but also complicated LCA enormously.
- The constant change of methods creates inconsistencies and uncertainties among practitioners. This is characteristic of tools in the process of development. Nonetheless, these inconsistencies mostly impede comparisons between products as well as over a given period.
- The increasing number of details treated augments the costs of application.
- LCA is currently limited in that its ecological calculations are based on single samples (that are rarely, if ever, resampled in subsequent periods) from a small group of products and businesses. So far, all methods of life cycle assessment are only able to give a static image of a "hypothetically possible, potential situation". No continuous LCA accounting similar to financial accounting is usually applied. However, for continuous environmental improvement continuous ecological accounting is necessary.

Concluding, today, product life cycle assessment is only able to give an image of "hypothetically potential" environmental impacts of a limited number of products. Background inventory data reduce costs of data collection to individual users but result in an even higher loss of representativeness, accuracy and relevance of the information provided.

By contrast, continuous environmental improvement requires continuous ecological accounting with relevant and representative information.

The LCA community has responded to the presented critique with a somewhat semantic distinction between a "threshold approach" and an "equivalency approach". The former only considers those processes of a life cycle which "lead to a surpassing of environmental thresholds" at the respective locations (White *et al.* 1995). The latter adheres to a "general prevention principle" adding all environmental interventions, no matter what impact they cause. However, neither this distinction nor one of these approaches reduces the validity of the criticism that the aggregation of interventions with local impacts which occur at different places does not provide accurate or representative information.

8.3.4 Site-Specific LCA

As mentioned before, the usefulness of data to external users of information can only be guaranteed with external auditing of site-specific information in accordance with international standards. The economic problem in general, as well as that of environmental protection, is ". . . how to secure the best use of resources known to any of the members of society, for ends whose relative importance only these individuals know. Or to put it briefly, it is a problem of utilization of knowledge which is not given to anyone in its totality." (Hayek 1945, p. 520).

Economically, it is obviously wiser to encourage economic actors to *collect the necessary data individually* than to promote the central collection of LCA data, including background inventory data. This means that every firm should concentrate on the accounting of those environmental interventions that can be measured fairly accurately: the site-specific environmental interventions of one's own firm. This allows the use of the established information channels of every organization, which are in any case more efficient than centrally planned collection of information. Furthermore, this results in higher quality and accuracy of data as well as in better representativeness of the actual situation. Likewise, tools which are compatible with established methods of accounting and management can be applied.

In order to collect *product-specific information*, incentives should be given for industry, retail trade, etc. to maintain the specific product information that has already been recorded and audited separately for each maufacturing and warehousing unit. From an economic point of view, the firms should be able to organize themselves to collect the necessary data to aquire a "green" product label. The concept of *site-specific LCA* is to compile an LCA with site-specific data on the life cycle steps of a product (Figure 8.11). All data have to be specifically collected, recorded and audited at each site and in every firm.

This is in complete contrast to a central collection of data. Also, no background data would have to be provided any more. The data used for decision making are specific, representative, collected individually, and usually have a consistent, verified standard of quality. Product-oriented accounting can only prevail if industry is given clear standards and a more active role, so that it can put its enterpreneurial power into action.

To encourage this development, governments must establish strong incentives for audited, site-specific ecological accounting, and firms must establish cooperation between suppliers, producers and customers (strategic environmental alliances) for the independent gathering of audited site-specific data of various steps of a product life cycle. Only standardized site-specific data

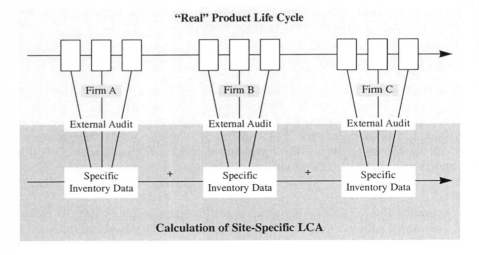

Figure 8.11   Collection of Data for a Site-Specific LCA

can be compared over time and between firms. Therefore, standardization organizations and/or governments have to define clear standards of site-specific ecological accounting (see Chapter 9). EMAS, BS 7750 and the draft of ISO 14001 are first steps in this direction. This also enables the data to be made easily verifiable and useful for external stakeholders. Hence, the information collected inside the firm could also be used for external purposes.

Also today, background inventory data are provided by industry, but the differences are that the calculated background inventory data are not representative (but an obscure industry average), that the data are not audited and that nobody really knows how the data were derived (no guarantee of consistent data quality).

If firm-specific and site-specific ecological accounting were standardized and audited the data could be passed on as product information from one company to the next. Thus, the ecological accounting of a firm would facilitate product-oriented accounting for subsequent firms in the product life cycle chain.

The next section deals with ecological investment appraisal to calculate the ecological improvements and impacts of capital investments, including measures to prevent pollution.

8.4   ECOLOGICAL INVESTMENT APPRAISAL

Methods of ecological investment appraisal have been employed for years to calculate the net ecological impact of investments for pollution prevention.

Some investments, such as clean-up facilities or pollution prevention devices, etc. are made exclusively for ecological purposes. However, not all environmental measures are effective, and some are more effective than others. Ecological investment appraisal sets out to determine whether, and if so by how much, the environmental impact can be reduced through a project.

In contrast to financial investment appraisals, future ecological reductions of investments are not discounted. Discounting would be contrary to the actual purpose of environmental protection, namely to reduce future environmental impacts and not solely to improve the present situation. Discounting reflects the inferior valuation of future benefits. The value of reducing environmental impacts is based on the actual state of the natural environment. However, if the environmental quality is worse in the future the value of reduction will be higher then than now. Two values must be taken into account when considering environmental impacts, namely the environmental impact added:

- caused by production, operation, maintainance and disposal
- reduced by the technology. This value can be subtracted from the value describing the EIA caused by the device.

Two main methods or key numbers for ecological investment appraisal are the:

- Ecological Payback Period (EPP)
- Ecological Rate of Return (ERR).

The Ecological Payback Period (EPP) measures how long it takes to reduce the environmental impacts caused by the investment. It calculates the relation between the environmental impacts caused by the technology, and the annual reductions in impacts that result from it. This key figure is especially interesting for *pollution prevention devices*. The ecological payback method does not suffer from the inherent weaknesses of the traditional financial payback method as no discounting is applied.

$$EPP = \frac{\text{EIA caused with the investment}}{\text{Annual reduction of EIA through investment}}$$

(EPP = Ecological Payback Period, EIA = Environmental Impact Added)

The investment is environmentally beneficial if the life-span of the investment is larger than the EPP.

Theoretically, all environmental impacts should be considered. However, in practice the EPP method has usually been calculated only for some of the substances affected by the investment (e.g. for CO_2 or water) or for energy (see for example Feist 1986, pp. 1ff. Fritsche *et al.* 1989, pp. 233ff, Spreng 1988a, pp. 41ff, Sutter and Hofstetter 1989).

The method of the Ecological Rate of Return (ERR) has also been applied for some years, especially for pollution prevention devices (see for example

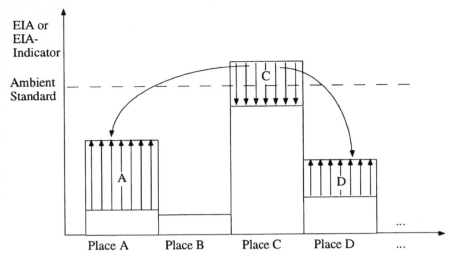

Figure 8.12 Ecologically Effective Clean-Up Measure with Negative ERR

ASVS 1990, p. 24). The ERR measures if the environmental impact added (EIA) has been reduced through the investment and, if this is the case, by how much. The ERR is a relation of:

$$\text{ERR} = \frac{\text{EIA reduced over the total time of the investment}}{\text{EIA caused with the investment}}$$

(ERR = Ecological Rate of Return, EIA = Environmental Impact Added)

Investments are ecologically efficient if the ratio is larger than one, and inefficient if it is smaller (for ecological efficiency see Section 7.3). The larger the ratio, the better the investment from the ecological viewpoint. Pollution prevention investments must have a positive ERR to be ecologically efficient. In the case where an investment does not reduce environmental impacts, the numerator and thus the whole equation is negative.

Seen from a global viewpoint, end-of-the-pipe technologies surprisingly often prove to be ecologically ineffective ($=$ ERR > -1). This means that the overall reduction in EIA they achieve is smaller than the EIA which they cause. Despite this fact, such investments are still made, mostly for regulatory reasons. However, such end-of-the-pipe investments can still make sense as the environmental interventions of the production and disposal of the devices occur at a different place from the reduction. For instance, in Figure 8.12, environmental impact added is reduced with a scrubber by the amount C at place C. The increased use of electric power which is generated at place A as well as the additional filter dust which is disposed of at place D cause more environmental impact added than the reduction achieved at place C ($C < A + D$). It may very well make sense to reduce environmental impacts to prevent threshold levels from being exceeded in certain, highly polluted areas, even if more EIA is caused in cleaner regions.

Figure 8.12 illustrates the reduction of the environmental impact added in a "hot spot" (i.e. highly polluted area) so that the ambient air quality falls under the threshold level (i.e. ambient air quality standard). The increase of pollution at the places of production and disposal (places A and D) is higher than the reduction of EIA at place C, but less problematic, when compared with the ambient goal. Situations with environmental clean-up activities that are ineffective from an overall viewpoint ($= ERR > -1$) but nevertheless effective considering the specific spatial circumstances (below the ambient standard) mainly occur for clean-up facilities in highly polluted industrial regions. Even then, however, it is desirable to find ecologically effective pollution prevention measures.

8.5 FROM INTERNAL TO EXTERNAL ECOLOGICAL ACCOUNTING

Chapter 8 has shown the structure and the principles of internal ecological accounting. Internal ecological accounting provides information for different internal stakeholders such as product, production, site, division and top management. It has also been shown that the concept of the balance-sheet cannot be applied consistently to ecological accounting. However, eco-asset sheets may be helpful for firms which directly impact ecological assets (e.g. mining, logging, etc.). Today's ecological accounting approaches focus mainly on emissions such as discharges of toxics. The costs related to these environmental interventions have been growing over the last decades whereas the costs of information technologies have decreased. Therefore, a systematic and cost-efficient system for the continuous accounting of environmental impact added is needed. As the current approaches of product life cycle assessment have often proved to be ineffective and inefficient, managers should focus, first of all, on site-specific accounting, which distinguishes EIA carriers, centers and drivers.

For time comparisons and for comparisons between entities, some standardization of the accounting method is necessary. For effective communication to external stakeholders, internal ecological accounting information has to be prepared in a transparent manner in line with generally accepted standards. This is why in Chapter 9, first, the basic conventions of accounting as defined by the International Accounting Standardization

Committee (IASC) are examined and basic assumptions and conventions of ecological accounting are defined.

For external ecological accounting, firms can refer to these conventions to increase the reliability, comparability and transparency of their environmental reports.

9
External Ecological Accounting

This chapter deals with ecological accounting and reporting for external purposes. After a short introduction, basic assumptions and qualitative characteristics of ecological accounting are discussed on the basis of the principles used in traditional financial accounting (Section 9.2). Section 9.3 deals with the consolidation of ecological data. The chapter ends with a summary (Section 9.4). How stakeholders react to the reporting of environmental impact added is a subject of discussion between management and academics. However, there is no question that ecological reporting has major potential influences on various important stakeholders including capital markets.

Thus, environmental information has become part of marketing and public relations for many firms. However, dubious claims and improper use of information by some firms in the past have diminished the reputational gains and therefore reduced some incentives for other firms to improve the environmental record. To increase marketing and reputational gains actual environmental leaders must be clearly distinguished from firms concentrating on "window-dressing". Environmental information is trustworthy to readers and comparable between firms only when widely accepted international standards of ecological accounting are established.

9.1 INTRODUCTION

External stakeholders put increasing pressure on firms in order to enhance the transparency of companies and to receive more information about the environmental impact added of business. Firms can only be successful if management is able to secure a continuous supply of material and non-material resources from crucial stakeholders such as suppliers, employees, investors, banks, etc. These stakeholders are only willing to exchange their resources as long as they consider the performance of the firm to be good (Freeman 1984). For most stakeholders the environmental performance is part of the overall corporate performance—and for some interest groups and individuals it is even the most important aspect. Therefore, the stakeholders ask for appropriate information for their assessment. Hence, management is challenged to report not only intentional policies, but actually to disclose environmental performance and achievements, including possible shortcomings. Powerful stakeholders, such as some environmental protection agencies, are able to require and enforce ecological accounting systems specially designed for their purposes (Chapter 11). Other stakeholders, such as the general public or environmental pressure groups, are only able to increase the attractiveness of external reporting (or to make the lack of environmental reporting a problem for the firm).

Managements of firms are sometimes still reluctant to communicate information about their environmental performance because they want to prevent regulatory bodies and environmental pressure groups from using the respective information against them. In addition, with improper use of environmental information by some firms in the past, the potential gains of environmental reporting decreased. However, this reluctance to publicly report is regarded with suspicion by many stakeholders and can often initiate especially strong reactions. For example, some firms may be thoroughly scrutinized by any kind of regulatory bodies, pressure groups, media, potential customers, etc. The development of regulation in the European Union, for example, shows a strong tendency to increase requirements for external ecological accounting and reporting.

Nevertheless, in Europe none of the professional accounting organizations or standard setting organizations is active in ecological accounting. (At least ". . . not much of real substance is taking place" to establish conventions of external ecological accounting (Gray 1994, p 285)).

Companies can, of course, use various means to communicate their environmental goals, efforts and performances. It is not intended here to cover conventional communication and marketing efforts or to deal with eco-marketing, but rather to focus on ecological reporting in the narrower sense of publishing *reports for accountability*. However, complementary aspects of communication are also mentioned.

The history of environmental reporting is young. The first reports were published in the 1980s (see for example Owen 1992). In the beginning, costs of environmental protection were the main issue. In the late 1980s LCAs of selected products and the first reports of discharges at some production sites were published. More comprehensive environmental reports, covering all businesses of a firm, have evolved only recently. However, so far the quality and information contents of environmental reports vary strongly. This is even true with special environmental reports for regulatory agencies such as the US Toxic Release Inventory (TRI). For further development and to increase the usefulness of environmental reports, some commonly accepted standards of external ecological reporting are needed.

With the existing methods of internal ecological accounting, management is able to analyse the origin (centers), the carriers and the drivers of environmental impact added. Recording, allocation and impact assessment are procedures that are also part of external ecological accounting. Today, allocation is often less of an issue in external ecological accounting than in product-oriented internal accounting. This is because external ecological accounting in most cases centers on a business and firm, or has a spatial focus. However, sometimes external stakeholders also request information on key products. More detailed information is also likely to be required to acquire green product labels.

The accounting technique is developed and implemented in many firms with the aim of communicating site-oriented information. However, this is not sufficient for external reporting. For external stakeholders, information of environmental impacts of firms is only useful if they know that the information is recorded in accordance with some basic conventions. In financial accounting, international conventions concerning the underlying assumptions and the qualitative characteristics of published data have been defined. These conventions have proved to be beneficial for users and providers. It therefore makes sense to discuss whether they could be applied to external ecological accounting.

The next section discusses the traditional conventions of accounting with regard to their applicability for external ecological accounting. After having developed conventions of ecological accounting and reporting, Section 9.3 deals with the most important question which has to be answered when establishing corporate reporting of environmental impact added.

9.2 CONVENTIONS OF ECOLOGICAL ACCOUNTING

Standardization can only take place if it is possible to develop a method of external ecological accounting which is genuinely accepted. Due to standardization a widespread application can be achieved as well as a comparison of ecological data between products, companies, etc. Only then are these data apt to influence market decisions of investors, clients, commerce, producers and suppliers.

In traditional financial accounting, certain fundamental qualitative accounting assumptions underlie the preparation of financial statements. They are usually not specifically stated because their acceptance and use are assumed. These are attributes that make the information provided in financial statements helpful to users (IASC 1993, p. 61). This is why in the next two sections these conventions relating to assumptions (9.2.1) and qualitative characteristics

---

Box 9.1
Conventions of External Ecological Accounting

Underlying assumptions

- Accrual
- Going concern

Qualitative characteristics

- Understandability
- Relevance
- Reliability
- Comparability

(9.2.2) are examined with regard to their applicability to ecological accounting (Box 9.1, see also Figure 5.4).

Ideally, external—traditional as well as ecological—accounting information ought to rely on internal accounting information. However, for efficiency reasons, the structure and contents of internal accounting must consider the conventions of financial accounting. Therefore, the development of conventions of external ecological accounting is crucial for the effectiveness of ecological accounting as a whole.

9.2.1 Underlying Assumptions of Ecological Accounting

In financial accounting, two important underlying assumptions can be distinguished according to the International Accounting Standards Committee (IASC):

- accrual
- going concern.

On the basis of *accrual*, ". . . the effects of transactions and other events are recognised when they occur (and not as cash or its equivalent is received or paid) and they are recorded in the accounting records and reported in the financial statements of the periods to which they relate." (IASC 1994, p. 41). The purpose of the accruals convention is that users of financial statements are informed not only of past transactions but also of future obligations (outflow) and resources (inflow). Future influences of past transactions are thus considered now.

Adopting the assumption of accrual in ecological accounting means that potential environmental impacts from an activity should not be recorded when the physical impact actually is *taking place* but rather when it *occurs* (when it is created). The accrual basis ensures that users of ecological statements are not only informed of past impacts on the environment, but also of future liabilities to the environment which will arise from past activities. Hence, the statements provide the type of information on past activities and other events that is most useful to users in making ecological decisions.[9]

"The financial statements are normally prepared on the assumption that an enterprise is a going concern and will continue in operation for the foreseeable future." (IASC 1994, p. 41). The expectation that a firm is a *going concern* implies that the organization has ". . . neither the intention nor the need to liquidate or curtail materially the scale of its operations . . ." (IASC 1994, p. 41). In the case where a substantial decrease of operations is expected, the financial reports should be prepared on a different basis, which will also have to be disclosed.

An application of the going concern basis means that the ecological statements should normally be prepared on the assumption that an enterprise will continue in operation for the foreseeable future, having neither the intention nor the necessity to increase materially the scale of its environmental impacts. If such an intention or necessity exists, the ecological statements may have to be prepared on a different basis and, if so, the basis used must be disclosed. A possible interpretation of this could be that a company must prepare its ecological statements on a different basis whenever an increase of its environmental impact might substantially change its influence on the environmental quality (eco-system).

For users of ecological statements both assumptions, accrual and going concern, are important. They imply that the potential environmental impacts taking place in the future are also important.

From a preventive viewpoint, ecologically interested stakeholders want to be informed about potential environmental impacts when they occur and not only when the interventions actually happen (accrual). The importance attached not only to current environmental interventions, but also to future interventions, is obvious. Today, in practice, ecological accounting measures environmental interventions when they take place. It can be argued for this manner of treatment that the time of interference is crucial to the natural environment. Nevertheless, to account for emissions when they are released, for example, results in a time lag between an activity and reporting its effects. From a managerial incentive point of view this perspective is problematic as the feedback (reporting of the environmental interventions) is not clearly and directly related to the cause (the activity).

The assumption of a going concern attaches importance to the future, as it attempts to prevent unexpected trend-breaks in environmental interventions.

9.2.2 Qualitative Characteristics of Ecological Accounting

In Section 5.1 the qualitative characteristics of financial statements have been discussed (see also Figure 5.4). Therefore, this section deals only with the application of these principles in ecological accounting.

In ecological accounting, qualitative characteristics are the attributes which make the information provided in ecological statements useful to users (interpreted according to IASC 1994, p. 42). "Qualitative characteristics are the attributes that make the information provided in financial statements useful to users." Therefore, the idea and contents of the qualitative characteristics which have been defined by the IASC (1994, p. 45) or financial statements can also be applied to ecological accounting. In this case the four main qualitative characteristics for ecological statements are as follows. The contents and form of these characteristics are strongly based on and interpreted according to IASC (1994):

- understandability
- relevance
- reliability
- comparability.

a) Understandability

The benefits of ecological statements (reports) must exceed the costs. Therefore, the benefit is determined by its *decision usefulness* and its ability to help to allocate resources efficiently, and also by better relationships to stakeholders, or by improvement in competitive advantage, etc. Hence, ecological accounting standards and ecological statements are only issued if they are seen to be beneficial and important to firms and their critical stakeholders. For firms, the costs of ecological statements arise from collection, processing, analysis, education, auditing, reporting, increased pressure of stakeholders, loss in comparative advantage, etc. But the direct costs and opportunity costs of collection, analysis, interpretation, etc. are also borne by users.

To increase the benefits, the information in ecological statements should be readily understandable to users, who are assumed to have a reasonable knowledge of environmental assessment and of the industry. Not only should environmental interventions be disclosed, but furthermore the information should be interpreted or at least presented in relation to well-known firms. This can be done with benchmarking against the best performer within the relevant industry, as well as with clear definitions to explain the scientific wording where necessary.

If information about complex matters is *relevant* for environmental impact assessment, it should by all means be included.

b) Relevance

The ecological information provided must be relevant to the users of ecological statements. The information prepared should help to make better ecologically oriented decisions by helping to evaluate past, present or future events, or by confirming or correcting past evaluations (*confirmative value*) (interpreted according to IASC 1994, p. 42). This means that the *predictive value* of the ecological statement is enhanced if unusual, abnormal and infrequent environmental impacts are separately disclosed. It also implies that, for example, the environmental impacts of accidents which abnormally decreased or increased production, and of reduced emissions because of strikes, etc., should be disclosed.

The relevance of information is affected by its nature and *materiality* (prospective impact). In some cases, the nature of information alone is sufficient to determine its relevance. For example, the emergence of a new environmental problem which is regarded as serious by society may affect the assessment of the risks and opportunities facing the environment, irrespective of what information science and management regard to be relevant or not. Thus, if the greenhouse effect is regarded as serious then information concerning CO_2 is relevant.

Information is material if its omission or misstatement could influence the decisions of users. In some cases, both nature and materiality are important, for example with regard to the installation of a new scrubber. The nature of the statement would be that the scrubber decreases the environmental impact caused by the company, while its materiality would focus on the potential environmental impact (e.g. in regard to a threshold level).

c)   Reliability

To be useful, information must also be reliable. For ecological data, this implies that it has a certain quality, and that its *ecological impact has been assessed correctly*. Because this is very difficult to judge, at least the *methods* by which the data have been determined should be presented as well as the reasons why they are disclosed the way they are.

Some information may be relevant but so unreliable in its nature or representation that its recognition may be potentially misleading. For example, if the validity and amount of an environmental impact is disputed, it may be inappropriate for the enterprise to recognize the maximum environmental damage, although it may be appropriate to disclose the amount and circumstances of the potential maximum environmental damage. *Qualitative judgement* is not normally sufficient, but where no other means can be applied, it should be clearly stated. In this way the information helps to faithfully represent the environmental impacts it either purports to represent or could reasonably be expected to represent.

Faithful representation also implies that environmental impacts are accounted for and presented in accordance with their substance and ecological reality and not merely their legal form (*substance over form*). The substance of an environmental impact of an enterprise is not always consistent with its legal form. For example, an enterprise may dump waste legally in one country even if it is forbidden at another place. Or a firm may dispose of an asset in such a way that the documentation purports to pass legal ownership to another party. Nevertheless, an agreement may exist which ensures that the enterprise continues to dump its hazardous waste on the property. In such circumstances, the reporting of a sale would not faithfully represent the transaction entered into.

To be reliable, information contained and methods used in ecological statements must be *neutral*, that is, *free from bias*. If, for example, a company emits benzene it should state this separately, and not cover this substance under an expression or an account for Volatile Organic Compounds (VOC), which generally are made up of less toxic substances, even if benzene is a VOC.

The preparers of ecological statements have to accept the uncertainties which inevitably surround many events and circumstances. Such uncertainties are recognized by the disclosure of their nature and extent and by the exercise of *prudence* in the preparation of the ecological statements. Prudence is the inclusion of a degree of caution in the exercise of the judgement needed in making the estimates required under conditions of uncertainty, in which connection assets or income are not overstated and liabilities or expenses are not understated. Prudence is also taken to mean that unrealized gains should not be reported, whereas unrealized losses that have already occurred should be disclosed.

If this approach were transferred to ecological accounting this would mean a precautionary approach. Ecological liabilities (the obligations a company has) and costs (e.g. environmental interventions and their impacts) should not be understated, and ecological achievements (e.g. reduction of emissions) not overstated. Furthermore, unrealized clean-up of landfills, etc. should not be reported, whereas unrealized (future) environmental impacts which have already occurred should be disclosed (e.g. waste caused which is currently stored in order to be dumped in the future).

To be reliable, the information in ecological statements must be as *complete* as possible within the limits of materiality and cost. An omission can cause information to be false or misleading and thus to be unreliable and deficient in terms of its relevance.

d) Comparability

Users must be able to *compare* ecological statements of an enterprise over time in order to identify trends in the ecological position and performance (longitudinal comparison). Furthermore, users should also be able to compare ecological statements of different enterprises in order to evaluate relative environmental positions, performance and changes in the environmental position (cross-firm comparisons). Hence, the measurement and display of ecological effects of comparable transactions and other events must be carried out in a consistent way throughout an enterprise and over time as well as for different enterprises.

Consistency has been recognized as an important qualitative characterstic for the preparation of financial statements (IASC 1994, p. 45). Here, it is assumed that accounting policies are consistent from one period to another, thus stressing the methodological uniformity during a period and when comparing periods. The purpose of this convention is to ensure comparability of accounting information over time. For ecological accounting, the assumption of consistency means that *a specific item must be treated with the same methods*, no matter in which period and where it occurs. Information in ecological statements should be comparable over time. This is certainly essential to allow comparison.

The convention of consistency has been strongly criticized with regard to environmental matters (Maunders and Burritt 1991, pp. 11ff., Gray 1994). It has been stated that the character of nature is non-linear (e.g. the release of one kilogram of sulfur dioxide will have completely different impacts depending on threshold levels or its time of occurrence) and that the limited absorptive capacities (threshold levels) of eco-systems differ vastly between seasons and regions. For environmental protection, time differences in releases and in impact levels are crucial (e.g. an additional kilogram of SO_2 emitted in eastern Europe will usually have a more severe environmental implication than one emitted in northern Norway). Therefore, it has been concluded that the assumption of consistency leads to wrong decisions concerning the environment.

However, this criticism is based on a misleading interpretation of the purpose of the convention of consistency. No doubt, the assumption of linearity is not valid for ecosystems, and therefore site-specific methods to assess emissions and other ecological interventions are vital in ecological accounting. Nevertheless, consistency does not mean that an item (e.g. an emission of one tonne of SO_2) must be treated in a fixed and rigid way no matter when and where it occurs. Furthermore, consistency does not require the same treatment but rather the application of the same methods for all places where firms' sites are located. Consistency allows methods to be applied which distinguish different cases in a consistent manner. For example, an impact assessment method may distinguish between countries with high and low pollution (e.g. by using different impact assessment factors). Time differences may also be considered by the applied accounting methods, for example by mentioning that the pollution has been emitted continuously over time and not in a once-only discharge. The time aspect could be relevant if the impact on nature is more severe with concentrated, once-only discharges. However, the methods used should be consistent over time despite these adaptations to spatial and time differences.

Interpreted correctly, the underlying assumption of consistency means that it is assumed that a specific item is treated in the same way by using the same clearly defined methods over time. But these methods may very well consider time and spatial differences. In other words, the methods of assessing an environmental intervention should be used in a consistent manner, but they should consider spatial and time differences.

Because users wish to compare the environmental position, performance and changes in the position of an enterprise over time, it is important that the ecological statements show *corresponding information* for the preceding periods, i.e. no information should be omitted without substantial reasons or without an explicit statement. Without the convention of consistency, users of an ecological statement could not rely on the information provided.

In any case users should be informed of the *accounting policies employed* in the preparation of ecological statements, changes in these policies, and the effects of such changes.

Consistency should not be confused with uniformity and should not be allowed to become an impediment to the introduction of improved accounting methods and standards, i.e. in order to internalize negative external effects better.

These qualitative characteristics are the main attributes that make information useful to readers of ecological statements. Nevertheless, they are confronted with some constraints.

9.2.3 Constraints on Relevant and Reliable Information

The application of the main qualitative characteristics and of appropriate accounting standards should normally result in ecological statements which convey what is generally understood as a *true and fair view* of information (interpreted according to IASC 1994, p. 46). However, IASC point out that the quality of ecological reporting information is impaired by three main constraints.

- *Timeliness.* Timeliness forbids undue delay in the reporting of information so that the information does not lose relevance. Nevertheless, time constraints must not be used as subsequent excuses for omissions in measuring and recording or in providing low data quality.
- *Balance between benefits and costs of ecological accounting.* The costs of computing more and better information about environmental impacts must not exceed the benefits of information for the natural environment. First, the benefits for the natural environment derived from ecological accounting information must in any case exceed the costs of providing it. Ecological, as well as economic-ecological efficiency are measures to decide whether the ratio between benefits and costs is positive.

- *Trade-off between qualitative characteristics.* In practice a balance between different qualitative characteristics is often necessary. Sometimes in ecological accounting and reporting (as in all accounting systems) different qualitative aspects have to be traded off against each other. For example, management may need to balance the relative merits of timely reporting and the provision of reliable information. In achieving a balance between relevance and reliability, the overriding consideration is how best to satisfy the ecological decision-making of users. Ecological impacts with a high degree of uncertainty could be stated qualitatively or be accounted for in a transitory account.

9.3 CONSOLIDATION

External ecological accounting can be product-, site-, or business- and company-oriented (corporations at group level). Many environmental reports exist for all three focuses. Group reports (company-oriented) are mainly published by multinational companies and therefore contain data which have to be aggregated from different enterprises. This raises questions of consolidation of ecological data.

The topic of consolidation is well known from financial accounting. Two main issues can be distinguished.

- The *method* of consolidation: how can data from different companies in different countries be aggregated?
- The *scope* of consolidation: what is the appropriate scope of consolidation?

The following sections firstly discuss the principles of consolidation in financial accounting (Sections 9.3.1 and 9.3.2). On this basis, methods for consolidation in ecological accounting are dealt with in Section 9.3.3.

9.3.1 Methods of Consolidation

Multinational companies use specific procedures for consolidation. These are defined by the main financial accounting standard setting organizations. In practice, three methods of consolidation are used. The method applied depends on the share with which a firm participates in another firm.

All major financial accounting standards (IAS, US GAAP and the Directives of the EU) require the following consolidation rules.

- *Full consolidation* is used by the parent firm[10] which controls the majority of the voting rights of a subsidiary (50% or more of the voting rights). Under the assumption of complete control[11] and economic unity of a group of firms, the parent company integrates all positions of the profit and loss account and of the balance sheet of the subsidiary into the group accounting. Minority interests are only reported for the minority's share of equity and profit.

- The *equity method* is applied for associates,[12] i.e. for holdings between 20% and 49%. It is assumed that the parent company has a significant influence on the subsidiary.[13] The equity method only considers the actual share of equities and no other financial figures such as debt, sales, assets or liabilites. Since equity consolidated investments are valued on an annual basis the changing value of such investments is reflected in the group accounts (Zenhäusern and Bertschinger 1993). Therefore, the equity method does not allow the real size, the economical debt-equity ratio (in comparison to the accounting debt–equity ratio) or the risk of a group to be assessed. (It is advisable for indebted companies to acquire only 49.9% of other firms, as no additional debt then appears in the group account.) For this reason, many financial analysts require additional information concerning total sales, liabilities, etc.
- The *proportionate method* is applied for investments between 1% and 19% of the share capital as well as for joint ventures, where two companies hold 50% each. According to the proportionate method, operational invest-ments[14] are reflected in the group accounts of the parent company with the book value (purchase price based on costs incurred). In most cases the value accounted for remains unchanged and therefore does not reflect an increase or decrease in value.

The consolidation procedure (i.e. for full consolidation) requires the elimination of *intercompany transactions* (e.g. between two subsidiaries where one is a supplier of the other). For example, the parent has three subsidiaries A (sales 200), B (sales 75) and C (sales 50). Companies B and C supply exclusively to company A. Thus the total sales of the group are 200 and not 325. The aim of this elimination is to avoid double recognition of accounting figures.

In environmental reports, the *methods of consolidation of ecological data* are practically never disclosed. Hence, external stakeholders cannot judge with which method the data of the environmental interventions of the group's subsidiaries are consolidated. Furthermore, as no standards exist, it is not clear if the subsidiaries have applied the same consolidation principles.

In practice, many firms consolidate ecological data by a method similar to that of full consolidation; but disregarding minority interests, and sometimes even investments up to 49.9%. Hence, the *consolidation practices for ecological accounting* can be assumed to *differ in most cases from those of financial accounting*. In this case, the disclosed emissions of a group do not necessarily reflect the actual environmental impact of the group. This fact must be carefully considered when calculating and interpreting eco-integrated figures such as sales per tonne of CO_2 emitted (see also Chapter 11).

9.3.2 Scope and Subject Matter of Consolidation

In financial accounting, the scope of consolidation shows which companies are and which ones are not integrated in the consolidated group figures. The

> **Box 9.2**
> **Scope and Subject Matter of Consolidation**
>
> In preparing consolidated ecological statements, the ecological statements of the parent and its subsidiaries are combined on a line-by-line basis by adding together items of environmental interventions. The environmental interventions consolidated must be in the same geographic range of impact (interpreted according to IAS 27 §26).

interpretation of group figures without knowing the scope of consolidation is useless. Moreover, for a meaningful analysis, the methods of consolidation must be known and all subsidiaries must apply the same accounting policies in similar circumstances, IASC (1995, IAS 27 §21).

To obtain reliable information about the total environmental impact added of a group, only environmental interventions *within the same geographical range of impact* may be aggregated. For instance, if the firm operates on a global scale only environmental interventions with a global impact should be aggregated (e.g. CO_2 concerning the greenhouse effect).

On a group level, the *aggregation* of environmental interventions with local impacts is meaningless. However, local environmental interventions *should be disclosed separately* from the aggregated environmental impacts in the external ecological statement of the group, and in any case they should be aggregated and assessed on a plant level.

9.3.3 Conclusions for Consolidation in Ecological Accounting

At least the following three main principles should be considered when consolidating environmental data in external ecological accounting.

1. *All subsidiaries should apply the same consolidation methods.* Thus, the top management and chief accountants should issue clear consolidation guidelines for ecological accounting.
2. In external ecological accounting, the *consolidation policies should be disclosed.* Meaningful interpretation of ecological statements of a group of firms is not possible without disclosure of the consolidation method used.
3. To avoid distortions when calculating eco-integrated key-numbers the *same consolidation principles must be used in ecological and financial accounting.* For financial accounting, international standards already exist. Thus, if there are no substantial reasons to do otherwise, the same principles should be applied in external ecological accounting as in financial accounting. According to the standards used in practice, full consolidation should be applied for subsidiaries which are controlled by the parent (at least 50% of

the voting rights). For stakes of 20% to 49% the equity method is used, whereas small holdings below 19% will be treated by the proportionate consolidation method.

If a subsidy is consolidated according to the equity method, additional economic information should be provided, such as:

- total sales
- total debt
- total profit or loss
- total assets.

This additional economic information allows the correct calculation of eco-integrated key figures such as profits per tonne of CO_2 emitted (see also Chapter 11).

9.4 SUMMARY

Environmental information has become part of marketing for many firms. However, inproper use by some firms in the past has diminished the reputational gains and therefore reduced some incentives to improve the environmental record. To increase marketing and reputational gains actual environmental leaders must be clearly distinguished from firms concentrating on "window-dressing".

Information in environmental statements is trustworthy to readers and comparable between firms only with the establishment of widely accepted international standards of ecological accounting. External ecological accounting implies the application of accounting principles and structures to collect, analyse and disclose environmental impact added. From an economic as well as from an ecological perspective it makes sense to investigate whether the accounting principles as formulated by the IASC are also suited for use in ecological accounting. It has been shown that, if interpreted in the appropriate sense, the application of the basic assumptions and conventions of financial accounting to external ecological accounting may provide a useful framework.

Common assumptions and conventions are the basis for standardization of external ecological accounting. Verification and auditing are only possible when clear, measurable standards are defined. In this field, considerable work remains to be done by accounting standardization organizations. Standards and audits reduce information costs and increase the usefulness for external stakeholders of the information provided by ecological accounting.

The next chapter deals with other ecological accounting systems, such as are established by tax agencies or environmental agencies.

10
Other Ecological
Accounting Systems

This chapter deals with special ecological accounting systems which establish a specific accounting relationship with a stakeholder group. After the introduction (10.1), ecological tax accounting (10.2) and other regulatory ecological accounting systems (10.3), such as the one established through the US Toxic Release Inventory (TRI), are discussed.

10.1 INTRODUCTION

Some powerful stakeholders supply the firm with such valuable resources, or are able to influence the company so strongly in some way, that they can enforce special accounting relationships. Historically, such critical stakeholders interested in ecological information are mainly regulatory bodies, particularly the environmental protection agency. Because it has legal enforcement powers, it can compel companies to deliver the required information. The agency needs information concerning environmental interventions to check how well the regulations are met, to assess the severity of environmental problems, and as a basis for designing environmental policies.

Environmental protection agencies typically apply "command and control" policies to regulate measures of environmental protection within their geographical areas. Usually, technical standards are defined for production technologies in order to regulate the discharge of pollutants. In this context, depending on national laws, the firms have to prove that they comply with the standards. This is also the case when applying for subsidies for environmentally benign technologies.

However, as with market-based regulations such as environmental taxes or emission trading, firms are required to monitor, record and report their releases. Some kind of ecological accounting is necessary for communication between the regulatory agency and the firm. In practice, the necessary information is often collected, prepared and communicated several times (in parallel) by various employees of the firm. Systematic corporate ecological accounting can therefore decrease costs of measurement, data keeping, reporting and coordination.

The difference relative to other traditional accounting systems lies mainly in the measurement and nature of the matter treated: every ecological accounting system measures the environmental impacts in physical units. As mentioned in Section 9.3, the users of specially designed ecological reports are often attentive readers of external ecological statements. However, their information needs cannot be covered by these more general public reports because of their specific requirements for detailed and often confidential information.

10.2 ECOLOGICAL TAX ACCOUNTING

Ecological tax accounting has started to become an important issue in most developed countries. However, little has been written about the consequences of environmental taxes on firms' accounting practices.

The impact of taxes on corporate accounting systems depends on the tax base. As nobody really likes to pay taxes, the regulators have to ensure that they receive correct and comparable information from all firms subject to the tax. The crucial point for the tax agency is to establish clear rules of monitoring, measurement and reporting. Therefore, specific accounting conventions and rules are needed which state in detail when, how and under which circumstances the taxed environmental interventions are to be measured and reported.

10.2.1 Approaches of Taxing

From an economic perspective, an optimal environmental tax exists when the marginal costs of environmental damage equal the marginal costs of prevention.[15] Economic theory distinguishes basically between two approaches to determine an optimal environmental tax.

- *Pigou tax*
  The goal of the Pigou tax is to internalize external costs; only the marginal environmental costs are internalized, not the total costs. Economic actors should make individual consumption and production decisions on the basis of prices which include all external costs.

  With a Pigou tax, the regulators would have to account for the external costs and allocate them to the goods which caused them. Then all other economic actors would have all information concerning the environmental impacts included in the prices. However, the calculation of external costs has proved to be impossible because the information about the marginal costs of environmental damage cannot be determined satisfactorily. Also, management may have every incentive to overstate marginal costs of prevention in order to keep the firm's costs as low as possible. So, because of information problems the ideal of a Pigou tax cannot be realized (see for example Pearce and Turner 1992, Frey *et al.* 1993). Therefore, to be informed about environmental impacts ecological accounting systems for firms becomes crucial.

- *Standard-price approach*
  In response to the problems with a Pigou tax, Baumol and Oates (1988) and Pearce and Turner (1992), propose a "standard-price-approach" to determine the ideal tax rate. They suggest taking a politically accepted level of environmental quality, or the discharge of a defined amount of a specific pollutant. Considering the reactions of the users of the goods taxed, the corrected price should be adjusted until the optimum tax-level is reached. The standard-price approach is therefore dynamic.

In practice all environmental taxes are based on the standard-price approach. However, in the political process, the tax rate is rarely, if ever, adjusted in such a way as to make possible an optimum result.

10.2.2 Tax Base for Environmental Taxes

Politicians and environmental agencies have the following choices for determining the tax base (Figure 10.1).

- *Inputs*
  One possible tax base is the inputs of economic processes (e.g. petrol, chemicals, energy) which cause environmental problems. The advantage of taking inputs as a tax base is that they can be measured easily and often appear in traditional accounting. However, accounting of the material flows is still necessary in most cases as the tax is based on the quantities used and not on the monetary value of the inputs. A problem is presented by the fact that no consideration is given to the way the inputs are used in the production process. Incentives are given for technologies which save input factors but not for all other prevention and emission reduction strategies. Also, firms can substitute the taxed inputs with less taxed but maybe more harmful goods. To levy a tax on inputs is only sensible if a strong link exists between the use of the input and an environmental intervention, and if substitutes are less harmful.
- *Desired outputs*
  Another possible tax base is the desired goods (desired outputs) that result from economic activities. Then, every product would have to be taxed according to the environmental impact added over its whole life cycle. The

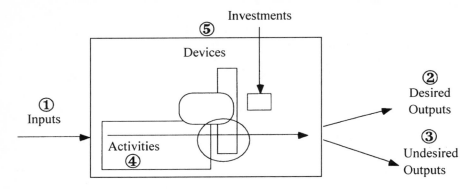

Figure 10.1 Alternative Tax Bases

measurement and reporting of sales are part of any traditional accounting system and therefore present no problem. However, to levy an environmental tax on purchases and sales is contrary to economic rationale, because no incentive is given to improve the design and production of the desired product. It is not the reduction of the consumption of the desired product but rather the external costs that is the actual environmental objective. Therefore, the environmental interventions should be taxed directly. Nevertheless, industrial products in particular are sometimes taxed on environmental grounds.

- *Undesired outputs*
  To tax environmental interventions (undesired outputs), especially emissions, is a very common proposal. The tax rate should ideally relate to the environmental harmfulness and the damage caused by the discharged substance. The tax base could be the actual source emissions (e.g. the emissions which are actually metered), using either a proxy of a source's emissions or a flat rate (OECD 1994b, p. 57). If the tax base is the actual environmental interventions, then it guarantees that all prevention efforts result in lower taxes—provided that the firms have an ecological accounting system to communicate their successful prevention of pollution.

  However, in the case of many sources of pollution (e.g. in traffic, or non-stationary polluters) the costs of monitoring can be exorbitantly high. In these cases, the eco-efficiency of the tax will be lowered. Therefore, output-oriented pollution taxes are discussed only for stationary emissions sources.

- *Activities*
  As with a tax levied on inputs, taxing environmentally harmful activities (e.g. driving a car) is only sensible if a clear link with environmental impacts exists. Such a link does not usually exist. Environmental taxes on activities can create some accounting problems, as neither traditional nor ecological

accounting systems are designed to measure and communicate the influence of taxes.[16]

- *Investments and devices*
  To levy a tax on investments and environmentally harmful devices is very problematic as the incentives are not clearly focused on the actual environmental interventions.

From an economic perspective taxes should be levied as directly as possible on "bads" (i.e. the environmental interventions) and not on goods. This results in the most effective and efficient reduction. In many countries (e.g. Germany) this view is gaining increased acceptance. Sometimes, however, the question arises of whether the regulatory bodies do not embrace the idea of environmental taxes merely to increase the public budget. This, of course, creates huge resistance from business. Therefore, fiscal neutrality is necessary whenever the (main and only) purpose is to change environmental behavior (see Section 6.2).

Traditional accounting systems obviously do not provide the necessary ecological information for levying environmental taxes. With input-oriented taxes, such as a tax on fossil fuels, the regulators do not have to be informed about the consumption of every firm. This is because such a tax can be levied once on the producer, or importer of the oil, coal, gas, etc. Nevertheless, if input-oriented environmental taxes are applied, the tax agency must establish special ecological accounting relationships with importers and producers of the goods taxed. To ensure consistent and correct reporting, the tax agency must establish clear ecological accounting rules. The same is true with a CO_2 tax where the tax base is the input of energies, because the emissions can be calculated on the basis of the carbon contents of the inputs and as no prevention technology for CO_2 emissions exists.

With taxes on discharged pollutants such as volatile organic compounds (VOC), the tax agency must be informed about the physical quantities of the taxed pollutant released into the environment by every firm. Therefore, specific ecological accounting systems measuring and reporting (taxed and regulated) environmental interventions are needed. Depending on the power of the environmental protection agency, as well as on the socio-political culture of a nation, the specifications of ecological tax accounting systems can vary widely with the object of taxation and between countries. However, those crucial aspects of ecological tax accounting which are of international nature have been discussed under the heading of internal and external ecological accounting.

The importance of environmental taxes, charges and fees is growing, at least in the developed world (see Section 6.1). With this development, the importance of ecological tax accounting systems is growing, too.

Not only environmental taxes, charges and fees, but also environmental regulations such as quantitative regulations of discharges into the natural environment affect business and corporate accounting. The next section addresses the nature of these regulatory ecological accounting relationships.

10.3 FURTHER REGULATORY ECOLOGICAL ACCOUNTING SYSTEMS

Environmental regulations can attempt to change prices or may directly focus on discharges of pollutants. The last section dealt with ecological tax accounting which provides information for government (i.e. tax) agencies to levy taxes, charges and fees. This section deals with other regulatory ecological accounting systems which serve to compute, analyse and report discharges of pollutants to environmental protection agencies in order to control quantitative environmental regulations.

As with ecological tax accounting, further regulatory ecological accounting systems are more or less developed in different countries. Therefore, it would go too far to examine the accounting policies and rules of different national environmental protection agencies. Among the most prominent regulations which have imposed specific regulatory ecological accounting systems are the following.

- US Toxic Release Inventory (TRI) and similar European regulations creating pollution release and transfer registers (PRTRs).
- US 33/50 program.
- US emissions trading programs.

10.3.1 The US Toxic Release Inventory (TRI)

The US Toxic Release Inventory (TRI) is an excellent example of a national regulatory ecological accounting system. The TRI was created by the US Congress in 1986 as part of the Emergency Planning and Community Right to Know Act. TRI data were first published in 1988, and usually the disclosed information is one year old when it is actually reported. On an aggregated level, the TRI defines a macro-economic ecological account. The TRI establishes an ecological accounting relationship for a list that now comprises over 600 toxic substances (Anonymous 1994b). Companies have to report releases of emissions into air, water and land, as well as locations and quantities of chemicals stored on-site, and off-site transfers of wastes for treatment or disposal at a separate facility. In 1990, the US Congress also forced plants to start recording the recycling of chemicals and pollution prevention activities (Hess 1994). In 1994 the US Environmental Protection Agency (EPA) received around 80,000 submissions for each TRI-listed chemical from 23,000 facilities (Anonymous 1994a, A1ff.). Every company has to publicly disclose the number and quantity of the releases for each site.

The information is publicly accessible for all interested stakeholders and is also used by eco-rating organizations. Eco-rating organizations using TRI data are, for example, the Investors Responsibility Research Center (IRRC) and the Center for Economic Priorities (CEP). Nearly three quarters of the TRI pollution releases came from public companies. It has been found, with a high statistical significance, that shareholders of these firms experience abnormally negative returns in response to the first release of the TRI information (Hamilton 1995, pp. 98ff.). This suggests that the published TRI information may influence investors and that environmental issues may profoundly influence the financial performance of companies.

The collection of data requires a very accurate ecological accounting system, and clear rules have to be established on how to measure and report the regulated emissions. Only then can consistency over time and comparability between firms be guaranteed. In the beginning, some firms were overwhelmed with problems of internal information collection so that they reported zero emissions. Others reported too much because they double-counted their emissions.

So far, the interpretation of the TRI data is difficult as the absolute numbers do not say anything about the eco-efficiency of the firms. This is because the sales, economic returns and the value added of the reporting companies are not mentioned. Thus, larger companies almost inevitably have higher emissions than smaller firms. However, larger firms are not more environmentally harmful just because of their size. This is why more recent reports based on TRI data often publish ratios, such as TRI releases per $1000 of sales (CEP 1993, IRRC 1993). However, these economic-ecological figures also do not consider spatial and time aspects of the releases.

Moreover, the main problem with the TRI system is that the quantity of toxins released says nothing about the actual impact. Nor is it distinguished according to the environmental impacts caused by the treatment facility. However, the location where the discharges take place is reported (see also Hess 1994, pp. 8ff.).

Nevertheless, the TRI system is a substantial step in the direction of external ecological accounting and public disclosure of environmental interventions. It certainly has had a very good performance record with respect to decreasing emissions. In 1993 regulated industries in the USA released a total of 2.81 billion pounds into the environment, compared to 3.21 billion pounds in 1992 (Hanson 1995, pp. 4ff.). Industrial releases overall also decreased between 1991 and 1992, namely by 6.5 per cent. Therefore, in 1994 the total emissions were 35% lower than in 1988 when the government began to publish TRI data, Hess (1994).

With the addition of 286 further chemicals to the list of 320 substances for which US manufacturers and users must file annual TRI reports, the reported amount released will, of course, increase. In order to lessen the reporting work load, EPA has proposed a rule under which facilities which release or transfer chemicals in quantities of less than 100 pounds annually would be exempted. The same would apply to facilities which annually transfer less than 1 million pounds of a chemical for recycling or energy recovery (Anonymous 1994a, *Environment Today* 1994, p. 6). A proposed rule EPA expected to issue in summer 1995 is intended to create a consolidated environmental database program with the effect of reducing the reporting costs of the industry (Hess 1995, p. 24).

In *European countries and Canada* pollution registers fulfil similar tasks to the TRI in the US (Hosbach *et al.* (1995). Macro-economic environmental accounting systems (i.e. of Norway and France) are also addressed in Section 7.6). The "Emission Inventories (EI)" of the Netherlands were established in 1990, followed by the Chemical Release Inventory (CRI) in the United Kingdom in 1991. The Canadian National Pollutant Release Inventory (NPRI) came in 1993 whereas in the EU the Polluting Emissions Register (PER) was introduced in 1995. Denmark has introduced a regulatory ecological accounting system which is the most advanced in Europe. In the spring of 1995, the Danish parliament passed a law requiring companies to report their impacts on the natural environment. The details of the accounting and reporting regulation are currently under review. About 3000 firms are expected to be covered by the regulation.

In the UK the main compiler of registers of emissions, effluents or wastes is Her Majesty's Inspectorate of Pollution (HMIP) (Deloitte Touche Tohmatsu *et al.* 1993, pp. 17ff., Roberts 1994, p. 20). HMIP issued its first "Chemical Release Inventory (CRI)" in 1994. It covered 1992 and 1993 emissions from a range of different industries. The 550-page document breaks down emissions by type, industrial sector and local authority. The CRI is seen as only a beginning, however, and will be widened over the coming years to cover all major industries. It is felt by the environmental pressure group Friends of the Earth to be only a pale shadow of the US Toxic Release Inventory, because it should give greater depth of information, including the names of individual companies and their emissions (Roberts 1994, p. 20).

The proposed Pollutant Emissions Register (PER) of the European Union has a similar approach to the TRI. As with TRI, no reporting will be necessary below minimal emission levels. The main reason to consider the establishment of PER is to improve the transparency and availability of information for citizens (EEC 1993b). The association of the European chemical industry (CEFIC) has been given the opportunity to make a proposal for a concrete model. The model is expected to include binding lists of pollutants which must be reported (IÖW 1993, p. 81). However, PER is not expected to be realized before the year 2000 (ÖB 1995).

Nevertheless, the OECD is currently working on a guideline for national pollutant registers (PRTRs: Pollutant Release and Transfer Registers) which are to be based on world-wide experience with national pollutant registers. The guideline will be written not only for developed but also for developing and newly industrialized countries (ÖB 1995, p. 5).

10.3.2 The US 33/50 Program

During the Reagan and Bush administrations the USA, EPA was faced with restrictions on its financial and administrative resources. Therefore, EPA had to find new approaches to environmental regulation. This is when the so called "33/50 program" was introduced. With the 33/50 program, companies were marketed by the US EPA as environmentally responsible, which voluntarily signed a legally binding agreement to cut emissions of the 17 widely used, most toxic chemicals in the USA by 33 per cent from 1988 to 1992, and then by 50 per cent in 1995. These 17 substances are also covered by the TRI (Hess 1994). Industry went beyond the interim goal, as TRI releases and transfers of these chemicals decreased by 46 per cent through 1992. 33/50 proved to be very successful as the relationship between regulators and management of firms changed from a command and control policy to a partnership between two cooperating parties.

However, with this new relationship an ecological accounting and reporting system covering these 17 "substances under contract" is needed. This regulatory ecological accounting system must be characterized by clear, mutually accepted accounting rules, so that measurement of performance is possible.

10.3.3 Emission Trading

One of the most sophisticated regulations to reduce corporate environmental impacts is emission trading. (For a discussion of emission trading see, for example, Tietenberg 1989, 1993; Hahn 1984; OECD 1994b.) The basic idea of emission trading is that firms may only release emissions to the extent they own emission certificates, granting them the right to pollute. The emission certificates are allocated at the beginning of the period and can be traded. The total level of environmental interventions is limited as only a defined number of tradeable emission allowances are available. The rationale behind emissions trading is that firms with low marginal prevention costs will reduce their emissions and sell the surplus emission allowances to those firms which have high marginal abatement/prevention costs. For the latter it is cheaper to buy emission certificates than to prevent pollution.

Different concepts and terms have been used in connection with emissions trading, such as "bubbles", "offsets", "netting" and "banking" (see for example Tietenberg 1993, Frey et al. 1993).

"Emission bubbles" are defined geographical areas in which a certain amount of discharges must not be exceeded. Regulators do not require who has to reduce how much, but rather leave it to the firms to reduce emissions where it is most cost-efficient. Therefore, the bubble concept gives some flexibility in satisfying regulatory standards which apply to a defined level of emissions in a specific region.

"Offsets" are employed when a firm wants to expand its production or to locate in an area where regulatory standards are not met. Then, the firm has to adhere to the strictest standards and compensate for its new emissions by buying tradeable permits from other sources in the area (i.e. by paying others to reduce emissions).

"Netting" is probably the most common form of tradeable permit. Here the "trade" takes place within a facility; therefore existing sources can be exempted from new source requirements, as long as no significant increases occur within the facility as a whole. (Source requirements are operating allowances, permits to enlarge production, etc.)

"Emission Banking" enables companies to "save" the reduced emissions for future use (OECD 1994b, p. 88).

With emissions trading a price is placed on environmental interventions. Thus, every kilogram released directly causes costs, whereas reductions of emissions are potential sales, i.e. income opportunities. Emissions trading therefore internalizes environmental interventions into traditional corporate accounting.

The regulators depend on correct information about the companies' releases in order to check whether the values of the certificates match with the actual releases. First, comprehensive emission trading requires a precise monitoring system (Stevenson 1992). Second, an ecological accounting system with clear rules and standards is necessary for the consistent and correct reporting of the regulated substances. Third, to detect the most cost-efficient opportunities of prevention, managers must have an internal ecological accounting system to inform them about where (environmental impact added center) what discharges (EIA driver) are caused by which cost carrier (i.e. EIA carrier). In addition managers must be informed about the marginal prevention and abatement costs in order to decide whether to buy or to sell pollution rights.[17] Therefore, internal ecological accounting must be coordinated with managerial accounting.

Tradeable permits have been introduced in some countries, notably the USA, Canada, Australia, Germany and Switzerland. The environmental interventions controlled through such programs are mainly air emissions with the aim of reducing problems such as photochemical smog, the depletion of the ozone layer and acid rain (OECD 1994b, p. 87). Empirical studies show that with emission trading environmental goals can be achieved in a more cost-efficient manner than with other regulations (Tietenberg 1992, Staehelin-Witt and Spillmann 1992). When introducing emission trading, the companies have to show emission allowances in traditional accounting (see Part B), and build up an efficient ecological accounting system to take full economic advantage of the new freedoms given with these new regulations.

10.3.4 Other Regulations and Standards Requiring Ecological Accounting

Another outstanding environmental regulation that establishes a regulatory ecological accounting relationship is the EU regulation on the Environmental Management and Eco-Audit Scheme (EMAS). In fact, EMAS is not an accounting standard but rather a standard for an environmental management system (see Part D). Nevertheless, the regulation substantially supports the emergence of ecological accounting, as it requires ecological accounting and public reporting of site-specific environmental interventions of firms which join the system voluntarily (EEC 1993). In contrast to the ecological accounting relations defined by TRI, 33/50 and emissions trading programs, EMAS does not clarify how many and which environmental interventions have to be accounted for. However, the accuracy of the reported data must be verified by an independent, certified auditor. EMAS therefore provides new opportunities for the accountancy profession, in relation both to consultancy and compliance (Hibbit 1994, pp. 97ff.).

As discussed in Part D, private standardization organizations (i.e. the British Standards Institute and the International Standards Institute) also have defined similar standards of environmental management systems (BS 7750, ISO 14001) which require some kind of ecological accounting system.

10.4 CONCLUSIONS

Today, in developed countries ecological accounting is part of regular business practice, although it often is not recognized as such. The reason for the fast emergence of ecological accounting lies in the importance for business of environmental issues, and in the fact that environmental impacts are not internalized in the market system and therefore not recognized in traditional accounting. Consequently, new accounting tools have emerged to consider environmental impact added.

Internal ecological accounting serves to communicate between internal stakeholders and supports internal decision making. Electronic data processing hardware and software now available can do much to facilitate information collection and qualitatively improve the practical implementation of ecological accounting. Special emphasis should be placed on the development of computer-supported management accounting systems, which make possible a simulation of changes of production technologies or inputs. They visually show the influence of various assessment models on the end result (measures of environmental impact added or EIA indicators).

Because of inherent problems of data quality, which can hardly be overcome in an economic way, firms *should not use background inventory data* to carry out product life cycle assessments. Management should primarily concentrate on site-, business- and firm-specific ecological accounting, where representative data and more accurate data quality allow decisions which can actually result in a reduction of environmental impacts. However, taken as a way of thinking, the philosophy of LCA is helpful in strategic management to anticipate potential major problems resulting from products.

External ecological accounting as an equivalent to financial accounting is booming. Nevertheless, the former is still a playground for various methods and perspectives. Therefore, conventions of external ecological accounting are needed to reduce the costs of information for users of ecological statements.

Despite many problems, traditional accounting has proved to be beneficial to business and society. Otherwise its basic principles would hardly have survived for more than one hundred years. The success of financial accounting as a tool to communicate with external stakeholders is largely based on underlying assumptions and conventions which reduce information costs and guarantee a certain standard of information quality. Therefore, some first suggestions for underlying assumptions and conventions of external ecological accounting have been proposed in this chapter.

External ecological accounting can be started on the basis of existing regulatory environmental reporting activities. Once a systematic and efficient ecological accounting system is established for reporting to regulatory agencies, it can be enlarged with little effort to include other, non-regulated environmental interventions and to calculate the overall environmental impact added of the firm.

In developed countries, environmental regulators have established more or less specifically defined ecological accounting and reporting relationships for communication with management. The regulatory accounting systems are mostly compulsory and represent good business practice. However, most firms have not linked the various regulatory accounting systems. This results in situations where the same data are collected several times by different employees to communicate with different regulatory bodies. In order to reduce costs of collection and reporting, regulatory ecological accounting should be coordinated and integrated with external and internal ecological accounting. Ecological accounting must be carried out as economically as possible—by linking internal with external and other ecological (regulatory) accounting systems. Then an optimal degree of synergies can be established. Well designed external and internal ecological accounting systems can substantially reduce costs and difficulties with environmental regulations.

So far, social and environmental responsibility is still reflected in the choice and implementation of various assessment models and procedures of ecological accounting, but also simply in the way such terms as "eco-balance", "life cycle assessment", "ecological accounting", etc. are used.

Despite these encouraging developments it must be kept in mind that just enlarging traditional accounting by an ecological accounting category will not substantially help to solve environmental problems unless an integration of environmental accounting with environmental management takes place.

PART D
Environmental Accounting for Environmental Management

Part D discusses how environmental accounting is linked with environmental management. Corporate environmental management deals with tools, processes, responsibilities and the organizational structure of environmental protection in firms.

Chapter 11 deals with the integration of ecological with traditional accounting. The Eco-Rational Path Method (EPM), often referred to as eco-integrated accounting, is the core method of integrating ecological with traditional accounting and the basis for strategic management of eco-efficiency (Section 11.2).

To support managerial decision making, eco-integrated accounting information must be communicated to internal and external stakeholders. Chapter 12 discusses environmental reporting. The main principles are dealt with as well as the characteristics which distinguish outstanding environmental reports from other such reports.

The link between environmental accounting and environmental management is made in Chapter 13. Sections 13.1 and 13.2 give an overview of the most important contemporary environmental management practices, and show how well these methods support the main tasks of environmental management.

Then, Section 13.3 deals with eco-controlling, the most comprehensive contemporary environmental management concept. Eco-controlling is the application of financial and strategic controlling to environmental management. It therefore works systematically with information from environmentally differentiated and ecological accounting.

Finally, general conclusions of the whole book are made in Section 13.4, and an outlook on the future development of environmental accounting is given.

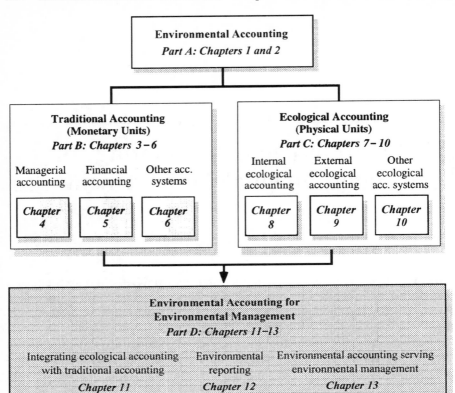

11

Integrating Ecological Accounting with Traditional Accounting

Ideally, environmental interventions (external costs) would all be expressed in the same units of measurement and therefore would implicitly be included in traditional accounting. However, as shown in Part B, traditional accounting does not adequately incorporate firms' environmental interventions, but rather shows the flow of funds. Insufficient internalization of environmental impacts is not a "fault" of traditional accounting but rather represents political priorities and reluctance. Nevertheless, the management of a company usually pursues not only economic objectives but also environmental, political and other goals. In addition it has to respond to the requirements of various stakeholders with diverse priorities. The integration of the results of ecological accounting with those of traditional accounting is therefore an important consideration of management, and it is necessary for the improvement of eco-efficiency.

Eco-efficiency is the ratio between value added and environmental impact added, or the ratio between an economic performance indicator and an ecological performance indicator (see also Section 7.3). The improvement of eco-efficiency therefore requires the integration of economic information (the flow of funds such as income, expense, revenues, costs, etc.) derived from traditional accounting with environmental information (environmental interventions such as emissions, resource use, etc.) derived from ecological accounting, (see also Figure 1.2, Part A).

Figure 11.1 shows traditional and ecological accounting. Environmentally differentiated traditional and ecological accounting are part of environmental accounting (the shaded area within the dash-line box in Figure 11.1). The integration of information of traditional and environmentally differentiated

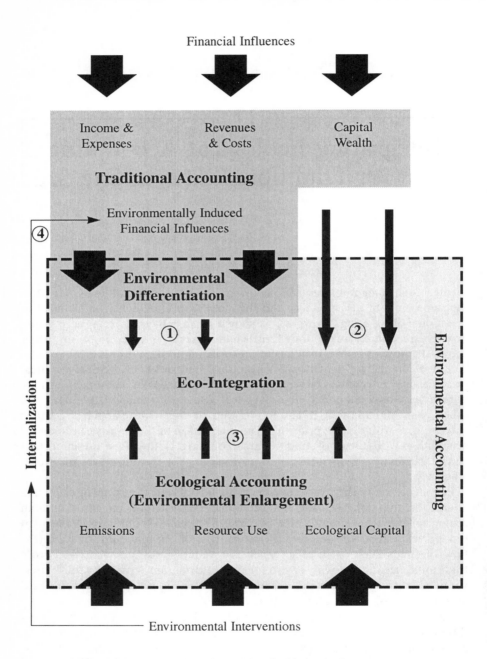

Figure 11.1 Integration of Traditional with Ecological Accounting

accounting with ecological accounting is also considered to be part of environmental accounting.

As consumer preferences and government policies increasingly favor a balanced approach by business to the environment, managers are paying more attention to the strategic importance of their environmental decisions (see for example Annighöfer 1990, Buchholz 1993, Kirchgeorg 1990, Marcus 1993, Meffert 1988, Roome 1992, Schmid 1989). Yet, while firms may be increasingly aware of the need to plan for the consequences of environmental actions, few tools are available to assist them in this process.

Section 11.1 shows the process of eco-integration and how the respective information can be used for decision-making. The Eco-Rational Path Method (EPM) has been developed to meet this requirement. It describes a structured decision process to pilot the companies' businesses to eco-efficiency. Strategic implications and eco-integrated portfolio matrices are discussed in Section 11.2. Finally, eco-integrated investment appraisal is treated in Section 11.3.

11.1 THE ECO-RATIONAL PATH METHOD (EPM)

The Eco-Rational Path Method (Schaltegger and Sturm 1992a), represents a straightforward practical procedure to integrate two dimensions: an economic dimension (left side) and an ecological one (right side). The integration process distinguishes three steps: accounting, judgement and decision (Figure 11.2).

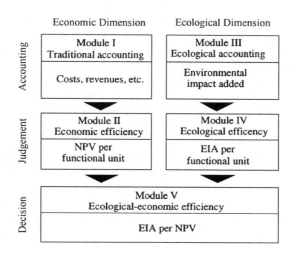

Figure 11.2   The Eco-Rational Path Method (EPM). Source: Schaltegger and Sturm 1992a, p. 206

In module one, the monetary results of traditional accounting, including the environmental compliance costs and the earnings, are evaluated.

Module three represents the evaluation of ecological harm in units of environmental impact added (EIA) calculated with ecological accounting. In module two, an economic performance indicator as a measure of economic efficiency, such as Net Present Value (NPV), Return on Net Assets (RONA) or the contribution margin (CM), is calculated. These key numbers are supplied by any well functioning economic controlling system.

Module four calculates ecological efficiency, as the quotient of EIA per product, product group or another functional unit. Both module two and four are the steps in which the data for isolated, ecological or economic efficiency judgements are supplied.

Module five integrates these four steps by confronting the economic with the ecological efficiency measure and by calculating the quotient EIA per unit of economic performance (e.g. EIA per created $ contribution margin of a product). In this module, a measure to implement sustainable development of a firm, its strategic business units, products, etc. is defined. The integration of economic with ecological performance indicators provides a measure for economic-ecological efficiency (eco-efficiency), thus allowing environmental issues to be incorporated into the decision making of internal and external stakeholders.[1]

The "factual" goal of eco-integrated strategic management is to integrate financial and ecological measures of business activities to achieve sustainable growth of an organization. Sustainable growth of an organization is characterized by economic growth with unchanged or reduced impacts on the environment (see Section 7.2). The "political" purpose of integrating and weighting economic and ecological effects is to include and meet requests of different stakeholders. Depending on the need for information and the goals of stakeholders, economic performance or growth can be measured in sales, revenues, contribution margin, net present value (NPV), etc. To support rational eco-integrated investment decisions *project related* financial and environmental information is necessary.

11.2 ECO-INTEGRATED PORTFOLIO ANALYSIS

This section suggests an eco-integrated portfolio approach (also eco-efficiency portfolio) to address strategic environmental issues (Ilinitch and Schaltegger 1995, see also Schaltegger and Sturm 1992a). On a conceptual basis, this matrix-oriented tool may help firms to evaluate the environmental and economic impact of specific products, strategic business units (SBUs), and industry mix. Additionally, this tool may support strategic decisions involving divestiture, acquisition, product development and marketing, communication with external stakeholders, and negotiation with environmental compliance groups, regulators, etc.

This section also discusses an eco-integrated approach to product and industry portfolio analysis, describes the eco-integrated portfolio matrix, and shows how the matrix may be used to evaluate strategic options. Examples from the paper and chemical industries illustrate uses of the matrix at the product, business, and corporate levels of analysis. The section concludes with implications for different management levels.

Portfolio approaches have been used for several decades to help diversified firms analyse their business mix (see, for example, Hofer and Schendel 1978; for other matrices, see Hill and Jones 1989, Pearce and Robinson 1991). While the dimensions of the models and corresponding matrices vary, each dimension addresses only economic aspects of the corporate portfolio. Although most managers would agree that environmental decisions affect economic success, the environmental dimension has only recently been explicitly incorporated into strategic portfolio analysis.

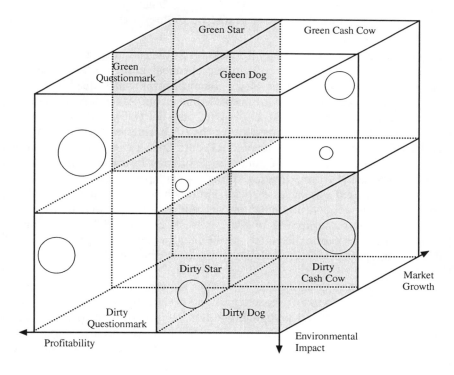

Figure 11.3   Eco-Integrated Portfolio Matrix (also Eco-Efficiency Matrix).
Source: Ilinitch and Schaltegger 1995

Figure 11.3 shows a three dimensional model of the *eco-integrated portfolio matrix*. By adding an ecological measure to any strategic portfolio matrix such as the Boston Consulting Group (BCG) matrix or the General Electric matrix, a three dimensional eco-integrated portfolio can be developed. The eco-integrated portfolio matrix involves quantifying the environmental impact added of business activities and comparing them with economic aspects such as growth and market share of the business examined. To facilitate discussion of the matrix, modified BCG matrix dimensions are used to represent the horizontal, economic plane in Figure 11.3. The vertical axis shows the environmental impact dimension, and the size of the circles assigned to specific products or industries may represent either total sales in dollars or the total environmental impact. This general approach is applicable to any firm or product group and can be employed in as many or as few details as managers desire (for an application see Box 11.1).

Box 11.1
Analysis of the US Chemical Industry
with the Eco-Integrated Portfolio Matrix

Figure 11.4 shows an exemplary application of the eco-integrated portfolio matrix for a competitor analysis in the chemical industry. This analysis works with the US operations of six chemical firms which display a wide range of variance on the environmental dimension: American Cyanamid, Ciba-Geigy Corporation (US), Dow, Du Pont, ICI (US), and Monsanto.

The source of toxic emissions data for the US businesses of these six firms is the US Toxic Release Inventory (TRI) data base. (The data were kindly provided, in pounds, by the Council on Economic Priorities, CEP, a non-profit organization investigating firms' social performance.) Using a standards-oriented impact assessment approach (see Section 8.2.3), sales-weighted units of environmental impact added were calculated for each firm. The analysis is limited to two years, 1989 and 1990, due to data constraints. The economic data—profit margin and sales growth—were drawn from public sources, including annual reports and the US Industrial Outlook.

Figure 11.4 shows each firm's profit, sales growth, units of environmental impact added due to toxic releases/thousand dollars of sales, and total units of EIA for both 1989 and 1990, highlighting changes from one period to the next. The arrows show the general direction in which the firm is moving, while the size of the circles represents the total EIA emitted of total sales by all US operations of each firm.

Several conclusions can be drawn from the relationship between the economic attractiveness of a firm and its environmental impact. First, the

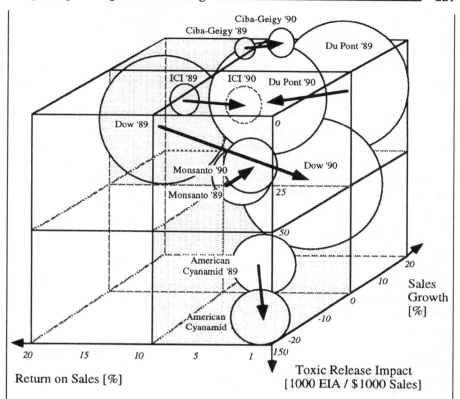

Figure 11.4 Eco-Integrated Portfolio Matrix Applied to Corporations (Comparison of Two Years)

six firms occupy substantially different static and dynamic economic and environmental positions. On the environmental dimensions, over the 1989–90 time frame, Ciba Geigy was the least polluting firm in both absolute and relative terms, American Cyanamid was the worst polluter per thousand dollar sales, and Dow had the largest absolute number of units of environmental impact added. Du Pont was the most environmentally improved over this time frame, reducing relative EIA units by roughly 35%. On the other hand, Dow moved in the opposite direction, increasing its relative EIA units by roughly 40% over this time frame.

The results are less straightforward on the economic dimensions. Evaluating change over this period is problematic, as sales growth and profitability for the entire industry declined between 1989 and 1990. In addition, two years is too short a period to display any definite trend at any rate. On the profitability scale, American Cyanamid's profit declined most on a percentage basis over this period (-67%), followed by that of Dow (-50%). ICI's profitability declined least (0%), followed by that of Du Pont (-14%). On the sales growth scale, again American Cyanamid experienced the greatest percentage decrease in sales growth (-200%), with Dow and ICI experiencing the greatest increases, at 71% and 100% respectively.

In matrix terms, American Cyanamid is moving towards the "dirty dog" position during this period, while Du Pont is moving towards the "green star" position. Dow's move towards a "dirtier" position was accompanied by strong sales growth yet a loss in profitability, while Du Pont's move towards a "greener" position was accompanied by its ability to maintain profit and sales growth. Ciba Geigy and ICI remained the "greenest" firms over the two year time frame, without experiencing an extreme loss of position in sales growth or profitability relative to their competitors.

The interpretation of these changes is complicated and should be qualified in several ways. First, the trend observed over this difficult two year period for the industry may not be the same as the trend in better economic times. Investigations over a longer period will soon be possible, as more TRI-data are published. Next, a phenomenon like Dow's increase of environmental impact added could result, hypothetically, from more accurate reporting of toxic releases rather than from an increase in EIA. Similarly, the change in Dow's sales growth could result from entering a rapidly growing, yet "dirtier", line of business. Finally, the TRI releases do not take non-pollutant related impacts on the environment into account (such as clear cutting, extinction of species, etc.).

However, this analysis seems to suggest that environmental sensitivity may have either positive economic effects on the firms investigated, or at least have no negative effects. Ciba and ICI did not suffer economically from their "green positions", while American Cyanamid seems to have been punished economically for its extreme "dirty position". Interestingly, the European firms' US operations were "greener" on average than those of US firms, possibly because of stronger regulatory and consumer pressures in Europe, and perhaps because the "Europeans" manufacture their "dirtier" basic chemicals outside the USA. Also, the firms which have made the greatest improvement in their environmental performance may not have reaped the economic benefits of lower clean-up costs, lower fines and consumer response over this short time frame.

The results of this analysis of the six chemical firms differ sharply from environmental rankings which are based on physical quantities not being assessed (see, for example, Rice 1993; Weir and Yamin 1993). Such inconsistencies occur for at least two reasons: (1) different evaluators use different objective measures of environmental performance; and (2) some rankings weight subjective data more heavily than objective data. Such inconsistencies may not only confuse or mislead those who attempt to use the data to make strategic decisions, but being listed may also damage the reputations and bottom lines of companies with low rankings by discouraging consumers from purchasing their products, discouraging investors from purchasing their stock, and attracting negative and costly attention from regulators, environmental "watchdog" groups, and the press. For these reasons, groups producing such rankings should be careful to clarify their rating system, and those using the rankings need to be educated regarding the biases associated with different data sources and weighting schemes.

The optimal position on the eco-efficiency matrix is the "*green star*": high economic impact and low environmental harm. An example of this sort of product might be a high market share, recyclable white paper produced by an energy-efficient mill which uses a non-chlorine bleaching process. Non-plastic coated paper and greeting cards made from recycled paper tend to be high value-added products for which demand is relatively large, yet which also have a relatively low environmental impact when produced in this way.

The opposite matrix cell, a "*dirty dog*" position, is no position anyone would endeavour to reach, although it may result from a combination of managerial decisions, the history of the firm, changing standards, increased industry risk, and new environmental issues. An example of a "dirty dog" might be bleached pulp produced by a smaller, older, energy intensive mill which uses a chlorine bleaching process. Such mills cannot achieve the economies of scale needed to gain market shares in their commodity markets. From an eco-integrated perspective, many products manufactured with such methods cause environmental harm without producing significant economic benefits.

Many intermediate positions exist between these two extremes. "*Dirty cash cows*" tend to possess high market shares in mature or declining "dirty" industries. An example of a "dirty cash cow" might be plastic coated, white paper from a relatively large and efficient pulp mill which uses chlorinated bleaching technologies and which benefited from the paper industry's lobbying for low emission standards or high pollution quotas. Such businesses can, in the short run, be highly profitable for both firms and the communities in which they operate, so that there is an economic incentive for continuing production. This position is very weak and risky in the long run, however, because of the increasing possibility that the potential loss of reputation, as well as the liability for a potential environmental disaster, could become actual costs for the company. Increasingly, stakeholders and "watchdog" groups search for ways to establish not only financial but criminal penalties for such actions. Depending on the firm's market share, plastic coated paper packaging materials, which are associated with high pollution releases but which also have a high and growing demand, may be positioned either as *"dirty stars"* or *"dirty question marks"*.

A counterpoint to the "dirty cash cow" might be the "green dog" or "green question mark". A "green dog" is in a weak position due to its lack of financial contribution, even though it is an environmentally attractive business. Examples of this position are high-priced, biodegradable paper products. These products may have experienced either limited success or failure in these markets, depending on their cost structure, their technology, and their ability to convince growing numbers of consumers that paying premium prices for environmentally sound products is worthwhile. Products which may be "green dogs" in a recessionary economy may have the long term potential to become "green question marks" or even "green stars" in a stronger economic climate. The strategic challenge for "green dogs" is to become financially more viable. This is sometimes achieved by a correct allocation of environmentally induced costs (see Section 4.3). A market must be created for the products, and/or the producer must capture market share. If consumer values and behavior can be changed, or if production costs can be lowered, "green dogs" may be very profitable sometime in the future.

In the coming decade, strategies which move firms toward "green cash cow" positions should enable them to achieve more sustainable growth. Likewise, the cost of operating in the "dirty cash cow" quadrant will surely increase. If "dirty cow" firms are unable or unwilling to develop environmentally sensitive products and invest in clean technologies, they may rapidly fall into the "dirty dog" corner. Late efforts to improve the environmental record of entrenched "dirty cash cows" may lead to an increase in costs without a similar increase in revenues. As a consequence, they may shift to the "green dog" position. For "dirty cows", environmental costs must be supervised and tracked closely. As they begin to rise, either a major clean-up effort or a quick divestiture is recommended.

While firms with "dirty cash cow" cultures may not be inclined towards "green" solutions, a conflict or trade-off between environmental and financial goals is not inevitable. Innovative pollution and risk prevention strategies and the substitution of environmentally positive inputs may improve the firm's environmental position. Such actions also can increase the contribution margin and net present value by lowering input and production costs or increasing sales and, therefore, may even move "dirty dogs" into the "green cash cow" quadrant (see for example Spitzer 1992, Spitzer *et al.* 1993).

Depending on the purpose of analysis a two dimensional eco-integrated portfolio matrix with one economic and one ecological performance indicator can be drawn (see Schaltegger and Sturm 1992a). The advantage of a three-dimensional portfolio matrix is that more measures can be integrated and shown visually. However, the portfolio and the interpretations are also complicated.

11.3 ECO-INTEGRATED STRATEGIES

As much has been written about environmental corporate and business strategies, this section is brief (see, e.g., Allenby and Fullerton 1992, Annighöfer 1990, Schreiner 1988, Steger 1988, Schmid 1989, Wells 1990).

The eco-integrated portfolio matrix has been used to *evaluate strategic options* on at least three levels: corporate, business, and product (for more examples of applications of such portfolios, see Ilinitch and Schaltegger, 1995). Table 11.1 shows the interaction of the three strategic levels, their respective stakeholder groups, and the types of decisions associated with each.

The interpretation of eco-efficiency portfolios is as delicate as the discussion with the BCG matrix suggests.[2] Nevertheless, the portfolios are mainly a way to visualize and integrate information from ecological and traditional accounting for strategic purposes. In practice, management also very much appreciates another use of eco-integrated accounting information, namely for investment appraisal (see Schaltegger and Sturm 1992a, Ilinitch and Schaltegger 1995).

On the *corporate strategy* level, firms are concerned with their portfolio of businesses and with the issues which impact on the firm as a whole. Much has been written about the economic impact of a firm's portfolio of businesses in terms of risk diversification, managerial complexity and economic profitability (see for example Hill and Jones 1989, Schendel and Hofer 1978). Understanding the relationship between environmental actions and economic results is increasingly important on the corporate strategy level, because environmental choices affect a firm's reputation as well as its bottom line. Environmental rankings which have appeared in the popular and business press vividly illustrate this point (see, for example, Crawford 1992, CEP 1993, Rice 1993, Speich 1992, Vaughan and Mickle 1993, Weir and Yamin 1993). Strategic options on the corporate strategy level include choosing which new businesses to enter, evaluating potential candidates for acquisition and divestiture, allocating scarce or constrained resources among business units, monitoring and enhancing the firm's reputation, and evaluating the ability to obtain market financing relative to its competitors.

On the *business strategy* level, options include evaluating the potential impact of new, complementary, and substitute products on the strategic business unit's (SBU) reputation and performance and assessing an SBU's strategic position relative to its competitors within an industry. Additional possibilities include acquisition of patents and production capacity, new plant locations, and product mix decisions.

Table 11.1 Strategic Dimensions of Eco-Integrated Portfolio Matrices

Stakeholder and Focus Level	Internal		External	
	Stakeholder Group	Focus (Examples)	Stakeholder Group	Focus (Examples)
Corporate Strategy Level	Top management (mgmt), strategic planning mgmt, environmental mgmt government, public & investor relations, finan. mgmt, legal mgmt, etc.	Corporate strategy & policy, environmental record & image of company, environmental compliance, etc.	Green investment, fund mgmt, investors, watchdog groups, government & regulatory agencies, etc.	Selection of shares, bonds etc., firms to blame, environmental compliance, etc.
Business Strategy Level	Division/SBU mgmt, competitor analysis mgmt, marketing mgmt, purchasing department, etc.	Relative position/strengths of company, potential assets & liabilities, etc.	Competitors, industry analysts, investment bankers, industry consultants, purchasing groups, etc.	Relative position & strengths of competitor, cost effective pollution prevention, contingent liabilities, etc.
Product Strategy Level	Product mgmt, marketing mgmt, patenting & licencing mgmt, manufacturing mgmt, etc.	Sales arguments, potential assets, comparison of technologies, evaluation of environmental impacts/ compliance, communication with agencies, etc.	Consumers, marketing consultants, green labelling groups, regulatory agencies, lawyers, manufacturers, etc.	Purchase, consumption, communications, environmental harm, compliance, product liability suits, purchase, liabilities, etc.

On the *product strategy* level, options include investment in technological innovations, the exploration of new uses of products, product marketing decisions, relaunches, environmental upgrades, and discontinuation of certain products.

While internal stakeholders such as top management, division managers or product managers may have access to the most accurate and specific data available, interested *external groups* such as investors, consumers and often also regulatory agencies must base their decisions on information available to the public, which tends to be more general and less reliable. Nevertheless, the actions of external stakeholders are a function of the economic and ecological information available about a company, its businesses and products. Also, firms must assess their position relative to that of their competitors by using externally available data. Therefore, it is important for corporate management to consider both internal and external data for its analysis.

An important consideration when comparing firms or products using the eco-integrated matrix is the industry environment in which the firm or product exists. It is impractical to assume that "dirty" industries can be eliminated from the industrial landscape, at least in the foreseeable future. So, *advanced firms in "dirty" industries should be identified and encouraged* on the basis of the improvement they achieve and their position within their industry, rather than be compared with a norm for all firms. Similarly, businesses which score significantly below their competitors in relatively "green" industries should be carefully scrutinized and encouraged to improve their records.

In order to simplify the discussion of the eco-integrated portfolio matrix, the traditional industry attractiveness yardsticks are applied of industry growth rate and firm market share or profitability to represent economic performance. These choices allow the use of familiar terms such as "cows" and "dogs" to discuss relationships between economic and environmental dimensions. The BCG dimensions also address the issue of sustainable growth as a key environmental concept (see for example Schmidheiny 1992, Shrivastava 1993, Shrivastava and Hart 1992). However, depending upon the use of the matrix, other economic measures may be preferable. For example, financial analysts may be interested in tracking pollution relative to total market return. Industry analysts may prefer to use environmental expenditure as a percentage of total cash flow or total debt capacity to evaluate firms' abilities to make long term commitments to environmental programs.

Eco-integrated matrices allow management to make not only a static but also a dynamic analysis by comparing the position of products, SBUs, or companies over time. All movements towards "green cash cow" positions represent sustainable growth of economic performance together with a reduction or maintenance of environmental impacts.

Economically or environmentally proactive strategies lead to better ecological and/or economic performance through innovation. Environmentally and economically reactive strategies, on the other hand, are characterized by being imitations performed with a time lag. No movement at all may be the result of poorly enforced or defensive strategies.

As general recommendations are always dangerous, it is very important also to analyse all the opportunities to convert "dirty dogs" into "green cash cows".

In practice the following different approaches to improve the "greenness" of products, businesses, companies, etc. can be observed.

- "*Repair approach*": in focusing on a specific product, the environmental intervention which causes most EIA units is investigated; for example a scrubber is added to the production step which releases the environmental intervention.
- "*Exchange approach*": for example, inputs which cause hazardous environmental interventions are replaced by other less harmful inputs.
- "*Quick strategic approach*": for example, the product with most environmental impact added per dollar yield is eliminated.
- "*Functional approach*": for example, management tries to find entirely new, "greener" ways to fulfil a certain function, i.e. to meet the wishes of buyers. This can be done by replacing a product with a service.

It is obvious that in many cases only the functional approach will lead to an overall improvement in the economic and ecological results.

11.4   SUMMARY AND IMPLICATIONS

In summary, this chapter has described a new tool for the analysis of economic and environmental performances of firms and products. The eco-integrated portfolio matrix approach provides a strategic framework for the evaluation of impacts of environmental actions on firm, SBU and product performance, both over time and relative to competitors in the same industry. The matrix can be used for several analytical purposes, such as evaluations of changes in product technologies or in a firm's business mix using data from internal ecological accounting. Using externally generated data of eco-rating organizations, the matrix may also help to evaluate competing firms' relative positions within a single industry environment.

The uses of this eco-integrated portfolio framework extend beyond internal evaluations of investment, technological and marketing decisions and external analysis of competitors. From an internal corporate perspective, firms may wish to consider whether current product lines are consistent with the image of their own policies. Products which are "dirtier" than desired can be identified and either targeted for environmental upgrading, written off, or sold to competitors with more compatible environmental strategies. Similarly, products which are "greener" may serve as bench-marks for other products, providing a road map for upgrading the firm's environmental image.

From an external market perspective, investors and analysts may be interested in evaluating a firm's or an investor's portfolio in terms of environmental exposure for either social or economic reasons. At present, environmental funds tend to use subjective evaluations of firms' environmental performance. This may cause fund managers to restrict their investment horizon unnecessarily by overlooking stocks which represent long-term environmental opportunities (risks) or which are improving their environmental and economic dimensions. A second, market-based use for the matrix is to support, buy, sell or hold recommendations for stocks. By tracking a firm's environmental opportunities (risks) relative to its economic benefits over time, analysts may begin to spot movements from a relatively attractive business mix to one which is considerably less attractive, due to changes in environmental standards and/or competitor responses.

Possible uses of the eco-integrated matrix are as a tool for analyses and communications, all of which are instrumental in effective strategic planning. The presentation and interpretation of environmental data is a challenge, particularly when comparing companies within an industry using external data. Sometimes, it may not be possible to determine whether environmental actions are the cause or the result of economic conditions. However, studies have shown that firms with the greenest environmental records do not seem to suffer undue economic hardships (Investors Environmental Report 1995b). Their examples should encourage managers to make investments to improve the environmental record of their firms.

Section 11.5 deals with eco-integrated investment appraisal, a tool which allows the detection of those investment opportunities which contribute most to eco-efficiency.

11.5 ECO-INTEGRATED INVESTMENT APPRAISAL

Eco-integrated investment appraisal enables management to measure and improve eco-efficiency.

It has been shown earlier in this book (Section 4.5) that investment appraisals must correctly consider (future) environmentally induced costs and revenues. Investments are commitments to a (future) strategic path of the firm. To repair and correct after investments have been transacted is often very costly (e.g. accumulated potential liabilities, repair costs, etc.). It is therefore vital that environmental aspects are considered early in the planning stage.

To correctly calculate the profitability of products and production devices all environmentally induced and other costs or revenues must be tracked, traced and allocated correctly. In the past, the calculation and allocation of environmentally induced costs received only a limited degree of attention. In particular, the costs of handling, machine occupation, personnel and raw materials have often not been considered when calculating the costs of waste generation. For the allocation of environmentally induced costs, the EIA caused by each cost center must be known.

The main purpose of eco-integrated investment appraisal is to *realize environmental protection in the most economic way*, i.e. to obtain the greatest possible improvement with a given budget. Economic use of scarce financial means for environmental protection is necessary to prove to shareholders that money is not wasted. Economically efficient environmental protection also serves "green" stakeholders, as it allows more environmental interventions to be reduced for the same amount of money.

Formulated in a more operative sense, one goal of eco-integrated investment appraisals is to get the greatest possible reduction of environmental impact added for the money spent (see Schaltegger and Sturm 1992a, Bretschger *et al.* 1993, Schaltegger *et al.* 1996).

As with products, businesses and firms, the Eco-Rational Path Method (EPM) can also be applied for investment appraisals.

Investments in prevention of environmental impact added are carried out to improve corporate environmental performance. Therefore, first of all, ecological efficiency must be ensured. As shown in Section 8.4, ecological investment analysis of an environmental protection device compares the EIA of production, operation and disposal with the reduced EIA over the whole useful life of the device. As the primary purpose of investments for environmental protection is to prevent future environmental impacts, the reduced EIA is not discounted.

Second, the economic efficiency of all alternatives must be calculated.[3] This can be done by calculating the net present value (NPV) including the option value. The NPV is the sum of all discounted payments and receipts over the life of an investment.

Third, the most economic of all ecologically efficient means must be ascertained. This can be done by calculating eco-efficiency, i.e. how much money has to be spent to reduce EIA by one unit:

$$\text{Eco} - \text{efficiency} = \frac{\Delta \text{ monetary unit}}{\Delta \text{ unit of EIA}} = \frac{\text{NPV}}{\Sigma \text{ net EIA}}$$

Table 11.2 gives an example of an eco-integrated investment appraisal of two alternatives to reduce emissions of a production process; to keep the example simple, it is assumed that no depreciation, taxes, etc. apply.

Alternatives A and B both cause costs. They serve the same goal and both are ecologically efficient as they lead to a net reduction of environmental

Table 11.2 Example of Eco-Integrated Investment Appraisal

	Investment A	Investment B
NPV	−200	−270
Σ net EIA	−100	−162
Eco-efficiency	1/2 = 0.5	81/135 = 0.6
Ranking	2	1 (best)

impact added. However, investment A gives a smaller reduction in environmental impacts for the money spent as its eco-efficiency is 0.5 compared to 0.6 for investment B.

The basic principle of calculating the eco-efficiency of investments is always the same, no matter whether the alternatives lead to economic benefits or costs or whether they cause or reduce environmental impacts. For further examples of eco-integrated investment appraisal see Schaltegger and Sturm (1992a).

It is in the interest of both environmentalists and managers to decrease environmental problems as much as possible with a certain financial budget. For management the calculation of economic-ecological efficiency of investments is valuable, as ecological goals are often fixed and have to be achieved in the cheapest way possible.

As will be shown in the next chapter, apart from its use for investment appraisal, the Eco-Rational Path Method (EPM) is also the foundation for integrated economic-ecological reporting (Chapter 12) as well as for eco-integrated controlling (Chapter 13).

12
Environmental Reporting

This chapter deals with the main questions and the basic principles of integrated economic-ecological reporting, i.e. the reporting of environmentally induced financial impacts and environmental impact added.

The main considerations with regard to the publication of an environmental report are why reporting should be carried out, what issues should be dealt with (what questions should be answered) and what distinguishes outstanding environmental reports from other such reports.

The following sections deal with the characteristics of sucessful environmental reporting in the context of seven of the most important questions of reporting.

- Why should reporting be carried out (Section 12.1)?
- Who should report (Section 12.2)?
- To whom (Section 12.3)?
- What are appropriate topics of environmental reporting (Section 12.4)?
- When is the ideal moment for environmental reporting (Section 12.5)?
- How often should reporting take place (Section 12.6)?
- How should reporting be done (Section 12.7)?

The chapter concludes with a discussion of the reaction of stakeholders to environmental reporting (Section 12.8).

12.1 WHY SHOULD REPORTING BE CARRIED OUT?

The managements of many companies have declared that they have not only economic but also environmental and social responsibilities. One part of taking these responsibilities is the reporting of the relevant achievements.

Financial reporting is established to ensure that financial stakeholders continue to provide financial resources for the company. Shareholders and lenders will only continue to supply their resources if they obtain useful information to assess whether they receive an acceptable return.

External ecological accounting and reporting serves to meet the information needs of stakeholders supplying resources such as labour, social acceptance, optimal regulations, etc. In addition, environmental issues exercise an influence on the price which a company must pay for its financial resources.

FASB (1994, FAS 1) defines the main objectives of financial reporting as, ". . . to provide information that is useful to present and potential investors and creditors and other users in making rational investment, credit and similar decisions. The information should be comprehensible to those who have a reasonable understanding of business and economic activities and are willing to study the information with reasonable diligence."

The objectives for environmental reporting can be defined very similarly: to provide information to present and potential stakeholders in making rational decisions. The information should be comprehensible to those who have a reasonable understanding of business and economic activities as well as of environmental impacts caused through these activities and who are willing to study the information with reasonable diligence.

An empirical study of Deloitte Touche Tohmatsu International et al. (1993, p. 27) concluded that the duty to the natural environment, public relations, future legal requirements (for Europe), competitive advantage and shareholder pressure are the main reasons for issuing an environmental report.

12.2 WHO SHOULD REPORT?

The first companies to issue environmental reports were from the chemical and oil industries. These companies took the lead as they were among the first to experience heavy pressure from external stakeholders. In the last decade many firms operating in sectors as diverse as power generation, waste management, computers, cosmetics, air travel, telecommunications and many others have been confronted with similar pressure and/or opportunities (Deloitte Touche Tohmatsu et al. 1993, p. 18). Even banking, once seen as untouched by environmental matters, has started with environmental reporting (e.g. Swiss Bank Corporation, National Westminster Bank). Today, no firm can seriously claim to have definitely no need for environmental reporting.

Small firms are less "quasi-public" (exposed to the public) than large multinationals. In addition, their management capacities are often more limited so that the costs involved with environmental reporting are relatively much higher for small than for large firms. For such small firms the inclusion of environmental matters in the financial annual report is a viable alternative to a special environmental report.

The credibility of reported information depends on the credibility of management and its environmental statement. Therefore, a clear commitment from top management is necessary. Ideally, this commitment should be supported with the activities of management and employees of the firm. In some cases even the private life of top managers can influence the credibility of the company as a whole.

12.3   REPORTING TO WHOM?

Environmental reports should focus on issues which certain, powerful stakeholders attempt to influence.[4] However, what information is crucial and of prime interest to which stakeholder?

This question can be answered in a systematic way, first by analysing the goals and the relative power of critical stakeholders. Second, those activities of the firm can be analyzed which have a considerable impact on the respective stakeholders. Then, it can be concluded for what reasons specific information concerning the firm's activities may be of prime interest for a specific stakeholder.

The "profile", i.e. the composition, importance and power of various stakeholders of a firm, determines the spectrum of addressees of an environmental report. The importance and power of a stakeholder is mainly determined by its value as a supplier of resources. A survey by Deloitte Touche Tohmatsu International *et al.* (1993, pp. 28 ff) showed that *employees* were the target group which was regarded as most important by the issuers of

Table 12.1   Percentage of Report Makers Targeting Particular Audiences. Source: Deloitte Touche Tohmatsu *et al.* 1993, p. 29

	Europe	North America	Japan
Employees	88	96	78
Consumers	43	26	89
Shareholders	65	78	33
Environmental campaigners	65	70	22
Local communities	65	70	56
Trade and industry customers	68	35	44
Media	65	39	56
Regulators	60	52	44
Financial community	53	48	22
Others	23	52	0

environmental reports. Table 12.1 lists the importance of various stakeholders as stated for Europe, North America and Japan.

A clear analysis of the user's needs helps to select the right information for the respective user. Checks, for example with pretests, reduce the risk of being misunderstood. A continuous two-way communication with critical stakeholders may help issues of interest to be identified very early. The report should be understandable for the target group and whenever technical and scientific language is necessary, explanations (e.g. glossaries) must be added.

12.4 WHAT SHOULD BE REPORTED?

All of us tend to be confronted with a flood of information. However, many decision makers and stakeholders often lack crucial information for environmentally important issues. Therefore, only that kind of information should be communicated to a stakeholder group which it considers to be of prime interest.

Twenty years ago, social reporting containing social as well as environmental issues was considered to be important. The main objective was to report the contribution of a company to society with information such as value added, number of employees, donations given, means and distances of transportation, etc. Yet, the trend of social reporting did not last. It was followed by safety-oriented reports which in turn became forerunners of todays environmental reports. Chemical and oil companies, being strongly exposed to safety requirements, were the first firms to publish safety reports.

Historically, environmental information was part of the financial annual reports. However, the information given—commented outlines of environmental policies—was very vague. Few if any quantitative data were given.

The first actual environmental reports already contained quantitative ecological data. A further improvement followed after the formulation of the "CERES Principles" (formerly "The Valdez Principles") (CERES 1992), which provide a general guideline to environmental reporting. In the last decade, environmental reports have become increasingly popular.

Today, environmental reporting comprises the communication of environmentally induced financial impacts as well as environmental impact added. Recently, many firms have started to issue a number of environmental reports, namely one for the whole group (corporate environmental report) plus several reports for all or the most important production sites. In this way, the firm takes account of the various information needs of different stakeholder groups. The corporate report is steadily gaining importance for actors in the financial markets.

12.4.1 Reporting Environmentally Induced Financial Impacts

Environmental compliance costs and potential liabilities can have a dramatic influence on the operations, liquidity and financial condition of a corporation (Table 12.2, see also Napolitano 1995). Therefore, most of the early environmental reports focused on costs of compliance, environmentally induced capital investments, etc. (see Table 12.3). Environmentally induced financial revenues or gains have rarely been mentioned in corporate reports even when the firm has profited from environmental issues.

However, the interpretation of environmental expenditures and capital investments is a delicate matter. First, there are no clear rules about how to determine what an environmental expenditure or an environmental investment is (see also Section 4.2.1). End-of-the-pipe technologies are obviously environmentally induced. Nevertheless, it is more difficult to detect how much of an integrated technology is environmentally related. Hence, the management has a large discretionary latitude in measuring environmentally induced financial impacts.

Second, the interpretation of the figures showing environmental expenditures and investments is ambiguous.

(a) Did the management spend more on environmental issues because it did more?
(b) Did the management spend more because it did not do enough in the past?

Table 12.2 Remediation Costs as Percentage of Pretax Income of Some US Corporations

	1992–1994	1994
Monsanto	9.2	7.0
Eastman Chemicals	n.a.	26.4
Alcan	n.a.	19.6
Mobil	32.4	27.2
Occidental Petrol	52.9	106.5

Table 12.3 Annual Environmentally Induced Capital Expenditures as Percentage of Total Capital Expenditures of Some US Corporations

	1992–1994	1994
Monsanto	n.a.	60.9
Eastman Chemicals	> 10.0	11.4
Alcan	0.1	11.0
Mobil	12.9	11.8
Occidental Petrol	7.6	6.1

(c) Did the management spend more because it did not effectively reduce the environmental impacts?

(d) Did the management spend more because its environmental protection activities were inefficient?

The questions show clearly that financial numbers alone do not say anything about the eco-efficiency of the firm. To provide further information, the financial figures must be put into the context of the environmental impact added of the company.

12.4.2 Reporting Environmental Impacts

In an analogy to the basic perspectives of ecological accounting (Section 9.1) the reporting of environmental impact added can also be:

- product-oriented
- site-oriented
- business- and company-oriented.

A first question to be answered for environmental reporting is therefore: should ecological information be reported for the whole company, or also for plants and strategic business units or even for products?

At the beginning of the 1980s there was a tendency to report the environmental impacts of selected *products* that had incurred public notoriety. Today, most environmental reports no longer include product-oriented information. Marketing tools such as "eco-labels", which are directly attached to products, have replaced the firms' reports of product-oriented information. Eco-labels are environmental information in an extremely condensed form. The information provided is often limited: mostly it simply states whether a more or less clear benchmark has been achieved. More informative eco-labels communicate product-oriented key-indicators such as use of water, emissions, etc. An excellent example of such an eco-label is the eco-profile of Scientific Certification Systems (SCS) (Figure 12.1).

Because of their simplicity, eco-labels are easily understandable particularly for customers who possess little if any knowledge about environmental sciences. By giving guidance, they usually provide the receivers with information on the basis of which they can decide whether or not to buy the company's product. Thus, the feedback mechanism is rather direct and is reflected in sales figures. Because of the simplicity of this system, eco-labels have to omit many informational aspects, and concentrate on only a few areas which are considered representative for the product's environmental benignity.

Today's corporate environmental reporting focuses on *sites* as well as on *businesses and firms*. Site-oriented environmental reports are typical for plants which are located in or near cities in the modern Western world. Site-specific

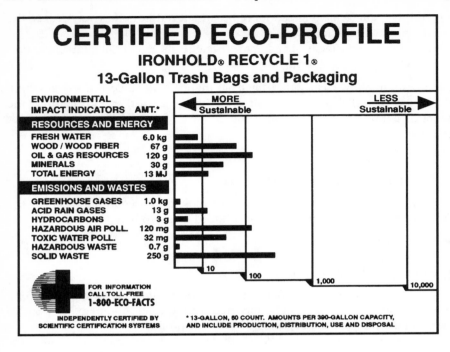

Figure 12.1 Example of an Informative Eco-Label. Source: According to Scientific Certification Systems. Reproduced with permission

reporting is a sign of advanced management which has established communications with environmentally aware and well educated citizens, local environmental pressure groups, etc.

More common than site-specific reports are corporate environmental reports, i.e. of transnational companies. First, large companies are more exposed to public opinion than small firms. Second, their contribution to the cause as well as to the solution of many environmental problems is considerable. For instance, transnational firms emit over 50% of all global greenhouse gases (UN 1992d, pp. 2 ff). Furthermore, these firms also have available the necessary resources for research and development as well as for solving the problems. Table 12.4 shows the consolidated ecological report of the Ciba concern. Recent reports provide details about the environmental interventions related to strategic business units. This allows possible environmental opportunities and business problems to be judged.

Table 12.4 Consolidated Environmental Report of the Ciba Group (in Tons per Year)

	1991	1994
Toxic waste disposal	**1,533,000**	**1,370,000**
• Recycling	1,277,000	1,136,000
• Incineration	224,000	197,000
• Landfill	32,000	37,000
CO_2 emissions	**1,200,000**	**1,260,000**
SO_2 emissions	**3,540**	**2,000**
NO_x emissions	**2,235**	**2,030**
Other air emissions	**8,180**	**5,920**
• Non-halogenated organic gases	5,480	4,940
• Halogenated organic gases	1,350	320
• Inorganic gases	1,140	580
• Total particulates	210	80
CFC, HCFC & halon	**n.a.**	**35.60**
• CFC	n.a.	9
• HCFC	n.a.	26
• Halon	n.a.	0.60

The main accounting emphasis for company-oriented reporting of environmental impact added is on *consolidated* environmental data (see also Section 9.1). The main addresses of consolidated figures are the investors.

In the best case, the application of the methods of impact assessment in ecological accounting provides information about *potential* environmental impacts (see for example Wenzel 1994). The actual environmental impact of most interventions depends to a large extent on the sensitivity of local and regional habitats as well as on the actual ambient environmental quality. One additional kilogram of discharged SO_2, for example, has *inter alia* a much more severe environmental impact in highly polluted regions of Poland than in remote northern Norway. Therefore, consolidation of environmental interventions in different regions becomes problematic or perhaps even impossible as soon as the intervention contributes to a non-global impact category. Table 12.5 shows examples of environmental impact categories with different spatial dimensions (global, sub-continental, regional, local).

Emissions which contribute to global problems such as the destruction of the ozone layer or the greenhouse effect can very well be consolidated on a global level. However, consolidated figures of emissions with a local and regional impact (e.g. toxics, heavy metals, water pollution) are merely artificial and cannot reflect the real environmental impacts at all (see also Section 9.3). Nevertheless, even for environmental interventions of local and regional impact, it could be argued that consolidation is not different from that of

Table 12.5 Spatial Impacts of Different Impact Categories. Source: Similar to Henshaw 1994

Spatial dimension Impact category	Global	Sub-continental	Regional	Local
Depletion of abiotic resources	+	+		
Depletion of biotic resources	+			
Global warming	+			
Ozone depletion	+	+		
Human toxicity			+	+
Eco-toxicity			+	+
Photochemical oxidant formation			+	+
Acidification			+	+
Nutrification			+	+
Land Use			+	+

financial statements. A given sum of money spent in Brazil does not have the same impact as if it were spent in England. However, this argument lacks validity as, in contrast to local environmental impacts, local money usually can easily be transferred to other places.

A discussion of where environmental interventions of regional impact have occurred can help in the correct understanding of consolidated information.

As this section shows, the mere reporting of environmental impacts is not sufficient to measure eco-efficiency.

12.4.3 Conclusions

Modern environmental reports focus on eco-integrated key-numbers as discussed in Chapter 11. Eco-integrated key-numbers are derived by calculating ratios between environmental figures and financial figures. Furthermore, the economic and the ecological dimensions are interconnected, for the ecological performance of a company influences its financial results. Also the environmental performance of a firm is often a function of its financial viability.

In addition to eco-integrated figures, stakeholders are interested in qualitative information describing the environmental policy of the firm, etc. Environmental reports which are required by regulators concentrate on legal requirements (Section 13.3). However, external ecological reports are distributed not only to civil servants but to a wider public. Employees, media, neighbours, etc. request information concerning publicly discussed environmental issues. Creditors and insurance companies request information concerning potential future problem-substances. Considering the potential and actual users of external environmental reports, it would seem reactive if only legally regulated environmental issues were disclosed. Nevertheless, a report without disclosure of the firm's legal compliance would be ridiculous. In summary, all ecological information which is *material* should be reported (see Section 10.2.1).

Besides financial and ecological information, an ideal environmental report should include the following *additional features* and answer the respective questions (Schaltegger and Sturm 1995, see also Fichter and Clausen 1994, p. 19).

- *Short presentation of the company and its business*
  What is the range of business in which the firm operates? Is the firm a major player in the market? Does it have enough economic potential to carry out advanced environmental management?
- *Environmental and general policy*
  Does a business and environmental policy exist? Is it publicly supported by top management? What are the contents of the policies? Are the policies known to employees and important stakeholders?
- *Quantitative environmental goals*
  What measurable environmental goals have been defined? What are the legal environmental standards? When are these goals to be met and by whom? What is the relevance of those goals to the firm's activities? Do ecological assets have to be considered (e.g. governmental organization, mining firm, etc.)?
- *Measures of environmental performance*
  How are environmental performance and progress measured? What are the main environmental performance indicators used in the ecological statement? Which information on environmental interventions is consolidated on the level of the firm? What are the weaknesses of these measures?
- *Description of environmental management program*
  What are the major characteristics of the firm's environmental management methods? Is the environmental management process audited? Have certificates, such as an EMAS certificate, been obtained? Why, or why not?
- *Past performance*
  Have the environmental goals been met? Does the firm comply with legal requirements? Did unusual accidents influence the environmental performance? What is the likelihood of new accidents? What measures have been taken to improve the environmental record further?
- *Criticism from various important stakeholders*
  What do supporters and critics think about the firm's environmental record and performance? Has the credibility of the firm improved?
- *Auditing reports*
  What was the result of external auditing?

Ecological accounting is still fairly new, as are the ways of presenting the figures. Few rules exist on what should be reported, and sometimes the careful reading of some environmental reports suggests that companies tend to disclose what is easily measurable and where environmental targets have been exceeded. Such disclosure practices are normal for the developing stage of environmental reporting.

However, this is changing with increasing practice. The management of a firm should take care not to give a (wrong) impression of "greenwashing" practices by only reporting successful achievements. Also, the quality of data, uncertainties, and the methods of collecting information should be disclosed to enable users to correctly interpret the published data. An interpretation and assessment of the information collected by management is necessary to guide external stakeholders through the "jungle of environmental data". (For ecological data, several assessment methods must be applied to avoid any bias).

12.5   WHEN SHOULD REPORTING TAKE PLACE?

Although the question is not the subject of lively discussions, management has to decide when to report environmental impact added. Basically the following possibilities exist:

- a separate environmental report is published at the same time as the financial report;
- a separate environmental report is published at another time than the financial report;
- the environmental report is integrated in the financial report.

Environmental matters can be included in the financial report or they can be published separately. Recently, most companies have preferred the third option, mentioning environmental matters in the financial report. Most firms tend to publish the environmental report some time after the financial statement. One reason for not releasing the environmental statement before the financial report is uncertainty about possible influences on shareholders. However, experience has shown that these fears are not justified when the corporate environmental management practices are credible and their necessity is explained in full detail. A second reason for the delay of environmental reports is that environmental information often still takes more time to collect than financial data.

Another possibility is to incorporate financial figures in the environmental reports. This allows eco-efficiency numbers to be calculated on the basis of the environmental report.

12.6 HOW OFTEN SHOULD REPORTING TAKE PLACE?

The question of the optimum interval for publishing environmental statements cannot be answered generally. It depends very much on the needs of the company's stakeholders and the specific situation (e.g. when major changes occurred). Some firms (e.g. Norsk Hydro in Norway, Henkel in Germany and Pirelli in Italy) regard an interval of two or three years as sufficient (Deloitte Touche Tohmatsu International *et al.* 1993, p. 29). However, as in the case of financial reporting, an increasing number of companies report their environmental impact added on an annual basis. Reporting at regular intervals is generally perceived better by readers than an irregular flow of information, as environmental issues are an increasingly important part of regular business activities. The establishment of systematic ecological accounting systems and computerized data collection and processing allow reporting at shorter intervals. In future, the reliability and cost-effectiveness of ecological accounting will be more strongly expressed by the ability of a firm to report on an annual basis.

12.7 HOW SHOULD REPORTING BE DONE?

The question of how environmental matters should be reported is closely connected with the question of what should be reported and to whom. A general answer is that firms should report in as honest and credible a way as possible.

Although companies mostly concentrate on written information, they should also use other information channels. One possibility is to organize an annual meeting for environmentally interested stakeholders, where management informs about the environmental report as well as about past developments and future plans

So far, more than three hundred firms have published separate environmental reports. Naimon (1995, p. 62) writes of 150 corporate environmental reports. However, we have collected over 300, many in the German language. It has been shown in Section 10.2.2 that the transfer of the basic assumptions and qualitative characteristics of financial statements to environmental reporting makes sense. The application of the principles of financial reporting and disclosure practices to environmental statements reduces the information costs for preparers and users.

Environmentally oriented information, especially when reported as figures of assessed impact, is often unfamiliar to many economically trained stakeholders. Some information can be expanded with figures and graphs. Nevertheless, even figures must be explained when they contain unusual information. This is why Management's Discussion and Analysis (MD & A) might even be more important for environmental than for financial statements. Here the future outlook and business strategies affecting environmental issues should be disclosed. Other important issues are expected future environmental problems, risks associated with them and possible ways of anticipating or responding to them. For some firms qualitative estimates of potential impacts on the ecological capital are relevant. Furthermore, many environmentally trained stakeholders are interested not only in a sensitivity analysis interpreting the reported environmental impact added, but also in a sensitivity analysis of the influence of different levels of production, different modes of responding, etc.

Important aspects of assessing the quality of environmental reports are the following.

- Corporate and environmental policy
- Corporate and environmental goals
- Environmental strategy and programs
- Environmental management systems
- Products and product policy
- Material and energy flows
- Environmental impact added indicators and EIA indices
- Assessment approaches, assessment results and interpretation
- Eco-integrated key figures
- Financial information (environmental investments, liabilities, etc.)
- Measures taken for improvement
- Audits (internal and external)
- Relationship with stakeholders
- Opinion of present public policy

To achieve an environmentally acceptable corporate identity, the general policy must be coordinated with the environmental policy—as well as with the environmental accounting and environmental management systems, the activities of the firm and the environmental reports. For example, if the company does not examine the possibilities of public transport for employees, environmental pressure groups may easily find this a weak point and accuse the company of "greenwashing", even if the environmental accounting and reporting systems are exceptionally well designed. Also, more superficial details of environmental reports, such as the paper chosen, should be considered. A company which tries to convey a "green" image while supporting the production of chlorine-bleached and unrecycled paper risks not being taken seriously.

12.8 HOW DO STAKEHOLDERS REACT?

The general purpose of environmental accounting and reporting is to establish mutually beneficial relationships with critical stakeholders to secure the supply of critical resources. The reactions of the users of environmental statements are therefore of major interest.

As discussed in Section 10.3.2 the main addressees of environmental reports are *employees*. It is commonly mentioned in speeches that well educated people are more motivated and proud of working for environmentally responsible firms than for laggards.

Also *media representatives* are attentive analysts of environmental reports as, in developed nations, environmental issues are of prime interest to readers. The media play an important role as an intermediate "judge and promoter" of environmental issues.

Other major addressees of ecological statements are *regulators*, although they have often established special accounting relationships. External ecological reports are an additional source of information which may support a positive attitude for advanced firms. From an administrative viewpoint proactive firms are easier to deal with than notorious laggards. This of course affects the administrative treatment of the respective firms.

Being public, an external ecological statement is naturally read by a wide range of stakeholders. Even academic institutions, and the newly established environmental management programs at business schools, offer sessions where environmental reports are analysed and compared.

Perhaps for many firms the most important new addressees of environmental reports are *actors in the capital markets*. These are not only eco-rating firms or environmental investment funds, but also financial analysts, institutional investors, banks, and shareholders. According to a variety of contradicting studies, the relation between environmental and financial performance is not a clear one (see for example Bragdon and Marlin 1972, Camejo 1992, Chen and Metcalf 1980, Cochran and Wood 1975, Cohen *et al.* 1995, Hamilton 1995, McGuire *et al.* 1981, Spicer 1978).

Eco-rating organizations and environmental funds have attracted a great deal of media attention. Managers of eco-rating organizations and environmental funds are among the most attentive analysts of environmental statements.

Much more powerful than environmental rating organizations and environmental funds are the rapidly emerging *environmental credit rating departments* of banks and insurance companies, which assess potential financial liabilities of corporate environmental problems. Being internal departments, they operate with a wide range of different criteria.

As with other business activities, such as marketing, the benefits of environmental accounting and reporting cannot easily be compared with their costs. However, the fact that environmental reporting is emerging and prevailing, and the statements of managers to this effect, support the impression that its economic benefits are also substantial.

13
Environmental Accounting Serving Environmental Management

Accounting will always remain just an information tool and never replace action.

This chapter deals with the role of environmental accounting as part of corporate environmental management. Section 13.1 gives an overview of important EU regulations (EMAS and Eco-label) as well as of British Standard 7750 and International Standard ISO 14001. How well different tools of corporate environmental management meet the main common requirements of those standards and regulations, is dealt with in Section 13.2. The chapter concludes with an examination of the concept of managerial eco-controlling and the role of environmental accounting (Sections 13.3 and 13.4).

13.1 STANDARDS OF CORPORATE ENVIRONMENTAL MANAGEMENT

As mentioned in Part A, Chapter 1, in the recent past new stakeholders defining standards of good practices of environmental management have influenced the arena of environmental accounting. The growing importance of environmental management is reflected in the number of important regulations and standards in force or being prepared, all with the aim of harmonising environmental management.

Among the most significant ones are British Standard BS 7750 (BSI 1992), the EU directive on the environmental management and audit scheme (EMAS) (EEC 1993), the regulation on the (also voluntary) Eco-Labelling system for products (EEC 1992) as well as the draft of the standard 14001 of the International Standards Organization (ISO) (ISO 1994a).

Standard setting organizations such as the British Standards Institute (BSI), the International Standards Organization (ISO), as well as national standardization organizations, have formulated standards against which management systems of firms can be audited. The standardization organizations are private and industry-financed. Their markets, i.e. sales, depend on the reputation of the organization for ensuring that the audited material achieves a high quality.

British Standard 7750, released in 1991, was the first standard for corporate environmental management systems. It substantially influenced ISO 14001, which was published as a draft in 1994.

A major motivation to establish environmental management systems stems from the European Commission (COM) with the regulation on the (voluntary) *European Environmental Management and Eco-Audit System (EMAS)* for production sites and firms (EEC 1993). EMAS enables companies to have their sites audited and, if they fulfil the requirements of the directive, to use a label which confirms that a specific site has an environmental management system in place and that it has successfully passed an external environmental audit.

As shown in Figure 13.1, an important part of EMAS is concerned with non-technical aspects of ensuring that an environmental management system is in place and functioning. To fulfil EMAS, a company must have implemented an environmental management system that helps to:

- formulate an environmental policy and goals for corporate environmental protection;
- secure efficient environmental accounting (or information management);
- evaluate environmental performance (and give decision-making support);
- plan and pilot the firm's activities;
- implement the plans;
- build up an effective and efficient organization;
- communicate with internal and external stakeholders (environmental reporting).

Furthermore, the existence and functioning of the corporate environmental management system is audited by an external verifier.

The firms which pass the requirements are free to display an EMAS logo on their letterhead, which is expected to become a mark of environmental excellence. It is expected that market-place pressure, especially in inter-corporate business relationships, will therefore urge companies to participate in EMAS (Fouhy 1995, p. 49).

The term "audit" seems misleading, because EMAS covers much more than a traditional legal compliance audit. For the implementation of the EMAS directive the European Standards Organisation CEN (Commission Européen de Normalisation) has obtained a mandate from the EU commission to formulate a precise environmental management standard. However, CEN has decided to wait for the ISO norms 14000ff.

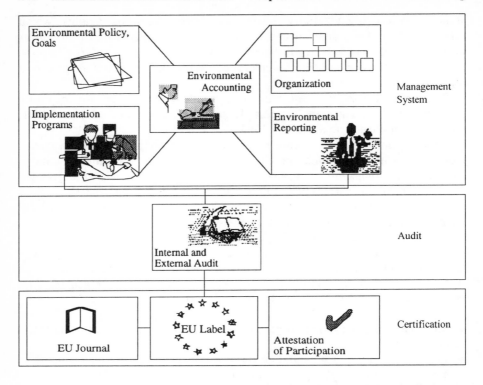

Figure 13.1 Core Parts of the EU Environmental Management and Eco-Audit System (EMAS)

Figure 13.2 shows the concept of the proposed ISO norm 14001. The main requirements for the environmental management system are similar to those of EMAS. The company must have established:

- an environmental policy;
- an environmental accounting system (or monitoring system);
- implementation plans;
- plans for correction;
- an effective and efficient organization.

As with EMAS, an external revision of the corporate environmental management system is necessary. However, in contrast to the European directive, ISO 14001 does not require external ecological reporting.

EMAS and ISO are both site-oriented. (ISO 14001 does not exclude the application of the standard to products). Just as with the quality standard ISO 9000, there will be strong pressure on companies to have their production sites

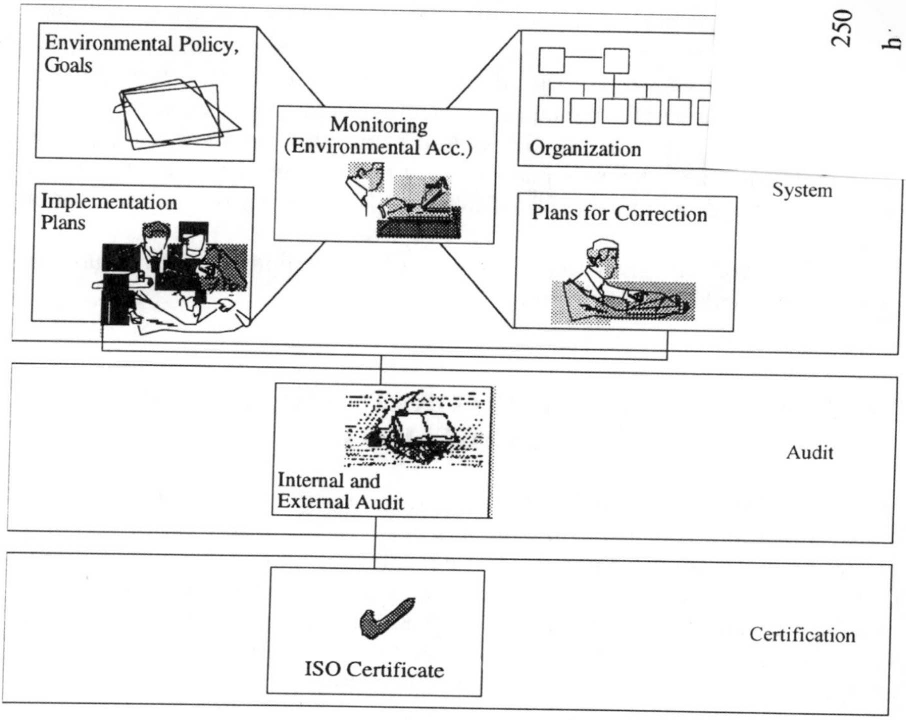

250 h

Environmental Policy, Goals	
	Organization
Monitoring (Environmental Acc.)	System
Implementation Plans	Plans for Correction

Internal and External Audit — Audit

ISO Certificate — Certification

Figure 13.2   Core Parts of the Proposed ISO Standard 14001

certified. It is likely that, especially in a business to business relationship, the fulfilment of an environmental management standard will be a common procurement requirement. The differences between the standards are minimal—apart from the fact that ISO 14001 does not require public disclosure of environmental impacts.

Politics and market pressure will determine which standard will prevail in the years to come. However, ISO can be favored. First, ISO 14001 is an international standard applying also the USA, Japan, south-east Asia, Switzerland, etc., whereas EMAS only covers the European Union. Second, ISO and its national standardization organizations are private organizations which have already established commercial relationships with firms (e.g. with ISO 9000). Third, a thorough study and comparison of the two standards shows that ISO 14001 will cause a smaller administrative work load for the firms involved.

BS 7750, EMAS and ISO 14001 define requirements for corporate environmental management systems (EMS). However, they do not specify w these requirements should be fulfilled. All standards emphasize the need for controlling tools for environmental management as well as the need for environmental, especially ecological, accounting as one important part of corporate environmental management. Nonetheless, the standards do not provide any methods for the decision making process of managers and implementation, i.e. through incentive systems. This freedom of action encourages the development of efficient tools for effective environmental management.

The next section gives an overview of contemporary environmental management methods of companies.

13.2 METHODS OF CORPORATE ENVIRONMENTAL MANAGEMENT

Here is not the place to further discuss various specific tools of environmental management, but rather to show the link between the main tools of corporate environmental management with environmental accounting and environmental management systems. For a discussion of environmental management tools and business strategy see, for example, Welford and Gouldson (1993). Figure 13.3 indicates that the contemporary methods of corporate environmental management are not particularily new, but that they rely on well known traditional management tools. Environmental accounting, environmental auditing, environmental reporting, eco-controlling and Total Quality Environmental Management (TQEM) stem from traditional accounting, auditing, reporting, controlling and TQM.

Eco-balancing corresponds to calculation (costing) whereas Life Cycle Assessment is nothing other than a special case of ecological accounting. It represents a single time ecological calculation (ecological costing) where the scope of calculation has been extended over the product life cycle (Section 8.3).

No matter what standard of environmental management is taken: BS 7750, EMAS, the EU regulation for a product eco-label or ISO 14001, all of them address some of the following key functions of "good environmental management":

- goal setting;
- information management;
- support of decision-making, organization and planning of environmental management programs;
- piloting, implementation and control;
- communication;
- internal and external auditing/review.

Traditional Economic management	→	Environmental Management
Calculation, Costing	→	Eco-Balancing, LCA
Accounting	→	Environmental Accounting
Auditing	→	Environmental Auditing
Reporting	→	Environmental Reporting
Total Quality Mgmt. (TQM)	→	Total Qual. Env. Mgmt. (TQEM)
Controlling	→	Eco-Controlling

Figure 13.3 Methods of Environmental Management Derive from Methods of Traditional Economic Management

Figure 13.4 gives an overview of various well-known methods of environmental management, see Schaltegger (1994). Other more "fancy" tools of environmental management, such as environmental business re-engineering, etc., are not explicitly shown here as they are usually derivatives of the tools mentioned. It also shows which tools support the key functions of environmental management.

- *Life Cycle Assessment*
  The main focus of Life Cycle Assessment is on data management (single calculations) and assessment (see Section 8.3). LCA also addresses some aspects of goal setting and decision support. However, other functions of corporate environmental management, such as piloting and communications, are not, or only very partially supported by LCA.
- *Environmental Accounting and Reporting*
  Traditionally, accounting is the core information management tool of a firm. All activities of management rely on or are at least influenced by accounting. Environmental accounting (see Chapter 2 for definition) is the application of established tools of accounting (i.e. tools of information management, analysis and communications) to environmental management, as has been shown in the previous chapters of this book.
  However, environmental accounting must be incorporated in a more comprehensive environmental management concept. Only then can the respective information be used for goal setting, piloting, implementation and communications.
- *Total Quality Environmental Management (TQEM)*
  TQEM is the application of the principles of Total Quality Management

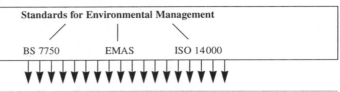

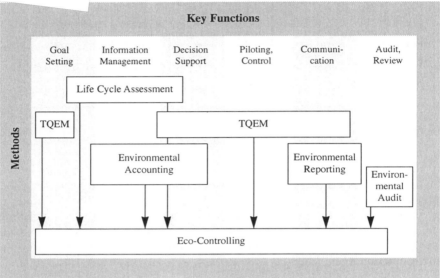

Figure 13.4 Functions and Tools of Corporate Environmental Management

(Deming 1982, 1983; Walton 1986) to environmental management. In this connection the term "quality" is expanded to include the aspect of environmental quality. TQEM is based on statistical tools, namely various charts for data analysis, piloting and internal communication. In addition, TQEM represents a statistical and engineering philosophy.

- *Environmental Auditing*
  The main tool of environmental auditing is the checklist. In the United States of America environmental auditing is understood merely as a check of compliance with regulations (Hall and Case 1992), whereas in Europe it is interpreted more as a management control system (Paasikivi 1994, EEC 1993). The European interpretation is formally expressed in the European regulation for the voluntary environmental management and eco-audit system (EMAS). Company-internal audits often serve to prepare for external audits by certified professionals.

- *Eco-Controlling*

  Traditionally, controlling is the core management concept to integrate and coordinate tools which specifically serve the key functions of corporate management. The controlling process and tools are based on accounting information. Eco-controlling is the application of controlling to environmental management. So far, it is the most comprehensive corporate environmental management concept, as it is designed with the purpose of integrating and coordinating other environmental management tools. All these functions are part of eco-controlling. Apart of its role in the positioning of a company's environmental strategy, eco-controlling is also an important tool for the management of the environmental performance of a production site in accordance with EMAS, ISO 14001 and BS 7750. Eco-controlling ensures that environmental issues are dealt with in a company-wide, continuous process, through its focus on the decision-making process and the possibilities it offers for incentive systems, i.e. internal taxes. With its focus on management function it enhances the acceptance of environmental issues within a company.

Figure 13.4 shows that environmental accounting and reporting, LCA, TQEM, environmental auditing, etc. are tools which have particular strengths in supporting specific functions of environmental management. Furthermore, it is also obvious that every comprehensive environmental management concept aimed at supporting real improvement must rely on some kind of environmental accounting. Environmental accounting supports information management, i.e. collection, analysis and decision, with environmentally induced financial data as well as with information on environmental impact added.

However, information does not replace action but it is rather a precondition for rational action. For actual and efficient improvement of the environmental record of a firm the collected and analysed environmental information must be fed into a continuous environmental management process. In traditional management accounting information is used as the main input for controlling and decision taking. Eco-controlling, by analogy, is the systematic process and concept for piloting corporate environmental management.

The next section deals with eco-controlling as it is the only approach which relies on environmental accounting and which is especially designed to coordinate and integrate other tools of corporate environmental management.

13.3 ECO-CONTROLLING

Only those who control themselves are not controlled by others.

Eco-controlling is the application of methods of financial and strategic controlling to environmental management. It attempts to provide a system for management decision support. Eco-controlling is among the most popular corporate environmental management approaches in continental Europe but is barely known in the Anglo-Saxon and American countries. Concepts of eco-controlling have been developed in the German speaking part of Europe (Austria, Germany and Switzerland) and are successfully applied by an increasing number of multinational as well as medium-sized and small firms.

Originally, eco-controlling was designed for manufacturing industry. Recently it has been applied to service industries (banking), to the management of fauna and flora (Buser and Schaltegger, in Schaltegger and Sturm 1995), and also to public environmental policy and public administration (Schaltegger *et al.* 1996).

13.3.1 Three Perspectives of Eco-Controlling

As financial and strategic controlling is defined in many different ways, it is no wonder that various concepts of eco-controlling have been published. Three main groups of eco-controlling approaches can be distinguished, Schaltegger and Kempke (1996).

- *Financially oriented* eco-controlling methods attempt to compute, analyze, pilot and communicate environmentally induced financial impacts (see for example Fischer 1993, Kloock 1990a, Schreiner 1988, Wagner and Janzen 1991). These methods rely on environmentally differentiated traditional accounting. The unit of measurement is in monetary terms (one-dimensional).
- *Ecologically oriented* eco-controlling approaches are based on satellite systems of ecological accounting which represent an enlargement of the existing accounting and controlling systems. Their purpose is to pilot corporate impacts on the natural environment (see for example Seidel 1988, Schulz 1989, Lehmann and Clausen 1991, Hallay and Pfriem 1992). The units of measurement are in physical terms (one-dimensional).
- *Economically-ecologically integrated* concepts of eco-controlling undertake an integration of the two above-mentioned approaches (Schaltegger and Sturm 1992a,b,c; 1995). Here the evaluation and piloting of financial as well as ecological impacts of economic activities are considered. The units of measurement are two-dimensional: monetary units per unit of environmental impact added.

All three eco-controlling perspectives can be used for strategic as well as for operative management.

The financial consequences of corporate environmental protection are no doubt very important. Nevertheless, the potential cost savings in environmental taxes, environmental liabilities, etc. can often only be detected, and eco-efficiency calculated, after environmental interventions of a firm have been analyzed. Therefore, controlling environmentally induced financial flows is necessary but not sufficient for comprehensive environmental management.

Also the mere controlling of environmental impacts which are caused by a firm is insufficient for effective and efficient environmental protection. Sustainable corporate environmental management can only be successful if it is economically sustainable for the firm, (i.e. if it enhances rather than reduces the competitiveness of the firm) and if satisfactory environmental protection can be guaranteed by the money spent.

The conclusion is that an integration of economic as well as of environmental information is necessary for an effective and efficient controlling-based environmental management.

The following section deals with integrated eco-controlling.

13.3.2 Process and Concept of Integrated Eco-Controlling

Eco-integrated controlling is an institutionalized, permanent, internal management process based on environmental accounting. The concept of eco-controlling corresponds with the methods of financial and strategic controlling. The issues to be managed are the firm's environmental and financial impacts. Eco-controlling can be divided into five modules (Figure 13.5).

- Goal and policy formulation.
- Information management (environmental accounting).
- Decision support system.
- Piloting and implementation.
- Internal and external communication.

Not only EMAS and ISO 14001, but also efficient environmental management in general, require an environmental policy as well as clear and measurable annual environmental protection goals. The goals should consider economic and ecological aspects.

The information management system is the core of any environmental management system. Only what is measured will be managed. The concept of environmental accounting attempts to increase the efficiency of information management.

Frequently, management suffers from excessively detailed information that hampers efficient working with the relevant data. Information concerning environmental interventions therefore has to be assessed according to its relevance. Furthermore, decision supporting tools, such as the Eco-Rational Path-Method (EPM) are needed, integrating economic with environmental aspects.

Effective environmental management requires incentive systems to pilot and implement the plans in the most efficient way. Internal communications play a core role in efficient implementation. However, communications with external

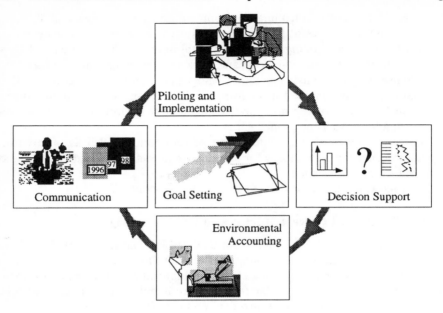

Figure 13.5 The Concept of Integrated Eco-Controlling

stakeholders also support internal processes and increase the gains from environmental management.

While it is important that a clear structure and plan for all modules exist, the steps do not necessarily have to be completed one after the other. Nevertheless, the modules are presented in the logical order of introduction.

Specific instruments are needed for each module to operate the eco-controlling process which provides management with a detailed analysis of the place, cause, extent and time of environmental impacts. However, the overall environmental impact caused by a company should always be kept in mind when dealing with partial problems. This is to avoid an ineffective and inefficient development (e.g. spending more and more on scrubbers for the reduction of less and less SO_2, instead of reducing worse impacts from NO_x).

The importance of each module of eco-controlling depends on the environmental issues the company is confronted with and on their effect on the business success of the company. However, companies should carefully consider whether they have given every module enough thought. Too often environmental management tools are introduced without a clear view on the company's environmental strategy.

13.3.3 Formulation of Goals and Policies

Unfortunately, the formulation of clear goals and policies as the first, most important step of environmental management is often neglected. Many top managers feel the pressure to do something for the environment and embark on an "environmental activism", which contains many isolated activities but no clear direction. For a company to be a good and efficient environmental performer and to reap the benefits of being an environmental leader in its markets, the "reason why" of investing in environmental management has to be very clear. It is therefore essential that top management is involved in the process of goal setting in order to ensure its commitment to the formulated environmental strategy.

To assess the exposure to and therefore the importance of different environmental issues for a company's overall performance is the first step of eco-controlling. Depending on this preliminary analysis the appropriate perspective and goals of eco-controlling will differ. The analysis should be conducted from the viewpoint of the company's stakeholders, their needs and their importance for the company's success. The degree of exposure to different environmental issues should guide a company's involvement and perspective in implementing eco-controlling. Here environmental science has to play its role by giving managers an indication of what the most dominant environmental issues are, from a scientific point of view. These are important because they are likely to influence the company's success sooner or later, be it through new legislation, through public or consumer perception and behaviour or otherwise.

Figure 13.6 shows an exposure portfolio. The firm's expected exposure to different environmental problems (e.g. greenhouse effect, depletion of the ozone layer, etc.) is shown on the horizontal axis. The importance assigned to these environmental issues by various stakeholders is depicted on the vertical axis. For most companies governmental stakeholders such as environmental protection agencies are the most powerful and therefore most important stakeholders where environmental issues are concerned.

This first module is, as mentioned, mainly a task for top management. Lower down in the organisation, line and staff managers should be involved in the formulation of the strategy by contributing to working groups, who investigate and formulate an opinion on topics of special importance in their field of competence.

The analysis of the firm's expected exposure to different environmental problems and the weight given to these aspects by various stakeholders enable management to focus on environmental issues with high priority for the firm (upper right quadrant). However, the upper left quadrant and the lower right quadrant in Figure 13.6 must also be observed, albeit less intensively. Issues with low public priority to which the firm contributes a lot may become a problem as soon as the stakeholders' perception changes. New investments in

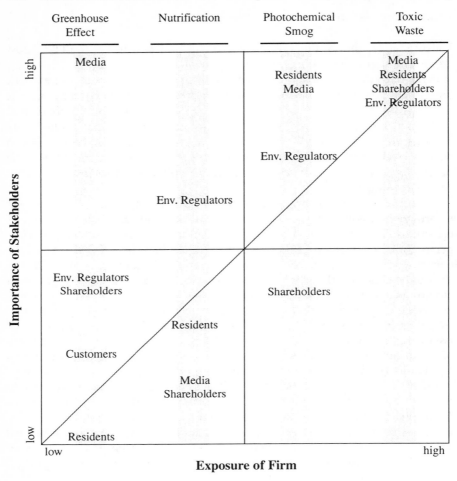

Figure 13.6 Key Environmental Issues and Environmental Exposure of a Company

production, on the other hand, can increase the firm's environmental impact when not anticipated early enough.

13.3.4 Information Management and Environmental Accounting

The recording of environmental information and environmentally induced financial information is necessary to build up a basis for decision making. Therefore, efficient environmental management requires well established

systems of environmentally differentiated accounting and ecological accounting (see Parts A, B and C).

Recording starts after setting up an environmental accounting system for the
company. The identification of potential sources of data is the first step in the
collection of data. Special attention has to be given to existing sources of
environmentally relevant data, such as management accounting for the
materials and the amount of energy used, site permits for some pollutants,
production statistics, technical specifications of the production machines, etc.

From an economic perspective it does not make sense to aim at a
comprehensive inventory of all mass and energy flows—apart from the fact
that this goal can hardly be achieved. Usually, the process of data collection
will be spread over several years, digging deeper each year until the marginal
benefit of more detailed data is equal to the marginal cost of collection.

The close relation between the methods and the terminology of management
accounting and ecological accounting ensures a quick understanding of the
process of the data collection by management and staff, who have to contribute
to the process, as well as by the users of data. Management accounting benefits
from an environmental data inventory in which environmentally induced costs,
for example energy or pollution abatement costs, can be allocated to the cost
centers and the cost drivers which cause them.

To focus on selected, "relevant environmental interventions" does not
provide the same span of information for strategies of pollution prevention. On
the other hand fewer resources have to be devoted to its collection and it may
still offer a sound basis for an efficient eco-controlling. Information
management needs careful considerations concerning the software required.

Contrary to common belief, the measurement of performance on economic
sustainability has also gone through a rapid development in recent years (Part
B). Increasing shareholder value is the new benchmark for economic success.
Shareholder value analysis turns away from traditional accounting figures and
focuses entirely on cash figures. In contrast to more traditional methods of
valuation of the success of a company or a strategy, shareholder value analysis
takes account of such key issues as the risk of a strategy or the time value of
money, and gives a clearer picture of the investments needed to achieve
economic success. Shareholder value analysis therefore is best suited to track
the economic dimension of sustainable development on a corporate level. For a
detailed discussion on the concept of shareholder value (see Rappaport 1986).

13.3.5 Decision Support System

The goal of the third module of eco-controlling is to provide decision makers
with a transparent and rational method for taking environmentally and
economically sound decisions in accordance with the data obtained in module
2 (Figure 13.7).

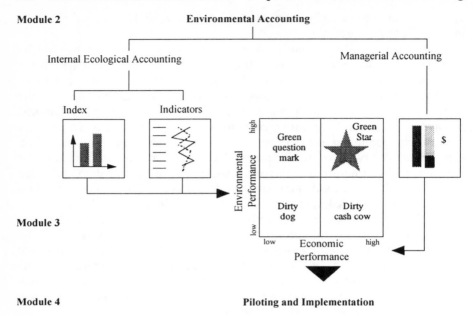

Figure 13.7 Decision Support System

The reason for collecting information on corporate environmental impacts as well as on environmentally induced financial impacts is to calculate eco-efficiency, in order to measure how well the firm's operations contribute to or conflict with sustainable development (see also Section 7.2). Further measures, such as environmental impact added indicators for specific environmental problems (e.g. greenhouse effect) are necessary to improve analysis of the different facets of environmental impacts, as well as to identify alternatives for cost efficient prevention and reduction.

As shown before, one effective way to visualize eco-efficiency is the eco-efficiency portfolio (Section 11.2).

13.3.6 Piloting and Implementation

Many of the existing environmental management tools fail to consider the importance of the implementation process.

Eco-controlling addresses different levels of the organisation and combines the very different tasks of shop floor environmental data collection and strategic environmental management. By using the language of managers, it helps to lower the barriers of implementation. Furthermore, it bridges the gaps between the different users of environmental management information.

Information has to be collected by production managers and passed on to the controller. The controller has to consolidate the data and prepare them for top management so that decisions can be taken. Line managers should have access to the data they need for their jobs, be it for the marketing of a product, the appraisal of a new investment for production equipment, or the control of operational performance on a site, etc.

Implementation is therefore crucial for eco-controlling. More and more companies have developed sophisticated systems of performance evaluation to remunerate their employees. The financial package offered to the employees can include 10–30% per-formance related pay. One way of ensuring the successful integration of eco-controlling is to link the remuneration package of managers to the eco-efficiency targets defined in eco-controlling. The range of possible performance indicators is unlimited, in principle. However, just as with payments linked to financial performance, the incentives have to be chosen with great care, and they must relate to the measures which can be influenced by the respective manager. Nothing creates more frustration than targets which cannot be achieved because of factors beyond the influence of the evaluated manager.

Environmental performance indicators should always have an economic and an environmental dimension. The performance indicators for upper management have a strategic dimension (e.g. 10% annual reduction of the firm's contribution to the greenhouse effect per dollar shareholder value). For lower management levels these performance indicators (eco-efficiency targets) must be specified further, (e.g. if oil usage is mainly responsible for the contribution to the greenhouse effect, the environmental performance indicator can be defined as oil usage per product unit manufactured). Furthermore, it is important that the people measured by the performance indicators are involved in the definition of the indicator.

If the decision support system has shown that the company's environmental problems relate to only a few clearly defined substances used, the establishment of an internal tax system should be considered. The "taxation" works in the same way as on a macro-economic level, adding costs to the most harmful substances. Being an internal system, the taxes are revenue-neutral for the company, but create a strong incentive for the different management levels (e.g. the product managers) to find environmentally less harmful and therefore internally "untaxed" solutions for their products. The implementation tools should also take careful account of a company's culture and existing management tools.

13.3.7 Communications

Internal and external communication (for environmental reporting, see also Section 9.3) are an integrated part of eco-controlling.

Internally, the necessity of environmental strategy for the success of a company has to be explained and the progress towards the targets must be documented. Managers should know what the environmental issues in their area of responsibility are and how the company is dealing with them. They should also have a clear picture of how they can use the information that eco-controlling can provide for improving the company's competitiveness.

Eco-controlling puts the focus of environmental management on a company's own processes. It does not include the environmental impact over the life cycle of its products.

The increasing importance of external communication of environmental issues is apparent from the fast-growing number of environmental reports. Although many of these reports still look very much like mere public relations brochures, more and more of them reflect a clear environmental strategy; and they report in some detail on the company's targets, the progress towards these targets and the environmental management tools used. While there are as yet no clear standards for environmental reporting, the interest in these reports from various groups of stakeholders is growing (see also Part A and Chapter 12).

The contents of the report should reflect the specific situation of a firm as well as the information needs of the stakeholders addressed. A balance between local site-oriented reporting and consolidated figures for the whole company has to be achieved. Site specific data will be of importance for the neighbors of plants, the local authorities, and the employees working on a specific site. If necessary, site specific data can be computed in detail. The data ought to be assessed according to its relevance for the specific environment of the plant. Consolidated, company-wide data are more relevant for shareholders, customers and top management trying to position the company. For multi-national companies only environmental interventions with a global impact should be consolidated. Environmental interventions with local impacts must not be aggregated but must rather be shown separately for different sites.

13.4 CONCLUSIONS AND OUTLOOK

Rational environmental management requires environmental accounting. Different accounting systems have developed which focus on specific information about specific topics and related sets of questions, since no accounting system can treat information with basically different units of measurement, nor can it provide meaningful answers to fundamentally different sets of questions. Existing accounting systems also have to be adapted to new developments which influence the topics traditionally dealt with.

Environmental topics exercise an increasing influence on the economic performance of firms. Thus, environmentally induced financial impacts have become an "established issue" of daily business.

Incomplete or inaccurate *managerial* accounting inevitably leads to wrong and inefficient investment decisions by management. Huge potentials for increasing a company's efficiency and financial performance remain undetected.

Incomplete or inaccurate *managerial* accounting inevitably leads to wrong and inefficient investment decisions by management. Huge potentials for increasing a company's efficiency and financial performance remain undetected.

Incomplete or inaccurate *financial or other* accounting systems mislead not only company directors but also investors, creditors, regulators, and the general public. As a consequence scarce financial resources are allocated inefficiently.

Hence, traditional accounting must differentiate between environmentally related and other financial flows. Furthermore, financial accounting standards should better incorporate environmental issues. Only when management and its stakeholders are informed about what activities, centers and carriers influence costs and revenues can it take the most economically rational decisions.

Environmental issues can only be considered accurately and in time (e.g. before they have material financial impacts) if environmental interventions are accounted for in physical units of measurement in separate *ecological accounting* systems. Thus, in the last decade, firms have introduced new, ecological accounting systems in order to be informed about environmental interventions and impacts (which are or could become financially relevant) before they actually occur. Furthermore, an increasing number of powerful stakeholders request information about the physical impacts on the natural environment caused by a firm, its profit centers, products, businesses, etc.

Internal ecological accounting supports management in investment decisions, whereas *external and other ecological* accounting systems help investors, creditors, regulators, environmentalists and the general public to take environmental and environmentally induced financial aspects into consideration. External ecological accounting can serve this function best if internationally accepted standards of ecological accounting are issued.

In addition to the adaptation (or differentiation) of traditional accounting and the development and introduction of ecological accounting, the integration of information created in both categories of accounting is vital for many managerial issues. *Integration of accounting information* can be achieved with the Eco-Rational Path Method (EPM) creating indicators of eco-efficiency.

Environmentally differentiated as well as ecological accounting provide the necessary information for decision making, piloting, implementation and communication (reporting). However, merely collecting and analyzing data does not improve the environmental record of a firm. The value of environmental accounting and the economic and ecological information it provides depend on how well the accounting information is incorporated into an effective and efficient concept of environmental management.

Accounting information becomes relevant for action only when it is part of the corporate (environmental) management system. Such *integration of environmental accounting into an environmental management concept* is done comprehensively with eco-controlling. The eco-integrated concept of eco-controlling also allows the integration of all important tools of environmental management of firms. Environmental accounting (including LCA) supports information management and decision making, and tools of Total Quality Environmental Management and environmental auditing help management to improve implementation, piloting and control, whereas environmental reporting is part of the communication process. What is important is that all steps and the supporting tools are coordinated. This is what the concept of eco-controlling is designed for. It is thus not surprising that eco-controlling has become the most popular environmental management concept in Europe.

Eco-controlling puts the focus of environmental management on the company's own processes. It does not attempt to include the environmental impact over the life cycle of its products. A management tool is adjustable to the specific situation of a production site and a firm.[5] A chemical company handling thousands of toxic substances will definitely need a more sophisticated concept of eco-controlling pursuing different goals than, for example, a furniture manufacturer or a service company.

More and more companies broaden their focus and state sustainable development as their main goal. It is widely agreed that sustainable development has an economic, an environmental and a social dimension.

Today, the tools for implementing sustainable development are becoming increasingly important for a company's success. The tools for assessing the social performance of a company are still in a very early stage of development. There is much less consensus here than with regard to the other two dimensions relating to how far the social responsibility and influence of a company goes. To date, most social initiatives of companies have been focused on human resource aspects within the company. But, for example, the effects of a company on the community have not yet been approached in a systematic way, although there is increasing agreement that social issues are the key to sustainable development, even from the corporate viewpoint.

Although the social dimension is not especially considered, eco-controlling is rapidly growing into a core management tool, going through similar stages of development to financial controlling.

Environmental accounting and eco-controlling create not only more information and knowledge, but also more knowledge about lack of knowledge. The statement of Socrates "I know that I do not know anything" shows that increased information and knowledge also raises new questions, often more than it provides answers.

Figure 13.8 shows the contributions of different accounting categories in a matrix with the dimensions "knowledge" and "knowledge about lack of knowledge". Traditional accounting has been developed for more than one hundred years, continuously eliminating problems so that good and appropriate methods of collection, analysis and reporting of information have prevailed. The area covered by "traditional accounting" in Figure 13.8 therefore resembles a "lying egg" with the longer end towards the dimension of contributing "knowledge". Ecological accounting, on the other hand, raises more new questions than it provides answers. Thus, the area of ecological accounting plotted in Figure 13.8 looks like a "standing egg" with its longer end towards the dimension "knowledge about lack of knowledge". Environmental accounting lies somewhere between those two accounting categories.

The future task for research in environmental accounting is mainly to extend the area covered in the direction of creating more "knowledge".

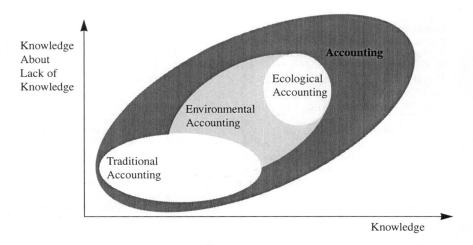

Figure 13.8 Contribution of Accounting to Knowledge and Knowledge About Lack of Knowledge

Endnotes

PART A: INTRODUCTION AND FRAMEWORK

1 National membership of selected environmental protection organizations (Cairncross 1991):

in ('000)	1975	1980	1985	1990
National Wildlife Federation [USA]	2,600 [1970]	4,600	4,500	5,800
Greenpeace [USA]	6	80	450	2,000
Sierra Club [USA]	153	182	363	566
Audubon Society [USA]	255	310	425	515
National Trust [GB]	539	1,047 [1981]	1,323	2,000
Royal Society for Nature Conservation [GB]	107	143 [1981]	166	250
Friends of the Earth [GB]	5	20 [1981]	30	200

2 Others may argue that because many companies did not (and many still do not) calculate their environmentally induced costs correctly, they simply did not (still do not) know if the sum of the marginal costs of collecting environmental information and the marginal costs of reducing environmental impacts are smaller than the marginal costs of environmental impacts from fees, fines, image problems, etc.

3 Well know examples of firms with high fines for environmental spills are Exxon and Occidental Chemical. Exxon faced a bill of as much as $16.5 billion, in addition to the already-paid $1.1 billion in state and federal criminal penalties and the $2 billion cleanup costs after the major oil spill in Prince William Sound in Alaska (*The Economist*, June 18, 1994, p. 62). Occidental Chemical has agreed to pay $120 million to the State of New York as a compensation for the contamination of the Love Canal, which was detected at the end of the 1970s (NZZ, 1994c. p. 19).

PART B: TRADITIONAL ACCOUNTING AND THE ENVIRONMENT

1 Externalities can be divided into external costs and external benefits. People who gain from external benefits do not contribute to the costs of producing the benefit.

When using the expression "externality", usually external costs are meant. See, e.g., Baumol and Oates (1988); Frey *et al.* (1993); Pearce and Turner (1994).

2   IASC defines the notions extraordinary and ordinary in IAS 8, 6 as follows:
   - *Extraordinary items* are income or expenses that arise from events or transactions that are clearly distinct from the ordinary activities of the enterprise, and therefore are not expected to recur frequently or regularly.
   - *Ordinary activities* are any activities which are undertaken by an enterprise as part of its business and such related activities in which the enterprise engages in furtherance of, incidental to, or arising from these activities.

3   See Maunders and Burritt (1991). Regardless of the accounting system it will never be possible to reflect all environmental effects. At the moment when a new product is developed or a new activity is initiated it is impossible to accurately estimate every possible prospective future risk.

4   See for example Johnson and Kaplan (1987a,b) or Rappaport (1986). One criticism has for instance resulted in the development of the concept of the "shareholder value" which is based on free cash flows. The shareholder value concept still uses the financial information collected. However, the basic idea is that the value of a company should not be based on a multiple of its earnings but on its financially quantified strategic value. Free cash flows concentrate strictly on real cash inflows and outflows as a consequence of a company's strategy, which leads to investment activities and future returns.

   In former times management was dedicated to maintaining liquidity. When it was recognized that liquidity today does not necessarily lead to liquidity tomorrow, new indicators were created. The consequences are countless books on accounting, many different accounting standards and conventions, etc. For further discussion see Rappaport (1986).

5   For example, the "Wirtschaftsring"-system ("Economic Circle"-system) is based on a special currency (called the WIR). This currency is used only between traders and retailers and it has a different interest structure than usual. Loans are credited with only very low interest rates. Mortgages can be raised with substantially lower interest rates than market rates. Other exponents of this colony model propose charging interest for debits (e.g. the Taler-community focus on a separate closed system of payments.) See also, e.g., Binswanger (1994); Kircher (1994).

6   The IASC was formed in 1973 to work for the harmonization and improvement of financial reporting. It does this primarily with the development and publication of International Accounting Standards (IAS). These standards are developed through an international process that involves national standard setting bodies, the preparers and users of financial statements and the worldwide accountancy profession (IASC 1995, p. 7). The FASB was founded in 1973. Since then, FASB has been responsible for the United States Generally Accepted Accounting Principles (US GAAP). It is a private organization without legal competences. The US government can, however, influence the GAAP through the SEC (Arthur Andersen *et al.* 1994, p. 39).

7   It has also been argued that the Exposure Draft E37 of IASC, the FASB Statement No. 2 and the CICA "Handbook" Section 3450, which deal with "Accounting for Research and Development costs" could be used as precedents for the suggested accounting for the costs of long-lived assets acquired as part of the clean-up of old waste sites. In this case, capitalization would be possible if, for example, an inactive dump site had a future use after the clean-up.

8   IAS 2, 89: "The cost of inventories may not be recoverable if those inventories are damaged, if they have become wholly or partially obsolete, or if their selling prices have declined. [. . .] The practice of writing inventories down below cost to net

realizable value is consistent with the view that assets should not be carried in excess of amounts expected to be realized from their sale or use." (IASC 1995, p. 89).

9 The "Hundred Group of the United Kingdom" ". . . believes that the environmental policy should be addressed in the annual report. Environmentally related disclosures should be made in the narrative section of the report not subject to audit. But it could change as more verifiable information became available." (*Financial Times* 1992)

10 Another argument against consumption taxes is that any kind of consumption tax causes a relatively higher burden for low-income families with many children than for rich singles. However, according to the Tinbergen rule (see Chapter 2), only one goal should generally be pursued with one tool (Tinbergen 1968). The discussed consumption tax is most effective for achieving environmental goals. Social goals, on the other hand, should be pursued with policies that directly help those who actually need support. To reduce possible negative social effects of a consumption tax and other policies, etc., direct grants should be given to those families which really deserve support.

PART C: ECOLOGICAL ACCOUNTING

1 It has to be acknowledged that this definition of eco-efficiency does not cover all aspects of sustainable development, such as socio-cultural, political and technological aspects. In calculating the value added, it is therefore not assessed if the value added was achieved by, for example, increasing economic opportunities for the poor, if products and services were oriented towards satisfying basic needs or if participative involvement of the workforce, neighborhoods etc. in decision-making and policies was practised.

2 The term "eco" does not refer exclusively to ecological efficiency but also to economic efficiency.

The basic idea of economic-ecological efficiency has also been taken up by the BCSD even though eco-efficiency has been defined somewhat differently: "Eco-efficiency is reached by the delivery of competitively-priced goods and services that satisfy human needs and bring quality of life, while progressively reducing ecological impacts and resource intensity throughout the life cycle, to a level at least in line with the Earth's estimated carrying capacity." (BCSD 1993, p. 9)

3 The first approach—called "ecological bookkeeping"—was put forward by the Swiss engineer Müller-Wenk in 1972 (Müller-Wenk 1972, 1978). Müller-Wenk's approach was later applied to cities, stressing the geographical perspective in accounting (Braunschweig 1982, 1988).

4 As discussed in Section 8.2.3, environmental impact assessment is also the general term for the assessment of environmental interventions, no matter whether the recorded interventions are of a site, product, nation or another system. In German speaking countries the term *Umweltverträglichkeitsprüfung* covers the assessment of site specific environmental interventions.

5 To reduce confusion with the more general philosophy of analyzing life cycles from social, political etc. perspectives, the term "Life-Cycle Analysis" has been changed to "Life-Cycle Assessment (LCA)" (SETAC 1991). Here, the latter term is used in order to conform with the standard.

6 Some professional accounting associations worth mentioning here are the Chartered Association of Certified Accountants (USA), the European Accounting Association (EAA), the Canadian Institute of Chartered Accountants and the Fédération des Experts Comptables Européens (FEE). Standardization organizations include the

International Standardization Organization (ISO); and regulatory bodies include the European Union (EU).

7 See, e.g., Braunschweig *et al.* (1994), Kalisvaart and Remmerswaal (1994), Kortmann (1994). Kalisvaart and Remmerswaal propose using a system of "country target effect scores" for the aggregation of the effect scores (contribution to greenhouse effect, etc.). In this connection, they divide the effect scores by national targets for the respective effects. They found eight national targets for the Netherlands: depletion of abiotic resources, greenhouse effect, eutrophication, photo oxidants, nutrification, depletion of the ozone layer, human toxicity and eco-toxicity.

8 See, e.g., Consoli *et al.* (1993) or Fava *et al.* (1991). SETAC is divided into SETAC US and SETAC Europe. The LCA working groups of SETAC Europe deal with: 1. Inventory, 2. Screening (development of a more rough, fast and cheap way to find out the most important impacts), 3. Impact assessment, 4. Case studies, 5. Conceptually related programmes (e.g. product designing programmes), 6. Education.

9 While we regard the accruals principle as beneficial if adopted by ecological accounting, Maunders and Burritt (1991, p. 11) criticize this. Their main criticism is that the "concern with measurement of a 'slice' through an entity's life means that longer-term, qualitative impacts of current activities are imperfectly represented . . .". Still, Maunders and Burritt acknowledge that their interpretations of the conventions may be criticized as selective.

10 "A parent is an enterprise that has one or more subsidiaries; a group is a parent and all its subsidiaries and a subsidiary is an enterprise that is controlled by another enterprise (known as parent)." (IASC 1995, IAS 27 §6).

11 "Control is presumed to exist when the parent owns, directly or indirectly through subsidiaries, more than one half of the voting power of an enterprise unless, in exceptional circumstances, it can be demonstrated that such ownership does not constitute control." (IASC 1995, IAS 27 §12).

12 "An associate is an enterprise in which the investor has significant influence and which is neither a subsidiary nor a joint venture of the investor." (IASC 1995, IAS 28 §3).

13 "Significant influence is the power to participate in the financial and operating policy decisions of the investee but is not control over these policies." (IASC 1995, IAS 28 §3).

14 Investments can be financial investments (for mere financial purposes) or operational investments (for strategic business purposes).

15 The marginal costs of environmental impact increase, whereas those of pollution prevention decline, with increasing environmental impacts. For further discussion see Section 1.3.

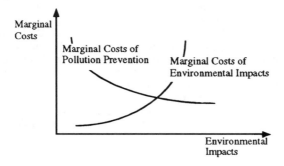

16 It is the purpose of tradition as well as ecological accounting to provide information for stakeholders to interpret the firm's activities. However, the emphasis is on the effects of the activities and the results. This is also the case with ecological tax accounting.

17 In Europe, emissions trading is applied in some cases in Germany, the Netherlands, and the two cantons (states) of Basel (Switzerland). Permits to pollute can only be sold by a company when it can prove that it is more than 20 per cent below regional emission standards. Even with this system of tradeable emission allowances, ecological accounting is needed to measure, report and prove that emissions have actually been reduced. See Schaltegger and Thomas (1994a,b).

PART D: ENVIRONMENTAL ACCOUNTING FOR ENVIRONMENTAL MANAGEMENT

1 EPM gives economic information (measured in monetary terms) and ecological information (measured in ecological terms) the same weight. Neither economic nor environmental performance is preferred. This can easily be changed by multiplying one or the other performance indicator by a factor. However, such a factor will always be biased. It has also to be considered that monetary flows (prices) already include an assessment, as they represent individual preferences in markets. Also, the ecological information is already weighted when methods of impact assessment are applied.

By converting EIA into dollar costs or by using officially defined monetary weighting factors, such as taxes, a direct subtraction of the costs from the economic performance indicator (e.g. the contribution margin) is possible.

2 The most obvious alternatives for strategic management referring to a static and/or dynamic eco-integrated portfolio analysis seem to be:
   ● elimination of "dirty dogs";
   ● milking of "green cash cows";
   ● investing in the "greening" of "dirty cash cows" and shifting them into a "green cash cow" position if possible;
   ● investing in order to improve the "economic health" of "green dogs" and shifting them to "green cash cow" positions, if possible.

3 In the past it has sometimes been argued by "deep green" environmentalists that it is unethical to calculate economic-ecological efficiency, because environmental impacts should be reduced almost regardless of costs. While it would of course be a paradisic situation if all environmental impacts vanished, it must be acknowledged from an economic as well as from a practical environmental perspective that scarce financial resources ought to be spent where most benefit is created. This can only be achieved by calculating the efficiency of investment.

4 Since financial analysts and investors can process only a limited amount of data, this could—in the extreme case—result in a substitution of financial information with ecological information. The kind of information reported will change if the marginal return of more ecological information exceeds the marginal loss of fewer financial data.

5 It has been shown with many small, medium and large firms (including Feldschlösschen Ltd., Flumroc Ltd., Mohndruck GmbH, Sarnafil Ltd., Wander Ltd., etc.) that with eco-controlling, it is possible to successfully manage and improve the eco-efficiency, the environmental performance and the environmentally induced financial impacts of the company and its production sites (see Schaltegger and Sturm 1995).

Bibliography

AAA/SEC (American Accounting Association's Securities and Exchange Commission Liaison Committee) (1995) Mountaintop Issues: From the Perspective of the SEC. *Accounting Horizons*, **9**, No. 1, March, 79–86.

AAF EU (Accounting Advisory Forum of the European Union) (1994) Environmental Issues in Financial Reporting. Working Document of the Accounting Advisory Forum, July, 6.

Abelson, R. (1991) Messy Accounting. *Forbes*, October 14, 172, 174.

Achleitner, A. (1995) (in German: *Die Normierung der Rechnungslegung*), *The Standardization of Accounting*. Zürich: Treuhand-Kammer.

Ackermann, J. (1995) How much Profit for Who? (in German: Wieviel Gewinn für wen). *Neue Zürcher Zeitung (NZZ)*, No. 11, 27.

ACN (Association Canadienne de Normalisation) (1993) L'ISO Choisit le Canada pour Jouer un Rôle Clé dans le Domaine de L'Environnement. *Environment Info*, **2**, No. 1.

Adams, J. (1992) *Accounting for Environmental Costs: A Discussion of the Issues Facing Today's Businesses*. Norwalk: FASB.

Advisory Committee on Business and the Environment 1993 *Report of the Financial Sector Working Group. London: ACBE*

Aeschlimann, J. (1994) Exxon Guilty—Now the Demands for Billions Emerge (in German: Exxon verurteilt—jetzt kommen die Milliardenforderungen). *Basler Zeitung*, 15 June, No. 137, 3.

AICPA (American Institute of Certified Public Accountants) (1994) Disclosure of Certain Significant Risks and Uncertainties. Proposed Statement of Position. Revised Draft. New York: AICPA.

AICPA (American Institute of Certified Public Accountants) (1995) Environmental Remediation Liabilities. Exposure Draft. Proposed Statement of Position. New York: Environmental Accounting Task Force, Accounting Standards Division, American Institute of Certified Public Accountants.

AIPP (American Institute for Pollution Prevention) with Aldrich, J. (1992) *A Primer for Financial Analysis of Pollution Prevention Projects*. Cincinnati: University of Cincinnati.

Alb, H. (1992) A Bridge Between Ecology and Economy (in German: Eine Brücke zwischen Ökonomie und Ökologie). *IO-Management Zeitschrift*, No. 6, 76–80.

Alfsen, K.; Bye, T. & Lorentsen L. (1993) *Natural Resource Accounting and Analysis. The Norwegian Experience*. Oslo: Statistisk Sentralbyrå.

Allenby, B. R. & Fullerton, A. (1992) Design for the Environment—a New Strategy for Environmental Management. *Pollution Prevention Review*, Winter, 51–61.

Annighöfer, F. (1990) Competitive Advantage with Strategic Environmental Management (in German: Wettbewerbsvorteile durch strategisches Umweltschutzmanagement). OFW (Ed.): *Environmental Management Between Ecology and Economy* (in German: *Umweltmanagement im Spannungsfeld zwischen Ökologie und Ökonomie*). Wiesbaden: Gabler.

Anonymous (1991) Private Organizations Entering Business of Certifying Environmental Status. *Inform*, 2, No. 10, October.

Anonymous (1992a) Study: "Green Fees" Can Be Levied to Cut Deficit, Spur Economy. *The Seattle Times*, November 18, A 12.

Anonymous (1992b): Decree for the Implementation of the Law on Free Access to Information Concerning the Environment (90/31/EU) (in German: Gesetz zur Umsetzung der Richtlinie des Rates vom 7. Juni 1990 über den freien Zugang zu Informationen über die Umwelt (90/313/EWG)). *Informationsdienst Umweltrecht*, No. 4, 251.

Anonymous (1992c) Law on Environmental Information Not Convincing—Part 1 (in German: Umweltinformationsgesetz nur halbherzig—Teil 1). *Ökologische Briefe*, No. 39, 23. September, 7–13.

Anonymous (1994a) Voluntary EPA Programs. *Nation's Business*, September, 64.

Anonymous (1994b) Is 33/50 a "Sham"?. *Occupational Hazards*, 56, Issue 8, August, 60–62.

AP (Associated Press) (1992a) Transcripts Show Chaotic Exxon Spill Response. First Concern Was Appearances; Dumping Toxic Waste also Discussed. *The Seattle Times*, 18. November, 1, 12.

AP (Associated Press) (1992b) Some Investors Turn to "Clean, Green" Companies. *The Seattle Times*, April 21, C3.

AP (Associated Press) (1994) Exxon Pays 20 Billion Dollars in Compensation (in German: Exxon zahlt 20 Milliarden Dollar Entschädigung). *Basler Zeitung*, No. 173, 10.

Arber, W. (1992) Why the Earth's Genetic Biodiversity Cannot be a Matter of Indifference. In: Koechlin, D. & Müller, K. *Green Business Opportunities. The Profit Potential*. London: Pitman Publishing, 21–32.

Archibald, R. & Conklin, D. (1993): Perched On the Leading Edge. *CA-Magazine*, January, 63–65.

Arora, S. & Cason, T. (1995) An Experiment in Voluntary Environmental Regulation: Participation in EPA's 33/50 Program. *Journal of Environmental Economics and Management*, 28, 271–86.

Arthur Andersen & Schweizerische Vereinigung für Finanzanalyse und Vermögensverwaltung (1994) *Transparent Accounting and Reporting of Banks* (in German: *Transparente Rechnungslegung und Berichterstatung von Banken*). Zürich: Arthur Andersen & Schweizerische Vereinigung für Finanzanalyse und Vermögensverwaltung.

ASVS (1990) *Solar 91*. Berne: ASVS.

Azzone, G. & Manzini, R. (1994) Measuring Strategic Environmental Performance *Business Strategy and the Environment*, 3, No. 1, Spring, 1–14.

Bailey, P. (1991) Full Cost Accounting for Life-Cycle Costs—A Guide for Engineers and Financial Analysts. *Environmental Finance*, Spring, 13–29.

BAK (Konjunkturforschung Basel AG) (1992–1995) *Economy and Environment. Northwest Switzerland* (in German: *Wirtschaft und Umwelt. Norwestschweiz*). Basel: BAK.

Barrett, M.; Beaver, W.; Cooper, W.; Milburn, A.; Solomons, D. & Tweedie (1994) American Accounting Association Committee on Accounting and Auditing Measurement, 1989–90. *Accounting Horizons (AH)*, **5**, No. 3, September, 81–101

Barth, M. & McNichols, M. (1994) Estimation and Market Valuation of Environmental Liabilities Relating to Superfund Sites. *Journal of Accounting Research*, **32**, Supplement, 177–209.

Basler & Hoffmann (1974) *Study Environment and Economy. Comparison of Environmental Impacts of PVC, Glass, Metal and Cardboard Containers* (in German: *Studie Umwelt und Volkswirtschaft. Vergleich der Umweltbelastungen von Behältern aus PVC, Glas, Blech und Karton*). Bern: Eidgenössisches Amt für Umweltschutz.

Battelle (1993) Life-Cycle Assessment: Public Data Sources for the LCA Practitioner. Washington D.C.: Report for the US Environmental Protection Agency.

Baumgartner, B. (1980) *The Controlling Concept. Theory and Practice* (in German: *Die Controller-Konzeption: Theoretische Darstellung und praktische Anwendung*). Bern: Haupt.

Baumol, W. & Oates, W. (1988) *The Theory of Environmental Policy (2nd edition)*. Cambridge: Cambridge University Press.

BCSD (Business Council for Sustainable Development) (1993) Getting Eco-Efficient. How Can Business Contribute to Sustainable Development? First Antwerp Eco-Efficiency Workshop, November, Organised in Association with UNEP–IEO (United Nations Environment Programme, Industry and Environment Office) and COM (Commission of the European Communities) Directorate-General XI.

Begley, R. (1994) TRI Releases Fall and "Wastes" Rise. Industry Disputes Expanding List. *Chemical Week*, April 27, **154**, No. 16, 9.

Bennett, M. & James, P. (1994) Financial Dimensions of Environmental Performance: Developments in Environment-Related Management Accounting. Manuscript presented to the British Accounting Association Conference, March 25.

Bertschinger, P. (1995) An Overview of the US Accounting Standards (in German: Die US-Rechnungslegungsstandards im Überblick. Internationale Entwicklung der Rechnungslegung von IAS zu US GAAP). *Der Schweizer Treuhänder*, No. 4, 269–80.

BEW (Bundesamt für Energiewirtschaft) (1994a) *Energy- and Material-balances of the Life Cycles of Buildings* (in German: *Energie- und Stoffflussbilanzen von Gebäuden während ihrer Lebensdauer*). Bern: EPFL & Universität Karlsruhe, Koordinationsgruppe für Ökobilanzen des Bundes.

BEW (Bundesamt für Energiewirtschaft) (1994b) *LCA of Buildings* (in German: *Ökobilanzen im Bauwesen*). Bern: Koordinationsgruppe für Ökobilanzen des Bundes.

BfK (Bundesamt für Konjunkturforschung) (1985) *Qualitative Growth* (in German: *Qualitatives Wachstum*). Berne: BfK.

Bierter, W. (1994) Eco-Efficiency: Megatons Instead of Nanogrammes (in German: Ökoeffizienz: Megatonnen statt Nannogramme). *Basler Zeitung*, 30 Juli, 15.

Binswanger, C. (1994) Der Gier des Geldes müssen Grenzen gesetzt werden. *Die Weltwoche*, 23 June.

Björness, S. (1992) *Ethical Investment Funds—A Spark for the Process Towards a "Better World?"* Fribourg: University of Fribourg.

Boehmle, M. (1992) The Annual Financial Report. Balance Sheet, Profit and Loss Account, Notes (in German: Der Jahresabschluss. Bilanz, Erfolgsrechnung, Anhang). Zürich: Verlag des Schweizerischen Kaufmännischen Verbandes.

Botkin, D. B. (1990) *Discordant Harmonies. A New Ecology for the Twenty-First Century*. Oxford: Oxford University Press.

Bragdon, J. & Marlin, J. (1972) Is Pollution Profitable? *Risk Management*, **19**, No. 4.

Braunschweig, A. (1982) Ecological Bookkeeping for the City of St Gall (in German: Die ökologische Buchhaltung für die Stadt St Gallen). St Gallen: mimeo.

Braunschweig, A. (1988) *Ecological Bookkeeping as Instrument of the Urban Environmental Policy* (in German: *Die ökologische Buchhaltung als Instrument der städtischen Umweltpolitik*). Chur: Rüegger.

Braunschweig A.; Förster R.; Hofstetter P. & Müller-Wenk R. (1994) Evaluation and Further Development of Assessment Methods for LCA—First Results (partly in German: Evaluation und Weiterentwicklung von Bewertungsmodellen für Ökobilanzen—Erste Ergebnisse). IWÖ-Diskussionsbeitrag No. 19, St. Gallen: IWÖ.

Brealey, R. & Myers, S. (1991) *Principles of Corporate Finance: Application of Option Pricing Theory*. New York: McGraw-Hill.

Bretschger, L.; Buse, I.; Mäder, S.; Schleininger R. & Schelbert, H. (1993) *Clean Air in the State of Zurich. Guidelines for an Efficient Air Policy* (in German: *Saubere Luft im Kanton Zürich. Leitlinie für eine effiziente Luftreinhaltepolitik*). Zürich: ZKB.

Broden, B. & Fryer, J. (1993) Environmental Taxes: Where Do We Go Now?, Taxes Can Curb Polluters While They Help Pay For Federal Services. *New Accountant*, January, 9–11, 28.

Brüggemann, A. (1994) Environmental Liability of Creditors (in German: Umwelthaftung des Darlehensgebers). SZW/RSDA 2/94, 71ff.

Brunn, H. (1995) Putting LCA Back in Its Track!. *LCA-News*, 5, No. 2, 2–4.

Bruntland Report: see WCED (1987).

BSI (British Standards Institute) (1992) *Specification for Environmental Management Systems*. BS 7750, London: BSI.

Büchel, K. (1996) System Boundaries. Schaltegger *et al.*: *LCA—Quo Vadis?* Basel: Birkhäuser.

Buchholz, R. (1993) *Principles of Environmental Management: The Greening of Business*. Englewood Cliffs, N.J.: Prentice Hall.

Bührle Corporation (1993) *Annual Report*. Zug: Bührle.

Bundesministerium für Umwelt, Jugend und Familie (1993) *LCA of Packaging Materials* (in German: *Ökobilanzen von Packstoffen in Theorie und Praxis). Eine Iststandserhebung*. Wien: IÖW.

Burch, R. (1994) Municipal Reporting on Sustainable Development. A Status Review. Ottawa: National Round Table on the Environment and the Economy, Working Paper No. 24.

Burt, T. (1994) EVC Institutions Reject Claims by Greenpeace. *The Guardian*, October 23.

BUS (Bundesamt für Umweltschutz) (1984) *Ecobalance of Packaging Materials* (in German: *Ökobilanzen von Packstoffen*). Berne: BUS.

Buser, H. & Schaltegger, S. (1995) Eco-Controlling for Fauna and Flora in Production Sites (in German: Öko-Controlling auf dem Firmenareal). *IO-Management*, May.

BUWAL (1991) *Ecobalances of Packaging Materials* (in German: *Ökobilanz von Packstoffen*). SRU No. 132/91. Bern: BUWAL.

BUWAL (1992) *The Concept of Eco-Scarcity*. Berne: EDMZ.

Byrd, J. & Zwirlein, T. (1994) Environmental Protection and Forward Contracts: Sulfur Dioxide Emission Allowances. *Journal of Applied Corporate Finance*, 109–10.

Cairncross, F. (1991) *Costing the Earth. What Governments Must Do. What Consumers Need to Know. How Business Can Profit*. London: Great Britain Books.

Cairns, D. (1995) *A Guide to Applying International Accounting Standards*. Central Milton Keynes: Institute of Chartered Accountants.

Camejo, P. (1992) The Greening of Wall Street. *The Environmental Forum*, November/December.

Campbell, K. & Stinson, C. (1993) Disclosure of Superfund Liabilities under Two Accounting Systems. Seattle: Working Paper.

Carlton, C. & Howell, B. (1992) Life Cycle Analysis: A Tool for Solving Environmental Problems? *European Environment*, **2**, Part 3, April, 2–5.

Cassils, J. (1991) Exploring Incentives: An Introduction to Incentives and Economic Instruments for Sustainable Development, Ottawa: National Round Table on the Environment and the Economy. Working Paper No. 13.

CEFIC (European Chemical Industry Council) (1993) *CEFIC Guidelines on Environmental Reporting for the European Chemical Industry*. Brussels: CEFIC.

CEP (Center of Economic Priorities) (1993) Several company reports. Washington, DC: CEP.

CERES (1992) *The Ceres Principles*. Boston: Ceres.

Chaddick, B.; Rouse, R. & Surma, J. (1993) Perspectives on Environmental Reporting. *The CPA Journal*, January, 18–24.

Chaterjee, P. (1993) Environmental Auditing Still Awaits Its Green Signal. *Financial Times*, February 5.

Chemical Marketing Reporter (1994a) TRI Exemption Plan Drawing Fire. *Chemical Marketing Reporter*, Aug. 8, **246**, No. 6, 4.

Chemical Marketing Reporter (1994b) EPA Final Rule Adds 286 Chemicals to TRI-List. *Chemical Marketing Reporter*, November 28, **246**, No. 22, 3.

Chemical Week (1994) UK Takes Step Toward TRI-Style Reporting. *Chemical Week*, September 21, **155**, No. 10, 20.

Chen, K. & Metcalf, R. (1980) The Relationship Between Pollution Control Records and Financial Indicators Revisited. *Accounting Review*, **55**.

Chynoweth, E. (1994) Environmental Reporting: Different Things for Different People. *Chemical Week*, **155**, No. 1, 106.

Ciba (1993) *Environmental Report 1993*. Basel: Ciba.

CICA (Canadian Institute of Chartered Accountants) (1992) *Environmental Accounting and the Role of the Accounting Profession*. Toronto: CICA.

CICA (Canadian Institute of Chartered Accountants) (1993) Environmental Costs and Liabilities: Accounting and Financial Reporting Issues, Research Report. Toronto: CICA.

CICA (Canadian Institute of Chartered Accountants) (1995) *Accounting Recommendations. Specific Items. Research and Development Costs*. Ottawa: CICA.

Clausen, J. (1993) Terminologies of the Eco-Audit (in German: Begriffliche Definitionen rund um das Öko-Audit). *Umwelt Wirtschafts Forum (UWF)*, Nr 3, 25–27.

Clausen, J. & Fichter, K. (1993) *Environmental Reporting* (in German: *Umweltberichterstattung*). Berlin: IÖW.

Clément, P. (1992) Environmentally Perverse Government Incentives, Ottawa: National Round Table on the Environment and the Economy. Working Paper No. 6.

Cochran, P. Wood, R. (1975) Corporate Social Responsibility and Financial Performance. *California Management Review*, **18**, No. 2.

Cohen, M.; Fenn, S. & Naimon, J. (1995) *Environmental and Financial Performance: Are They Related?* Washington D.C.: Investor Responsibility Research Center (IRRC).

Colby, S.; Kingsley, T. & Whitehead, B. (1995) The Real Green Issue. Debunking the Myths of Environmental Management. *The McKinsey Quarterly*, No. 2, 132–143.

COM (Commission of the European Communities) (1993). Amended Proposal for a Council Regulation (EEC) Allowing Voluntary Participation by Companies in the Industrial Sector in a Community Eco-Management and Audit Scheme, COM/93 97 final. 16 March, Brussels: EEC.

Consoli, F. *et al.* (1993) *Guidelines for Lifecycle Assessment: A Code of Practice*. Brussels: SETAC.

Cooper, C. (1992a) The Non and Nom of Accounting for (M)other Nature. *Accounting, Auditing and Accountability Journal (AAAJ)*, **5**, No. 3, 16–39.

Cooper, C. (1992b) M[othering] View on: "Some Feminisms and Their Implications for Accounting Practice". *Accounting, Auditing and Accountability Journal (AAAJ)*, 5, No. 3, 71–75.

Council of the European Communities, The (1993) Council Regulation (EEC) No. 1836/93 of 29 June 1993 allowing voluntary participation by companies in the industrial sector in a Community eco-management and audit scheme. *Official Journal of the European Communities*, 10 July, No. L 168/1–18.

Cowe, R. (1994) Greenpeace Campaign Targets Investors Over PVC Flotation. *The Guardian*, 22 October.

Crawford, C. (1992) Campaign for Cleaner Corporations. America's Corporate Polluters. CEP: Research Report.

Daily, G. C. & Ehrlich, P. R. (1992) Population, Sustainability and the Earth's Carrying Capacity. *Bio Science*, 10, No. 42, 761–71.

Daly, H. E. (1968) On Economics as a Life Science. *Journal of Political Economy*, No. 76, 392–406.

Daly, H. E. (1992) Allocation, Distribution and Scale: Towards an Economics that is Efficient, Just and Sustainable. *Ecological Economics*, No. 12.

Dangerfield, A. (1995) Accounting in Accordance with IAS. End of the Honeymoon? (in German: Rechnungslegung nach IAS. Ende der Flitterwochen?). *Index*, No. 2, 26–30.

Deloitte & Touche (undated) *EMS Overview*. Deloitte & Touche.

Deloitte Touche Tohmatsu International, IISD & SustainAbility (1993) *Coming Clean. Corporate Environmental Reporting. Opening up for Sustainable Development.* London: Deloitte Touche Tohmatsu International.

Deming, E. (1982) *Out of the Crises*. Cambridge, Mass.: MIT.

Deming, E. (1993) *The New Economics for Industry. Government, Education*. Cambridge, Mass.: MIT.

Deml, M. (1994) *Green Money–Annual Report for Ethical Investment 1995/6*. (in German: *Grünes Geld–Jahrbuch für ethisch-ökologische Geldanlagen 1995/6*). 2nd edition. W.U.: Vienna.

Dierkes, M. & Preston, L. (1977) Corporate Social Accounting and Reporting for the Physical Environment. *Accounting, Organizations and Society (AOS)*, 2, No. 1, 3–22.

Dirks, H. (1991) Recognition and Measurement Issues in Environmental Cleanup Costs. *Environmental Finance*, Summer, 233–6.

Ditz, D.; Ranganathan, J. & Banks, D. (Eds.) (1995) *Green Ledgers. Case Studies in Corporate Environmental Accounting*. Washington D.C.: WRI.

Dixit, A. & Pindyck, R. (1993) *Investment under Uncertainty*. Princeton: Princeton University Press.

Dixit, A. & Pindyck, R. (1995) The Options Approach to Capital Investment. *Harvard Business Review*, May–June, 105–15.

Dobyns, L. & Crawford-Mason, C. (1991) *Quality or Else*. New York: Houghton Mifflin.

DOE (Washington State Department of Ecology) (1992a) Guidance Paper: Economic Analysis for Pollution Prevention. Olympia WA.

DOE (Washington State Department of Ecology) (1992b) *Success Through Waste Reduction*. Volume I. Olympia: DOE.

DOE (Washington State Department of Ecology) (1992c) *Success Through Waste Reduction. Proven Techniques for Washington Businesses*, Volume II. Olympia: DOE.

DOE (Washington State Department of Ecology) (1993a) *Pollution Prevention Planning in Washington State Businesses Volumes I–III*. Olympia: DOE.

DOE (Washington State Department of Ecology) (1993b) *Success Through Waste Reduction. Pollution Prevention Planning in Washington State Businesses*. Olympia: DOE

DPA (1994a) The Contamination of a Neighbourhood in the USA. Chemical Company Pays 120 Million Dollars (in German: Die Verseuchung einer Siedlung in den USA. Chemiefirma zahlt 120 Millionen Dollar). *Neue Zürcher Zeitung (NZZ)*, June 23, No. 144, 19.

DPA (1994b) Exxon Has to Pay 286 Million Dollars to Fishermen. (in German: Exxon muss den Fischern 286 Millionen Dollar zahlen). *Basler Zeitung*, August 13.

Drucker, P. (1990) The Emerging Theory of Manufacturing. *Harvard Business Review*, May/June, 94–102.

DuPont (1993) *Corporate Environmentalism. Progress Report.* Wilmington: DuPont.

Eckel, L. & Fisher, K. & Russel, G. (1992) Environmental Performance Measurement. *CMA Magazine*, March, 16–23.

Economist, The (1992) Do It Our Way. *The Economist*, 6 May, 90.

Economist, The (1993) Waste and the Environment. A Lasting Reminder. *The Economist*, 29 May.

Economist, The (1994a) Corporate Liability. UnExxonerated. *The Economist*, 18 June, 62.

Economist, The (1994b) After Valdez. *The Economist*, 18 June, 20.

Economist, The (1994c) Where there's muck. . . . *The Economist*, 9 December.

Economist, The (1994d) Insurers Get that Sinking Feeling. *The Economist*, 20 August, 57–58.

Economist, The (1994e) Morals Make the Money. *The Economist*, 3 September, 76ff.

Economist, The (1995) Environmental Policy. Could Try Harder. *The Economist*, 21 October, 62ff.

Edward, F. (Ed.) (1992) *Environmental Auditing: The Challenge of the 1990s.* Calgary: University of Calgary Press.

EEC (The Council of the European Communities) (1992) Council Regulation (EEC) No. 880/92 of 23 March 1992 on a Community Eco-Label Award Scheme. *Official Journal of the European Communities*, No. L 99, 1 July.

EEC (The Council of the European Communities) (1993) Council Regulation (EEC) No. 1836/93 of June 1993 Allowing Voluntary Participation by Companies in the Industrial Sector in a Community Eco-Management and Audit Scheme. *Official Journal of the European Communities*, No. L 168, 1–18.

EEC (The Council of the European Communities) (1994) Environmental Issues in Financial Reporting. Working Document for the Accounting Advisory Board Forum. New York: Draft.

EFFAS (European Federation of Financial Analysts Societies) (1994) *Environmental Reporting and Disclosures. The Financial Analyst's View.* London: Working Group of Environmental Issues of the Accounting Commission of the European Federation of Financial Analysts' Societies, Authors: Müller, K.; de Frutos, J.; Schüssler, K. & Haarbosch, H.

Eichenberger, H. (1994) Environmental Management: Change the Challenge to an Opportunity (in German: Umwelt-Management: Aus der Not eine Tugend machen). *Atag Ernst & Young Praxis 1/94, 18–25.*

EIRIS (1989) *The Financial Performance of Ethical Investments*, London: EIRIS.

EIU (The Economist Intelligence Unit & American International Underwriters) (1993) *Environmental Finance. Evaluating risk and exposure in the 1990s.* New York: EIU.

ENDS-Report (1994) The Elusive Consensus on Life-Cycle Assessment. Environmental Impact Analysis No. 38. ENDS Report 231, April, 20–25.

Environment Canada, Solid Waste Management Division (1995) The Life-Cycle Concept. Backgrounder. *Ecocycle*, No. 1, 6.

Environment Today (1994) EPA Would Lift Thresholds for TRI's Form R. *Environment Today*, Sep. 6.

EPA (US Environmental Protection Agency) (Ed.) (1978) SAM/IA: *A Rapid Screening Method for Environmental Assessment for Fossil Energy Process Effluents*. Authors: Schalit L., Wolfe K. (Authors), EPA–600/7–78–015. Washington D.C.: US EPA.

EPA (US Environmental Protection Agency) (1986) Environmental Auditing Policy Statement. *Federal Register*, **51**, No. 131, 25004–10.

EPA (US Environmental Protection Agency) (1992a) *Life-Cycle Assessment: Inventory Guidelines and Principles*. Washington D.C.: Franklin Associates.

EPA (US Environmental Protection Agency) (1992b) Life Cycle Impact Analysis. Part I: Issues, Authors: Ream, T. & Mohin, T. Research Triangle Park: Research Triangle Institute: EPA.

EPA (US Environmental Protection Agency) (1992c) *Total Cost Assessment. Accelerating Industrial Pollution Prevention Through Innovative Project Financial Analysis*. Washington D.C.: US EPA.

EPA (US Environmental Protection Agency) (1993a) Life-Cycle Assessment: Public Data Sources for the LCA Practicioner, Draft Final, Report to the US: EPA. Washington D.C.: Battelle.

EPA (US Environmental Protection Agency) (1993b) *Life Cycle Design Manual. Environmental Requirements and The Product System*. Washington D.C.: EPA.

Epstein, M. (1995) *Measuring Corporate Environmental Performance*. Chicago: Irwin.

Ernst & Young (1992) Lender Liability for Contaminated Sites. Issues for Lenders and Investors, Ottawa: National Round Table on the Environment and the Economy. Working Paper No. 3.

ESU (1994) *Eco-Inventories of Energy Systems* (in German: *Ökoinventare von Energiesystemen*). Zurich: ETH/PSI.

Eurostat (1994) *Environmental Protection Expenditure: Data Collection Methods in the Public Sector and Industry*. Luxembourg: Office for the Official Publications of the European Communities.

Ewer, S.; Nance, J. & Hamlin, S. (1992) Accounting for Tomorrow's Pollution Control. The Problems CPAs will Face—And Suggested Solutions—When Dealing With Future Environmental Laws. *Journal of Accountancy*, July, 69–74.

FASB (Financial Accounting Standards Board) (1974) *Accounting for Research and Development Costs*. Norwalk: FASB.

FASB (Financial Accounting Standards Board) (1975) *Classification of Short-Term Obligations Expected to be Refinanced*. Norwalk: FASB.

FASB (Financial Accounting Standards Board) (1980) *Accounting for Preacquisition Contingencies of Purchased Enterprises*. Norwalk: FASB.

FASB (Financial Accounting Standards Board) (1993) Miscellaneaous Accounting. *SEC Docket*, Vol. 54, No. 6.

FASB (Financial Accounting Standards Board) (1995) *Accounting Standards—Current Texts*. Norwalk: FASB.

FASB EITF (Financial Accounting Standards Board Emerging Issues Task Force) (1990) *Issue 90–8: Capitalization of Costs to Treat Environmental Contamination*. Norwalk: FASB.

FASB EITF (Financial Accounting Standards Board Emerging Issues Task Force) (1993a) *Accounting for Regulatory Assets*. Norwalk: FASB.

FASB EITF (Financial Accounting Standards Board Emerging Issues Task Force) (1993b) *Interpretation No. 14: Reasonable Estimation of the Amount of a Loss (An Interpretation of FASB Statement No. 5)*. Norwalk: FASB.

Fava, J.; Denison, R.; Jones, B.; Curran, M.; Vigon, B.; Selke, S. & Barnum J. (Eds.) (1991) *A Technical Framework for Life-Cycle Assessment*. Smugglers Notch, Vermont: SETAC.

Fava, J.; Jensen, A.; Pomper, S.; DeSmet, B.; Warren, J. & Vignon, B. (Eds.) (1992) *Life-Cycle Assessment Data Quality: A Conceptual Framework.* Wintergreen: SETAC.

Feder, B. (1993) Sold: $21 Million of Air Pollution. *The New York Times,* March 30, C1.

FEE (Fédération des Experts Comptables Européens) (1993) *Environmental Accounting and Auditing: Survey of Current Activities and Developments.* Paris: FEE.

FEFSI (Fédération Européenne des Fonds et Sociétés d'Investissement) (1994) *Quarterly Statistics,* 30 September. Brussels: FEFSI.

Feist, W. (1986) *Energy- and Emissions-Balances of Insulation Materials* (in German: *Primärenergie- und Emissionsbilanzen von Dämmstoffen*). Darmstadt: IWU.

Fenn, S. (1995) Great Heat. *Technology Review,* **98,** No. 5, 62ff.

FER (Fachkommission für Empfehlungen zur Rechnungslegung (1994) *10th Annual Report* (in German: *10 Jahresbericht*). Zürich: FER.

Ficher, K. (1993) Environmental Management Standards: BS 7750 (in German: Umweltmanagement-Standards: der BS 7750. Die Vorreiterrolle Grossbritanniens bei der Standardisierung des Umweltmanagements). *Informationsdienst,* No. 3–4, 14–15.

Fichter, K. & Clausen, J. (1994) A Good Environmental Report—Your Benefit (in German: Ein guter Unweltbericht—Ihr Nutzer). *Unternehmen und Ummelt,* No. 3.

Financial Times (1992) Management Account. Men in Grey Get the Green Jitters. June 11, 41.

Finnveden, G. (1994) Some Comments on the Level of Spatial Detail in the Characterisation. Hofstetter, P.; Jensen, A.; Schaltegger, S. & Udo de Haes, H. (Eds.): *First Working Document on Life Cycle Impact Assessment Methodology.* Zürich: SEATC/ETH.

Fischer, R. (1993) Ecologically Oriented Controlling (in German: Ökologisch orientiertes Controlling). *Controlling,* No. 3, 140–146.

Förschle, G. (1993) Accounting for Measures of Environmental Protection from an Accounting Perspective (in German: Die Bilanzierung von Umweltschutzmassnahmen aus bilanztheoretischer Sicht). *Der Betrieb,* **46,** No. 24, June 18, 1197–203.

Fouhy, K. (1995) New Payback for Environmental Commitment. *Chemical Engineering,* March, **102,** No. 3, 49.

Frank, M. & Ruppel, E. (1976) Thermodynamics and Energy Analysis of Products (in German: Thermodynamik und Energieanalyse von Produkten) Berlin: TU-Diskussion paper.

Freedman, J. (1995) Results of IMA Co-Sponsored Survey Being Released at Corporate Environmental Accounting Conference. *Management Accounting,* **76,** No. 10, 68.

Freeman, E. (1984) *Strategic Management. A Stakeholder Approach.* Marshfield, Mass.: Pitman Publishing.

Frey, R. L. (1993) *Strategies and Instruments* (in German: *Strategien und Instrumente*). Frey *et al.*: *Economics for the Environment.* (in German: *Mit Ökonomie zur Ökologie*). Basel/Stuttgart: Helbing & Lichtenhahn, Poeschel, 67–110.

Friedman, B. (1992) *All about Environmental Auditing.* New York: McGraw Hill.

Friedrichs, R. (1987) Accounting for Measures of Environmental Protection (in German: Rechnungslegung bei Umweltschutzmassnahmen). *Der Betrieb,* No. 51/52, December 18, 2580–88.

Fritsche, U.; Rausch, L. & Simon, K. H. (1989) *Environmental Impacts of Energy Systems* (in German: *Unweltwirkungsanalyse von Energiesystemen (GEMIS)*). Wiesbaden: Hessisches Ministerium für Wirtschaft und Technik.

Fritzler, M. (1994) Who Knows What a Tortured Sheep Is? (in German: Wer weiss schon, was ein "gedipptes" Schaf ist?) *Future-Magazin,* No. 4, 20.

Gahrmann A., Hempfling R. & Sietz M. (1993) *Valuation of Measures of Corporate Environmental Protection* (in German: *Bewertung betrieblicher Umweltschutzmassnahmen. Ökologische Wirksamkeit und ökonomische Effizienz*). Taunusstein: Blottner.

Gallhofer, S. (1992) M[othering] View on: "The Non and Nom of Accounting for (M)other Nature". *Accounting, Auditing and Accountability Journal (AAAJ)*, **5**, No. 3, 40–51.

GEFIU (Gesellschaft für Finanzwirtschaft in der Unternehmensführung) (1993) Questions of Accounting for the Clean-Up of Contaminated Goods (in German: Bilanzielle Fragen im Zusammenhang mit der Sanierung schadstoffverunreinigter Wirtschaftsgüter). *Der Betrieb*, **46**, No. 31, August 6, 1529–32.

Georgescu-Roegen, N. (1971) *The Entropy Law and the Economic Process*. Cambridge, Mass.: Harvard University Press.

Goodfellow, J. & Willis, A. (1991) The Name of the Game? *CA-Magazine*, March, 43–50.

Gorry, G. & Morton, M. (1989) A Framework for Management Information Systems. *Sloan Management Review*, Spring, 49–61.

Gottschalk, E. (1994) Many "Nice Guy" Funds Fail to Make Nice Profits. *Wall Street Journal (WSJ)*, July 7, C1, C16.

Gray, R. (1990a) *The Greening of Accountancy: The Profession After Pearce*. London: The Chartered Association of Certified Accountants, Certified Accountants Publications, Research Report 17.

Gray, R. (1990b) The Accountant's Task as a Friend to the Earth. *Accountancy*, June, 65–69.

Gray, R. (1992) Accounting and Environmentalism: An Exploration of the Challenge of Gently Accounting for Accountability, Transparency and Sustainability. *Accounting, Organizations and Society (AOS)*, **17**, No. 5, 399–425.

Gray, R. (1994) Environmental Accounting and Auditing: Survey of Current Activities and Developments. *Accounting & Business Research*, **24**, No. 95, 285–86.

Gray, R. & Laughlin, R. (Eds.) (1991) Green Accounting, Special Issue of *Accounting, Auditing and Accountability Journal (AAAJ)*, **4**, No. 3

Gray, R. & Owen, D. (1993) *The Developing Approaches to Environmental Disclosure. The Second Year of the Association's Award Scheme*. London: ACCA.

Gray, R., with Bebbington, J. & Walters, D. (1993) *Accounting for the Environment*. London: Chapman Publishing.

Gray, R.; Owen, D. & Maunders, K. (1987) *Corporate Social Reporting: Accounting and Accountability*. Hempstead: Prentice Hall.

Grayson, L., Woolston, H. & Tanega, I. (1993) *Business and Environmental Accountability. An Overview and Guide to the Literature*. London: Technical Communications.

Greenberg, R. & Unger, C. (1991) Getting Started—Introducing Total Quality Management Measures into Environmental Programs. *Corporate Quality & Environmental Management*, 35–39.

Greenpeace (1994) Greenpeace Intervenes in ECV Flotation. *Greenpeace Business*, No. 22, December.

Grimsted, B.; Schaltegger, S.; Stinson, C. & Waldron, C. (1994) A Multimedia Assessment Scheme to Evaluate Chemical Effects on the Environment and Human Health. *Pollution Prevention Review*, Summer, 259–68.

Grittner, P. (1978) *Attempt to Explain a Thermodynamic Theory of Product. The Example of Aluminium and Copper* (in German: *Kersuch der Begründung einer thermodynamischen Theorie des Wertes von Produkten am Beispiel von Aluminium und Kupfer*). Bamburg: Schadel.

Guineé, J. & Heijungs, R. (1993) A Proposal for the Classification of Toxic Substances within the Framework of Life-Cycle Assessment of Products. *Chemosphere*, **26**, No. 10, 1925–44.

Gunn, T. (1992) *Creating Winning Business Performance. 21st Century Manufacturing.* New York: Harper Business.

Günther, E. (1993) *Ecologically Oriented Controlling—Concept of a System for Piloting and Empirical Validation* (in German: *Ökologieorientiertes Controlling—Konzeption eines Systems zur ökologieorientierten Steuerung und empirische Validierung*). Augsburg.

Günther, E. & Wagner, B. (1993) Environmental Orientation of Controlling (in German: Ökologieorientierung des Controlling). *Die Betriebswirtschaft*, **53**, No. 2, 143–66.

Günther, K. (1991) LCA as Basis for Environmental Audits (in German: Öko-Bilanzen als Grundlage eines Umwelt-Auditings). Steger (Hrsg.): *Umwelt-Auditing. Ein neues Instrument der Risikovorsorge.* Frankfurt: FAZ, 59 ff.

Gurlit, E. (1992) The Access of the Public to Environmental Information. The US as the Leading Example for Europe (in German: Der Zugang der Öffentlichkeit zu umweltbezogenen Informationen—Das U.S.-amerikanische Vorbild und die Entwicklung auf europäischer Ebene. Weidner, H. Zieschank R. & Knoepfel, P. (Eds.): *Umweltinformation, Berichterstattung und Informationssysteme in zwölf Ländern.* Berlin: Sigma WZB.

Gutscher, H. (1993) Eco-Efficiency in Practice (in German: Öko-Effizienz in der Praxis). Public Speech at the MUBA-Conference 19 March. Basel: Muba.

Haasis, H. (1992) Environmental Costs in Accounting (in German: Umweltschutzkosten in der betrieblichen Vollkostenrechnung). *Wirtschaftsstudium (WiSt)*, **3**, March, 118–22.

Hahn, R. (1984) Market Power and Transferable Property Rights. *Quantitative Journal of Economics*, **99**, 753–765.

Hall, R. & Case, D. (1992) *All About Environmental Auditing.* Washington D.C.: Federal Publications.

Hallay, H. (1989) Terms around Eco-Auditing (in German: Begriffe rund ums Öko-Audit). *Umswelt-Wirtschaftsformum (UWF)*, No. 4.

Hallay, H. (1992) Eco-Controlling—The Management Tool of the Future (in German: Öko-Controlling—ein Führungsinstrument der Zukunft). Glauber/Pfriem (Eds.): *Ökologisch Wirtschaften. Erfahrungen, Strategien, Modelle.* Frankfurt: Fischer, 114–23.

Hallay, H. & Pfriem, R. (1992) *Öko-Controlling. Umweltschutz in mittelständischen Unternehmen.* Frankfurt: Campus.

Hamer, G. (1986) Satellite Systems and National Accounts (in German: Satellitensysteme in Rahme der Westerentwicklung der Volkswirthschaftlichen Gesamtrechnung). *Zeitschrift für Wirtschafts- und Sozial-statistik*, No. 1, 60–80.

Hamilton, J. (1995) Pollution as News: Media and Stock Market Reactions to the Toxics Release Inventory Data. *Journal of Environmental Economics & Management*, January, **28**, No. 1, 98–113.

Hamner, B. & Stinson, C. (1992) Managerial Accounting and Compliance Costs. Seattle: University of Washington, discussion paper.

Hansen, U., Lübke, V. & Schoenheit, I. (1992) Testing Firms as a Method of Socio-Ecological Management (in German: Der Unternehmenstest als Informationsinstrument für ein sozial-ökologisch verantwortliches Wirtschaften). *Zeitschrift für Betriebswirtschaft (ZfB)*, **63**, No. 6, 587–611.

Hanson, D. (1995) Toxic Release Inventory: Chemical Industry Again Cuts Emissions. *Chemical & Engineering News*, April 3, **73**, No. 14, 4–5.

Harris, P. (1994) Green Accounting Seeks Hidden E-Costs. *Environment Today*, **5**, No. 6, 1, 17ff.

Hautau, H.; Lorenzen, U.; Sander, D. & Bertram, M. (1987) *Methods of Monetary Valuation of Environmental Impacts* (in German: *Monetäre Bewertungsansätze von Umweltbelastungen*). Göttingen: Vandenhoeck & Ruprecht.

Hawkshaw, A. (1991) Status Quo Vadis. *CA Magazine*, March, 25.

Hayek, F. (1945) The Use of Knowledge in Society. *American Economic Review*, No. 4, 519–30.

Hector, G. (1992) A New Reason You Can't Get a Loan. *Fortune*, September 21, **126**, No. 6, 107–10.

Heigl, A. (1989) Tax Incentives for Investing in Environmental Protection (in German: Ertragssteuerliche Anreize für Investitionen in den Umweltschutz). *Betriebswirtschaftliche Forschung und Praxis (BFuP)*, **41**, No. 1/89, 66–81.

Heijungs, R.; Guinée, J.; Huppes, G.; Lankreijer, R.; Udo de Haes, H. & Sleeswijk, A. (1992) *Environmental Life Cycle Assessment of Products. Guide and Backgrounds.* Leiden: CML.

Held, M. (1986) *Environmental Accounting in Firms* (in German: *Ökologisch Rechnen im Betrieb*). Tutzinger Materialie No. 33. Tutzing: Evangelische Akademie Tutzing.

Henn, C. & Fava, J. (1984) *Life Cycle Analysis and Resource Management.* New York.

Henrieques, D. (1992) Building a Better Nuclear Nest Egg. *New York Times*, April 12, F 17.

Henshaw, C. L. (1994) Spatial Detail in LCA. Hofstetter, P.; Jensen, A.; Schaltegger, S. & Udo de Haes, H.: *First Working Document on Life Cycle Impact Assessment Methodology.* Zürich: SEATC/ETH.

Hess, G. (1994) The Right Direction; Industry-Wide Emissions are Declining Steadily, While the EPA Looks into Expansion of the Toxics Release Inventory. *Chemical Marketing Reporter*, Aug. 15, **246**, No. 7.

Hess, G. (1995) EPA Proposal Seeks to Ease Reporting Burden in Industry. *Chemical Marketing Reporter*, Feb. 20, **247**, No. 8, 24.

Heuvels, K. (1993) The EU Eco-Audit Regulation in Practice. Experiences of a Pilot Study (in German: Die EG-Öko-Audit-Verordnung im Praxistest. Erfahrungen aus einem Pilot-Audit-Programm der Europäischen Gemeinschaften). *Umwelt-Wirtschaftsforum (UWF)*, No. 3, 41–48.

Hibbit, C. (1994) Green Reporting: It's Time the UK Profession Responded. *Accountancy*, October, **114**, No. 1214, 97–98.

Hilary, R. (1993) *The Eco-Management and Audit Scheme: A Practical Guide.* London: Technical Communications.

Hill, C. & Jones, G. (1989) *Strategic Management: An Integrated Approach.* Boston: Houghton Mifflin.

Himelstein, L. & Regan, B. (1993) Fresh Ammo For The Eco-Cops. What Price Pollution? New Methods Try to Calculate It to The Dollar. *Business Week*, November 29, 93–94.

Hines, R. (1991) On Valuing Nature. *Accounting, Auditing and Accountability Journal (AAAJ)*, **4**, No. 3, 27–29.

Hirschman, A. (1970) *Exit, Voice and Loyality: Responses to Decline in Firms, Organizations and States.* Cambridge: Harvard University Press.

Hofer, P. & Schendel, D. (1978) *Strategy Formulation: Analytical Concepts.* St. Paul: West.

Hofstetter, P. (1995) Time Aspects in Life Cycle Assessment, Zürich: Manuscript.

Holmark, D.; Rikhardsson, P. & Jørgensen H. (1995) *The Annual Environmental Report. Measuring and Reporting Environmental Performance.* Copenhagen: Price Waterhouse.

Hopfenbeck, W. & Jasch, C. (1993) *Eco-Controlling. New Philosophy Pays! Audits, Environmental Reports and LCA as Management Tools* (in German: *Öko-Controlling. Umdenken zahlt sich aus! Audits, Umweltberichte und Ökobilanzen als betriebliche Führungsinstrumente*). Landsberg: Verlag Moderne Industrie.

Horngren, C. & Foster, G. (1987) *Cost Accounting. A Managerial Emphasis (6th edition).* Englewood Cliffs: Prentice Hall.

Hosbach, H.; Karlaganis, G. & Saxer, H. P. (1995) Pollution Register Creates Transparency and Improves the Awareness of Polluters (in German: Schadstoff-Emissionsregister schaffen Transparenz und fördern das Umweltbewusstsein der Verursacher). *BUWAL-Bulletin*, No. 3, 31–34.

Hrauda, G.; Jasch, C.; Puchinger, V. & Rubik, V. (1993) *LCA of Packaging Materials in Theory and Practice. State of the Art* (in German: *Ökobilanzen von Packstoffen in Theorie und Praxis—Eine Iststandserhebung*). Wien: Österreichisches Bundesministerium für Umwelt, Jugend und Familie & Institut für Ökologische Wirtschaftsforschung (IÖW)

Hubbard, H. (1991) The Real Cost of Energy. *Scientific American*, **264**, No. 4, April, 18–23.

Hueting, R. (1987) The Economic Aspects of Environmental Accounting. *The Journal for Interdisciplinary Economics*, **2**, 55–71.

Hundred Group of Finance Directors Environmental Working Party, The (1992) *Statement of Good Practice: Environmental Reporting in Annual Reports.* London: Hundred Group.

IASC (1992a) Property, Plant and Equipment. International Accounting Standard. Proposed Statement. Exposure Draft 43 (E 43), May, 9, London: IASC.

IASC (International Accounting Standards Committee) (1992b) XIV World Congress of Accountants. Environmental Issues. *IASC Insight*, October, 6.

IASC (International Accounting Standards Committee) (1993) International Accounting Standards 1993. Hertfordshire, IASC.

IASC (1994) Future Work Programme. *IASC Insight*, September, 12.

IASC (International Accounting Standards Committee) (1995) International Accounting Standards 1995, London: IASC.

ICC (International Chamber of Commerce) (1991a) *The Business Charter for Sustainable Development. Principles for Environmental Management.* Paris: ICC.

ICC (International Chamber of Commerce) (1991b) *WICEM II. Second World Industry Conference on Environmental Management.* Rotterdam: ICC, UNEP, UNCED.

IISA (International Institute for Sustainable Development) (1992) *Business Strategy for Sustainable Development. Leadership and Accountability for the 90s.* Manitoba: IISD.

Ilinitch, A. & Schaltegger, S. (1993) Eco-Integrated Portfolio Analysis: A Strategic Tool for Managing Sustainably. Paper presented at the Academy of Management Annual Conference, Atlanta.

Ilinitch, A. & Schaltegger, S. (1995) Developing a Green Business Portfolio. *Long Range Planning*, No. 3.

INSEE (Institut National de la Statistique et des Etudes Economiques) (1986a) *Les Comptes Satellites de l'Environnement-Méthodes et Resultats.* Ministre de l'Environnement. Serie C 130. Paris: INSEE.

INSEE (Institut National de la Statistique et des Etudes Economiques) (1986b) *Les Comptes du Patrimoine Naturel.* Ministère de l'Environnement, Serie C 137–138. Paris: INSEE.

Insight (1992) *"Big Cap" Social Profiles.* New York: Franklin Research and Development Corporation.

Institute for Pollution Prevention with Aldrich, J. (1992) *A Primer for Financial Analysis of Pollution Prevention Projects.* Cincinnati: University of Cincinnati.

International Environmental Reporter (1995) Danish Proposal Would Require Industry to Set up Separate "Green" Accounting System. *International Environmental Reporter,* February 22, 143–44.

International Environmental Reporter (1995) Commission to Suggest Ways to Reorient Tax System from Labor to Resource Depletion. *International Environmental Reporter,* February 22, 143.

IÖW (Institut für Ökologische Wirtschaftsforschung) (1993) *Environmental Reporting* (in German: *Umweltberichterstattung*). Berlin: IÖW.

IRRC (Investor Responsibility Research Center) (1993) Various company reports. New York: IRCC.

ISO (International Standards Organization) (1994a) Environmental Management Systems. Specification with Guidance for Use. Committee Draft ISO/CD 14001, London: ISO.

ISO (International Standards Organization) (1994b) Life-Cycle Impact Assessment, Draft to be included in WG 1-document on Life-Cycle Assessment—General Principles and Procedures. London: ISO.

ISO (International Standards Organization) (1994c) ISO TC 207: Environmental Performance Evaluation Framework Document on Definitions, Principles and Methodology, Final Draft. Toronto: ISO, Environmental Management Subcommittee No. 4.

Jacobs, M. (1991) *Short-Term America. The Causes and Cures of Our Business Myopia.* Boston: Harvard Business School Press.

Johanson, P. (1990) Valuing Environmental Damage. *Oxford Review of Economic Policy,* **6**, No. 1, 34–50.

Johnson, H. & Kaplan, R. (1987a) *Relevance Lost. The Rise and Fall of Management Accounting.* Boston: Harvard Business School Press.

Johnson, H. & Kaplan, R. (1987b) The Rise and Fall of Management Accounting. Management Accounting Information is Too Late, Too Aggregated, and Too Distorted to be Relevant. *Management Accounting,* January, 22–29.

Johnson, L. (1993) Research on Environmental Reporting. *Accounting Horizons,* **7**, No. 3, 118–23.

Johnson, L. (Ed.) (1991) *The FASB Cases on Recognition and Measurement.* Illinois: Irwin.

Kalisvaart, S. & Remmerswaal, J. (1994) The MET-Points Method. A New Single Figure Performance Indicator Based on Effect Scores. Brussels: Paper presented at the Fourth SETAC-Europe Congress.

Kamphausen, P., Kolvenbach, D. & Wassermann, B. (1987) The Treatment of Environmental Problems in Firms. Liabilities for Orphaned Waste Sites (in German: Die Beseitigung von Umweltschäden in Unternehmen. Haftung für Altlasten—Rechtsschutz—Versicherungsschutz—steuerliche Behandlung). *Der Betrieb,* No. 3, February 20, Supplement.

Karl, H. (1992) More Environmental Protection with Eco-Auditing. The Eco-Audit Scheme of the EU (in German: Mehr Umweltschutz durch Umwelt-Auditing? Audit-Konzeption der Europäischen Gemeinschaft). *Zeitschrift für angewandte Umweltforschung (ZAU),* **5**, No. 3, 297–303.

Karl, H. (1993) European Initiative to Introduce Environmental Audits. Critical Evaluation from an Economic Perspective (in German: Europäische Initiative für die

Einführung von Umweltschutz-Audits—Kritische Würdigung aus ökonomischer Sicht). *List Forum für Wirtschaftspolitik*, **19**, No. 3, 207–220.

Karr, J. (1993) Protecting Ecological Integrity. *The Yale Journal of International Law*, **18**, No. 1, Winter, 297–306.

Kaspereit, H. (1992) *The Environmental Dimension of Accounting* (in German: *Die ökologische Dimension im betrieblichen Rechnungswesen*). Freiburg i.B.: Diplomawork.

Keidanren (Japan Federation of Economic Organizations) (1991) *Keidanren Global Environment Charter*. Tokyo: Keidanren.

Kinder, P., Lydenberg, St. & Domini, A. (1991) *The Social Investment Almanac. A Comprehensive Guide to Socially Responsible Investing*. New York: Henry Holt.

Kircher, N. (1994) Choked by Interest Rates. Payment with Talent—A New System as a Flintstone (in German: Im Würgegriff des Zinses. Zahlen mit Talent—Ein neues System sorgt für Zündstoff). *Schweizerische Handelszeitung*, 10 March.

Kirchgeorg, M. (1990) *Environmentally Oriented Behavior of Firms: Typologies and Explanations* (in German: *Ökologieorientiertes Unternehmensverhalten: Typologien und Erklärungsansätze auf empirischer Grundlage*). Wiesbaden: Gabler.

Kirkman, P. & Hope, C. (1992) Environmental Disclosure in UK Company Annual Reports. Cambridge University Engineering Department Research Paper No. 16/92.

Kleiner, A. (1991) What Does it Mean to be Green? *Harvard Business Review*, July–August, 38–47.

Klich, T. (1993) Suitability of Qualitative Instruments of Planning and Analysis for the Purposes of Environmental Controlling (in German: Eignung qualitativer Planungs- und Analyseinstrumente für Zwecke des Umweltschutz-Controlling). *Zeitschrift für Betriebswirtschaft (ZfB)*, No. 2, 105–17.

Kloock, J. (1990a) Environmental Cost Accounting (in German: Umweltkostenrechnung). Scheer (Hrsg.): *Rechnungswesen und EDV*. Heidelberg, 129–56.

Kloock, J. (1990b) Environmental Protection and Clean Water (I) (in German: Umweltschutz in der betrieblichen Abwasserwirtschaft (I)). *Wirtschaftsstudium (WISU)*, No. 2, 107–13.

Kloock, J. (1990c) Environmental Protection and Clean Water (II) (in German: Umweltschutz in der betrieblichen Abwasserwirtschaft (II)). *Wirtschaftsstudium (WISU)*, No. 3, 171–75.

Knight, P. (1994) What Price Natural Disasters? *Tomorrow*, 48–50.

Knudsen, A. (1992) Financial Reporting in the 1990s and Beyond. A Position Paper of the Association for Investment Management and Research. Philadelphia: AIMR.

Koechlin, D. & Müller, K. (1992) Environmental Management and Investment Decisions. Koechlin, D. & Müller, K. (Eds.): *Green Business Opportunities. The Profit Potential*. London: *Financial Times*/Pitman.

KOM (1992) Proposal for a Regulation (EU) of the Commission for a Voluntary Eco-Audit System for Firms (in German: Vorschlag einer Verordnung (EWG) des Rates, die freiwillige Beteiligung gewerblicher Unternehmen an einem gemeinschaftlichen Öko-Audit-System ermöglicht). KOM (91) 459 endg., Ratsdokument 5218/92.

Koordinationsgruppe des Bundes für Energie- und Ökobilanzen (1994a) *LCA of the Life Cycle of Buildings* (in German: *Energie- und Stoffflussbilanzen von Gebäuden während ihrer Lebensdauer*). Bern: BEW, EPFL, Universität Karlsruhe.

Koordinationsgruppe des Bundes für Energie- und Ökobilanzen (1994b) *LCA of Buildings* (in German: *Ökobilanzen im Bauwesen. Die Anwendung der Energie- und Stoffflussanalyse (E+S) im Bauwesen. Illustrationsbeispiel*). Bern: BEW/BUWAL / AFB/BFK/EMPA.

Kortmann, J. (1994) *Towards a Single Indicator for Emissions—An Exercise in Aggregating Environmental Effects*. Amsterdam.

Kreikebaum, H. (1992) Integrated Environmental Protection with Strategic Planning and Controlling Tools (in German: Integrierter Umweltschutz (IUS) durch strategische Planungs- und Controlling-Instrumente). Steger, U. (Hrsg.): *Handbuch des Umweltmanagments*. München: Beck.

Kreuze, J. & Newell, G. (1994) ABC and Life-Cycle Costing for Environmental Expenditures: The Combination Gives Companies a More Accurate Snapshot. *Management Accounting*, **75**, No. 8, 38–42.

Kurz, R. & Spiller, A. (1992) Environmental Auditing: Internal Risk Controlling or Market-Oriented Environmental Check? (in German: Umwelt-Auditing: Internes Risikocontrolling oder marktorientierte Umweltverträglichkeitsprüfung?) *Zeitschrift für angewandte Umweltforschung (ZAU)*, **5**, No. 3, 304–09.

Lascelles, D. (1993) *Rating Environmental Risk*. London: Centre for the Study of Financial Innovation.

Laughlin, B. & Varangu, L. (1991) Accounting for Waste or Garbage Accounting: Some Thoughts from Non-Accountants. *Accounting, Auditing and Accountability Journal (AAAJ)*, **4**, No. 3, 43–50.

Leggett, J. (1995) *Climate Change and the Financial Sector* (in German: *Die Klimaveränderung und der Finazsektor*). Hamburg: Greenpeace.

Lehmann, S. (1990) LCA and Eco-Controlling as Tools or Corporate Pollution Prevention (in German: Ökobilanzen und Öko-Controlling als Instrumente einer präventiven Umweltpolitik in Unternehmen). Kozmiensky (Hrsg.): *Vermeidung und Verwertung von Abfällen*, Berlin: EF-Verlag, 101–09.

Lehmann, S. (1991) LCA and Eco-Controlling. Theory and Practice (in German: Ökobilanz und Öko-Controlling. Die Instrumente: theoretische Entwicklung und praktische Umsetzung). *IÖW-Informationsdienst*, No. 2/91, 14–15.

Lehmann, S. & Clausen, J. (1991) Eco-Controlling. Information Tool for Environmental Management (in German: Öko-Controlling. Informationsinstrument für ökologische Unternehmensführung). *Wechselwirkung*, No. 51, October, 11–15.

Leibenstein, H. (1966) Allocative Efficiency versus X-Efficiency. *American Economic Review (AER)*, **56**, 392–415.

Linfors, L. (1994) *Summary and Recommendations. Product Life Cycle Assessments—Principles and Methodology*. Brussels: SETAC.

Lobos, I. (1992) Boeing Will Pay Fine Over Hazardous Waste. EPA Assesses Largest Charge of Its Kind. *The Seattle Times*, 14 January, B1.

Löhrer, G. (1993) How Environmental Protection Pays (in German: Wie sich die Umwelt rechnet). *Bilanz*, No. 10, 20–21.

Lutz, E. & Munashinghe, M. (1991) Accounting for the Environment. *Finance and Development*, March, 19–21.

MacLean, T. (1989) Full Cost Accounting, mimeo.

Mansley, M. (1995) *Long Term Financial Risks to the Carbon Fuel from the Climate Change*. The Delphi Industry Group.

Marcus, A. (1993) *Business and Society. Ethics, Government and the World Economy*. Boston: Irvin.

Marshall, J. (1993) A Nearly Useless Energy Tax. *The New York Times (NYT)*, April 11, 13.

Mauch, S.; Iten, R.; von Weizsäcker, E. & Jesinghaus, J. (1992) *Ecological Tax Reform. The Cases of Europe and Switzerland* (in German: *Ökologische Steuerreform. Europäische Ebene und Fallbeispeil Schweiz*). Chur: Rüegger.

Maunders, K. & Burritt, R. (1991) Accounting and Ecological Crisis. *Accounting, Auditing and Accountability Journal (AAAJ)*, **4**, No. 3, 9–26.

McGuire, J.; Sundgren, A. & Schneeweis, T. (1981) Corporate Social Responsibility and Firm Financial Performance. *Academy of Management Journal*, **31**.

McKey, B. (1991) Clean Air Rules Affect Small Firms. *Nations Business*, July, 28.
McMurray, S. (1992) Monsanto Doubles Liability Provision For Treating Toxic Waste to $245 Million. *Wall Street Journal (WSJ)*, March 23, A7.
Meadows, D.; Meadows, D. & Behrens, W. (1992) *The New Limits to Growth*. Boston: MIT Press.
Meffert, H. (1988) *Strategic Management and Marketing* (in German: *Strategische Unternehmensführung und Marketing*). Wiesbaden: Gabler.
Meffert, H. (1991) *Strategic Management and Marketing: Contributions to a Market Oriented Business Policy* (in German: *Strategische Unternehmungsführung und Marketing: Beiträge zu einer marktorientierten Unternehmungspolitik*). Wiesbaden: Gabler.
Meyer, C. & Stenz, T. (1995) Dynamic of the Swiss Accounting. Breakthrough of Internationally Comparable Accounting Standards (in German: Dynamik in der Schweizer Rechnungslegung. Durchbruch international vergleichbarer Normen). *Neue Zürcher Zeitung*, No. 20, 27.
Monty, R. (1991) Beyond Environmental Compliance: Business Strategies for Competitive Advantage. *Environmental Finance*, 1, No. 1, 3–11.
Moore, D. (1991) At the Drawing Board. *CA Magazine*, March, 54–56.
Moore J. (1993) Voluntary Environmental Audits—The Risks and Benefits. Seattle: Manuscript
Mooren, C.; Müller, H. & Muhr, M 1991 Environmental Subsidies in Investment Appraisal (in German: Umweltorientierte Fördermassnahmen des Staates in betrieblichen Investitionskalkülen). *Zeitschrift für angewandte Umweltforschung (ZAU)*, 4, No. 3, 267–82.
Morgan, N.; Palleson, M. & Thomson, R. (1992) Environmental Impact Assessment and Competitiveness, November. Ottawa: National Round Table on the Environment and the Economy, Working Paper No. 7.
Morrow, M. (1992) *Activity-based Management. New Approaches to Measuring Performance and Managing Costs*. New York: Woodhead-Faulkner.
Müller, K.; de Frutos, J.; Schüssler, K. & Haarbosch, H. (1994) *Environmental Reporting and Disclosures. The Financial Analyst's View*. London: Working Group on Environmental Issues of the Accounting Commission of the European Federation of Financial Analysts' Societies (EFFAS).
Müller-Wenk, R. (1972) Ecological Bookkeeping: An Introduction (in German: Ökologische Buchhaltung. Eine Einführung). St Gallen: mimeo.
Müller-Wenk, R. (1978) *Ecological Bookkeeping* (in German: *Ökologische Buchhaltung*). Frankfurt: Campus.
Müller-Wenk, R. (1993) Öko durch Ökobilanzei (in English: Eco with Ecobalances). *Ciba News*, No. 4, 3ff.
Münchner Rückversicherung (1995) *Jahresbericht (Annual report)*. Munich: Münchner Rückversicherung.
Naimon, J. (1995) Corporate Reporting Picks Up Speed. *Tomorrow*, January–March.
Napolitano, G. (1995) Company-Specific Effect of Environmental Compliance. *The Quarterly Accounting Review*, June.
National Pollution Prevention Center for Higher Education (1995) *Pollution Prevention Educational Resource Compendium: Accounting*. Ann Arbor: University of Michigan.
Neeley, L. & Imke, F. (1987) *Accounting. Principles and Practices*. Cincinnati: South-Western Publishing.
Newell, G., Kreuze, J. & Newell, S. (1990) Accounting for Hazardous Waste. Does Your Firm Face Potential Environmental Liabilities? *Management Accounting*, May, 58–61.

Nitkin, D. & Powell, D. (1993) Corporate Sustainable Development Reporting in Canada. Ottawa: National Round Table on the Environment and the Economy, Working Paper No. 17.

Nordic Council of Ministers (1995) *LCA-Nordic Technical Reports*, Various Numbers. Copenhagen: Nordic Council of Ministers.

Noreen, E. (1987) Commentary on H. Thomas Johnson and Robert S. Kaplan's "Relevance Lost: The Rise and Fall of Management Accounting". *Accounting Horizons*, December, 110–16.

Norsk Hydro (1994) *Environmental Report*. Oslo: Norsk Hydro.

NPI (1995) *Report on Socially Responsible Investment Funds in Continental Europe*. London: NPI.

Nussbaum, R. (1995) *Environmental Management and Ethics. Environmental Management Expressing Strategic and Ethic Rationality* (in German: *Umweltbewusstes Management und Unternehmensethik—Umweltbewusstes Management als Ausdruck erfolgsstrategischer und ethischer Rationalität*). Bern: Haupt.

NZZ (Neue Zürcher Zeitung) (1994a) Exxon Guilty in the Valdez Case. High Claims (in German: Exxon im Fall Valdez für fahrlässig befunden. Grosse Forderungen an den Erdölkonzern). *Neue Zürcher Zeitung (NZZ)*, June 15, No. 137, 19.

NZZ (Neue Zürcher Zeitung) (1994b) Mild Judgement of Exxon Case (in German: Mildes Urteil gegen Exxon). *Neue Zürcher Zeitung (NZZ)*, No. 187, 20.

NZZ (Neue Zürcher Zeitung) (1994c) Environmental Protection with Market Support. Results of the Emissions Trading Programme in the U.S.A. (in German: Umweltschutz mit der Unterstützung des Marktes. Bilanz des Handels von Schadstoff-Zertifikaten in den USA). *Neue Zürcher Zeitung (NZZ)*, No. 304, 23.

NZZ (Neue Zürcher Zeitung) (1995) Increasing Importance of Accounting Standards in Accordance with IAS (in German: Wachsende Bedeutung der Rechnungslegung nach IAS). *Neue Zürcher Zeitung (NZZ)*, No. 60, 13.

ÖB (Ökologische Briefe) (1995) Clean Environment with Public Access to Information? (in German: Saubere Umwelt durch öffentlichen Informationszugang?) *Ökologische Briefe*, No. 26, 5–6.

OECD (Organisation for Economic Co-Operation and Development) (1992) *OECD Guidelines for Multinational Enterprises*. Paris: OECD.

OECD (Organisation for Economic Co-Operation and Development) (1993) *Systèmes d'Information et Indicateurs d'Environnement*. Paris: OECD.

OECD (Organisation for Economic Co-Operation and Development) (1994a) *Natural Resource Accounts: Taking Stock in OECD Countries*. Paris: OECD Environment Monographs, No. 84.

OECD (Organisation for Economic Co-Operation and Development) (1994b) *Managing the Environment: The Role of Economic Instruments*. Paris: OECD.

OECD (Organisation for Economic Co-Operation and Development) (1995) *PRTR Guidance to Governments Document, Data Management and Reporting for a National Pollutant Release and Transfer Register, Pollution Prevention and Control Group*. Paris: OECD.

Orgland, M. (1990) *Environmental Investment Funds. An Assessment of their Chances of Success in Different Industrial Countries*. St. Gallen: HSG.

OTA (Office of Technology Assessment, US Congress) (1994) *Industry, Technology and the Environment: Competitive Challenges and Business Opportunities*. Washington, DC: US Government Printing Office.

Ottoboni, A. (1991) *The Dose Makes the Poison. A Plain-Language Guide to Toxicology*. New York: Van Nostrand Reinhold.

Owen, D. (Ed.) (1992) *Green Reporting. Accountancy and the Challenge of the Nineties.* London: Chapman & Hall.

Paasikivi, R. (1994) Towards a European Standard. *EEE Bulletin,* Winter, 8–10.

Pariser, D. & Neidermeyer, A. (1991) Environmental Due Diligence: The Internal Auditor's Role. *Journal of Bank Accounting and Auditing,* Winter, 22–30.

PCEQ (President's Commission on Environmental Quality) (1991) *The Report of the President's Commission on Environmental Quality,* Washington D.C.: PCEQ.

PCEQ (President's Commission on Environmental Quality) (1993) *A Framework for Pollution Prevention,* Washington D.C.: PCEQ.

Pearce, J. & Robinson, R. (1991) *Strategic Management: Formulation, Implementation, and Control.* Homewood: Irwin.

Pearce, D. W. & Turner, R. K. (1992, 1994) *Economies of Natural Resources and the Environment.* New York: Harvester Wheatsheaf.

Peat Marwick, Mitchell, & Co. (Ed.) (1987) *Law Regulating Accounting Standards* (in German: *Bilanzrichtliniengesetz*). 2nd edition. München: Beck.

Peglau, R. & Schulz, W. (1993) Environmental Audits: Expert Knowledge and Perspectives (in German: Umweltaudits: Sachstand und Perspektiven). Umwelt und Energie. *Handbuch für die betriebliche Praxis,* No. 3, Berlin: Haufe.

Pekelney, D. (1993) Emissions Trading: Applications To Improve Air and Water Quality. *Pollution Prevention Review,* Spring, 139–48.

PERI (Public Environmental Reporting Initiative) (1994) *PERI Guidelines.* May. London: PERI.

Perriman, R. (1995) Is LCA Losing Its Way? *LCA-News,* 5, No 1, 4–5.

Peskin, H. (1991) Alternative Environmental and Resource Accounting Approaches. Constanza, R. (Ed.): *Ecological Economics: The Science and Management of Sustainability.* New York: Columbia University Press, 176–93.

Petrauskas, H. (1992) Manufacturing and the Environment: Implementing Quality Environmental Management. Speech at the University of Michigan, November 20.

Pfriem, R. (1991) Eco-Controlling and Organizational Development (in German: Öko-Controlling und Organisationsentwicklung von Unternehmen). *IÖW-Informationsdienst,* 6, No. 2/91, 1–14.

Pieth, R. (1995) Black Market for Ozone Killers (in German: Schwarzmarkt für Ozonkiller). *Cash,* No. 29.

Pilko, G. (1990) Negotiating a Fair Division of Environmental Costs. *Mergers & Acquisitions,* March/April, 58–62.

Pohl, C.; Ros, M.; Waldeck, B. & Dinkel, F. (1996) Imprecision and Uncertainty in LCA. In: Schaltegger, S. (1996) *Life Cycle Assessment (LCA)—Quo Vadis?* Basel/Boston: Birkhauser.

Pojasek, R. & Cali, L. (1991a) Measuring Pollution Prevention Progress. *Pollution Prevention Review,* Spring, 119–29.

Pojasek R. & Cali L. (1991b) Contrasting Approaches to Pollution Prevention. *Pollution Prevention Review,* Summer, 225–35.

Polimeni, R.; Fabozzi, F. & Adelberg, A. (1986) *Cost Accounting. Concepts and Applications for Managerial Decision Making.* New York: McGraw-Hill.

Popoff, F. & Buzzelli, D. (1993) Full-Cost Accounting. *Chemical and Engineering News (C&EN),* January 11, 8–10.

Power, M. (1991) Auditing and Environmental Expertise: Between Protest and Professionalisation. *Accounting, Auditing and Accountability Journal (AAAJ),* 4, No. 3, 30–42.

Price Waterhouse (1991) *Environmental Accounting: The Issues, The Developing Solutions.* New York: Price Waterhouse.

Price Waterhouse (1992a) *Accounting for Environmental Compliance: Crossroad of GAAP, Engineering, and Government. A Survey of Corporate America's Accounting for Environmental Costs.* New York: Price Waterhouse.

Price Waterhouse (1992b) *Environmental Litigation Support.* New York: Price Waterhouse.

Price Waterhouse (1993) *Environmental Costs: Accounting and Disclosure.* New York: Price Waterhouse.

Price Waterhouse (1994) *Progress on the Environmental Challenge. A Survey of Corporate America's Environmental Accounting and Management.* New York: Price Waterhouse.

PWMI (1992) Eco-Profiles of the European Plastics Industry. Report 1. Brussels: European Center for Plastics in the Environment.

Rabinowitz, D. & Murphy, N. (1992) *Environmental Disclosure: What the SEC Requires. Understanding Environmental Accounting & Disclosures Today.* New York: Executive Enterprises Publications Co., 23–37.

Raftelis, G. (1991) Financial Accounting Measures as Part of Pollution Prevention Assessment. *Environmental Finance*, Summer, 129–50.

Rappaport, A. (1986) *Creating Shareholder Value. The New Standards for Business Performance.* New York: Free Press.

Rat der EG (1993) Regulation (EU) No. 1836/93 of the Commission of the 29 June 1993 for the Voluntary Scheme to Joint the EU-Eco-Audit System (in German: Verordnung (EWG) Nr. 1836/93 des Rates vom 29 Juni 1993 über die freiwillige Beteiligung gewerblicher Unternehmen an einem Gemeinschaftssystem für das Umweltmanagement und die Umweltbetriebsprüfung). *Amtsblatt der Europäischen Gemeinschaften*, No. L 168/1–168/18.

Ream, T. & French, C. (1993) *A Framework and Methods for Conducting a Life-Cycle Impact Assessment.* Research Triangle Park, NC: US EPA.

Reitmayr T. & Heissenhuber A. (1993) Classification of Ecologically Oriented Systems of Accounting and Enlargement to an Economic-Ecological System of Key Figures for Agriculture (in German: Klassifizierung ökologisch orientierter Rechnungssysteme und Erweiterung zu einem ökonomisch-ökologischen Kennzahlensystem für den Bereich der Landwirtschaft). *Zeitschrift für Umweltpolitik und Umweltrecht (ZfU)*, No. 3, 281–310.

Rensch, H. (1992) Who Profits from LCA? (in German: Wem nützen Ökobilanzen?) *Neue Zürcher Zeitung (NZZ)*, 23/24 January, No. 18.

Repetto, R. (1992) Accounting for Environmental Assets. *Scientific American*, June, 64–70.

Repetto, R.; Dower, R.; Jenkins, R. & Geoghegan, J. (1992) *Green Fees: How a Tax Shift Can Work for the Environment and the Economy*, November. Washington D.C.: World Resource Institute (WRI).

Reuters (1995a) Dirty Industry Must Show Green Accounts Soon (in German: "Schmutzige" Industrie soll schon bald "grüne" Bilanzen vorlegen. Gesetzesentwurf sieht Veröffentlichung von umweltbelastenden Faktoren bei der Produktion vor). *Nordschleswiger*, January 19, 1995.

Reuters (1995b) Industry Association Excluded Pro Kemi (in German: Branche schloss Pro Kemi aus). *Nordschleswiger*, February 25, 1995.

Reuters (1995c) First Regulation for LCA (in German: Erster Normentwurf für Öko-Bilanz). *Nordschleswiger*, May 10, 1995.

Rice, F. (1993) Who Scores Best on the Environment? *Fortune*, 26. July, 114–22.

Rifkin, J. (1985) *Entropy.* Frankfurt-am-Main: Ullstein.

Rikhardsson, P. (1994) The Measurement and Reporting of Corporate Environmental Performance. Aspects and Developments. Paper presented at the Second Nordic Network Conference "Business and Environment", Sandvika, December.

Roberts, M. (1994) UK Takes Step Toward TRI-Style Reporting. *Chemical Week*, Sept. 21, **155**, No. 10, 20.

Roberts, R. (1994a) SAB 92 and the SEC's Environmental Liability, Speech at the 1994 Quinn, Ward & Kershaw Environmental Law Symposium. Baltimore: The University of Maryland School of Law, April 8.

Roberts, R. (1994b) Update on Staff Accounting Bulletin, No. 92. Speech at the 1994, Midwinter Meeting Toxic & Hazardous Substances & Environmental Law Committee Program, American Bar Association, *Vista*, May 7.

Roberts, R. (1994c) Environmental Liability Disclosure Developments, Speech at the Environmental Law Institute, Corporate Environmental Management Workshop on Environmental Reporting & Accountability. Washington D.C., June 6.

Roberts, R. & Hohl, K. (1994) Environmental Liability Disclosure and Staff Accounting Bulletin No. 92. *Business Lawyer*, **50**, No. 1, November, 1–17.

Robinson, W. (1995) Versatility of Structured Settlements. *Pennsylvania CPA Journal*, **66**, No. 2, 15.

ROI (Risk & Opportunity Intelligence)/Environmental Auditors (1994) *SYBERR System Based Environmental Risk Rating*.

Römer, G. (1990) Environmental Protection and Controlling (in German: Umweltschutz und Controlling). *Controller Magazine*, No. 1, 3–10.

Roome, N. (1992) Developing Environmental Management Strategies. *Business Strategy and the Environment*, No. 1, 11–24.

Ross, A. (1985) Accounting for Hazardous Waste. Cleanups May Have a Significant Financial Impact. *Journal of Accountancy*, March, 72–82.

Roussey, R. S. (1991) *Environmental Liabilities in the 1990s*. New York: Arthur Andersen.

RTI (Research Triangle Institute) (1993a) *A Framework and Methods for Conducting a Life-Cycle Impact Assessment*. RTI, US EPA.

RTI (Research Triangle Institute) (1993b) *Life-Cycle Assessment: Guidelines for Assessing Data Quality*. RTI, US EPA.

Rubenstein, D. (1994) *Environmental Accounting for the Sustainable Corporation*. Westport: Quorum.

Rück T. (1993) *Eco-Controlling as Management Tool* (in German: *Öko-Controlling als Führungsinstrument*). Frankfurt: Gabler.

Rückle, D. (1989) Investment Appraisal for Environmental Investments (in German: Investitionskalküle für Umweltschutzinvestitionen). *Betriebswirtschaftliche Forschung und Praxis (BFuP)*, **41**, No. 1/89, 51–65.

Salamitou, J. (1991) The Environmental Index: an Environmental Management Tool for Rhône Poulenc. *Integrated Environmental Management*, No. 4, November, 7–9.

Samdani, G. (1995) Professional Environmental Auditors Guidebook. *Chemical Engineering*, **102**, No. 3, 10–12.

Sandor, R. & Walsh, M. (1993) Environmental Futures: Preliminary Thoughts on the Market for Sulfur Dioxide Emission Allowances. Manuscript.

Schaltegger, S. (1993) Strategic Management and Measurement of Corporate Pollution. Ecological Accounting: A Strategic Approach for Environmental Assessment, SMRC-Study No. 183, Minnesota: SMRC, University of Minnesota.

Schaltegger, S. (1994a) Contemporary Environmental Management Practices (in German: Zeitgemässe Instrumente des betrieblichen Umweltschutzes). *Die Unternehmung*. No. 4, 117–31.

Schaltegger, S. (1994b) *Eco-Controlling for the Swiss Army* (in German: *Öko-Controlling für das Eidgenössische Militärdepartement (EMD)*). Bern: EMD.

Schaltegger, S. (Ed.) (1996) *Life Cycle Assessment (LCA)—Quo Vadis?* Basel: Birkhäuser.

Schaltegger, S. (1996) Accounting for Eco-Efficiency. In: Hens & Devuyst (Eds.): *Environmental Management*. London: Routledge.

Schaltegger, S. & Kempke, S. (1996) Eco-Controlling—The State of the Art (in German: Ökocontrolling—überblick bisheriger Ansätze) *Zeitschrift für Betriebswirtschaft (ZfB)*, No. 2.

Schaltegger, S. & Kubat, R. (1994) *Glossary of Life Cycle Assessment. Terms and Concepts*. Basel: WWZ, Study No. 45.

Schaltegger, S. & Kubat, R. (1995) *Glossary of LCA. Terms and Definitions*. WWZ-Study No. 45. Basel: WWZ.

Schaltegger, S. & Stinson, C. (1994) Issues and Research Opportunities in Environmental Accounting. Basel: WWZ Discussion Paper No. 9124.

Schaltegger, S. & Sturm, A. (1990) Ecological Rationality. Starting Points for the Development of Environmental Management Tools (in German: Ökologische Rationalität. Ansatzpunkte zur Ausgestaltung von ökologieorientierten Managementinstrumenten). *Die Unternehmung*, No. 4, 273–90.

Schaltegger, S. & Sturm, A. (1991) The Method of Ecological Accounting (in German: Methodik der ökologischen Rechnungslegung) 3rd edition. Basel: WWZ, discussion paper No. 33.

Schaltegger, S. & Sturm, A. (1992a) *Environmentally Oriented Decisions in Firms. Ecological Accounting Instead of LCA: Necessity, Criteria, Concepts* (in German: *Ökologieorientierte Entscheidungen in Unternehmen. Ökologisches Rechnungswesen statt Ökobilanzierung: Notwendigkeit, Kriterien, Konzepte*). Bern/Stuttgart: Haupt.

Schaltegger, S. & Sturm, A. (1992b) Eco-Controlling as Management Tool (in German: Öko-Controlling als Management- und Führungsinstrument). *IO-Management*, No. 6, 71–75.

Schaltegger, S. & Sturm, A. (1992c) Eco-Controlling: An Integrated Economic-Ecological Management Tool. Koechling & Müller (Eds.): *Green Business Opportunities. The Profit Potential*. London: Pitman/*Financial Times*, 229–40.

Schaltegger, S. & Sturm, A. (1993) Environmental Management (in German: Ökologieorientiertes Management). Frey *et al.* (Hrsg.): *Mit Ökonomie zur Ökologie*, 2nd edition, 179–201.

Schaltegger, S. & Sturm, A. (1994) *Environmentally Oriented Decisions in Firms. Ecological Accounting Instead of LCA: Necessity, Criteria, Concepts* (in German: *Ökologieorientierte Entscheidungen in Unternehmen. Ökologisches Rechnungswesen statt Ökobilanzierung: Notwendigkeit, Kriterien, Konzepte*) (2nd edition). Bern/Stuttgart: Haupt.

Schaltegger, S. & Sturm, A. (1995) *Eco-Efficiency with Eco-Controlling. For the Implementation of EMAS and ISO 14001* (in German: *Öko-Effizienz durch Öko-Controlling. Zur praktischen Umsetzung von EMAS und ISO 14001*. Zürich/Stuttgart: vdf/Schäffer-Poeschel.

Schaltegger, S. & Sturm, A. (1996) Managerial Eco-Control in Manufacturing and Process Industries. *Greener Management International*, February.

Schaltegger, S. and Thomas, T. (1994a) PACT for a Pollution Added Credit Trading (in German: PACT für einen Schadschöpfungs-Zertifikatshandel). *Zeitschrift für Umweltpolitik und Umweltrecht (ZfU)*, No. 3, 357–81.

Schaltegger, S. & Thomas, T. (1994b) Pollution Added Credit Trading (PACT). New Dimensions in Emissions Trading. WWZ-Discussion Paper No. 9410. Basel: WWZ. Forthcoming in *Ecological Economics*.

Schaltegger, S.; Kubat, R.; Hilber, C. & Vaterlaus, S., with Sturm, A. & Flütsch, A. (1996) *Innovative Management of Public Environmental Policy. New Public Environmental Management: NPEM* (in German: *Innovatives Management staatlicher Umweltpolitik. New Public Environmental Management: NPEM*). Basel: Birkhäuser.

Schendel, D. & Hofer, C. (1978) *Strategy Formulation: Analytical Concepts*. St Paul: West.

Schierenbeck, H. (1994) *Glossary of Banking and Insurance* (in German: *Bank- und Versicherungslexikon*) (2nd edition). München: Oldenbourg.

Schmid, U. (1989) *Environmental Protection—A Strategic Challenge for Management* (in German: *Umweltschutz—Eine strategische Herausforderung für das Management*). Frankfurt: Lang.

Schmidheiny, S. (Ed.) (1992) *Changing Course: A Global Business Perspective on Development and the Environment*. Cambridge, Mass.: MIT Press.

Schreiner, M. (1988) *Environmental Management in 22 Sessions* (in German: *Umweltmanagement in 22 Lektionen. Ein ökonomischer Weg in eine ökologische Wirtschaft*). Wiesbaden: Gabler.

Schreiner, M. (1991) *The Environmental Challenge of Accounting* (in German: *Ökologische Herausforderungen an die Kosten- und Leistungsrechnung*). Freimann, J. (Hrsg.): *Ökologische Herausforderung der Betriebswirtschaftslehre*. Wiesbaden: Gabler.

Schulz, E. & Schulz, W. (1994) *Environmental Controlling in Practice.* (in German: *Umweltcontrolling in der Praxis*). München: Vahlen.

Schulz, W. (1985) *The Monetary Value of Better Air Quality* (in German: *Der monetäre Wert besserer Luft*). Frankfurt: Lang.

Schulz, W. (1989) *Corporate Environmental Information Systems* (in German: *Betriebliche Umweltinformationssysteme*). *Handbuch Umwelt und Energie, Heft UE.* Freiburg: Haufe-Verlag, 33–98.

Schulz, W. (1991) *Eco-Controlling* (in German: *Ökocontrolling*). OFW (Hrsg.): *Umweltmanagement im Spannungsfeld zwischen Ökologie und Ökonomie*. Wiesbaden: Gabler, 221–42.

Schwab, N. & Soguel, N: (1995) *Contingent Valuation, Transport Safety and the Value of Life*. Boston: Kluwer.

Schweizer Rück (1995) *Annual Report, 1994*. Zurich: Schweizer Rück.

SCS (Scientific Certification Systems) (1992) Several product evaluation forms. San Francisco: SCS.

SEC (Securities and Exchange Commission) (1989) Management's Discussion and Analysis of Financial Condition and Results of Operations. Release Nos. 33-6835; 34-26831; IC-16961; FR-36. Washington, DC: SEC.

SEC (Securities and Exchange Commission) (1993) SAB No. 92. Washington D.C.: SEC.

Seidel, E. (1988) *Ecological Controlling* (in German: *Ökologisches Controlling*). Wunderer (Hrsg.): *Betriebswirtschaftslehre als Management- und Führungslehre*. Stuttgart: Poeschel, 367–82.

Servatius, H. (1994) Strategic Environmental Controlling. The High School of Environmental Navigation (in German: *Strategisches Umwelt-Controlling—Die hohe Schule der Umweltnavigation*). Tagungsband des FGU Berlin, UTECH 23 February, 103–38.

SETAC (Society of Environmental Toxicology and Chemistry) (1991) *A Technical Framework for Life-Cycle Assessment*. Washington D.C.: SETAC.

SGCI (1991) *Responsible Care*. Zürich: SGCI.

Shorthouse B. (1991) Using Risk Analysis To Set Priorities for Pollution Prevention. *Pollution Prevention Review*, Winter, 41–53.

Shrivastava, P. (1993) Crisis Theory/Practice: Towards a Sustainable Future. *Industrial and Environmental Crises Quarterly*. **7**, No. 1 .

Shrivastava, P. & Hart, S. (1992) Creating Sustainable Corporations. Paper presented at the Academy of Management Annual Meeting, (Las Vegas August).

Sietz, M. (1991) Methods of Environmental Auditing (in German: Methoden des Umwelt-Auditing). Steger, U. (Hrsg.): *Umwelt-Auditing. Ein neues Instrument der Risikovorsorge*. Frankfurt: FAZ, 45–58.

Simon, B. (1991) Sharks in the Water. *Financial Times*, November 27, 16.

Skellenger, B. (1992) Limitation of Liability Clauses Gaining Popularity Among Environmental Consultants. *ANEP Environline*, No. 3, Spring, 4–5.

Solomon, C. (1993) Clearing the Air. What Really Pollutes? Study of a Refinery Proves an Eye-Opener. *The Wall Street Journal*, March 29, front page.

Solow, R. (1992) *An Almost Practicable Step Toward Sustainability*. Washington D.C.

Speich, C. (1992) Tender Buds Sprout. Bilanz-Test of Business Reports (in German: Zarte Knospen spriessen. Bilanz-Test Geschäftsberichte). *Bilanz*, No. 5 , 163–68.

Spicer, B. (1978) Investors, Corporate Social Performance and Informational Disclosure: An Empirical Study. *Accounting Review*. **53**.

Spindler, E. (1993) The Eco-Audit Regulation (in German: Öko-Audit-Verordnung). *Umwelt-Wirtschaftsforum (UWF)*, No. 3, 34–35.

Spitzer, M. (1992) Calculating the Benefits of Pollution Prevention. *Pollution Engineering*, September 1, 33–38.

Spitzer, M. (1994) Stakeholder's Action Agenda: A Report of the Workshop on Accounting and Capital Budgeting for Environmental Costs. Washington D.C.: EPA.

Spitzer, M. & Elwood, H. (1995a) *An Introduction to Environmental Accounting as a Business Management Tool: Key Concepts and Terms*. Washington D.C.: US EPA.

Spitzer, M. & Elwood, H. (1995b) US Environmental Protection Agency Design for the Environment Program. Environmental Accounting Project. Washington D.C.: US EPA.

Spitzer, M.; Pojasek, R.; Robertaccio, F. & Nelson, J. (1993) Accounting and Capital Budgeting for Pollution Prevention. Environmental Protection Agency. Paper presented at the Engineering Foundation Conference, January 24–29. San Diego: C.A.

Staehelin-Witt, E. (1993) Valuation of Environmental Goods (in German: Bewertung von Unweltgütern). In: Frey, R. et al. *Economics for the Environment* (in German: *Mit ökonomie zur Ökologie*). Basel/Stuttgart: Helbling and Lichtenhahn/Schäffer-Poeschel.

Staehelin-Witt, E. & Spillmann, A. (1992) Emissions Trading. A Market Based Approach for the Swiss Environmental Policy (in German: Emissionshandel. Ein marktwirtschaftlicher Weg für die schweizerische Umweltpolitik). WWZ-Study No. 40. Basel: WWZ.

Stastny, D. (1993) *Environmental Auditing*. Wien: Schriftenreihe 19/93 des Instituts für Ökologische Wirtschaftsforschung Wien.

Stavins, R. (1992) Harnessing the Marketplace. We Have to do More with Less. *EPA-Journal*, May/June, 21–25.

Steen, B. & Ryding, S. (1994) The EPS-Environ-Accounting Method. An Application of Environmental Accounting Principles for Evaluation and Valuation of Environmental Impact in Product Design. Stockholm: IVL-Report B 1080.

Steger, U. (1988) *Umweltmanagement*. Wiesbaden: Gabler, FAZ.

Stevenson, R. (1992) Monitoring Pollution at Its Source. *The New York Times (NYT)*, April 8, C1, C6.

Stinson, C. (1993) Environmental Accounting a Growth Industry. *Puget Sound Business Journal*, February 5–11.

Stipp, D. (1992) Market Heats up in Recycled CFCs. *Wall Street Journal (WSJ)*, April 29, B1.

Stockwell, J.; Sorensen, J.; Eckert, J. & Carreras, E. (1993) The US EPA Geographic Information System for Mapping Environmental Releases of Toxic Chemical Release Inventory (TRI) Chemicals. *Risk Analysis*, **13**, No. 2 , 155–64.

Sturm, A. (1993a) Eco-Controlling. From LCA to a Management Tool (in German: Öko-Controlling. Von der Ökobilanz zum Führungsinstrument). *Gaia*, No. 2, 107–20.

Sturm, A. (1993b) Eco-Controlling. The Next Challenge for the Profession (in German: Öko-Controlling: Die nächste Herausforderung an den Berufsstand). *Index* Nr. 2/93, 30–35, Rio realisieren: Öko-Controlling (Continuation). *Index*, No. 3/93, 44–48.

Surma, J. (1993) *Tackling Corporate America's Environmental Challenge*. New York: Price Waterhouse.

Surma, J. & Vondra, A. (1992) Accounting for Environmental Costs: A Hazardous Subject. *Journal of Accountancy*, March, 51–55.

Susskind, L. & McKearnan, S. (1995) Enlightened Conflict Resolution. *Technology Review*, **98**. No. 3.

SustainAbility (1993) What Do We Mean By Sustainability? EPE Workshop, Module 1, Letter 1.1.

SustainAbility; Spold & BiE (Business in the Environment) (Eds.) (1992) *The LCA Sourcebook*. London: Spold/SustainAbility.

Sutter, P. & Hofstetter, P. (1989) The Ecological Payback Period (in German: Die ökologische Rückzahldauer). *Schweizer Ingenieur und Architekt*, No. 49, 1342–46.

Tanega, J. (1994) Environmental Disclosures and Optimal Control Strategies of Stochastic Systems. Kingston: Manuscript.

Tanega, J. (1995) Environment and the Capital Markets, Kingston: Manuscript.

Tellus (1992) *The Tellus Institute Packaging Study*. Boston: Tellus.

Tietenberg, T. (1989) Marketable Permits in the US: A Decade of Experience. Roskamp, K. (Ed.): *Public Finance and the Performance of Enterprises*. Detroit: Wayne State University Press.

Tietenberg, T. (1993) *Environmental and Natural Resource Economics*. Glenview: Foresman.

Tinbergen, J. (1968) *Economic Policy: Principles and Design* 3rd edition. Amsterdam, North Holland.

Todd, R. (1992) Zero-Loss Environmental Accounting Systems. New York: Manuscript.

Töpfer, K. (1992) Corporate Auditing of Environmental Protection (in German: Betriebliches Umweltschutz-Auditing). *IO-Management*, No. 6, 81–86.

Töpfer, K. (1993) The Discussion About LCA Has Just Started (in German: Die Diskussion um die Ökobilanz wird nun erst richtig beginnen). *Handelsblatt*, 28 September, B1.

Turney, P. & Anderson, B. (1989) Accounting for Continuous Improvement. *Sloan Management Review*, Winter 37–47.

UBA (Umweltbundesamt) (1992) *LCA—Expert Knowledge—Perspectives* (in German: Ökobilanzen—Sachstand—Perspektiven). Berlin: UBA

Udo de Haes, H. & Hofstetter, P. (1994) Definition of Terms. Proceedings of the SETAC Conference on Impact Assessment. Zurich; SETAC, July 8–9.

Udo de Haes, H. (Ed.) (1995): The Methodology of Life Cycle Impact Assessment. Report of the SETAC-Europe Working groups on Life Cycle Impact Assessment (WIA). Leiden: SETAC.

Ullmann, A. (1976) The Corporate Environmental Accounting System: A Management Tool for Fighting Environmental Degradation. *Accounting, Organizations and Society (AOS)*, **1**, No. 1, 71–79.

UN (United Nations) (1990) *Environmental Assessment. Procedures in the UN System.* Geneva: UN.

UN (United Nations) (1991a) Accounting for Environmental Protection Measures. New York: United Nations Economic and Social Council. Commission on Transnational Corporations, Intergovernmental Working Group of Experts on International Standards of Accounting and Reporting.

UN (United Nations) (1991b) *Environmental Accounting for Sustainable Development.* Note by the Secretariat. Geneva: UN.

UN (United Nations), Preparatory Committee for the United Nations Conference on Environment and Development (1991c): Integrated Economic-Environmental Accounting. Progress Report of the Secretary-General of the Conference, United Nations Conference on Environment and Development, August 12–September 4. Geneva: UN.

UN (United Nations) (1991d) *Transnational Corporations and Industrial Hazards Disclosure.* New York: UN.

UN (United Nations) (1992a) *Environmental Accounting: Current Issues, Abstracts and Bibliography.* New York: UN.

UN (United Nations) (1992b) *Environmental Disclosures: International Survey of Corporate Reporting Practices.* New York: UN.

UN (United Nations) (1992c) *International Accounting and Reporting Issues: 1991 Review.* New York: UN.

UN (United Nations) (1992d) *Climate Change and Transnational Corporations: Analysis and Trends.* New York: UN.

UN (United Nations) (1994) *Environmental Management in Transnational Corporations.* Report on the Benchmark Corporate Environmental Survey. New York: UN.

UNEP (United Nations Environment Programme) (1991) Managing Change: Discussion Paper for the Executive Director's Advisory Group on Commercial Banks and the Environment. Geneva: UNEP.

UNEP (United Nations Environment Programme) (1994) Company Environmental Reporting. A Measure of Progress in Business and Industry Towards Sustainable Development. Technical Report No. 24. New York: UN.

US EPA (Environmental Protection Agency), Office of Pollution Prevention and Toxics. (1991) *Total Cost Assessment. Accelerating Industrial Pollution Prevention through Innovation.* Washington D.C.: EPA.

US EPA (Environmental Protection Agency) (1995) *Design for the Environment. EPA's Environmental Network for Managerial Accounting and Capital Budgeting,* March. Washington: EPA.

US EPA (Environmental Protection Agency), Office of Research and Development (1993) *Life Cycle Design Guidance Manual. Environmental Requirements and the Product System.* Washington D.C.: EPA.

US EPA (Environmental Protection Agency), Risk Reduction Engineering Laboratory Office of Research and Development (1992) *Life-Cycle Assessment: Inventory Guidelines and Principles.* Cincinnati: U.S. EPA.

U-Tech (Hrsg.) (1994) *Environmental Audits—New Ways of Environmental Management* (in German: *Umweltaudits—Neue Wege zum Umweltmanagement*). Berlin.

UWF (Umwelt-Wirtschafts-Forum) (1993) Eco-Audit and Environmental Verification (in German: Öko-Auditing und Umweltbetriebsprüfung). *UFW*, No. 3, September.

Van Dieren, W. (1995) *To Count With Nature. The New Club-of-Rome Report: From Gross National Product to Eco-National Product* (in German: *Mit der Natur rechnen. Der neue Club-of-Rome Bericht: Vom Bruttosozialprodukt zum Ökosozialprodukt*). Basel: Birkhäuser.

Van Someren, T. (1993) Environmental Audit as Part of an Environmental Management System (in German: Umwelt-Audit als Teil eines Umweltmanagementsystems). *Umwelt-Wirtschaftsforum (UWF)*, No. 3, 36–40.

Vaterlaus, S. (1993) Integrated Economic-Ecological Accounts of Nations (in German: Integrierte ökonomisch-ökologische Gesamtrechnung). Basle: WWZ, paper No. 4/12.

Vaughan, D. & Mickle, C. (1993) *Environmental Profiles of European Business*. London: Royal Institute for International Affairs.

Vaughan, S. (1994) *Greening Financial Markets*. Geneva: IAE.

Vedsø, L. (1993) *Green Management*. Copenhagen: Systime.

Vinten, G. (1991) The Greening of Audit. *Internal Auditor*, October, 30–36.

Von Weizsäcker, E.; Jesinghaus, J.; Mauch, S. & Iten, R. (1992) *Environmental Tax Reform* (in German: *Ökologische Steuerreform*). Zürich: Rüegger.

Wachman, R. (1992) Management Account. Men in Grey Get the Green Jitters. *The London Evening Standard*, June 11, 38.

Wachman, R. (1994) Green Row Over EVC Flotation. *The London Evening Standard*, October 21.

Wagner, B. (1995) Working materials: Environmental Management (in German: Arbeitsmaterialien: Umweltmanagement). Kontaktstudium Management der Universität Augsburg. Augsburg: Scriptum.

Wagner, G. & Janzen, H. (1991) Ecological Controlling—More than a Slogan? (in German: Ökologisches Controlling—Mehr als ein Schlagwort?). *Controlling*, 3, No. 3, 120–29

Wainman, D. (1991) Balancing Nature's Books. *CA-magazine*, Toronto, March.

Walleck, A.; O'Halloran, B. & Leader, C. (1991) Benchmarking Worldclass Performance. *The McKinsey Quarterly*, No. 1, 3–24.

Walton, M. (1986) *The Deming Management Method*. New York: Perigée.

Watson, G. (1993) *Strategic Benchmarking*. New York: John Wiley & Sons.

WCED (World Commission on Environment and Development) (1987) *Our Common Future*. Oxford: Oxford University Press.

Weir, D. & Yamin, P. (1993) Toxic Ten. America's Truant Corporations. *Mother Jones*, January/February, 39–42.

Welford, R. (1994) *Environmental Management and Business Strategy*. London: Pitman Publishing.

Welford, R. & Gouldson, A. (1993) *Environmental Management and Business Strategy*. London: Pitman Publishing.

Wells, R. (1990) Environmental Performance Will Count in the 1990s. *Marketing News*, March 19, **24**, No. 6.

Welser, M. (1994) Environmental Aspects of Consulting Firms (in German: Umwelt-Aspekte in der Unternehmensberatung). *Atag Ernst & Young Praxis* 1/94, 34–39.

Wenzel, H. (1994) Information on Spatial Detail in LCA. The Significance of the LCA Application. Hofstetter, P.; Jensen, A.; Schaltegger, St. & Udo de Haes, H.: *First Working Document on Life Cycle Impact Assessment Methodology*. Zürich: SEATC/ETH.

White, A. & Becker, M. (1992) Total Cost Assessment: Catalyzing Corporate Self Interest in Pollution Prevention. *New Solutions*, Winter, pp. 34ff.

White, P. (1995) *Environmental Management in an International Consumer Goods Company*. Resources, Conservation and Recycling. Brussels: SETAC.

White, P.; De Smet, B.; Udo de Haes, H & Heijungs, R. (1995) LCA Back on Track. But is it One Track or Two? *LCA-News*, 5, No. 3, 2–4.

Whittington, G. (1992) *The Elements of Accounting. An Introduction*. Cambridge: Cambridge University Press.

WICE (World Industry Council for the Environment) (1994) *Environmental Reporting. A Manager's Guide*, Paris: WICE.

Wildavsky, A. (1993) Accounting for the Environment. Berkeley: Manuscript.

Williams, G. & Phillips, T. (1994) Cleaning up Our Act: Accounting for Environmental Liabilities. Current Financial Reporting Doesn't Do the Job. *Management Accounting*. 30–33.

Wingår, B. (1992) Environmental Monitoring and Reporting in Norway. Weidner, H.; Zieschank, R. & Knoepfel P. (Eds.): *Umweltinformation. Berichterstattung und Informationssyteme in zwölf Ländern*. Berlin: Sigma WZB, 99–140.

WIR (1994) *Geschäftsbericht 1994*. Basel: WIR.

Worldwatch Institute (1995) *State of the World*. New York: Norton.

Würth, S. (1993) *Umwelt-Auditing*. Frankfurt: Schriftenreihe der Treuhand-Kammer, Bd. 118.

WWF (World Wide Fund for Nature, International) (1992) *Methodology for the Calculation of Sustainable National Income*. Glands: WWF International.

WWF (World Wide Fund for Nature) (1993) Sustainable Use of Natural Resources: Concepts, Issues and Criteria. Gland: WWF International Position Paper.

WWF (World Wide Fund for Nature) (1994) Keine Hoffnung für Shir Khan? *Panda Magazine*. No. 4. Zürich: WWF.

Wynn, L. & Lee, E. (1993) *Life-Cycle Assessment: Guidelines for Assessing Data Quality*. Research Triangle Park, NC: US EPA.

Young, P. (Ed.) (1985) *Cost Allocation: Methods, Principles, Applications*. Amsterdam: North Holland.

Zenhäusern, M. & Bertschinger, P. (1993) *Corporate Accounting* (in German: *Konzernrechnungslegung*). Bern: Haupt.

Zünd, A. (1978) The Meaning of Controlling—Controller (in German: Begriffsinhalte Controlling—Controller). Haberland/Preisler/Meyer (Hrsg.): *Handbuch Revision, Controlling, Consulting*. München, 1–25.

Zweifel, P. & Tyran, J. (1994) Environmental Impairment Liability as an Instrument of Environmental Policy. *Ecological Economics*, **11**, 43–56.

Zyber, G. R. & Berry, C. G. (1992) Assessing Environmental Risk. *Journal of Accountancy*, March, 43–48.

Index